GOD REMEMBERS

AMSTERDAM STUDIES IN THEOLOGY AND RELIGION
(AmSTaR)

The *Amsterdam Studies in Theology and Religion* (AmSTaR) is a peer-reviewed publication of VU University Press in cooperation with VISOR (VU Institute for the Study of Religion, Culture and Society) and the Faculty of Theology. It publishes dissertations and scholarly monographs on a wide range of issues pertaining to theology and religion. The series is open to publications in English, German and Dutch.

Editorial Board

Prof. dr. C. van der Kooi
Dr. J.W. van Saane
Prof. dr. J.T. Sunier
Dr. P.G.A. Versteeg

Executive Editor

Dr. A.W. Zwiep

Volume 2

Vol. 1   C. van der Kooi, E. van Staalduine-Sulman, A.W. Zwiep (eds.), *Evangelical Theology in Transition: Essays Under the Auspices of the Center of Evangelical and Reformation Theology* (2012)
Vol. 2   B.J. Pakpahan, *God Remembers: Towards a Theology of Remembrance as a Basis of Reconciliation in Communal Conflict* (2012)
Vol. 3   P.B.A. Smit, *Tradition in Dialogue: A Historical Study of the Notion of "Tradition" in the International Bilateral Dialogues of the Anglican Communion* (forthcoming).

God Remembers

Towards a Theology of Remembrance
as a Basis of Reconciliation
in Communal Conflict

B.J. Pakpahan

VU University Press

VU Uitgeverij | VU University Press
De Boelelaan 1105
1081 HV Amsterdam
The Netherlands

E-mail: info@vu-uitgeverij.nl
Website: www.vu-uitgeverij.nl

© 2012 Binar Jonathan Pakpahan
© 2012 cover design Heleen ten Voorde (VU Dienst Communicatie)

ISBN 978 90 8659 603 4
NUR 700

All rights reserved. No part of this book may be reproduced, stored in a retrieval system, or transmitted, in any form or by any means, electronic, mechanical, photocopying, recording, or otherwise, without the prior written consent of the publisher.

To my church

Huria Kristen Batak Protestan (HKBP)

(Batak Protestant Christian Church)

Contents

List of Abbreviations xi

Acknowledgments xiii

Chapter 1. Introduction

1. Signs of a Growing Culture of Remembrance................................1
2. To Remember or to Forget? 3
3. What is Remembrance? 7
4. Shared Memory and Reconciliation 8
5. Remembrance of Conflict in the Church 12
6. Christian Remembrance 14
7. The Research Question 17
8. Development of the Argument...18

Chapter 2. The Wounds of the Past in the Huria Kristen Batak Protestan

1. Huria Kristen Batak Protestan (HKBP)......................................21
   - 1.1 A Brief History of the Church 21
   - 1.2 The Influence of Batak Culture in HKBP 22
   - 1.3 The Structure of the Church... 25
2. The HKBP 1992–1998 Crisis 30
   - 2.1 The Beginning of the Conflict.. 32
   - 2.2 Conflict between Ephorus and Secretary General.............35
   - 2.3 The 51st General Synod... 37
   - 2.4 The Inauguration of Rev. S.M. Siahaan as Acting Ephorus 43
   - 2.5 The Extraordinary General Synod February 11–13, 1993 47
   - 2.6 Two Conflicting Groups 50
3. The Confrontations 52
   - 3.1 Legal Confrontation 52
   - 3.2 Physical Confrontation.. 57
   - 3.3 Separation of Congregations...60

- 4. Reconciliation Efforts 62
  - 4.1 Reconciliation Effort within the Church 62
  - 4.2 Reconciliation Effort by Communion of Churches in Indonesia (PGI) 65
  - 4.3 Reconciliation Effort by Government Representatives 69
  - 4.4 1998 Reconciliation General Synod 70
  - 4.5 After 1998 Reconciliation General Synod 74
- 5. Analysis of the Conflict 77
  - 5.1 An Anthropological Analysis 77
  - 5.2 A Political-Theological Analysis 81
  - 5.3 A Church-Political Analysis 85
  - 5.4 Was the 1998 Reconciliation General Synod Enough? 88
- 6. Conclusion 90

Chapter 3. Biblical Meaning of Remembrance

- 1. Social Memory in Biblical Context 92
- 2. Remembrance in the Old Testament 96
  - 2.1 The Role of Memory in the Old Testament Community 96
  - 2.2 "Zākhar" as the Central Expression for Remembrance in the Old Testament 100
  - 2.3 Etymology, Occurrences, Contexts, and Usages 101
  - 2.4 Hebrew Psychology of Memory 105
- 3. Aspects of Remembrance in the Old Testament 108
  - 3.1 God Remembers People 108
  - 3.2 People Remember God 113
  - 3.3 The Cultic Representation of the Past 117
- 4. Remembrance in Connection with Forgiveness and Reconciliation 120
  - 4.1 Hosea: God Remembers Sins 121
  - 4.2 Malachi 3:16: The Book of Remembrance 123
  - 4.3 Nehemiah 9:1–37: The Great Confession of Sins 126
  - 4.4 Jeremiah 31:34: God Remembers Sins No More 129
- 5. Remembrance in the New Testament 130
  - 5.1 The Role of Memory in the Early Communities in Jesus' Time 130
  - 5.2 Linguistic Analysis of Memory in the New Testament 136
  - 5.3 Anamnesis in Hebrews 10:3: The Memorial of Sins 139

6. Anamnesis in the Eucharist 142
    6.1 The Four Texts 142
    6.2 The Eucharist and the God who Remembers 145
    6.3 The Eucharist and Passover 146
    6.4 The Eucharist and Sacrificial Act 152
7. Conclusion 154

Chapter 4. Towards a Theology of Remembrance

1. Johann Baptist Metz: Memoria Passionis as Dangerous Memory 157
    1.1 The Bourgeois Church, Middle Class Religion, and Post-Bourgeois World 163
    1.2 Political Theology 165
    1.3 Memory and Time 168
    1.4 Dangerous Memory: Memoria Passionis 172
    1.5 Memory of Suffering? 176
    1.6 Flora Keshkegian: Redeeming Memories for Healing and Transformation 177
2. Alexander Schmemann: The Eucharist and Liturgical Memory 185
    2.1 Crisis in the Church 187
    2.2 Liturgical Theology 190
    2.3 The Central Place of the Eucharist 193
    2.4 Liturgy of Time 196
    2.5 Sacrament of Remembrance 200
    2.6 Joyous Communal Memory 204
    2.7 Liturgical Theology and Political Theology in Dialogue 205
    3. Miroslav Volf: The End of Memory 208
    3.1 Volf's View on Forgiveness 212
    3.2 The Role of Memory 215
    3.3 Remember Truthfully 217
    3.4 A Community of Remembrance 220
    3.5 The End of Memory? 222
4. Metz, Schmemann, and Volf in Dialogue 226

Chapter 5. Remembrance in the Liturgy of the Eucharist

1. Liturgy and Remembrance 232
    1.1 The Contribution of the Three Theologians in the Liturgy of the Eucharist 240
    1.2. Elements of the Eucharist 242
2. The Elements of Eucharist in the BEM Document 247
    2.1 The Elements of the BEM Eucharistic Liturgy 252
    2.2 Lima Liturgy of the Eucharist 260
3. The Liturgy of HKBP 265
    3.1 Order of the Sunday Service 266
    3.2 The Preparation Service for the Celebration of the Eucharist 271
    3.3 The Eucharistic Liturgy after the Preparation Service 276
    3.4 The Eucharistic Liturgy without Preparation Service 281
4. Eucharistic Liturgy: A Space for Healing Memories 286
    4.1 Proposed Preparation Service of the Eucharist 287
    4.2 Proposed Eucharistic Liturgy after Preparation Service 290
5. Conclusion 296

Chapter 6. God Remembers

1. The Importance of Remembrance 299
2. To Create a Redemptive Memory 301
3. The Eucharist and Justice 306
4. Epilogue 309

Bibliography

1. Books 312
2. Articles in Books and Journals 319
3. Dictionaries and Encyclopedias 324
4. Internet Resources 324
5. Newspaper Articles 325

Indexes

1. Index of Names 326
2. Index of Biblical References ....

List of Abbreviations

AMIN	Angowuloa Masehi Indonesia Nias/Christian Communion of Indonesia in Nias
BAKORSTANASDA	Badan Koordinasi Stabilitas Nasional Daerah/The Jakarta Agency for the Coordination of Support for the Development of National Stability
CCA	Christian Conference of Asia
FKW-HKBP	Forum Kerukunan Warga HKBP/ Member's Peace Forum of HKBP
GKPA	Gereja Kristen Protestan Angkola/Christian Protestant Angkola Church
GBKP	Gereja Batak Karo Protestan/Protestant Karo Batak Church
GKPI	Gereja Kristen Protestan Indonesia/Christian Protestant Church in Indonesia
GKPPD	Gereja Kristen Protestan Pakpak Dairi/Pakpak Dairi Christian Protestant Church
GKPS	Gereja Kristen Protestan Simalungun/Simalungun Christian Protestant Church
HKBP	Huria Kristen Batak Protestan/Batak Protestant Christian Church
HKBP SAI-Tiara	HKBP side that was produced by Sinode Agung Istimewa Tiara (SAI Tiara) or the Extraordinary General Synod in Tiara Center, the group under the leadership of Ephorus Rev. P.W.T. Simanjuntak
HKBP AP-SSA	HKBP Aturan Peraturan-Setia Sampai Akhir or HKBP Order & Implementation/Be Faithful until the End group understood themselves as being faithful to the Church Order, under the leadership of Ephorus Rev. S.A.E. Nababan
KSPPM	Kelompok Studi Pengembangan dan Pemberdayaan Masyarakat/Study Group of People Development and Empowerment
LWF	Lutheran World Federation
PGI	Persekutuan Gereja-gereja di Indonesia/Communion of Churches in Indonesia
RMG	Rheinische Missionsgesellschaft
STT HKBP	Sekolah Tinggi Teologi HKBP/HKBP Theological Seminary
TEN Team	Tim Evangelisasi Nehemia/TEN or Nehemiah Evangelization Team

UEM	The United Evangelical Mission, also known as VEM
VELKD	United Evangelical Lutheran Church of Germany
VEM	Vereinte Evangelische Mission, also known as UEM
WCC	World Council of Churches

Acknowledgments

"Jesus, remember me when you come into your kingdom!" (Luke 23:42). This was the plea of one of the two criminals that was hung on the cross with Jesus. His plea resembles his hope of Jesus' remembrance and his trust for his salvation. Before saying that, the criminal confessed that he deserved to be crucified because of what he had done. This small scene on the cross has all the elements that we are going to explore in this research on the theology of remembrance: a powerful confession that is followed by the request to Jesus's remembrance, the suffering on the cross, rejection, a story of the past hurt, and the hope of salvation. The journey towards a theology of remembrance brings us to a similar hope that the criminal expressed on the cross, that God remember us. In the end, we will come to an understanding of remembrance in Christian theology, thus, I present to you this dissertation.

As a result of my dissertation this book would not have been possible without the help of many people.

First of all I remember God's love in my life and how God's remembrance led me to finish this dissertation. I would like to thank my *Doktorvater* Prof. Van der Borght for his never-ending spirit to help me right from the start, his encouragement, his faith in me, and his father-teacher role while helping me finding my own theological basis. I also would like to thank Prof. Singgih for the questions and conversations that helped me remember my own roots. I thank Prof. van de Beek for the powerful discussions I had.

I thank the financial help from Yayasan Tanoto, and Mbak Ratih as my contact person; also Stichting Mission from PKN, and the administrator Pak H. Lems; and Fam. Liem who helped me during my ministry year in GKIN. Thank you A*m*ST*a*R through Dr. Arie Zwiep for having accepted this dissertation into the publication series, and Jan Oegema of VU University Press for his involvement.

Much appreciation goes to Okke Postma who helped me edit my English, which was furthered by Susanne Sitohang and Julie Whittenberg.

I thank my wife Dorta for her support and encouragement that literally speeded up the writing of the dissertation. I am always indebted to a great person whom I admire, my father, and my wonderful mother; my brother Darta & Marina, my sister Iyuth, the ones who were always there for me.

I will always remember the kindness of Tante Tina Haisma Saragih and Oom Luitzen Haisma; Szaszi and Minette; and Beatrix. Lastly, I want to thank the institutions and the people in it that helped me grow, my church HKBP, Jakarta Theological Seminary, the Faculty of Theology of VU University Amsterdam, the GKIN Church, Perki in the Netherlands.

I thank you all for all your help, support, and prayer. It has been quite a journey that brought so much life-experience. After more than four years in the Netherlands, I feel ready now for a new journey in Indonesia. I will always remember my days in the Netherlands with a grateful heart.

Binsar Jonathan Pakpahan
Jakarta, June 2012

Chapter One

Introduction

1. Signs of a Growing Culture of Remembrance

> For memory is a blessing: it creates bonds rather than destroys them. Bonds between present and past, between individuals and groups. It is because I remember our common beginning that I move closer to my fellow human beings. It is because I refuse to forget that their future is as important as my own. What would the future of man be if it were devoid of memory?[1]

With these words in *From the Kingdom of Memory,* Elie Wiesel has expressed his positive view on memory. The opinion is remarkable, coming from the pen of a person who carries with him very painful memories as a Jewish survivor of a concentration camp during World War II, an experience that tore his family apart. In fact, Wiesel's biggest fear is forgetfulness. He wants to remember what happened in the past, and to be an agent of memory. For him, memory is the answer to hatred. He remembers for the sake of the generations to come, in order to offer hope to his generation.

Wiesel is one of the defenders of memories of past atrocities who want to remember for the sake of the victims. For him, memory helps people to connect to what happened in the past and to remember the story of the people who suffered. His voice also resonates with many others who advocate remembrance as a place of learning so that similar events will not happen again in the future. For Wiesel, to remember is actually to live your life and to have your identity or a sense of self through memories. It is a revival of one's existence by preventing the past from disappearing and to call upon the future. In his own words:

> Memory is a passion no less powerful and pervasive than love. What does it mean to remember? It is to live in more than one world, to prevent the past from fading and to call upon the future to illuminate it. To remember is to revive fragments of existence, to rescue lost beings, to

---

[1] Elie Wiesel, *From the Kingdom of Memory: Reminiscences* (New York: Schocken Books, 1995), 10.

cast harsh light on faces and events, to drive back the sands that cover the surface of things, to combat oblivion and to reject death.[2]

The shift in the purpose of remembering past conflict as preserving the story of the winner to one of creating space for the voice of victims has developed mainly in the previous century. In the case of conflict, typically it would be the winners who used to write the history about what had happened. Winners usually wanted to preserve their power by writing their own version of the story that told what really happened. The memory of the winner would become "the story", a story that had to be accepted by the side that lost, and thus would become history. However, the winner's story does not always truly portray what really happened. We can always find a different side of the coin to any story.

This way of remembering the past has been changed thanks to the way people look at the importance of memories. We have erected many memorials in the last century to remember communal catastrophes in the past, such as the Auschwitz memorials in different places in the world, the WTC memorial after 9/11, Bali Bomb monument, and many others.

Instead of trying to forget as a means to come to terms with the past atrocities, more and more in recent decades, peoples and nations have become convinced that remembering is a better option. For many Jewish institutions and individuals, remembering prevents forgetting and hinders repetition of the same kind of shameful acts of genocide. In South Africa, the Truth and Reconciliation Commission tried to recover the truth about the excessive violence during the apartheid era. The aim of the commission provided a mechanism for a process of forgiveness and reconciliation in order to help the country move on and to build a post-apartheid rainbow nation. In Australia, the official institution of a special day of remembrance, Australian National Sorry Day on May 26, expresses the intention to recognize the wrong being done to indigenous people in Australia in the twentieth century in order to restore the broken relation between the Australian authorities and aboriginals. These three cases offer different purposes and approaches in their remembrance of the past communal conflict, and consequently render different results. The important common point to recognize here is that they do not want to forget what has happened in their past.

---

[2] Elie Wiesel, *All Rivers Run to the Sea: Memoirs Volume 1, 1928–1969* (London: Harper Collins, 1996), 150, as in Robert Vosloo, "Reconciliation as the Embodiment of Memory and Hope" in *Journal of Theology for Southern Africa, vol. 109* (March 2001), 25–40.

This call to remember a painful past instead of forgetting it is reinforced by a growing commitment on the part of the international community to protect human rights. A new impetus for national and international human rights laws came at the end of the 20th century, as countries in several regions of the world moved from dictatorship to democracy and began to address their social and cultural legacies of the past regimes of violence. The efforts that have been made include establishing truth commissions, opening state files, removing officials from office, publicizing the name of the perpetrators and the victims, providing reparations and apologies, providing public services to treat trauma, creating memorials to commemorate victims, and promoting public educational programs to incorporate the experience into the official historical records.

The improved media technology has also influenced people's effectiveness in keeping memories. Modern technology has helped everyone to get easier access to news and archives. These abundant resources of information and stories have created space for more voices to be heard. We can also find videos and voice recordings of the past wars or events on the Internet. Once something is put on the Internet, it stays there as accessible to all and forever.

2. To Remember or to Forget?

The perception of a growing culture of remembrance has stimulated research on memory and remembering and has pressed persistent questions about this shift in dealing with past atrocities. The first question that comes to mind is whether remembrance is the right way in dealing with the past. If a memory is too painful to bear, would it not be better to forget it? What good does a memory of the painful past bring? How can we deal with it? What if the past is too painful, so that it seems better to let go of the memory?

Bringing back the painful past can bring the pain back as well. This is why many prefer to forget about past wounds and try to bury a bitter past. The fear is that talking about the old wounds is the same as repeating the same bitter memories of the past. It can be considered as a way of opening the same wound again. Many choose not to talk about past injuries and are thus choosing the idea of letting go of the past by forgetting it. The most painful things are usually the ones we try to forget because they hurt too much to remember.

Remembrance can also lead to retribution, or even to vengeance. Unresolved past experiences can come back and haunt us again in the future, and easily lead us to another act of violence. Many stories of violence happened as a result of unresolved memories. People with unresolved experiences of violence during their childhood tend to repeat the violent act in their adulthood. At a communal level, the memory of past conflict that is being transmitted to the next generations can lead to future vengeance. Those generations then share the remembrance of the pain without having to experience what really happened in the past. With the memory of victimization, a group of people can one day choose to take revenge against something that happened to their previous generation. This is why remembrance of past hurt is a risky matter.

Remembering the past can trap people in romanticizing the past, or it could even become a sort of re-vengeance in turn. We must be aware of the danger that memories—and how we remember them—can be manipulated, and thereby even manipulate us. The memories of those who were originally slaves, immigrants, or indigenous peoples and those who colonized them are somewhat different. The official story of history is usually the story of the people who have the power. History is the story of the winner. This could lead to never-ending prejudices among those who maintain the version of that story.[3]

Inevitably, the memory of events is multilayered, and often fractured. How they are remembered is influenced by age, gender, nationality, and political or religious affiliations of the individual or group remembering. Memory is further colored by the circumstances of those remembering, both in the past (for example whether they experienced occupation, served in the armed forces, were the member of the resistance, or an inmate in a concentration camp or death camp), and in the present.[4]

The difficulties of dealing with memory have invited people to use the term "forgive and forget." It means: what has been forgiven will be forgotten.[5] However, this sentence has been used with a different sense, which is to let the past stay in the past. But does that work? Simply to forget actually is not to forgive, and to forgive is not the same as to forget. For if you totally forget that someone once hurt you, you cannot

---

[3] See Geneviève Jacques, *Beyond Impunity: An Ecumenical Approach to Truth, Justice and Reconciliation* (Geneva: WCC Publications, 2000), 29.

[4] Isabel Wollaston, *A War Against Memory: The Future of Holocaust Remembrance* (London: SPCK, 1996), 1–2.

[5] See the play of the word in Lewis B. Smedes, *Forgive and Forget: Healing the Hurts We Don't Deserve* (New York: Harper & Row Publishers, 1984).

forgive that person. Of course, you may not need to forgive them since you no longer remember the pain. Often though, forgetting is not permanent. The memory is not eradicated, and it can be resurrected. Thus, in order to forgive, you have to first remember. Perhaps after you have forgiven, you can subsequently forget, maybe permanently. But the two processes—to forgive and forget—are distinct, not to be merged. To forget, especially to forget a wrong done to someone else (or to presume the right to forgive a wrong done not to you but to a third party), is considered by many not to be a moral virtue but rather a morally reprehensible condoning of evil.[6] To forget a crime that has been done, especially to a third party, is considered supporting evil. This is why the act of remembering is also important for the way of forgiveness.

Paul Ricoeur has written an extensive work *Memory, History, and Forgetting*. From a philosophical point of view, he has analysed the depth of oral memory as the most original form of memory. Not only written documents, but also—and even more so—oral storytelling is important for memory. Because of the nature of memory that is connected to individual's voices, and the incomplete nature and the subjectivity of history and archivization, forgetting will always be present in remembrance. For Ricoeur, forgetting and forgiveness comes separately and together. He explains,

> Separately, inasmuch as they each belong to a distinct problematic: for forgetting, the problematic of memory and faithfulness to the past, for forgiveness, guilt and reconciliation with the past. Together, inasmuch as their respective itineraries intersect at a place that is not a place and which is best indicated by the term "horizon": Horizon of a memory appeased, even of a happy forgetting.[7]

The problem of forgetting also comes in three different modes. Forgetting can come as a result of a blocked memory, this is the first mode. A person can subconsciously decide to block a certain event from her or his mind. The second mode of forgetting comes in the form of manipulated memory, where the memory that is presented has already been manipulated. The third mode is a commanded forgetting, which is in the form of amnesty. In amnesty we are asked to not remember what happened, not to "silence evil but to state it in a pacified mode, without anger."[8]

---

[6] See Solomon Schimmel, *Wounds Not Healed by Time: The Power of Repentance and Forgiveness* (New York: Oxford University Press, 2002), 48–49.

[7] Paul Ricoeur, *Memory, History, Forgetting,* trans. Kathleen Blamey & David Pellauer (Chicago: The Chicago University Press, 2006), 412

[8] Ricoeur, *Memory*, 456.

Ricoeur also introduces the concepts of happy memory and of happy forgetting. Happy memory receives its place in the mnemonic modes of memory: reminding, reminiscing, and recognizing.[9] Happy memory is by voluntarily wanting to remember because it brings a desired good to the one who remembers. It makes us able to remember without mourning. It is not motivated by "suspicion or by the excessive primacy accorded to phenomena of deficiency, even to the pathology of memory."[10] Happy forgetting is in parallel with happy memory. A happy forgetting can be a necessity for the possibility of remembering. A happy forgetting is when we choose to have the happy memory, and for this reason only we want to remember some things and forget other events or circumstances.

His idea of happy forgetting is an outcome of his epilogue in the book about forgiveness.[11] In the epilogue, Ricoeur turns to the religious idea of forgiveness as the eschatology of forgetting. It is difficult but not impossible to do.[12] With the light of forgiveness, memory, history and forgetting can be seen in the light of eschatology, "the wish for a happy and peaceful memory, something of which would be communicated in the practice of history and even in the heart of insurmountable uncertainties that preside over our relations to forgetting."[13] His epilogue shows that the religious concept of forgiveness is being considered seriously through philosophical hermeneutics. For him, with reference to Hannah Arendt, "forgiveness has the effect of dissociating the debt from its burden of guilt and in a sense of laying bare the phenomenon of the debt, as the dependence on a received heritage ... it should release the agent from his act."[14]

---

[9] Ricoeur uses the idea of mnemonic memory from Edward S. Casey, *Remembering: A Phenomenological Study* (Bloomington, Indiana: Indiana University Press, 2000). Mnemonic is any learning technique that helps us remember.

[10] Ricoeur, *Memory*, 37. Ricoeur also mentions that when Augustine said, "The power of memory is prodigious my God. It is a vast immeasurable sanctuary (X, 8)," it is precisely a happy memory. We can say that happy memory also includes the use of memory as a place where one can be at peace.

[11] He claims that the epilogue came as reflection on the previous chapters and was not intended as something that would be exclusively written for the book. See Paul Ricoeur, "Memory, History, Forgiveness: A Dialogue Between Paul Ricoeur and Sorin Antohi," an interview with Sorin Antohi, translated from French and annotated by Gil Anidjar, a transcript of conversation that took place at Pasts, Inc., Center for Historical Studies, Budapest on March 10, 2003. The interview is available online at http://www.janushead.org/8–1/Ricoeur.pdf, accessed March 2010.

[12] Ricoeur, *Memory*, 457.

[13] Ricoeur, *Memory*, 459.

[14] Ricoeur, *Memory*, 489.

3. What is Remembrance?

A lot of multidisciplinary researches on the meaning of remembrance have taken place. Since many researches and in-depth analysis have their own definitions, we opt to start with a lexicographic description of the word. "Remembrance" is derived from the verb "remember", and often connected with the word "memory". According to the *Oxford Dictionary*, "remembrance" is: n. the act of remembering or process of being remembered; a memory or recollection, while the verb "remember" means: "keep in memory, not forget; (also absol.) bring back into one's thought, call to mind (knowledge or experience, etc)".[15] The *Dictionary of Philosophy and Psychology* mentions that remember derives from the Latin word: re + *memiri*, which is to be mindful in thought; to exercise memory. Moreover, remembrance is a term used in a very loose way to cover memory, recollection, and retention, or the result of the memory function generally.[16] Thus, according to the lexicographic understanding, remembrance means an action of the mind to recall something of the past. To remember is to exercise the memory of the past and bring it back into the present.

However, remembering has also a deeper understanding than what we have said above. The *Stanford Encyclopedia of Philosophy* (SED) mentions that there are two major groups of memory. The first group is non-declarative memory. This is the kind of memory where we do not have to declare or seek for the truth because it is more of a habit or procedure. In this group, we have skill memory, which is the remembrance of how to drive, play guitar or run because it is our procedural, habit, and skill memory. We also remember facts that happened, for instance our birthday, or our graduation day, which is called propositional memory.

The second group is the declarative memory, where we seek to find the truth about the event that we had. This declarative memory includes semantic memory which is the memory or facts that related to conceptual information underlying our general knowledge of the world, for example, the apartheid system in South Africa. Another memory that belongs to declarative memory is recollective memory or episodic memory, which is memory for experience events and episodes, such as

---

[15] See H. W. Fowler et al. (eds.), *The Concise Oxford Dictionary of Current English* 9th edition (New York: Clarendon Press, 1995).

[16] James Mark Baldwin et al. (eds.), *Dictionary of Philosophy and Psychology Vol. II* – copyright 1901 (Gloucester, Massachusetts: Peter Smith, 1960).

the conversation you had, or the argument, or feelings about something that happened to you. Declarative memory demands from us to find out what really happened; it needs facts, while non-declarative memory does not really represent the past.[17]

Declarative memory is considered as a basic need in order to have a sense of one self. This form of memory functions to maintain a hold on one's identity. One can barely live without this type of memory. Remembrance in this form of memory is thus an active and dynamic act of the mind. What we are going to study in more depth in this research is the declarative form of remembrance, especially in the case of communal conflict.

4. Shared Memory and Reconciliation

Remembering and forgetting also have a connection with the sense of one's identity. In her research on the role of memory with regard to identity issues in traumatic situations, Nicola King says, "Reading the texts of memory shows that "remembering the self" is not a case of restoring an original identity, but a continuous process of "*re*-membering", of putting together moment by moment, of provisional and partial reconstruction."[18] It means that remembering is a part of self-construction. Our memory is also connected with our identity.

Collective memory also shapes the identity of a community. It is a high point of any specific group that unifies after having a certain feeling towards an event. Yael Zerubabel, in his award-winning research on the role of collective memory in the making of the Israeli nation, said that the commemorative narratives of specific events often suggests one's unique character, while their examination within the context of the master commemorative narrative indicates the recurrence of historical patterns in the group's experience.[19] In other words, the events and groups of individuals are influencing each other. Yet, this remembering of one's identity cannot avoid configuring the other in ac-

---

[17] See the complexities of the understanding of memory in John Sutton, "Memory", *The Stanford Encyclopedia of Philosophy (Summer 2010 Edition)*, http://plato.stanford.edu/archives/sum2010/entries/memory/, accessed April 15, 2011.

[18] Nicola King, *Memory, Narrative, Identity: Remembering the Self* (Edinburgh: Edinburgh University Press, 2000), 175. King tries to contribute to the growing field of trauma and holocaust studies and to explorations of the workings of memory.

[19] Yael Zerubabel, *Recovered Roots: Collective Memory and the Making of Israeli National Tradition* (Chicago: The University of Chicago Press, 1994), 7.

cordance with some model of cognitive apprehension.[20] One's identity always has the tendency of putting others in the construction of his/her memory. Either victims put perpetrators in their memory's framework or it will be the other way around.

In the social sphere, remembering memories is not easy. The task has a complex relation to time. What is important to note is that memory is not history.[21] King states, "Memory can create the illusion of a momentary return to a lost past; its operations also articulate the complex relationship between past, present and future in human consciousness."[22] This is why we should deal cautiously with memories. Stories told, as memory of the past, are not the same as the real event. Memories of victims differ from those of perpetrators. Victims and perpetrators recall an event differently; yet each tends to think that they have the true meaning in their own opinion. This is why an act of remembering by both sides is not only difficult, but also risky. King notes,

> In the case of traumatic memory, this may be a process of repetition with a difference, as we revisit painful or otherwise significant moments of the past with changed and changing emotion and understanding… memories—initially perhaps unbidden, visual, sensory, immediate—became text as soon as we begin to describe them to ourselves and others, to put them into sequence or turn them into stories.[23]

Traumatic memories are reiterated through stories, while the stories may not be the real history. It is this narrative experience that will become memory.

Avishai Margalit in his book *The Ethics of Memory* explains further how a personal story becomes a collective memory.[24] Margalit tries to clarify the terms of shared memory and common memory. A common memory "aggregates the memories of all those people who remember a certain episode which each of them experienced individually. A

---

[20] Edith Wyschogrod, *An Ethics of Remembering: History, Heterology, and the Nameless Others* (Chicago: The University of Chicago Press, 1998), 9–10.
[21] See James V. Wertsch, *Voices of Collective Remembering* (Cambridge: Cambridge University Press, 2002), 33–66. Wertsch explains more about the difference between remembering and history, and remembering vs. re-experiencing.
[22] King, *Memory*, 11.
[23] King, *Memory*, 175.
[24] Avishai Margalit, *The Ethics of Memory* (Cambridge: Harvard University Press, 2003). Some of his important questions are: "Are we obligated to remember people and events from the past? If we are, what is the nature of this obligation? Are remembering and forgetting proper subjects of moral praise or blame? Who are the 'we' who may be obligated to remember: the collective 'we', or some distributive sense of 'we' that puts the obligation to remember on each and every member of the collective?"

shared memory integrates and calibrates the different perspectives of those who remember the episode into one version."[25] Thus, a shared memory needs cooperation between people who experienced the event and agreement to a certain extent about what actually happened. This shared memory is then kept in different ways. A traditional society will have a hierarchy of storytelling from their leader or priest, and modern society will have institutions such as archives, monuments, street names, etc. Nevertheless, a shared memory does not guarantee that the event will be connected with everyone in the community. Margalit says, "The significance of the event for us depends on our being personally connected with what happened."[26] Once the story or stories of individuals have become a shared story, the community will have the responsibility to see to it that the memory is preserved, but it is not the responsibility of each one to remember everything.

Shared memory is not the same as history because it is an agreement on the story of an event; it can be a closed memory after the members of society have agreed upon it. History always looks for alternative lines in its search for historical descriptions. This is why tradition is also a form of shared memory because it is a sanctified and authorized story for the community. He also says that, "History is regarded as a systematic and critical collective memory. But collective memory is really more akin to conventional wisdom than to common sense."[27] Thus, shared memory is important for the society, and could become part of history, but it is not history.

He proposes that the natural communities of memory are families, clans, tribes, religious communities, and nations. This means that story of the past has a chance of survival in these communities. The story of the past can come in two forms, as positive memories and as negative memories. These memories have layers of shared story among different communities and these layers can influence each other. However, it seems natural that in their shared story more authority will be afforded to larger communities.

Margalit believes that there should be a universal ethical community that ought to have some minimal shared moral memories. What should humanity remember? He says, "Striking examples of radical evil and crimes against humanity, such as enslavement, deportations of ci-

---

[25] Margalit, *The Ethics of Memory*, 51–52.
[26] Margalit, *The Ethics of Memory*, 53.
[27] Margalit, *The Ethics of Memory*, 63.

vilian populations, and mass exterminations."²⁸ Even though he is not sure about how we can create such shared story for humanity—because it will take a lot of political effort and willingness from leaders of the world—he is convinced that it will be really detrimental not to do it. He also believes that by preserving shared memory of past atrocities we will be able to protect humanity in the future. We have to remember because by doing so we may be able to prevent negative forces from rewriting the past and thereby controlling collective memory.

David E. Lorey and William H. Beezley, editors of *Genocide, Collective Violence, and Popular Memory: The Politics of Remembrance in the Twentieth Century*, explain in their book that,

> At the very center of all these issues of recovery, reconciliation, and looking forward in history—here in particular, is the social processing of memories of genocide and collective violence. All the faces of history are present in this connection: history as imagined; history as practiced by historians, policy-makers and others; history as battleground of ideas, ideals, and ideologies; history as therapy; history as taught in the schools; and history as the patrimony of a society or nation.²⁹

To summarize, memory is like a battleground for everything. Restoring collective remembrance is central for the work of reconciliation. Therefore, it is important to grow towards a common story, shared by victims and perpetrators. Charles Villa-Vicencio emphasizes the importance of this common storytelling,

> We need to tell one another stories. It is perhaps the only basis for recognizing and yet transcending our differences. It is perhaps the only basis for gaining and understanding of both ourselves and the hopes and fears of others. It is the only basis on which different stories, different memories, and different histories can emerge as the basis for an inclusive nation-building exercise."³⁰

---

[28] Margalit, *The Ethics of Memory*, 78.

[29] David E. Lorey and William H. Beezley (eds.), *Genocide, Collective Violence, and Popular Memory* (Wilmington, Delaware: SR Books, 2002), xiv.

[30] Charles Villa-Vicencio, "Telling One Another Stories", in *The Reconciliation of Peoples: Challenge to the Churches*, eds. Gregory Baum & Harold Wells, (Geneva: WCC, 1997), 31. Villa-Vicencio also quotes H. Richard Niebuhr who says, "Where common memories is lacking, where men [sic] do not share in the same past, there can be no real community, and where community is to be formed common memory must be created....The measure of our distance from each other in our nations and our groups can be taken by noting the divergence, the separateness and the lack of sympathy in our social memories. Conversely, the measure of our unity is the extent of our common memory." H. Richard Niebuhr, *The Meaning of Revelation* (New York: Macmillan, 1967), 115.

5. Remembrance of Conflict in the Church

The observation of the culture of remembrance, the questions about forgetting or remembering, the role of remembrance in identity formation and the building of a shared story on the way to reconciliation, all these aspects also touched me at a personal level. The inspiration came when I heard a guest lecturer, Fransisco Budi Hardiman, an Indonesian Catholic philosopher, deliver a paper at Jakarta Theological Seminary. He tried to explain the connection between remembering and an event through a philosophical analysis. Victims tend to recall their negative experiences again and again. Or it could go the opposite way, when they tend to forget it. In trauma, to remember and to forget are a part of a physical mechanism that you can never let go off. When victims try to forget, they are in fact remembering. Remembering and forgetting is a movement in the mind of the victims.[31]

His lecture inspired me because it was in some way exactly connected with what was happening in the Church of which I am a member and a pastor: the Huria Kristen Batak Protestan (HKBP) or the Batak Protestant Christian Church. HKBP was founded by the Reinische Missionsgessellscaft (RMG) in 1861.[32] Its members belong mainly to the Batak ethnic group that comes from the region of North Tapanuli in North Sumatra, Indonesia. HKBP, a member of Lutheran World Federation and of the World Council of Churches, has a total membership of 4.1 million in 3,176 local churches, and is served by 1,445 ministers.[33]

The story related here began when there was a crisis at the HKBP Great Synod in 1992 when the Church had to choose new leadership (the leaders of the HKBP as a whole). There was no final decision during this Great Synod. Afterwards, the military took over the Assembly and appointed a new transitional ephorus (bishop) to be in charge of the HKBP to organize a new Great Synod.[34] This caused division within

---

[31] Fransisco Budi Hardiman, "Melampaui Mengingat dan Melupakan" (Paper presented at the 69th Dies Natalis of Jakarta Theological Seminary, September 2003).

[32] This is considered the starting date of the Church when four missionaries got together and discussed the future of the mission. They are Rev. van Asselt, Rev. Betz, Rev. Klammer, and Rev. Heine. However, the work of the mission had already started in 1824 when Burton and Ward from the Baptist Church in England came in 1824.

[33] For more information about the Church, visit their website at http://www.hkbp.or.id. See Almanak HKBP 2011 (Tarutung: HKBP, 2010).

[34] This appointment was made under the letter of Bakorstanasda Sumbagut No. Skep/3/Stada/XII/1992 in 23rd of December 1992. Bakorstanasda or Badan Koordinasi Pertahanan Daerah Sumatera Bagian Utara (The Region's Defense Coordination Office of North Sumatra).

the Church between those who followed the new leader that had been appointed by the government and the people who thought that this government involvement was outrageous and still were loyal to the old ephorus.[35] The conflict lasted officially until 1998. An older version of the official profile of the Church contains the following statement about that period,

> For about six years (1993-1998) HKBP has undergone a serious crisis, before the reconciliation in 1998. Thank God, HKBP has not fallen apart. However, the crisis had resulted in a number of drawbacks, among others: there are still some congregations which have not yet been reinstalled in full harmony; there has been no improvement in the ministry as a whole, particularly in terms of preparations for facing the challenges of the 21st century; a number of buildings and other facilities need repairs or rehabilitations; and ecumenical relations need improvements.[36]

From the official statement we can recognize that the problem is enormous, not only buildings and facilities that need to be repaired were neglected, but ecumenical relations had also been shattered. However, the statement does not say anything about victims or perpetrators. There was nothing mentioned about how the crisis started, what really happened during it, and what had been done afterwards to reconcile. There is a sense of silence intended to drop the problem and leave it behind. This raises questions: have people really been reconciled–—especially since "there are still some congregations which have not yet been reinstalled in full harmony"? How did and does the Church deal with this?

Actually, the six year conflict resulted in huge damage within the Church. Both ministers and lay people were physically and otherwise injured and even killed during the conflict. Many churches have been divided, and even after the official end of the conflict many refused to go back to the old congregation and preferred to establish new congregations, albeit within the denomination at large. Many of the assets of

---

[35] For instance see, Moksa Nadeak et al., *Krisis HKBP: Ujian bagi Iman dan Pengamalan Pancasila* (Eng: *Crisis of HKBP: A Test of Faith and Pancasila's Application*) (Tarutung: Biro Informasi HKBP, 1995), and Saut Sirait, *Politik Kristen di Indonesia: Suatu Tinjauan Etis* (Eng: *Christian Politics in Indonesia*) (Jakarta: BPK-GM, 2001). However, take note that both books were written by the group that remained loyal to the old ephorus.

[36] HKBP, *The Profile of HKBP Walking into the Third Millennium* (Tarutung: HKBP, 2002), 3. We are using the quote from the year 2002 because it would be for another eight years the most complete official statement about the conflict when compared to recent versions. Compare to more recent Almanak HKBP 2010 that mentions the case in HKBP history section, to the following statement, "1992 - The election of new HKBP leaders could not take place, and there were separations in HKBP until 1998."

the Church were gone. Many members of the Church moved to other denominations and never came back even after the so-called reconciliation. There are still congregations in Jakarta and Bandung that refuse to be reconciled. The hurt is still there. In brief, the conflict is really too deep to be left behind.

In some sense, the decision not to talk about the past trauma seems to make common sense because there is nothing positive to be gained from passing on the story. Just as the many painful stories of the past hurt, the retelling and remembrance of the painful past could evoke hidden anger from hearers and from the people who experienced the conflict. There is also the danger that remembrance can become a form of vengeance. People feared that encouraging the remembrance of the case would lead to yet another dispute about whom to blame in the conflict, and this could even lead to a judicial matter. These kinds of reasons can be surmised about why people choose to be silent about the past hurt and instead take the road to the future without a coherent story.

However, the stories of the past might well be too important to be silenced. Is keeping quiet the best solution for this conflict? What about the victims? How should we deal with deep and collective wounds?

What has happened in my Church is an illustration of the sort of reality that exists in many churches, which is the inability to come to terms with conflicts within Christian communities and the inability to forgive and to reconcile. Instead, many churches have opted to forget about past conflicts. In recent decades in many churches, the coming to light of sexual abuse of pastoral relations and the systematic effort to cover up and to forget such abuse, illustrates in a painful way that Christian communities in many ways have yet to embrace this new culture of remembrance.

6. *Christian Remembrance*

The command to remember has always been central in Christian faith. In fact it is the basis of Christianity. Christians are called to remember their identity, and the saving act of God through the life, death and resurrection of Jesus. The idea of remembrance is central in Christian theology. Christian liturgy is the response that Christians make to God's saving action. The Bible is full with the command to remember God's saving deeds. This is why a deeper understanding of the idea of remembrance in Christian faith can contribute to the ongoing discussion of remembrance, especially when it is connected with communal trauma and conflict.

Long before the development of modern social science on memory, Augustine has reflected on the profound nature of human's memory.[37] Augustine struggled with the notion of memory in his Confessions. He sees memory as a dynamic, active, and continuous notion that helps us to recognize God. Augustine says that memory is "a great field or a spacious palace, a storehouse for countless images of all kinds which are conveyed to it by the senses."[38] At first we might think that Augustine is saying that memory is like a hard disk of a computer that keeps memories and stores them. Memories can be recalled and brought out from their storage when needed, each through their own gateways. Nevertheless, he goes further and says, "The power of memory is prodigious, my God. It is a vast immeasurable sanctuary. Who can plumb its depths? And yet it is a faculty of my soul. Although it is part of my nature, I cannot understand all that I am. This means, then, that the mind is too narrow to contain itself entirely."[39] Thus, even though memory is like a storehouse, one cannot fully control what is in it, nor fully control the ability to recall the content whenever desired.

This view on memory is connected with his view on time. Augustine sees that there are three different times, a present of past things (memory), a present of present things (perception), and a present of future things (expectation).[40] He thinks that there is actually no real presence except our present perception of what the past was, what the present is, and what the future will be. What has happened to us will be kept in memory and will be used to recognize our present and future. Therefore, memory is constantly being reshaped by our perception through time. In other words, my feelings towards something are kept in my memory. They can be recalled when I want to use them, but my memory does not evoke exactly the same feelings as when I experienced the original feelings.

---

[37] See Gary Wills, *St. Augustine's Memory [Introduction and Commentary]* (New York: Viking Penguin, 2002). Wills sees 7 points in Augustine's understanding of memory: (1) Memory as dynamic; (2) Memory as constructive; (3) Memory as the self; (4) Memory as guide to conduct; (5) Memory as the basis of community; (6) The dialectic of memory; (7) Memory as pathway towards God. We shall review some of these that are related to our topic.

[38] Augustine, *Confessions* (Harmondsworth: Penguin, 1961), Book X, 8. We shall compare it with the translation of Gary Wills.

[39] Augustine, *Confessions*, Book X, 8.

[40] Augustine, *Confessions*, Book XI, 20.

Augustine compares memory to a mental stomach and the feelings to food. He gives the example of sad feelings (pictured as food) that have been digested by my memory (pictured as stomach). The sad feelings stay in my memory, but do not have the same taste as when they first entered my stomach. He says, "Yet, while I remember these feelings by drawing them from my memory, they do not produce any emotional effect in me."[41] Augustine seems to have an optimistic view of being able to recall past emotions without re-experiencing it. It could also mean that in Augustine's view, we should be able to recall our hurtful past without re-experiencing the pain.

However the process of remembering is also dynamic and full of reinterpretation of what is in the memory. The memory of the past is re-experienced when the person who remembers gives a meaning to it. This is why the process of forgetting is an interesting thing. He says, "When I remember memory, my memory is present to itself by its own power; but when I remember forgetfulness, two things are present, memory, by which I remember it, and forgetfulness, which is what I remember."[42] This means forgetting is also remembering that we forget something. We cannot realize that we forget something if we do not know that we had the memory in the first place. He says, "For we do not entirely forget what we remember that we have forgotten; if we had completely forgotten it, we should not even be able to look for what has been lost."[43]

Remembering for Augustine is more than just recalling something into one's mind. It is an active process. This idea of active remembrance is important later on in our research when we explore how victims and perpetrators can remember their past and give a new meaning to it.

Christian remembrance in the case of conflicts is linked with forgiveness and reconciliation.[44] It is a way of breaking the cycle of negative

---

[41] Augustine, *Confessions*, Book X, 14.
[42] Augustine, *Confessions*, Book X, 16.
[43] Augustine, *Confessions*, Book X, 19.
[44] See L. Gregory Jones, *Embodying Forgiveness: A Theological Analysis* (Grand Rapids: Eerdmans, 1995); Geiko Müller-Fahrenholz, *The Art of Forgiveness: Theological Reflections on Healing and Reconciliation* (Geneva: WCC Publications, 1997); Gregory Baum & Harold Wells (eds.), *The Reconciliation of Peoples: Challenge to the Churches* (Geneva & New York: WCC & Orbis Books, 1997); Desmond Tutu, *No Future without Forgiveness* (New York: Doubleday, 1999); Raymond G. Helmick & Rodney L. Petersen (eds.), *Forgiveness and Reconciliation: Religion, Public Policy, and Conflict Transformation* (Pennsylvania: Templeton Foundation Press, 2001). Philosophers have also struggled with the issue of forgiveness and remembrance especially in the communal context, see Donald W. Shriver Jr., *An Ethic For Enemies: Forgiveness in Politics* (Oxford University

remembrance. Forgiveness is a tool that we can use to break the cycle of vengeance. It "breaks the power of the remembered past and transcends the claims of the affirmed justice and so makes the spiral of vengeance grind to a halt."[45] If it is done correctly, the memory of the hurtful past can be turned into a positive remembrance. The research for the present study tries to look for a contribution of positive remembrance from Christian theology that can be used to break this circle of violence.

In situations where trauma has hurt people, individually and collectively, forgiveness is an important step to take in order to be able to achieve a real reconciliation. This is where remembrance takes its role in forgiveness and reconciliation: remembrance in Christian faith is the step towards forgiveness. To forgive means to be able to remember what needs to be forgiven. Therefore, to remember is an essential factor in forgiveness and reconciliation, but the question remains, how can we do it?

7. The Research Question

Realizing that my own Church has not been able to deal with a traumatic internal conflict, and that Christian faith has its own source to remember in a better way, I come now to the main question of this research: How can the current culture of remembrance be informed by a deeper understanding of remembrance in biblical, theological, and liturgical resources of the Christian tradition in order to deepen reconciliation after the 1992-98 conflict in the HKBP?

In order to answer this question we will answer the following questions:

1. What was at stake in the 1992-98 conflicts within the HKBP?
2. Which biblical resources can contribute to a culture of remembrance?
3. Which 20th century theological resources can contribute to a culture of remembrance?
4. Which liturgical resources, especially from the Lutheran tradition, can inform and deepen a praxis of remembrance?

Throughout this study we shall keep in mind that our focus is not on forgiveness; rather, we will investigate the step that is needed before forgiveness, which is remembrance.

Press, 1997); Martha Minow, *Between Vengeance and Forgiveness* (Boston: Beacon Press, 1998); Trudy Govier, *Forgiveness and Revenge* (New York: Routledge, 2002).

[45] Miroslav Volf, *Exclusion and Embrace: A Theological Exploration of Identity, Otherness, and Reconciliation* (Nashville: Abingdon Press, 1996), 121.

8. Development of the Argument

The exploration of the research question will be accomplished by dividing this research into several in-depth analyses of what remembrance is. This present chapter functions as an introduction to the research as a whole.

The second chapter offers a case study that will suggest that the new culture of remembrance will be good for the Church as well. This chapter will investigate the experiences and questions that prompted this research, which is the 1992–1998 conflict within HKBP. This chapter will investigate what happened before, during and after the conflict. The main resources for this chapter are from newspapers articles, official documents of the Church, and some analysis that has been made about the topic. Here, we will see how both sides in the conflict remember what had happened and that everybody claimed to be the victim of the other based on the same event. There will be some cultural analysis as well as theological. We will also see the role of the state in the conflict, in which the ruling administration tended to take sides. At the end of the chapter we will see that the Church decided to leave the problem unresolved. The question will be raised whether the way to fully reconcile is by forgetting the past event.

Chapter three offers a deeper exploration on the biblical understanding of remembrance. The chapter will explore the idea of remembrance in the Old and New Testament. First, we will see how the communities of Old and New Testament perceived memory, and how they remembered. We will see that the theme of memory and the calling to remember were very strong in Israel's tradition. After this survey we will do linguistic analysis on the word "remember" and its derivatives. We will also work through exegetical analysis on a few biblical verses or parts that are relevant to our research. In the New Testament the call to remember will quickly lead us to the call to remember Jesus in the Eucharist. Here we will explore the meaning of anamnesis and its development as a biblical theme of the New Testament.

The following chapter, number four, offers a deeper exploration into Christian theology. Here, we will analyse theologians that have been dealing with the theme of remembrance and memory. Three theologians have been identified as using the theme of memory in their theological exploration, namely Johann Baptist Metz, Alexander Schmemann and Miroslav Volf. These three theologians are from different denominations and pursue different theological interests. All of them have their own use of "remembrance" and "memory" in their theology which proved to be very powerful when combined together, especially in the theme of communal remembrance of the past injustices. The in-depth analysis of their theology informs our understanding of remembrance as a theological concept.

Chapter five explores a deeper understanding of remembrance in Christian liturgy. This chapter will describe which liturgical sources can be found within the liturgy of the HKBP in order to remember in such a way that is contributes to reconciliation. Or to be more specific, we will trace how victims and perpetrators can remember in liturgy the past event in such a way that the painful memories are transformed in the memory of the loving Christ. We will explore what remembrance means in liturgy and how it can bring healing to the past memories. We will explore ecumenical liturgical resources to find the place in liturgy for communal remembrance and healing. The transformation of individual past hurt into communal memories of Christ through liturgy and its elements opens a space of healing for both victims and perpetrators. The chapter will suggest a liturgy of remembrance that could bring healing to past memories.

The sixth chapter offers the conclusions of the entire research project.

As to methodology, this research has been done through analysing recent pertinent literature on the subthemes. For the chapter on the conflict within the HKBP, some archival research has been done as well.

Chapter Two

The Wounds of the Past in the Huria Kristen Batak Protestan

In this chapter we will analyse an example that illustrates that churches have to deal with trauma just as people and other institutions do. The case that we will explore in what follows is an example of a communal conflict in the Huria Kristen Batak Protestan (shortly: HKBP) or The Batak Protestant Christian Church, where the memory of the past hurt still haunts the present. The HKBP experienced a conflict in 1992 that divided the Church into two groups with separate leaderships and offices. The conflict that lasted until late 1998 has created legal and physical confrontations between the two factions. These confrontations have resulted not only in material damages in the Church, but also death of some of its members and even ministers. This kind of conflict has resulted in serious trauma among its members.

The Church claimed that reconciliation has taken place and that peace is now in place. However, we will question this claim by ascertaining whether or not the Church has really reconciled. Lasting signs of the conflict can still be seen in the lives of the many congregations, as will be explored more later on in this chapter. In a complex and deep case such as the HKBP conflict, it is difficult to determine who the perpetrators were and who the victims were. Both conflicting parties have their own stories and thus their own memories.

This chapter will explore what happened during the conflict and how people deal with the wounds. We shall explore the reconciliation efforts that have been made after the conflict and try to analyse whether those efforts were enough to have a sustainable reconciliation and to move on to the future. The Church conflict will be displayed by what both conflicting sides have written on the case, by reviewing official church documents, and by portrayals of the case by local and national media. We will try to explore the conflict from both sides and give our own analysis at the end of this chapter.

1. Huria Kristen Batak Protestan (HKBP)

1.1 A Brief History of the Church

HKBP or Huria Kristen Batak Protestan (Eng: Batak Protestant Christian Church) was officially founded by the Rheinische Missionsgesellschaft (RMG, now known as The United Evangelical Mission or UEM based in Wuppertal, Germany) on October 7, 1861.[1] However, the work of the mission had already started as early as 1824 when Richard Burton and Nathaniel Ward were sent by the Baptist Missionary Society from England. After the failed attempt of these two missionaries, due to politics by agreement of the Dutch and the British, two American missionaries, Henry Lyman and Samuel Munson came in 1834. They were killed by the native people before they were able to spread the Gospel. Only in 1857 a Dutch missionary, G. van Asselt came to southern part of the Batakland and worked there, and managed to baptize the first convert in Batakland on March 31, 1861, with the help of two other Dutch missionaries Dammerboer and Betz. The RMG started their work in Batakland in 1861 and took over the work of the mission there. Reverend I. L. Nommensen, who is also known as the Apostle of the Batak people, was the first ephorus of HKBP. Nommensen entered the area of Batak Toba in 1863 and baptized the first converts in Silindung area in 1865.[2] Missionaries started training catechists, evangelists, and ministers in the year 1883.[3] As a religious organization, HKBP was acknowledged by the colonial government of Netherlands in the Staatsblad No. 360, in the year 1932, and re-acknowledged by Indonesian government on 2 April 1968, with their Letter of Recognition No. Dd/P/DAK/d/135/68.

Although HKBP claimed herself to be a fellowship of believers from all over the world, the Batak reference in the Church's name indicates

---

[1] This is considered to be the starting date of the church when four missionaries got together and discussed the future of the mission. They are Rev. Heine, Rev. Klammer, Rev. Betz, Rev. van Asselt.

[2] For more history on the church, see J.S. Aritonang, *Sejarah Pendidikan Kristen di Tanah Batak* (Eng: *Mission Schools in Batakland* (Leiden: Brill, 1994)) (Jakarta: BPK GM, 1988); J.R. Hutauruk, *Kemandirian Gereja* (Eng: *Church's Independency*) (Jakarta: BPK GM, 1993); Andar M. Lumbantobing, *Makna Wibawa Jabatan Dalam Gereja Batak* (Eng: *The Significance of Position's Authority in Batak Church*) (Jakarta: BPK GM, 1996); Lothar Schreiner, *Adat dan Injil: Perjumpaan Adat dengan Iman Kristen di Tanah Batak* (Eng: *Culture and Gospel: The Encounter of Culture and Christian Faith in Batak Land*) (Jakarta: BPK GM, 2000).

[3] See Edward O.V. Nyhus, *An Indonesian Church in the Midst of Social Change: The Batak Protestant Christian Church, 194-957* (Ph.D. Diss.: University of Wisconsin, Madison, 1987), 27-28.

that HKBP is a church that is connected to the Batak people. HKBP uses Batak language in most of their congregations as the main worship language. This shows that HKBP is closely related with the Batak culture.

The real independence of HKBP happened in July 11, 1940 during World War II. During the war, the Dutch Colonial Government arrested German missionaries because they were considered to be an enemy. Because of that action, Batak ministers took over the leadership of the Church. Rev. K. Sirait was elected to be the first *voorzitter* of HKBP, which later on was acknowledged as the first ephorus of the Church. Afterwards, the Church grew and congregations outside Batakland were established.[4]

Currently, the headquarters of HKBP are in Pearaja Tarutung, North Tapanuli region in the province of North Sumatra, Indonesia. Until 2011, HKBP had 14 people at the rank of ephorus and 9 secretary generals.[5] HKBP, a member of Lutheran World Federation since 1952, and of the World Council of Churches, has a total membership of 4,1 million, 3,176 local churches, and 1,445 ministers.[6]

1.2 The Influence of Batak Culture in HKBP

As a church that was established in Batakland, HKBP has been influenced by the Batak culture. Genealogically-anthropologically speaking, there are six sub tribes of the Batak tribe, namely Toba, Karo, Pakpak or Dairi, Simalungun, Angkola, and Mandailing. They have their own languages and dialects.[7] HKBP mainly consists of Batak Toba people and uses the Batak Toba language as its main language. According to Lothar Schreiner, there are three common identifications of Batak culture:[8]

1. The genealogy lineage is divided by *marga* or family name based on a patrilineal distinction and exogamy practice.
2. Traditional religion revolves around the belief of ancestor's spirits.
3. Traces of Indian religion and cultures, which came along with the Hindu influence.

The Batak people value their *marga* (familial surnames) and *adat*. *Adat* is often translated as customary law while its true meaning serves a deeper

---

[4] For more information about the independence movement of HKBP, see Hutauruk, *Kemandirian Gereja*.
[5] The official record of important dates of the church has always been noted in the church's official lectionary and information book (*Almanak*). The book notes that during 1992–1998, HKBP had two ephoruses.
[6] See HKBP, *Almanak HKBP 2011* (Tarutung: HKBP, 2011).
[7] Lumbantobing, *Makna Wibawa*, 1.
[8] Schreiner, *Adat dan Injil*, 7–8.

philosophy. Adat can be seen as a harmony and balance that include the relation with the creator, nature, the past, present and future. Pedersen says, "For their protection against each other and to preserve the equilibrium in the microcosm the Bataks established a means of harmonizing the supernatural powers around them for their own welfare. This harmony was embodied in the notion of *adat*."[9] This means there is a totality in the harmony of life, both physically and mentally. The Batak people are conservative when it comes to changing this harmony belief system. Tobing says, "it is an undeniable fact that the Toba-Batak are conservatives by nature: foreign elements have only been accepted when they could be brought in an organic relation with their original cosmic views."[10]

Batak culture has a lineage of patrilineal genealogy and has a strong remembrance of, and roots, in their family tree. Their extended family can be traced back to the first person who has that *marga* (family name) which could mean twenty generations prior to them. *Adat* Batak also teaches that one should pay respect to his/her elder family members. Batak people have an exclusive designation for every member of the family. This "title" explains their position in the family and supersedes their given name. For instance, *tulang* (male family member from mother sides—consequently their spouses will be called *nantulang*); *namboru* (female family member from the father's side—consequently their spouses will be called *amangboru*); *bapauda* (younger brother of the father or anyone lower than his level in the same family name); *bapatua* (older brother of the father or anyone higher than his level in the same family name); etc. Thus, even without mentioning names, a Batak person will know who the person is and what their position in the family is by referring to the title of the position in the family. Everyone has a unique place in the eye of *adat*. There are three main groups in the explanation of relationship of the Batak people: *dongan sabutuha, hulahula,* and *boru*. Tobing explains this connection,

> The term *dongan sabutuha* (womb companions) i.e. those who originate from one womb" points to agnatic relationship. The *dongan sabutuha* are also called "dongan samarga" …in principle are all male members of one

---

[9] Paul B. Pedersen, *Batak Blood and Protestant Soul: The Development of National Batak Churches in North Sumatra* (Grand Rapids, Michigan: William B. Eerdmans Publishing Company, 1970), 35. There are some good books about the origin of the Batak people, one of them is W. M. Hutagalung, *Pustaha Batak: Tarombo dohot Turiturian ni Bangso Batak* (Pematangsiantar: Tulus Jaya, 1991).

[10] Philip Oder Lumban Tobing, *The Structure of the Toba-Batak Belief in the High God* (Amsterdam: Jacob van Campen, 1956), 18.

marga. The term *hulahula* principally points to one's father-in-law and his nearer *dongan sabutuha* belonging to his *na marsaompu* (connected as far as their great-grandfather in common). *Boru* (English: girl) principally indicates one's son in law and his nearer *dongan sabutuha*.[11]

It is customary that the last saying in a family gathering is the saying of the oldest person. A man is not fully grown into his manhood if he is not yet married. As long as he is not married, he cannot have a say in a formal family meeting. A married man will be called by his surname in public display and not by his first name.

Pedersen says that "*Adat* was design to avert disaster, restore harmony, promote fertility, preserve health, and assure the welfare of the group."[12] This view on the importance of balance, harmony, and especially *adat* has an effect on any violation of the system. The neglect of *adat* is believed to lead to a negative impact on oneself and also the entire society, for example on issues such as infertility, disease, and crop failure.

In local stories and poems, Batak people are often described as diligent workers in order to achieve the goals of happiness, descendants, and honour (*hamoraon, hagabeon, hasangapon*). The children are expected to exceed their parents. Sometimes the will to achieve the three things mentioned above is so great that Batak people often do brave things. They will not hesitate to move outside of the original hometown in order to get better education or work. Batak people regard family honour very highly and will defend it with everything that they can muster.[13]

In connection with the view on harmony and their traditional religious belief, Pedersen says, "The Toba Batak organization of time also suggests a unified world view, with each twenty four hour a day and twelve month a year viewed as a totality." [14] They view time as something concrete and associate it with "a part of God's High Body." In the Batak traditional view of the cosmic universe, time and space formed an essential unity; in other words, Batak culture highly values balance and harmony. The concept of time in Batak culture philosophy is best described in a saying *tinatap tu jolo tinailihon tu pudi* (look ahead, see to the past). This phrase is often mentioned when people are planning something ahead. The past is very much as close to the present as the future. Based on this philosophy, Batak people very keenly remember

---

[11] Lumbantobing, *Makna Wibawa*, 73.
[12] Pedersen, *Batak Blood*, 36.
[13] See Bungaran Antonius Simanjuntak, *Melayu Pesisir dan Batak Pegunungan* (Jakarta: Yayasan Obor Indonesia, 2010), 164.
[14] Pedersen, *Batak Blood*, 26.

their origins, their ancestors and their roots. Bungaran Simanjuntak mentions that the future is decided by the present and the past.[15] His remark shows that Batak culture is very adept in the remembrance of their identity and roots. It is normal for a Batak to keep track of his lineage in the family tree, from the first generation of the *marga* to their own generation. A group of *marga* often will build statues or monuments to remember and honour their ancestors, as a remembrance of the glory days as well as a motivational symbol to do better in the future. The cost of building such monument will be divided among the descendants.[16] Thus, collective memory in the form of family statues and monuments is very much alive in Batak people.

1.3 *The Structure of the Church*

To have a clearer view of the problem in HKBP, we should look at the Church Order. The most updated Church Order of HKBP prior to the 1992 conflict is the Church Order of 1982-1992.[17] The Church Order of 1982 is divided into two parts: namely *Aturan* (Eng: Order) and *Peraturan* (Eng: Order of Implementation). The Church Order of 1982-1992 based the ecclesiological foundation of the Church on the Confession of Faith of the Church, which was written in 1951. The Confession of Faith of HKBP is based on the Barmen Declaration of 1934.

To understand the situation and the theological background of the Church, we will analyse the ecclesiological foundation of the Church in article 8 of the Confession, as it also explains the relation of church towards nation.[18]

    A. We believe and confess:

    [That] The church is the fellowship of believers in Jesus Christ, who are called, gathered, sanctified and confirmed by God in His Spirit (1 Cor. 1:2; 1 Pet. 2:9; Eph. 1:2,22; 1 Cor. 3:11).

    With this doctrine we reject and oppose:

---

[15] See Simanjuntak, *Melayu Pesisir*, 165–166.
[16] See Ibrahim Gultom, *Agama Malim di Tanah Batak* (Jakarta: Bumi Aksara, 2010), 46–47.
[17] HKBP, *Aturan dan Peraturan Huria Kristen Batak Protestan HKBP 1982–1992* (Tarutung: HKBP, 1982).
[18] We will use the translation that was written by L. H. Purwanto with minor adjustments, *Indonesian Church Orders under Scrutiny: The Relation between the Church Members and the Church Office-Bearers: How It Is and How It Should Be* (Kampen: Theologische Universiteit van de Gereformeerde Kerken in Nederland te Kampen, 1997), 80–82.

1. The church that was established by man by his/her own will; by those who want to separate themselves from the (our) church, especially when the separation is not based on the fact that the [existing] church has a teaching which is contradictory with the Word of God.
2. The opinion that says: Only leaders, church meetings, and church members have the right over the church; only Christ has power over the church; and we can only follow the teaching that goes with teaching of Christ. The church is not ruled by "democracy" but by "christocracy".
3. The opinion that says that the church should become a state church. The obligation of the state is different from the ordination of the church.
4. The opinion that says that the church is based and bound to local custom; and the opinion that only based the church on organization.

B. We believe and confess:

[That] The church is holy. The ground of the church's holiness is not the holiness of its individual members, but the holiness of Christ, the Head of the Church. The church is holy because Christ has made it holy, and therefore God considers it as holy. Because of its holiness, the church is called the holy people, temple of the Holy Spirit, the house of God (1 Pet. 2:9; Eph. 2:22; 3:21; Rev. 1:6; 1 Cor. 3:16).
With this doctrine we reject and oppose the view that says that humans can achieve their holiness by their own effort, and we also want to overcome the despair which causes separation among the church members because of their sin.

C. We believe and confess:

[That] The church is catholic. That the Catholic Church is the communion of saints, the communion of those who believe in Jesus Christ and His gifts, that is Gospel, the Holy Spirit, faith, love, and hope. They are people from every country, nation, ethnic group, and language, although they have different cultures and ways of life.
With this doctrine we reject and oppose the understanding that regards the church as a nation's religion and the idea that there is no unity between churches.

D. We believe and confess:

[That] The church is one, as it is according to Eph. 4:4; 1 Cor. 12:20, "There is one body, which is the church. As it is, there are many members, yet one body." The oneness that is mentioned here is different from the worldly meaning of the word; instead it is the oneness in spirit (John 17:20-21).
With this doctrine we reject and oppose all separations that are not according to the teaching of faith, but only following their own will.

E. Marks of the true church.

We believe and confess that the marks of the true church are:
1. Where the gospel is purely preached.
2. Where the two sacraments are administered in accordance with the Word of Jesus Christ.
3. Where discipline is imposed to prevent sin.

The Church confesses that she is "the fellowship of believers in Jesus Christ, who are called, gathered, sanctified and confirmed by God in his Spirit." The starting point of the Church is the congregation. This is further expressed in "the church is the communion of saints". The church is not ruled by humans, but by Christ.

The Barmen Declaration was a statement of the Confessing Church in Germany during the time of the Nazi ruling. The intention of the Declaration was to oppose the German Christians that supported the Nazi's on the basis of strong nationalism and anti-Semitic sentiments. The influence of the Barmen Declaration on the Confession of Faith of HKBP in the matter of church-state and church-nation relationship become clear from statements such as "The Church rejects and opposes the opinion that says that the Church should become a state church (point A.3); and the understanding that regards the church as a nation's religion (point C)." We will see later that this theological foundation was neglected during the time of the conflict.

Fridz Sihombing, a pastor of HKBP, wrote an eloquent analysis on the influence of the Barmen Declaration on the conflict of the Church in his doctoral theses which he defended at the Kirchliche Hochschule Wuppertal in 2007 with the title *Versöhnung, Wahrheit und Gerechtigkeit: Die ökumenische Bedeutung der Barmer Theologischen Erklärung für den Weg der Kirchen in Indonesien.*[19] He defended the argument that during the time of conflict, HKBP did not use the theological basis of the Confession which was based on the Barmen Declaration. The ecumenical nature of the Declaration and the sharp separation between church and nation were totally ignored during the time of conflict. The involvement of the government and Sihombing's analysis on it shall be observed in the later part of this chapter.

---

[19] Fridz Pardamean Sihombing, *Versöhnung, Wahrheit und Gerechtigkeit: Die ökumenische Bedeutung der Barmer Theologischen Erklärung für den Weg der Kirchen in Indonesien* (Wuppertal: Neukirchener, 2007). One of the purposes of his research was to prove that the reconciliation in HKBP in the Reconciliation General Synod in 1998 does not have a future because it was produced without justice and truth towards the victims.

How has the Confession influenced the structure of the Church? Based on the Church's constitution and regulations and implementations, its organizational structure is described in the following way:

> What forms HKBP is that every one of the congregations is united under one resort, is united under one District, and united under one Central (catholic fellowship), that make HKBP into its presence.[20]

In the Order of Implementation, this article was explained as:[21]

> 1. Congregation. The congregation is a communion of HKBP members at a certain place. According to article 13 of the Order of the Church, the congregation is led by the minister, preacher teacher, and the church's council.[22] Meetings in the church are presided by the *resort* minister.
> 2. Resort. The resort is an assembly of a number of congregations led by a *resort* minister. The resort minister is assisted by the resort council.
> 3. District. The District is an assembly of a number of resorts led by a *praeses*. The *praeses* is proposed by the Central Council to the General Synod of ministers which eventually votes for them. The *praeses* is assisted by a District Council. The District meeting is attended by all resort ministers in the district, and one representative from each resort.
> 4. HKBP as a whole. HKBP is an assembly of all congregations, resorts, and districts led by an ephorus. The Ephorus is appointed by the General Synod from the participating ministers in the General Synod. The Ephorus is assisted by the Central Council. The Central Council of the Church consists of 11 ministers and 11 non-ministers appointed by the General Synod. The General Synod is the highest decision maker organ in the Church and is led by the ephorus, attended by all members of the Central Council, all resort ministers, 1 or 2 representative(s) from each resorts, all praeses, chairperson of the minister's conference, and representatives from institutions.

Thus, HKBP considers itself as a church that is formed starting from the communion of members on the local level, in a specific area, all the way to the HKBP as a whole. In terms of organisational structure, HKBP has a hierarchical structure with the ephorus on the top level.

Until 2004, the ministry of the Church was organized on four levels. a. HKBP as a whole, led by the ephorus (bishop); b. Districts, led by a

---

[20] HKBP, *Aturan dan Peraturan*, article 11.

[21] See also Purwanto, *Indonesian Church Orders Under Scrutiny*, 86–87. Purwanto described the structure of HKBP based on the explanation that was given by the Church in its Book of Implementation.

[22] Purwanto noted the inconsistency of the Church Order on the structure of the congregation compared to its Book of Implementation. According to Article 13, the congregation is led by the deputy *resort* minister, while the Book of Implementation said it was led by minister, preacher teacher, and the church's council.

praeses (superintendent); c. Resort, led by a resort pastor; and d. Local congregation led by a teacher preacher. A secretary general is also part of the HKBP leadership role along with the HKBP Central Council. At the synod level, the HKBP is led by the ephorus. In fact, the ephorus has a strong position in the Church as a whole. The Order of Implementation (*Peraturan*) Chapter 1 D.2.a.1 stated that, "It is the ephorus that shall lead HKBP and its representatives in the relation with the government, church, or any other institutions." The secretary general of HKBP is obliged to manage all departments and bureaus in the organizational structure of the HKBP. We shall return to the tasks of ephorus and secretary general later on.

The highest decision making body in HKBP at that time is the General Synod. There is also a Central Council of the Church that consists of both ordained and non-ordained members of the Church. This Central Council has the task to: a.) To help the ephorus to guide the whole HKBP, according to the Church Order, Confession, Church Law, and Rules that are set by the General Synod; and b.) To maintain and guide the efficiency of the treasurer and finance of the Church.

Besides the ordination of pastors, HKBP also recognizes the ordination of teacher's preacher, *bibelvrouw* (women's Bible preacher), and deaconess. These three ordained ministry positions have their own three years theological education. After 2004, the Church introduces a new structure. However, we will only focus on the previous structure of the Church, because it was connected with the period of time that we will investigate.

At synod level, HKBP had 14 departments and bureaus. The departments were established to help the Church to accomplish the church's calling, leading all HKBP members to a mature Christian life being able to perform their service and witness in the midst of the church, the society, and the world. These departments, such as the Department of Sunday School, the Department of Youth, the Department of Church Music and Choir, etc., were arranged to be under the leadership of the ephorus, as it was written in Order of Implementation III.A: "Departments are under the leadership authority of the ephorus through the secretary general of HKBP as an intermediary. The directors of all departments are appointed by the Central Council. Church's matters at synod level were directly led and handled by the ephorus with the secretary general as intermediary.

2. The HKBP 1992-1998 Crisis

The story began with a crisis at the HKBP General Synod in 1992 when the Church had to choose new leaders. There was no final decision during this General Synod until the very end of that Assembly. Afterwards, the military took over the Assembly and appointed a new transitional ephorus to be in charge of HKBP to organize a new General Synod.[23] This has caused division within the Church between those who followed the new leader that had been appointed by the government, and those who thought that this government had overstepped its authority and remained loyal to the old ephorus.[24]

Protests of all sorts were raised against this decision, both from international and national churches. However, the government insisted that they were in no position to interfere into the internal problems within the Church. They claimed that the appointment of the new ephorus was intended only to help HKBP in solving their problems and also to keep stability in society.[25] With the government's recognition of his position, the new ephorus claimed the Church's assets, which resulted in direct and indirect confrontations within the congregations. Some of the congregations were divided into two or even three groups. The military was often involved in the process of taking over a church. They claimed that the old ephorus was illegal and that therefore the government refused to recognize him. The crisis caused many divisions within the Church as a whole and in local congregations.

This conflict came to an end through the 1998 Joint General Synod in Pematangsiantar, North Sumatra. The official profile of the Church stated this problem clearly,

> For about six years (1993-1998) HKBP has undergone a serious crisis, before the reconciliation in 1998. Thank God, HKBP has not fallen apart. However, the crisis had resulted in a number of drawbacks, among oth-

---

[23] This appointment was made under the letter of Bakorstanasda Sumbagut No. Skep/3/Stada/XII/1992 in 23rd of December 1992.

[24] For instance see, Moksa Nadeak et al., *Krisis HKBP: Ujian bagi Iman dan Pengamalan Pancasila* (Eng: *Crisis of HKBP: A Test of Faith and the Exercise of Pancasila*) (Tarutung: Biro Informasi HKBP, 1995), and Saut Sirait, *Politik Kristen di Indonesia: Suatu Tinjauan Etis* (Eng: *Christian Politics in Indonesia*) (Jakarta: BPK-GM, 2001). However, note that these books were written by the group that remained loyal to the old ephorus.

[25] Einar Sitompul, "Kemandirian Gereja: Refleksi Singkat Krisis HKBP" (Eng: "Church Independency: A Short Reflection of HKBP Crisis"), in *Gereja di Pentas Politik: Belajar dari Kasus HKBP* (Eng: *Church in the Political Platform: Learning from HKBP Case*), ed. Einar Sitompul (Jakarta: Yakoma-PGI, 1997), 94.

ers: there are still some congregations which have not yet been in full harmony; there has been no improvement in the ministry as a whole, particularly in terms of preparations for facing the challenges of the 21st century; a number of buildings and other facilities needs repairs or rehabilitations; and ecumenical relations need improvements.[26]

Surprisingly, HKBP did not mention anything about the cause of the crisis nor what happened during that time, even though it lasted for six long years. From the official statement we can observe that the problem was enormous: not only buildings and facilities needed repair, but also ecumenical relations had been shattered. The statement did not mention anything about victims or perpetrators. One is left with a sense of silence concerning all aspects of the causes and perpetuation of the crisis, which gives rise to a possible desire to drop the problem and leave it behind.

Actually, the six years of conflict resulted in huge damage within the Church. Both ministers and lay people were injured and even killed during the conflict. Many churches experienced splits. Even after the conflict was declared resolved, many members refused to go back to the old congregation and preferred to establish a new congregation—within the denomination. Many of the Church's assets were gone. Many members of the Church moved to other denominations and never came back even after the so-called reconciliation. In January 2005 up until 2010, there was still conflict in one of the congregations in Jakarta between the two parties that separated during the conflict.[27] This is just one of the cases among many after the official reconciliation in 1998.

We will try to see and investigate what really happened during the time of crisis, and what the elements are that caused it. This is not an easy task to do since files about details of the conflict are scattered and

---

[26] HKBP, *The Profile*, 3.
[27] The conflict happened within a congregation in HKBP Pondok Bambu between the two conflicting parties of the crisis of 1992–98, in Jakarta in January 2005. This conflict started after the minister rejected to allow one of the groups use the same church building any longer to have their own Sunday service. After a while, the congregation decided to appoint their own pastor. See "Mau Diusir Pendeta dari Gereja: Jemaat HKBP Pondok Bambu Mengadu ke Pimpinan HKBP" (Eng: "Being Forced Out of the Church: The Congregation of HKBP Pondok Bambu File Their Report to the Leaders of HKBP") and "Tentang Kasus di HKBP Pondok Bambu: Pendeta Jangan Sok Berkuasa di Tengah Masyarakat" (Eng: About the HKBP Pondok Bambu Case: Minister Must Not be Arrogant in the Midst of the Society") in *Narwastu Pembaruan* No. 20/2005, (March 2005), 18–19. See Binsar T. H. Sirait, "Jemaat Pagi HKBP Pondok Bambu Angkat Pendeta" (Eng: The Morning Worship of HKBP Pondok Bambu Appointed Their Pastor") in *Reformata* Edition 250, Year III (April 2005), 23.

there are so many different point of views about the conflict. We will build an account of what really happened at the 51st General Synod in 1992, and will try to understand the reasons behind the conflict. Our research will use official materials produced by each party in the conflict, and newspapers articles and reports by ecumenical bodies.

2.1 The Beginning of the Conflict

An earthquake shook Tarutung, North Sumatera on April 27, 1987. That earthquake killed two persons, injured twenty-two persons, and damaged around 300 buildings in the area.[28] This incident soon was followed by the forming of "Tim Evangelisasi Nehemia/TEN" (Nehemiah Evangelization Team) in Jakarta to be sent to the region acting as a relief team for the victims.

At that time, HKBP was led by Rev. S.A.E. Nababan as ephorus and Rev. O.P.T. Simorangkir as secretary general after being elected during the HKBP 48th General Synod on January 23-28, 1987. The earthquake happened three months later and soon became a challenge to Rev. Nababan's leadership. The challenge focussed on the decision whether to approve the sending of such an evangelization team to the region or not, and whether the theological foundation of the group matched those of the Church. Rev. Nababan decided to support the group's activities in the region. The team had been formed as an initiative of some members of HKBP congregations in Jakarta. They had learned that a lot of people had returned to animism by bringing offers to sacred places in the area. They wanted to evangelize the area. Some HKBP pastors were part of the team.[29]

According to another source of information released after the 1992 conflict, HKBP did not recognize the legality and authority of the team. The main reason for the rejection of the team was the suspicion that the members of the team were charismatic.[30] In a later document, the Rev. P.W.T Simanjuntak's side, who later on became the opposition of Rev. Nababan, noted that the TEN team, "who were not ordained pastors, had done a number of activities which were contrary to the Dogma, Confession and

---

[28] A record of the earthquake is found in http://www.sinarharapan.co.id/berita/0503/30/sh02.html, accessed October 2007.
[29] Nadeak, *Krisis HKBP*, 64.
[30] HKBP Information Bureau, *Building the Truth: The Streamlining of the Information about the Batak Christian Protestant Christian Church (Huria Kristen Batak Protestan: HKBP)* (Tarutung: HKBP, 1994), 5. Charismatic means the belief in the gifts of the Holy Spirit through the baptism in the Holy Spirit and to be manifested in the form of signs, miracles, speaking in tongues, prophecy, healing, among other gifts of the Spirit in 1 Cor. 12:1–11.

Service Order of HKBP, namely to give blessing by the laying on of hands, to emphasize the greatness of the Holy Spirit and the importance of tithing which is a characteristic of another church denomination."[31]

Eleven pastors questioned the current ephorus' decision to bring TEN into the region at a retreat camp at Parapat.[32] They concluded that the TEN activities had to be stopped. This group was led by Rev. P.M. Sihombing, the former secretary general in the period before Rev. Nababan' leadership, and happened to be the main contender of Nababan for the ephorus position during the 1987 General Synod. The general meeting of all pastors in HKBP discussed the matter from November 4-8, 1987. A special team was formed to investigate the accusation and the members concluded that the TEN team had done nothing that was contrary to the Church's teachings. But the report did not lay to rest the controversies about the TEN Team. Soon, two undersigned book-length treatments of the accusation again questioned the decision of the ephorus.[33]

The HKBP Central Council meeting on August 25-27, 1988, decided to do two things with regard to the people who were protesting the presence of TEN Team. First, they were presented with a warning letter. Secondly, the meeting invited the accusers to substantiate their allegations. In response, five ministers and a lay member who signed the books apologized and were soon given back their position in the ministry. Nineteen ministers stood firm on their decision of to reject the TEN team decision of the ephorus and refused to apologize.

The situation deteriorated after this. The General Synod in November 10-15, 1988, rejected all charges that were presented by the 19 ministers because of lack of evidence supporting their stance. The General Synod decided to punish those who had gone astray, and dismissed them from any structural position in the church. They were granted three months to apologize. At the meeting of ministers in every district, duly led by each praeses as the head of the district, and attended by Rev. Dr. A.A. Sitompul as the chairperson of the HKBP's Meeting of Ministers,[34] the nineteen pastors were dismissed from their current structural position in their own districts.[35]

---

[31] HKBP Information Bureau, *Building the Truth*, 5.
[32] Because of this retreat camp, this group was then known as *parritrit* group.
[33] *Quo Vadis HKBP* (signed by 27 ministers and 11 lay people) (*not published*), and *Nunga Lam Patar* (Eng: It Is Clearer) (*not published*).
[34] It was a structural position in HKBP at that time.
[35] Nadeak, *Krisis HKBP*, 66-68.

The decision to dismiss the ministers from their organisational position was taken during the months of May, June, and August 1989. This decision was taken according to the Order of Implementation of HKBP Article II.A.6, "It is the ministers' assembly in their own districts, led by praeses, and attended by the Chairperson of the Meeting of Ministers who will give his/her consideration. The general meeting of the praeses will decide the dismissal."[36] In brief, the actions that were taken by the Church to dismiss the 19 pastors seemed to have been taken in the right ordered manner according to the Church's Order.

The number of people affected by Rev. Simanjuntak's side was even greater than just the 19 pastors. They noted, "By trickery, Nababan dismissed 19 pastors who took part at the retreat together with a number of teacher-preachers, Bible Women Preachers, Deaconesses, and 104 students of the Teacher Preacher School. He also expelled 20 elders and 514 congregation members of HKBP at Pulo Brayan, a suburb of Medan, on March 5, 1989."[37]

It soon became obvious that the dispute went much deeper than the evangelization activities of TEN team. There were also suspicions from Rev. Nababan's side that the protest against the TEN team was supported by one of the local newspapers owner in Medan, the capital of North Sumatera. They suspected that a major reason behind the published one-sided stories was purely economical. They said that the owner of the newspaper had already established a university in the North Tapanuli region, and was feeling threatened by the plan of some business person in Jakarta who supported TEN's program of establishing a new university there.[38]

In September 1990, Gen (ret.) Maraden Panggabean, the then chairperson of Supreme Advisory Council (one of five state's High Councils that was in charge of giving advice to the President) came into the picture by forming a "Peace Team" that included seven prominent members of HKBP with the purpose of solving the problem in the HKBP. This team was formed based on a memo of the Minister of Religion Affairs no. MA/132/1990 dated September 6, 1990.[39] The team made several visits to congregations in order to find facts about the conflict through seminars and discussions. The secretary general of HKBP, Rev. O.P.T.

---

[36] Nadeak, *Krisis HKBP,* 68.
[37] HKBP Information Bureau, *Building the Truth,* 5. This research cannot confirm these figures on the other side's account because there was no note on it.
[38] Nadeak, *Krisis HKBP,* 65.
[39] Nadeak, *Krisis HKBP,* 69.

Simorangkir, later on agreed on the agenda of the team and supported the activity of the team by covering some of the expenses from the HKBP treasury on his order. The team's intention and the outcome of their investigations were not very clear. However, this shows that the government kept an eye on the affairs of HKBP, and that the secretary general agreed with the government's decision.

At the 1991 Meeting of Ministers, a procedure for re-admission of the dismissed pastors was accepted. The 1991 HKBP Meeting of Ministers decided to accept one of the *parritrit* members back as a full minister because he had shown his regret and loyalty.[40] The Meeting also decided to stay open for any of the *parritrit* members who would like to return to their ministry if they were willing to obey the procedures. This decision aimed at the eighteen remaining ministers who were still under the Church's Discipline.

2.2 *Conflict between Ephorus and Secretary General*

One of the factors that worsened the conflict was the unclear role division between the ephorus and secretary general of HKBP. In the Order of Implementation, the ephorus is the leader of all HKBP. The tasks of the ephorus, sometimes close to those of the secretary general, included: (a) To become the shepherd for all congregations and office bearers; (b) To lead the General Synod, Central Council's Meeting, and Praeses Meeting; (i) To decide on pastor's mutations (pastor's tour of duty) in urgent cases; and (j) To give the final decision on a never-ending dispute.[41] These tasks were sometimes in conflict with the description of the tasks of the secretary general, especially in these points: (a) To lead all HKBP Central Office's administration, and all departments meetings; (b) To provide and prepare all materials and works that are connected with the General Synod and Central Council Meeting; (c) To represent the ephorus in tasks accordingly.[42]

The Church also has several bureaus that help the internal office matters, such as the Personnel Bureau, the Financial Bureau, etc. Another article described the roles of those Bureaus and Departments of HKBP. The Order of Implementation Chapter III A. explained "These departments are under the leadership of the ephorus represented by the secretary general." The general understanding was that those offices were

---

[40] Decision of 1991 HKBP Meeting of Ministers, Decision Number VII. Point 1, on *Parritrit*.
[41] Implementation of Church Order, Chapter I. D. 2. a.2.
[42] Implementation of Church Order, Chapter I. D. 2. b.2.

led by the secretary general who is more in charge of keeping the main office running well.

However, the job descriptions of the two top leaders of the Church intersected each other in practice. The secretary general was in charge of the administration matters, but it was the ephorus that had a final say on the mutation of pastors. It was also unclear to whom the Heads of the Departments had to report, to the ephorus or to the secretary general.

Those behind Rev. Simanjuntak were of the opinion that the leadership of Rev. Nababan was causing conflict. The official Information Bureau of HKBP after the 1992 conflict broke stated, "The attitude and leadership style of the Rev. Dr. S.A.E. Nababan showed harshness, stiffness and an authoritarian attitude. He often threatened his staff members, namely the praeses, pastors of parishes and staff members of headquarters."[43] This opinion on his style of leadership created tension between him and the Secretary General Rev. O.P.T. Simorangkir. The administrative work of the secretary general was considered being taken over by Rev. Nababan. Rev. Simanjuntak's side suspected that Rev. Nababan tried to concentrate power in own hands by, "decisions on the pastors' tour of duties, the sending of the Church workers to study in Indonesia as well as abroad, the policy of financial support, etc."[44] His side claimed that Nababan had stripped him from his official duties without any clear reason. However, the Nababan side would argue that according to the Church Order, the ephorus is indeed the leader of all HKBP.

This dualistic overlap of leadership in HKBP was taken seriously. The 50th General Synod in April 8-12, 1991, charged the Central Council of the Church with the task to define more precisely the exact function of the ephorus and the secretary general. The idea to create the position of a deputy ephorus was rejected by the meeting. The synod recommended that the duty delegation should be given to the secretary general or one of the praeses.[45] The meeting also urged the Central Council to explain further the phrase "These departments are under the leadership of the ephorus represented by the secretary general."[46]

---

[43] HKBP Information Bureau, *Building the Truth*, 3.

[44] HKBP Information Bureau, *Building the Truth*, 4. The book continues that this situation was to cause a "chaos within the friendship among the pastors…"

[45] HKBP, *Decision of 1991 HKBP Meeting of Ministers*, Decision Number V. Point 4, on deputy ephorus.

[46] HKBP, *Decision of 1991 HKBP Meeting of Ministers*, Decision Number V. Point 16, on role of ephorus and secretary general.

2.3 The 51st General Synod

The 51st General Synod of HKBP took place from November 23-28, 1992, at Sipoholon Seminary near Tarutung, North Sumatra, Indonesia. The General Synod was attended by 534 participants, mainly ministers of the Church. The synod was expected to discuss three extra items on the agenda at the request of the Police National Headquarters: a. To discuss and legalize the new Constitution of HKBP for the term 1992-2002; b. To elect the office bearers of HKBP for the term 1992-1998; and c. To resolve the conflicts within HKBP. The National Police could bring such questions to the agenda of the Church, because at that time, every organization or mass events needed a legal permit from the National Police Headquarters, signed by the Chief Commander of the Indonesian Police. For any and all sizeable gatherings this was standard practice.

The agenda of the synod, approved by the National Police Headquarter in Jakarta, was different from the actual proposals by the then ephorus.[47] Rev. Nababan proposed two sessions of the General Synod, in June 1992 to discuss and approve the new 1992-2002 HKBP Constitution, and in November 1992 to elect the new office bearers based on the new Constitution. The first request for holding a General Synod was refused and Rev. Nababan as ephorus of HKBP presented a new schedule for approval to the authorities: a session to discuss and approve the New Constitution on November 23-25, 1992, and a session to choose the new office bearers in late January 1993. However, without the knowledge of Rev. Nababan, the secretary general also held a meeting with some of the members of the Central Council to organize the Synod and based on that meeting he sent a letter to the National Police Headquarters proposing three main agenda points for the Synod, which was then to become the General Synod.[48] This proposal given by the secretary general was followed by a recommendation from The Commander of the 23rd Regiment, Colonel Daniel Toding, who accepted the agenda for the Synod as proposed by the secretary general.

Two organizing committees for the Synod, one appointed by the ephorus and one by secretary general, produced their own invitations and materials for the General Synod. Based on the agreement between the Nababan committee and the authorities (the Kodim or *Local Mili-*

---

[47] See Nadeak *et.al., Krisis HKBP*, 74.
[48] We will explain the conflict between the secretary general and the ephorus at the later part of this chapter. This conflict eventually contributed to the two letters sent by both of them proposing two different contents of the General Synod.

tary Office 0210 and North Tapanuli Local Police), only the ephorus was to send out invitations for the General Synod. However the other committee continued its work. For that reason another meeting between the two conflicting committees had to be organized on the registration day for the General Synod in the office of the local military in Tarutung under the supervision of Commander of 23rd Regiment, Colonel Daniel Toding. That meeting produced an agreement that committed both parties to work together. Later on that evening Colonel Daniel Toding announced to the participants of the synod that a steering committee was formed with him as the head of the committee with Humuntar Lumban Gaol and B.A.S. Tobing (from the ephorus side), and Rev. Halasson Silitonga and Rev. S.M. Siahaan as members.

The military seemed to have a special role in the Synod because both parties admitted that they had a tactical post in the Synod complex with 400 armed soldiers under the order of the Commander of 23rd Regiment.[49] Soon after the General Synod was officially opened on the November 24, it began a heavy and slow process. The tedious and slow pace of the Synod was due to protests, objections, and questions that were raised by some number of participants towards the rule and the agenda of the Synod. Rev. Nababan noted that these protesters were usually the same persons that had repeatedly objected to the process of the Synod. They were identified to be on Rev. Simorangkir's side.[50]

The third day was again dominated by protests and interruptions. The main issue on the third day was the status of the Central Council membership of Elder M. H. Rajagukguk. This became an issue because, according to the Order of Implementation, he was supposed to have retired and should be considered only as a guest of the Synod. Even so, the secretary general's side wanted him to stay as a full delegate from the Central Council. After some heavy discussions, the meeting turned sour because some participants vehemently disagreed to let the Synod go to

---

[49] Nadeak, *Krisis HKBP*, 74–75.
[50] Saut Sirait & Gomar Gultom, "Kronologi Sinode Agung ke 51 HKBP" (Eng: "The Chronology of the 51st General Synod of HKBP"). This 7 page report was claimed to be the official chronological report of the Synod by Rev. Nababan's side. However, a small book was published in 1994 by Rev. Simanjuntak's side written by Rev. S.M. Siahaan with the title, "Laporan dan Informasi Sinode Godang HKBP ke -51, tanggal 23 s/d 28 Nopember 1992 yang gagal & Notulen Pertemuan Fungsionaris HKBP Periode 1986–1992 dengan Ketua Bakorstanasda Sumbagut/Panglima KODAM I BB" (Eng: "The report and Information on the Unsuccessful 51st HKBP General Synod & Minutes of the Meeting between HKBP 1986–1992 Boards with the Commander of Northern Sumatra Military).

a vote on any decision. The situation was so heavily protested by the same people from the day before, that the moderator had to suspend the meeting until the next day. One of the items contested in every session of the synod was whether or not the Rev. Nababan could run for a second term as ephorus of the Church. Rev. Nababan's side reported that there were signals that the military did not want Nababan to go for a second term.[51]

On the last day of the Synod, November 28, 1992, Ephorus Nababan issued a letter of complaint to North Tapanuli Region Police Office with the request for a restraining order against some people that had been identified as trouble makers during the whole synod. Soon after the Synod was opened that day, some participants asked Rev. Nababan not to stand for a second term. Apparently the protests were so hard to ignore that a special meeting of the Central Council had to be conveyed to discuss the matter. Rev. Nababan indicated at that time that he did not have the ambition for a second term, but he would not refuse the responsibility if the Synod wanted him to do so. According to his opponents, this statement was a trick. Finally later that day, Rev. Nababan gave the authority to the oldest pastor in HKBP, Rev. T.P. Simorangkir to chair the meeting during the agenda item on the analysis of the Report of Office Bearers of HKBP. The chance to respond was given to the participants and 104 participants took the opportunity to speak to the issue. Among those speakers were 68 participants who wanted Nababan to accept a new mandate and 24 who asked him not to go for a second term and resign.[52]

After 10 o'clock that evening, Nababan took over the chair of the meeting from Rev. T.P Simorangkir. That decision was heavily contested by some participants, because they suspected Nababan tried to influence the meeting in an illegal way. According to them Rev. T.P. Simorangkir was still chairing the session. The situation truly went from bad to worse. Protesters started yelling and screaming and began moving towards the front of the auditorium. Rev. Nababan called on the police to control the situation. However the police did not seem to be able to do anything because the protesting participants managed to get to the front of the room and started to make a lot of noise.

According to the report released by Rev. Nababan's side, Nababan then had a discussion with the Deputy of North Sumatra Military Intel-

---

[51] Sirait, "Kronologi Sinode", 4.
[52] This number was coming from Nababan's side, Sirait and Gultom, "Kronologi Sinode", 5.

ligent Corps, Lieutenant Colonel Ginting, about what to do. Lieutenant Colonel Ginting claimed that is was the authority's responsibility to calm things down. At 10:10 p.m., Nababan closed and suspended the Synod for an indeterminate period of time. Finally Nababan left the room on the advice of Lieutenant Colonel Ginting with an escort of police officers to return to his residence in Pearaja (only a fifteen minute drive from where the General Synod took place).

Lieutenant Colonel Ginting called upon the Central Council members to meet after Nababan left. According to Rev. Nababan's side, Ginting chaired the meeting and claimed that it was now the authority of the secretary general to chair the Synod, after the ephorus had left, to deal with the government.[53] According to the story written by Rev. S.M. Siahaan, Ginting asked the Central Council whether the Synod could continue or otherwise be handed over to the government. Rev. Siahaan wrote that Humuntal Lumban Gaol, one of the members of the Central Council, asked the authorities to take over the General Synod to make it in order again. Ginting then advised that a meeting with the Military Commander Toding should take place. The secretary general went to the military commander's office, which was near the venue. There a meeting was held between some members of the Central Council, the secretary general, Lieutenant Colonel Ginting and Colonel Toding.[54] According to Sirait, the secretary general and Colonel Toding had a private meeting afterwards for some 10 minutes.[55]

After this event, the reporting by the two sides became totally different. We will first give both accounts of the events before proceeding with a further analysis.

In the first version, Colonel Toding and Secretary General Simorangkir both sat down on the seat of the meeting chairperson. Rev. Simorangkir then said, "according to the HKBP Statue and Constitution, the representative of the ephorus hands over the authority to lead this Synod to the Military Commander." Then the Military Commander granted time to the secretary general to read the Official Decision of HKBP 51st General Synod. The content of the decisions were: a) Because of the poor health of the ephorus, and according to the HKBP Statue and Constitution, a caretaker team shall be formed to continue the ephorus' duties. The team consists of Rev. A. A. Sitompul, Rev. W. Sihite, Rev. S.M. Siahaan, Rev. Bonar Situmorang, and Elder A. Padang Situmorang; b) These caretak-

---

[53] Sirait and Gultom, "Kronologi Sinode", 6.
[54] Siahaan, 17–18.
[55] Nadeak, *Krisis HKBP,* 77; Sirait & Gultom, "Kronologi Sinode", 6

ers shall work under the coordination of the secretary general and are to prepare the next General Synod.[56]

The participants reacted strongly against the announcement that was made by the secretary general. Members of Central Council that were in the meeting with Humuntal Lumban Gaol, Rev. B.H. Situmorang, and Rev. T.P. Simorangkir reacted by saying that this was not according to the decision of the Central Council. Most of the participants moved forward towards the chair and protested against the decision. Some of them yelled and pleaded with the secretary general not to sell the Church to the government. They demanded that the decision should be withdrawn. After looking at the strong reactions and protests of the participants, Colonel Toding declared that the decision was withdrawn. Later on, a crowd of more or less 400 participants walked towards the Central Office of HKBP to see the ephorus in his residence.

The report of the events by the other side was quite different. They noted that during the meeting between the Central Council and the Military Commander, they tried to contact Nababan up to three times. Apparently Nababan claimed to be sick and therefore he was unable to attend the closing session. The members of Central Council had to meet to take some decisions on the confusing end of the Synod. Members of the Central Council (except B.A.S. Tobing) decided to give the authority to the secretary general, as prescribed in Order of Implementation of HKBP where the function of the secretary general is to act as ephorus in case of sickness and other emergencies. There were some members (Rev. T.P. Simorangkir, Ms. N.D. Gultom, C.E. Sitorus, and Rev. B.H. Situmorang) of the Central Council who thought that the mandate given was only for settling down the unrest inside the meeting building.

Secretary General Rev. O.P.T. Simorangkir then took over the chair as acting ephorus and upheld the decision that caretakers should be appointed. The official result of the HKBP 51st General Synod was read by the secretary general and stated the following decisions:

1. In a situation of emergency, the authorities can stop and dismiss the Synod.
2. According to the HKBP 1982-1992 Church Order, the terms of office bearers of ephorus, secretary general, and the rest of Central Councils and praeses are officially over.
3. To maintain the survival of HKBP as an organization, the HKBP 51st

---

[56] Nadeak, *Krisis HKBP*, 76, Sirait & Gultom, "Kronologi Sinode", 6. This account was also written in a number of witness reports made by some ministers that were given to Ephorus Nababan.

> General Synod appointed the following caretakers: Rev. W. Sihite (Chair), Rev. A.A. Sitompul (Vice Chair), Rev. B.H. Situmorang, Rev. T.P. Simorangkir, and Elder A.P. Situmorang (members). The tasks of the caretakers were to control the running of HKBP as organization and church, to prepare and hold an extraordinary General Synod to choose new office bearers, to maintain the status quo of HKBP without taking any principal decisions on personnel and finance, to keep the general peace and order in HKBP, and to maintain the coordinating relations and ask for guidance from the government.

After the decision was read, the ministers loyal to Rev. Nababan started screaming, protesting, and accusing the secretary general, that he had sold the Church to the government. They requested that the government would cancel such decision and asked the government to interfere and take over HKBP's situation.[57]

Colonel Daniel Toding, as the representative of the state cancelled the decision read by the secretary general and dismissed the Synod. Later on that morning some of the supporters of Nababan went to see him in his residence and Nababan met them and said that he was still the ephorus of HKBP and that he was in good health.

While Nababan thought that he was still the ephorus, the secretary general's side interpreted the dismissal of the Synod differently. What did the dismissal mean for HKBP? The book written by the Information Bureau of the secretary general's side said,

> The closing of the Synod's session meant that the term of office bearers of the HKBP (ephorus, secretary general, Central Council and praeses) had been concluded on Saturday, November 28, 1992 at 24.00 hours. They no longer had responsibility on all things concerning the leadership and management within the HKBP. Since November 29, 1992, the leadership of HKBP had been vacant and therefore it was delivered to the government and security officers.[58]

The secretary general's party was interpreting the dismissal as a handing over of authority in the Church to the government.

---

[57] There seemed to be an inconsistency between the two books that were published by Rev. Simanjuntak side. The book called *Building the Truth* claimed that the participants were asking the government to take over, see page 12, while the small book written by Rev. S.M. Siahaan said that the participants through Rev. Titus Simanjuntak asked that the government carry out the decision that were read by the secretary general, see 24.

[58] HKBP Information Bureau, *Building the Truth*, 13.

2.4 The Inauguration of Rev. S.M. Siahaan as Acting Ephorus

The rough last session of the HKBP 51st General Synod left a big question to who the legitimate leader of HKBP really was. Rev. Simorangkir's side was of the opinion that "since the November 29, 1992, the leadership of HKBP had been vacant and therefore it was delivered to the government and security officers."[59] Major General Pramono, the regional commander of BAKORSTANASDA (Badan Koordinasi Stabilitas Nasional Daerah/The Jakarta Agency for the Coordination of Support for the Development of National Stability), and who was also the regional military commander, invited the Central Council of HKBP to hold a meeting at his office on the December 16, 1992. Rev. Nababan was invited to this meeting but he did not attend it. There were 18 members of the Central Council who attended the meeting and Rev. Simorangkir as the secretary general. This time the Central Council was divided into two factions, 13 members, including the secretary general, were against Nababan, and 6 members were on Nababan's side.

Major General Pramono explained that his intention to invite the Central Council of HKBP was to solve the crisis of HKBP. He wanted the future HKBP to be ordered according to the needs of the congregations, and that HKBP would stick to religious purposes only, in contrast to what has been happening in recent times. There had been some disturbances in the congregations.[60] His institution did not have any intention to take sides and his sole purpose was that HKBP would be in peace again. The General also mentioned that his current priorities were to protect the stability of national security.

Questions can be raised as to the intentions of General Pramono. What did he mean by "HKBP would stick to religious purposes only"? Was this an indication that the government felt annoyed with the social activities that were advocated by the Church?

During that meeting, General Pramono insisted that the General Synod had failed to reach its objective and that the current goal should be how to elect new leaders of the Church. He claimed that the leadership of Nababan and Simorangkir had failed and that it was time to choose new leaders of the Church through an extraordinary General Synod. Then he proposed that pastors of the Church should organize the Extraordinary General Synod and that a senior pastor should become acting ephorus to take care of the extraordinary synod. The

---

[59] HKBP Information Bureau, *Building the Truth*, 13.
[60] Siahaan, *Laporan dan Informasi*, 60.

members of the Central Council who were in favor of choosing new leaders of the Church proposed three names: Rev. Dr. W. Sihite, Rev. Dr. A.A. Sitompul, Rev. Dr. S.M. Siahaan. Those members who were loyal to Nababan refused to propose any name. The General insisted that both Nababan and Simorangkir had to be removed from their current positions, and that HKBP had to act accordingly if the Church did not want the army and police to interfere.[61] The meeting ended with the promise of the General to deliver the issue to the related institutions in the government such as Department of Religious Affairs, the Department of Interior Affairs, the head of National Police, and the head of National Army.

Over the following weeks, tension remained high, and the HKBP headquarters in Pearaja, Tarutung, was surrounded by the military. A decision was issued on December 23, 1992, with the letter No. SKEP/3.Stada/XII/1992 by Major General Pramono as the Chief of Regional BAKORSTANASDA that appointed Rev. Dr. S.M. Siahaan as the acting ephorus with as main tasks: to prepare and hold an Extraordinary General Synod with the goal to elect new office bearers of HKBP in midst February 1993, according to the 1982 Church Order. The BAKORSTANASDA decree claimed the intervention was necessary for reasons of national security given the upcoming session in March 1993 of the People's Consultative Assembly, which was expected to re-elect President Soeharto. It cited two other decrees giving the government responsibility to settle the HKBP dispute. One was a BAKORSTANASDA decree dated February 27, 1991; the second was a Ministry of Religious Affairs decree dated October 21, 1992, stating that the military had decided to intervene long before the synod was convened. The December 23, 1992 decree also cited a report from the military commander, Colonel Toding, on the failure of the synod to elect a new ephorus, and a report by the Committee of the 51st Synod about matters the synod was unable to resolve. Simorangkir prepared the latter report. The decree also called for a special General Synod to be convened, in cooperation with BAKORSTANASDA, no later than mid-February 1993 to elect new officials for HKBP.

Protests were raised against this new decree. The HKBP led by Rev. Nababan filed a lawsuit against the regional military commander and BAKORSTANASDA chief, General Pramono. Some 4,000 HKBP members marched to the provincial parliament in Medan on December 28,

---

[61] Siahaan, *Laporan dan* Informasi, 78–79.

demanding the decree to be revoked. Others gathered at the governor's mansion, and still others marched to the regional military headquarters. Security forces lined their route. A major Jakarta newspaper, *Suara Pembaruan*, wondered aloud whether BAKORSTANASDA had not gone too far and said the action constituted unacceptable interference in the internal affairs of the Church.[62] On December 28, 1992, around ten thousand members and office bearers of HKBP marched to voice their protest to the North Sumatera Governor office and the Regional Military Office, rejecting the interference of the government in HKBP. Moksa Nadeak observed that this was the first people's demonstration ever in Indonesia since one during the New Order administration that started in 1966 and that was directed against the military office.[63] On the following day there were similar protests at local military offices in Tebing Tinggi, Pematangsiantar, and Tarutung. The protesters asked that the appointment letter should be withdrawn.

Interestingly, the Interior Minister, Rudini, and a senior minister close to President Soeharto, Admiral Sudomo, the Coordinating Minister for Political Affairs and Security, publicly opposed the BAKORSTANASDA action, both claiming that they joined with church leaders in supporting Rev. Nababan. They thus stood in direct opposition to Commander of the Armed Forces, General Try Sutrisno, who backed General Pramono.[64]

On December 31, the day that Rev. Siahaan was to be inaugurated, thousands of HKBP members occupied the church at HKBP headquarters in Pearaja to prevent the ceremony from taking place. There were also demonstrations in Jakarta. The effort to take over church buildings, as well as other protests throughout the Toba Batak area of North Sumatra, continued for the next two weeks. Major General Pramono ignored the protests and kept to his plan to have the inauguration of the acting ephorus in the church at the central office of HKBP in Pearaja, Tarutung. The inauguration should take place in the central church because it is the ephorus' traditional venue. Because a large number of people gathered at the central office in Pearaja to refuse the inauguration on December 31, 1992, the event was moved to Sipoholon, the place of the previous General Synod. Military force was used to secure the

---

[62] "Penunjukan Pejabat Ephorus HKBP," Suara Pembaruan, December 28, 1992.
[63] Nadeak, *Krisis HKBP*, 82.
[64] "Sudomo, Try to Seek Solution to Row over Bishop's Appointment," *Jakarta Post*, December 31, 1992; "State Should Stay Out of Church's Conflict: Rudini," *Jakarta Post*, January 2, 1993.

event. Moksa Nadeak described the situation as if "there is a war going on or an inauguration of a military general."[65] On the January 16, 1993, Rev. Siahaan's group managed to take over the central office in Pearaja from Nababan's supporters with the help of the military.

Rev. Siahaan, the appointed acting ephorus was a minister of the Church, and the former dean of the Education Faculty of the Nommensen University in North Sumatra, a university that belonged to the Church. Answering the issue of government intervention, the Rev. Siahaan's side wrote this in their official statement,

> It is good to know that the HKBP as a religious institution is a social organization which belongs to the domain of the Republic of Indonesia. Therefore it is subject to the *construction* (Ind: *pembinaan*; can also be translated as *guidance*) of the government according to Chapter 12 of the Constitution, No. 8/1985 concerning social organizations. This chapter explains that such a construction (guidance) is necessary towards good and self-supporting growth.

They continued, "The contribution of the intervention mentioned above in the HKBP obviously was not a cause but a result of Dr. Nababan's leadership that had created the procrastination and had spread tensions."[66] Obviously, Rev. Siahaan's side considered the interference of the government as necessary and appreciated it. Both factions had a different opinion on the legality of the interference of the government. On January 9, 1993, the Indonesian government issued a decree banning all individuals and organizations from commenting on the HKBP crisis. By the terms of the decree, only Sudomo, the Coordinating Minister for Political Affairs and Security, and General Pramono, the regional military commander, had the authority to make public statements on the issue. By this time, Sudomo had clearly changed his stance, telling the press that the BAKORSTANASDA move against HKBP was "justified and not an act of interference."[67]

What happened next was that Rev. Nababan sought legal help to solve the problem. He filed a lawsuit against the Chief of BAKORSTANASDA and the chosen new leaders who were appointed in the Extraordinary Assembly to the State Court in Medan, Pematangsiantar, Tarutung, and some other municipalities in North Sumatra. The chief judge of the first trial in Medan suspended the finality of the appointment letter by BAKORSTANASDA on January 18, 1993, while the process of the lawsuit

---

[65] Nadeak, *Krisis HKBP,* 82.
[66] HKBP Information Bureau, *Building the Truth,* 14–15.
[67] "Sudomo Bans All Comments on Church Conflict," *Jakarta Post,* January 11, 1993.

was in place. Then on February 6, 1993, the chief judge was replaced by another judge who then changed the previous provisional decision of suspending the finality of the appointment letter to allow it to take place. The court in Tarutung and Pematangsiantar then dismissed the lawsuit. This dismissal was understandable since the government was in favor of Rev. Simanjuntak's side and many suspected that the law was under the control of the then administration.[68]

During April and May 1993, under military protection, thugs used considerable violence to wrest control of many parsonages and church buildings from the majority of ministers who remained loyal to Nababan. The thugs were often members of Pemuda Pancasila, a youth organization related to Golkar, the political party of the government. They were hired by the Simanjuntak faction. Horrific stories of torture in police and military detention centers also began to appear. There was some violence from the Nababan side too, but this was legally prosecuted, while none on the Simanjuntak side were prosecuted for their offences.

2.5 *The Extraordinary General Synod February 11-13, 1993*

The acting Ephorus Rev. Siahaan then managed to get a permit from the government to hold an Extraordinary General Synod on the February 11-13, 1993, with only one item on the agenda: the election of new office bearers, namely a new ephorus, a secretary general, members of the Central Council and praeses for 16 districts. The opening and the closing ceremonies were held at a HKBP church in Medan, the capital of North Sumatera and the sessions took place at the Tiara Convention Center in the same city. The Extraordinary General Synod was attended by a representative of the Minister of Religious Affair of Indonesia, Major General R. Pramono and the governor of North Sumatra.

The Extraordinary General Synod claimed to gather 464 out of 562 participants of General Synod. This means that the synod had reached its required quorum. Nadeak argued that Rev. Siahaan replaced 87 of the original participants of the previous General Synod. Military and even local governmental support pushed the participants to come to the event, sometimes by force.[69]

---

[68] Nadeak, *Krisis HKBP,* 132–134.
[69] Nadeak, *Krisis HKBP,* 84. Further, Nadeak mentions some governmental letters asking HKBP pastors in their region to attend the Extraordinary General Synod. For instance, a letter No. 005/554, dated on January 28, 1993 from the Regent of Deli Serdang, addressed to Resort Minister and Teacher Preacher at HKBP Resort Dolok

During the Extraordinary General Synod, Rev. Dr. P.W.T. Simanjuntak was chosen as the new ephorus with Rev. Dr. S.M. Siahaan as secretary general. They were also able to appoint new praeses for districts and members of the Central Council.

Other decisions that were made during the Extraordinary General Synod were:

- To authorize the newly appointed Central Council to re-assign the *parritrit* group who were released from their ministries duties during the Nababan leadership.
- To dismiss the committee of the 1992–2002 HKBP Constitution that was originally formed based on the 50th General Synod to propose the 1992–2002 Church Order. The Extraordinary General Synod instructed the ephorus and the Central Council to form a new committee to carry out the same task and to continue to use the 1982–1992 Church Order until the new Church Order would be implemented.
- The office bearers of the Central Office of HKBP for the term 1986–1992 were officially dismissed from November 29, 1992, at 00.00 hours.
- Rev. Dr. S.A.E Nababan would no longer have the right to represent HKBP either in Indonesia or outside Indonesia, and all correspondences that would come from him should be rejected in all HKBP units.

The Extraordinary General Synod basically established a new team of leadership in the Church and dismissed the previous one. They emphasized that the previous office bearers had already been dismissed on the date of the last synod, and therefore Rev. Nababan had no right whatsoever to represent the HKBP at any occasion.

After the Extraordinary General Synod, the separation was obvious and the two conflicting groups called themselves by different names. Rev. Nababan's side called themselves HKBP *Aturan Peraturan-Setia Sampai Akhir* group (HKBP AP-SSA), that is "Order & Implementation/Be Faithful until the End", based on 1 Peter 1:25. They understood themselves as being faithful to the Church's Order and Confession, es-

---

Masihol, saying that they should send their representative to the Extraordinary General Synod. Rev. Daniel T. Siahaan told a story about his experience as youth pastor in HKBP Palembang, South Sumatera during the conflict. He describes that he was invited along with Rev. Ben Parhusip and the Praeses of South Sumatera District, the Rev. Amir Hasan Silitonga, to the Provincial Military Police office to meet Colonel Dj. Purba. The Colonel asked them whether the pastors from Palembang region were ready to attend the Extraordinary General Synod. He also said that the tickets for the pastor's travel had been prepared. See Daniel T. Harahap, "Gereja yang Luka dan tak Menyerah (1): Sebuah Kesaksian Seorang Pendeta di Masa Konflik HKBP 1991–1998," http://rumametmet.com/2007/03/20/gereja-yang-luka-dan-tak-menyerah-1/ accessed November 2007. This personal story illustrates that the military were in full support of the Extraordinary General Synod.

pecially in rejecting outside interference in choosing the new ephorus. Rev. P.W.T. Simanjuntak as the new ephorus of the Church claimed to be the true HKBP leader and often referred to the HKBP that was produced by Sinode Agung Istimewa Tiara (*SAI Tiara*); that is the Extraordinary General Synod in Tiara Center. From now on we will refer to Rev. Nababan's group as the AP-SSA group and Rev. Simanjuntak's side as the SAI Tiara group.

Several protests were listed by the AP-SSA group with regard to the decision of the Extraordinary General synod since they did not agree with the formation of the synod in the first place.[70]

1. The Extraordinary General Synod meeting was held at a convention hall of the Tiara Hotel and was protected by the North Sumatra BAKORSTANASDA, while in the Order of Implementation of the Church Order chapter VI article 21 mentioned that "every church meeting is a closed meeting and will be held inside the church."
2. The Extraordinary General Synod replaced 87 legitimate participants of the previous synod and 22 members of Central Council along with 17 praeses who were not invited.[71]
3. The extraordinary session chose an ephorus that was not fit according to the Order of Implementation Chapter 1 D article 2.a.3 that mentions, "The condition of being an ephorus is that he/she must be an ordained minister for at least 20 years, must be a resort minister for at least 3 years, and never been sanctioned by the Church." Rev. P.W.T. Simanjuntak (the chosen ephorus) was sanctioned and dismissed from his office duties in 1979 by the then Ephorus G.H.M. Siahaan. Rev. S.M. Siahaan (the chosen secretary general) had been accused of corruption in 1976 for manipulating university funds and had been sentenced to six months in prison; he was also accused of taking funds from HKBP's Education Foundation in Pematangsiantar, North Sumatra.[72]

The praeses of 17 districts were chosen based on the names suggested by Rev. S.M. Siahaan, while in the Order of Implementation Chapter

---

[70] Nadeak, *Krisis HKBP*, 86.

[71] Rev. Nababan was also not invited. Rev. Simanjuntak's side explains that the extraordinary session was held when the previous office bearers had already been dismissed and therefore they were not invited because they were not on the invitation list based on the Order of Implementation of the Church Order that states only Resort Ministers can be present as formal participants. See HKBP Information Bureau, *Building The Truth*, 18–19.

[72] "Penunjukan Pj. Ephorus Undang Protes" (Eng: "The Acting Ephorus Appointment resulted in protests"), Sinar Pagi, December 29, 1992. Also reported in *Asia Watch* 3, January 25, 1993, see http://www.hrw.org/reports/pdfs/i/indonesa/indones2931.pdf, accessed October 2007. The dismissal letter of Rev. Siahaan as a dean was officially given by the Foundation of the University with the letter number 052/SK/DP/Nomm/1976.

IV D Article 2.c.13 says, "That Central Council will propose the praeses candidates twice as much as the number of districts." Even before the Extraordinary General Synod was held, Rev. Siahaan has already replaced every praeses by force and chose a district coordinator instead, a position that did not exist in HKBP.

We observe that objections of the Nababan's side focused on the involvement of the government. This interference was seen as an outrageous act against the independence of the Church as a religious institution. This was also the main reason why they identified themselves with "Be faithful until the end". They wanted to implement the Church Order and to be independent from any outside interference.

2.6 Two Conflicting Groups

After the 1993 Extraordinary General Synod, HKBP was practically separated into two parties. One was led by Rev. P.W.T. Simanjuntak as ephorus, and the other was led by Rev. S.A.E. Nababan. The two different leadership teams each had their own staff, church products, lectionaries and signatures on every letter that was produced by HKBP. The way to differentiate them was to see whose signature was on the letter. After Rev. Simanjuntak took over the physical headquarters, Rev. Nababan was constantly on the move, running the leadership most of the time through constant communication. He managed to establish a crisis headquarter in Pematangsiantar but put no address on the letterhead. He sometimes did sign communications on letterhead paper with the central office in Tarutung as the address. Meanwhile, the team of Rev. Simanjuntak's side solely occupied the central office of HKBP.

The separation infiltrated every aspect of the life of HKBP. The theological seminary in Pematangsiantar soon divided into two schools when Rev. Nababan's supporters moved to the Tomuan area. The "Immanuel" Bulletin of the Church became divided into two separate publications. The HKBP Hospital in Balige was already taken over by Rev. S.M. Siahaan during his period as acting ephorus. He replaced the director of the hospital. HKBP SAI Tiara leadership took over the university of the Church in Medan and Pematangsiantar with the help of government's officials. The Church's theological schools for Teacher Preacher, Bibelvrouw, and Deaconess were also divided.

During the conflict period, ministers continued to be ordained, but neither side recognized the validity of the other side. Rev. Simanjuntak's side ordained more ministers than the faction that was loyal to Rev. Nababan. From February 1993 to September 1994 alone, Rev. Simanjuntak's side ordained 103 ministers.[73] Rev. Nababan's side noted in their annual lectionary of 1995 that HKBP had 230 ordained ministers, and had ordained 24 ministers during this same period.

Both parties claimed to be on the correct side of the crisis and tried to defend their own actions and blame the other party for being out of order. Some of the objections from Simanjuntak's side towards Nababan's side were expressed in the following way:

> Those conflicts and problems are not actually caused by the government intervention after the failure of Dr. S.A.E. Nababan to conduct the 51rd (ed. correction: 51st) General Synod of the HKBP which took place from 23 to 28 Nov 1992 at Sipoholon Seminary, Tarutung, in order to discuss and take a vote on the synod's three main agenda items. Nevertheless, the symptoms of the conflicts had turned up before the synod took place, caused by the actions of Dr. S.A.E. Nababan himself who had manipulated the official events in the HKBP in order to realize his personal ambition, although such actions were contrary to the constitution of HKBP.[74]

Rev. Simanjuntak's side thus blamed the conflict mainly on the conduct of Rev. Nababan. In fact, they thought that trouble had already started brewing in HKBP soon after his election as ephorus in 1986. The official Information Bureau of HKBP stated that the cause of the conflict lies in the personality and leadership style of Rev. Nababan, and the decision he took over the pastor's tour of duty.[75]

Rev. Simanjuntak side claimed that Rev. Nababan had tried to secure his second term in office as ephorus by trying to change the Church Order. Rev. Nababan actually proposed to hold the General Synod in two sessions; the first one would discuss and vote the new 1992—2002 Church Order, and the second one would elect new HKBP leaders. HKBP SAI Tiara suspected that Rev. Nababan would first try to change the Church Order since the existing Order made it impossible for him to stand for a second term as ephorus, because of an article in the Order required an ephorus candidate to be a parish pastor for at least three years. Rev. Nababan had never been a parish pastor, but he had been able to escape this rule at the 1987 election, because of a rule in the Article of Transition that stated, "All pastors that have served in general ministry for more than nine years, will be considered the same as

---

[73] HKBP, *Minutes of HKBP Meeting of Ministers 5–8 November 1991* (Tarutung: HKBP, 1994), 68–71. Compare this figure to the number of ministers in 1991 which is 531 ministers with 90 vicars. Thirty nine of the 90 have been ordained before the conflict started in late 1992. See HKBP, *Minutes of…1991*, 100.
[74] HKBP Information Bureau, *Building the Truth*, 1.
[75] HKBP Information Bureau, *Building the Truth*, 3.

those who served three years as a parish pastor." This transitional Article would end in 1992. If this article were not renewed, Rev. Nababan would have no chance of standing for election with regard to the ephorus office for a second term. Therefore, his opponents tried to stop Rev. Nababan's attempt to change the rules in order to qualify for a second term as ephorus.[76]

Rev. Nababan's side mainly raised the Church Order objections against Rev. Simanjuntak side. They found a lot of violations of the Church Order, beginning with the request to organize the synod before the 51st General Synod by Rev. O.P.T. Simorangkir as secretary general to the Chief of Indonesian National Police. According to HKBP AP-SSA group, this request constituted a violation of the Church Order, because the Order stipulated that only the ephorus was to represent HKBP in dealings with governmental institutions.

One of the major issues in the conflict was the appointment letter of Rev. S.M. Siahaan as acting ephorus by the Chief of BAKORSTANASDA. The interference of the government in this case was considered outrageous. The results of the Extraordinary General Synod, performed under the coordination of the illegitimate acting ephorus, had to be rejected as illegitimate. Rev. Nababan refused to accept any of the decisions made by Rev. Siahaan as acting ephorus or Rev. Simanjuntak as the elected ephorus. Rev. Nababan's side listed a lot of violations of the Church Order especially because of the involvement of the government. HKBP AP-SSA claimed that their side was constitutional and they therefore refused to recognize the leadership of HKBP SAI Tiara.

3. *The Confrontations*

3.1 *Legal Confrontation*

The first legal action was filed by Rev. Nababan against the Letter of Appointment by the Chief of BAKORSTANASDA and the installment of Rev. Siahaan as acting ephorus. The argument was developed that

---

[76] This is also the content of an open letter of distrust against Rev. Nababan as ephorus on November 20, 1992, during the 51st General Synod. This letter was read by Secretary General Rev. O.P.T. Simorangkir on behalf of 13 members of Central Council of HKBP saying that, "the source of all HKBP conflicts are in the person of Rev. Dr. S.A.E. Nababan, LLD that ever since he led HKBP never acted on the basis of the Church Order and in an authoritarian manner", see Rev. O.P.T. Simorangkir, "The Secretary General of HKBP Report to the 51st General Synod," (not published), 22.

HKBP was a legally independent institution, making it impossible for BAKORSTANASDA to intervene in the internal problems of the Church. On January 11, 1993, the court headed by Lintong Oloan Siahaan ordered the Chief of BAKORSTANASDA to delay the implementation of their decision. On February 6th, the judges of the case were replaced and the decision taken by the previous judges were overturned and the new court issued a dispensation to allow the implementation of the decision of Chief of BAKORSTANASDA. The court in Medan finally decided that there was nothing wrong with the decision of BAKORSTANASDA in the HKBP case. Subsequently, the lawyers of Rev. Nababan appealed to the Supreme Court.

Rev. P.W.T. Simanjuntak side also filed a lawsuit against Nababan at the State Court in South Jakarta. The suit was about the legality of the actions by side that was lead by Rev. Nababan. The court twice instructed the latter to attend the court through newspaper published summons, but Nababan never attended the trial proceedings. Nadeak argues that Rev. Simanjuntak filed a suit against Nababan that was served to an unknown address and as a consequence Rev. Nababan never knew about the suit. Rev. Nababan only learned about the decision of the court through newspapers, and he immediately filed a case against the court's decision by stating that Rev. Simanjuntak's side should have known his correct address, because Nababan was filing a lawsuit in the Medan court at the same time. Eventually the court in Jakarta granted the appeal of Rev. Nababan in October 1995 and cancelled the previous court decision.[77]

Soon after the new HKBP leaders under Ephorus Rev. P.W.T. Simanjuntak started working, the first major decision made was to change the pastor's tour of duty by shifting two hundred parish pastors from their places. Since many rejections of the re-assignment decision took place, Rev. Simanjuntak dismissed 110 pastors whom the new leadership deemed to have resigned from HKBP. However, some congregations refused this decision and remained supportive of their pastors.

As Rev. Nababan got fewer options inside the country, he turned for outside help. Rev. Nababan had very good relations with Vereinte Evangelische Mission (VEM) based in Wuppertal, Germany. The VEM was the mission body that sent Rev. Nommensen to Batakland to become the first ephorus of the Church. The mission body acknowledged

---

[77] The State Court in Pematangsiantar refused Rev. Nababan's lawsuit against Rev. Simanjuntak about the legality of his position regarding the Extraordinary General Synod in Medan. Rev. Nababan appealed on this decision to the High Court in Medan.

Nababan as the only leader of HKBP and criticized the Indonesian government for interfering in the Church's issue. Interviews with Rev. Nababan were published in German newspapers, causing bad publicity for President Soeharto's national administration. VEM supported Nababan by financial means as early as January 1993. They sent the money through *Persekutuan Gereja-gereja di Indonesia* (PGI/Communion of Churches in Indonesia) with the stipulation that only Rev. Nababan could use the funds to rebuild his leadership and to pay for the costs of the legal actions.

Rev. Simanjuntak's side was clearly unhappy with the decision of VEM and PGI. They consider this action as a conspiracy "stirring up the unity of HKBP, and opposing and undermining the policy of the Indonesian government."[78] They said, "Nababan has shifted the status of the Church from a religious institution into a political institution which undermined the government by inciting some groups in society."[79]

The mutual attacks clearly were getting worse. Both sides claimed that the other side had to be punished according to the Church Order for not obeying the Church leaders. Rev. Simanjuntak's side dismissed Rev. Nababan from all his office ministries in HKBP with a letter numbered 122/108/II/94, dated February 26th 1994. The dismissal meant that he was not allowed to teach, preach, and speak on behalf of HKBP.

Even local newspapers in North Sumatera were taking sides. One of the largest selling newspapers in North Sumatera, *The Sinar Indonesia Baru,* was clearly in favour of the HKBP led by Rev. Simanjuntak. In their publications, they referred to Rev. Nababan's side as "a group of people calling themselves as SSA",[80] or as "SAE Nababan's group".[81] This local North Sumatera newspaper published extensively on the conflict and on some editions published four news items about the conflict in one day.[82] The HKBP AP-SSA protested against the one-sided infor-

---

[78] HKBP Information Bureau, *Building the Truth,* 22.
[79] HKBP Information Bureau, *Building the Truth,* 25.
[80] For instance, see "Tidak Ada Lagi Kebaktian Bergilir di HKBP Tanjung Sari" (Eng: "No More Turns in Services in HKBP Tanjung Sari"), *Sinar Indonesia Baru*, April 3, 1994, 11.
[81] The newspaper often did not refer to Nababan as Reverend anymore and only used S.A.E. Nababan in their publications, while Simanjuntak was always referred to as Ephorus Rev. Dr. P.W.T. Simanjuntak. For instance see "Jemaah HKBP Agar Hidup dalam Kearifan Menghadapi Masalah yang Ada" (Eng: "HKBP Congregation Must Live Wisely to Overcome Existing Problem") in *Sinar Indonesia Baru*, April 4, 1994, 14.
[82] For instance, this newspaper used to publish several stories daily on the conflict such as these four different titles in one day's publication: "3 Sintua Penentang SAI Dikeluarkan dari HKBP Padangsidimpuan" (Eng: "3 Elders Who Rejected SAI Were

mation by this newspaper.⁸³ Meanwhile, there was another local newspaper, the weekly *Sentana*, who often issued the news of HKBP with positive attitudes towards Rev. Nababan's side.

The involvement of the government in the case became very clear in the events that happened after the extraordinary synod. The government finally gave its full support to Rev. Simanjuntak's side after President Soeharto received them at the presidential palace on March 22, 1994. The President said that he only acknowledged the HKBP that was the result of the Extraordinary General Synod in Medan, 1993. This strengthened the position of Rev. Simanjuntak, and the military and the police officially gave them full support. Bandung, the capital of West Java province was one of the areas where the separation of the congregations was very obvious. Within 24 hours after the President's acceptance of the Rev. Simanjuntak's group, the provincial military commander in West Java made a statement during a ceremony in Bandung, saying that he would discipline those who were involved in continuing the HKBP conflict.⁸⁴ In Siantar-Simalungun, a local military commander also warned the local civil servant units to stay away from AP-SSA group because of what the President had said.⁸⁵ In North Tapanuli, the Region Secretary threatened to dismiss any civil servant that was still involved in the AP-SSA group.⁸⁶

Dismissed from HKBP Padangsidimpuan"); "Kebaktian Minggu Dua Kali di Gereja HKBP Resor Binjai/Langkat Ditiadakan" (Eng: "Two Times Service in HKBP Resort Binjai/Langkat is Dismissed"); "8 Tersangka Perusak Rumah dan Mobil Warga HKBP di Duri Ditahan Polisi" (Eng: "8 Persons Suspected of Vandalizing the House and Car of HKBP's Member in Duri were arrested by the Police"); "Ephorus Pimpin Kebaktian di HKBP Tanjung Sari Dihadiri 3000 Orang" (Eng: "Ephorus led the service in HKBP Tanjung Sari—Attended by 3000 Congregational Members"). They were all printed in *Sinar Indonesia Baru*, April 25, 1994, 12. This is one of the instances where the newspaper published multiple intense stories on the conflict in one edition.

⁸³ There was an official letter by Forum Keprihatinan Warga HKBP (HKBP Member Solidarity Forum), a communication forum among HKBP SSA followers, sent on February 28, 1995, with the number 28/FKW/SUMBAGUT/II/1995 towards the editor of *Sinar Indonesia Baru* asking them to apologize and revise their news about HKBP SSA.

⁸⁴ "Pangdam III Siliwangi: Anggota ABRI yang Turut Perkeruh HKBP akan Diceklek Batang Lehernya" (Eng: "Military Commander III Siliwangi: Members of the Army who Make HKBP Situation get Worse Will be Choked"), *Sinar Indonesia Baru*, April 23, 1994, 1–2.

⁸⁵ "Danrem 022/PT, Kolonel Inf. Sunarto: Korpri Unit Hankam Siantar-Simalungun Bersih dari SSA" (Eng: "Regional Military Commander 022/PT, Colonel Inf. Sunarto: Civil Servant Corps Defense and Security Unit in Siantar—Simalungun should be cleared from SSA"), *Sinar Indonesia Baru*, April 29, 1994, 12.

⁸⁶ "Kakansospol Taput Letkol N. Simanjuntak: Dr. SAE Nababan Sudah Dilarang Muspida Taput Berkotbah Tanpa Izin. Sekwilda: Pegawai Pemda Taput yang Terlibat

On June 6, 1994, 230 pro-Nababan pastors, wearing their liturgical robes, went to the House of Representatives in Jakarta. They demanded that the government should restore the freedom of worship and that religious activities should be based on Pancasila (the foundation of the Indonesian state) and the 1945 Constitution. They signed a statement demanding that the military relinquish their right to use churches and liquidate the security units it had set up to secure Simanjuntak's leadership. The Jakarta Post noted that the government had confusing stances on HKBP during the three different hearings between commissions of the House of Representatives with the Minister of Home Affairs, the Minister of Religious Affairs, and the Armed Forces Chief General.[87]

The three government officials had different views on the Rev. Simanjuntak's group visit to the President. Yogie S. Memed, the Minister of Home Affairs told the House Commission II (Commission of Domestic Politics) that the government only recognized Rev. P.W.T. Simanjuntak as the current ephorus of HKBP. General Chief of Indonesian Armed Force, General Feisal Tanjung however, said to the House Commission I (Commission of Security Affairs) that, "The fact that President Soeharto recently received Simanjuntak and Siahaan does not mean that the government has recognized their leadership."[88] Tanjung also stated that the military had played no part in the HKBP conflict after the 1993 extraordinary General Synod. He mentioned that the armed forces were under strict orders not to interfere with the matter. Meanwhile Tarmizi Taher, Minister of Religious Affairs declined to comment on HKBP matter and claimed that the government would not interfere in this problem. These comments were made on the same day by three qualified government officials and resulted in three different answers. The most confusing answer came from General Feisal Tanjung who said that the acceptance of Rev. Simanjuntak's group did not mean that the government recognized their leadership. This was in contradiction

---

Kemelut HKBP akan Ditindak. Supir Mobil Pemda yang Mengangkut Massa SSA akan Dipecat" (Eng: "Chief of Local Social and Political Unit of North Tapanuli: Liut. Col. N. Simanjuntak: Dr. SAE Nababan Has Been Forbidden by Local Government to Preach Without Permit. Region Secretary: Any Civil Servant in North Tapanuli who is Involved in HKBP Case Shall Be Disciplined. Driver of Local Government Vehicle that Carried Supporter of SSA Shall Be Dismissed"), *Sinar Indonesia Baru*, March 18, 1994, 1–2.

[87] "Govt Has Confusing Stance on HKBP Rift," *Jakarta Post*, June 8, 1994, 1. This occasion was also noted by *Kompas* the biggest selling newspaper, "Sengketa HKBP Hendaknya Diselesaikan Kekeluargaan" (Eng: "HKBP Dispute should be Resolved in a Peaceful Way"), June 8, 1994.

[88] See "Govt Has Confusing Stance".

to previous statements from military officers that documented through several newspaper articles which put Rev. Simanjuntak's side in a favorable light.[89]

3.2 *Physical Confrontation*

Some severe physical confrontations took place during the conflict. They sometimes involved a third party. Most of the skirmishes happened during a take-over of church assets, i.e. houses, churches, and offices. Both sides would prepare themselves for the inevitable confrontations. If HKBP AP-SSA planned to take over a church, then HKBP SAI Tiara would try to defend it and *vice versa*. A third party would appear when one of the conflicting sides asked for their help, mainly the police (and military) and local youth organizations.

The confrontations often ended with victims on both sides. Some would have minor injuries such as bruises; other would suffer heavier injuries that involved some stitching; and in some cases people were killed. Neither side formally gave notice of the casualties. Information about them was scattered in local newspapers and letters. HKBP AP-SSA was the victim of most occasions. As briefly described below, HKBP SAI Tiara take-overs of church assets were protected through the presence of government officials, while protesters against it were usually arrested.

Nevertheless, both sides claimed to be the victims during the time of crisis. Both reported some events where their members had become victims of violent actions by the other party. The HKBP SAI Tiara side noted that,

> In their fight to take a number of church buildings by force, the supporters of Nababan were not reluctant to perform brutality and despicable deeds which have claimed a number of lives as well as properties: Elder Mr. Petrus Pakpahan of HKBP Church in Jalan Helvetia Medan, the death of a student of the HKBP Theological Seminary at Pematangsiantar Mr. Albiner Sitanggang at Pangururan Samosir, the damaging of HKBP churches in Glugur Medan, Tebing Tinggi and in other places. Furthermore, the Nababan's supporters who formed the group of "Be Faithful

---

[89] It is also worth to note a statement from Rudini, the former Minister of Home Affair in a one day seminar on the expression of religious life in Jakarta on February 17, 1993. He said that what happened in the HKBP is the result of outside interference and he claimed that he had refused any government's involvement in the HKBP problem when he was still a minister. "Rudini: Sejak Awal Saya Menentang Campur Tangan Pemerintah dalam Masalah HKBP" (Eng: "Rudini: I Have Refused Any Government's Interference in the HKBP Problem in the First Place"), *Sentana* 4th Week of February, 1994, 1.

Until the End" (SSA), besides doing some terrors and intimidations, killed a police officer, Sergeant Pangkirimon Tambun, sadistically. The murder took place at the HKBP Church at Siraituruk near Porsea.[90]

The highlighted events noted by HKBP SAI Tiara included the loss of some people's lives.

The event in Siraituruk village where a police officer was killed was an accumulation of an earlier tragedy. Nadeak and friends note in their book that the day before the officer got killed, an attack by 400 military and police officers was made against Rev. Nababan's followers that celebrated an event at HKBP Narumonda. The officers receded when a crowd of 5,000 gathered to chase them out of the church. After Rev. Nababan led a service in the church the following day, military officers made a new assault. Some hundred houses got damaged, and twenty persons were severely injured. People from nearby villages such as Sitorang, Silaen, Sigumpar, Parparean, Narumonda and Porsea had to move to Siraituruk for days. While they were guarding their village, a police officer who happened to pass through the area, became a victim of their anger. He was beaten to death.[91]

The victims were not only coming from HKBP SAI Tiara side, in fact most victims belonged to Rev. Nababan's side. Elder S. Siagian of Pasir Padang Village was stabbed in his eye and was beaten after trying to escape an attack from HKBP SAI Tiara side. Herbert Hutasoit, who was the secretary of Forum Kerukunan Warga (Member's Peace Forum) HKBP AP-SSA, was found dead with gunshot wounds at a paddy field on June 1, 1994.[92] Leopold Sitompul died after getting injured during an attack by security forces of HKBP SAI Tiara on June 25, 1995 in Binjai, North Sumatra.[93] The conflict spread outside Sumatra as well. In Jakarta, 600 people attacked HKBP Sudirman that was occupied by Rev.

---

[90] HKBP Information Bureau, *Building the Truth*, 24–25. Rev. Laurensius Maringan Napitu was convicted for involvement in the attack on the church that caused the death of Petrus Pakpahan. He was sentenced to ten months in prison and one year probation. See "Pendeta Laurensius Maringan Napitu Dihukum Percobaan 1 Tahun Atas Kematian St Drs Petrus Pakpahan di Helvetia Medan" (Eng: "Rev. Laurensius Maringan Napitu was Sentenced 1 Year Probation on the Death of St Drs Petrus Pakpahan in Helvetia Medan") in *Sinar Indonesia Baru*, September 29 1994, 1 & 11. However, the news later on stated that the cause of death of Petrus Pakpahan was not of the attack.

[91] Nadeak, *Krisis HKBP*, 120–122.

[92] "Herber Hutasoit Dibunuh Sadis" (Eng: "Herber Hutasoit was Brutally Murdered"), *Sentana*, 1st Week of June 1994, 1. No suspect was arrested.

[93] This event was highlighted by many local newspapers in North Sumatra, and the news heading on the front page of *Mimbar Umum* was "250 Preman Mengamuk di Binjai, 18 Terluka" (Eng: "250 Thugs Went Wild in Binjai, 18 were Injured"), June 26, 1995.

Nababan's side. No one was arrested in the incident that was stopped by the police.[94] There were many similar stories of take-over attempts in other parts of Indonesia outside of Sumatra, such as in Bogor, Bandung, etc. While benefitting from the HKBP Bandung case, Rev. Simanjuntak made a statement expressing his concern about the use of external force in the case of HKBP.[95] Apparently, both sides were worried about the use of external force by the other side.

Rev. Simanjuntak's side seemed to use external help to secure or obtain buildings that were still occupied by Rev. Nababan's faction. HKBP SAI Tiara would call on youth organizations such as Pemuda Pancasila to help them on such Subdistrict and Chief of Local Military occasions.[96] Rev. S.T. Bakara, one of the acting praeses linked to Rev. Simanjuntak's side, signed a note for the hiring of external security forces in the District V Office in Pematangsiantar.[97] In HKBP Sigumpar, the Chief of Local Military of Silaen area arrested the biblevrouw of HKBP AP-SSA that led the church at the time of the takeover by the HKBP SAI Tiara.[98]

The police arrested some ministers who refused to accept the HKBP SAI Tiara side. In the first days after the election of Rev. Siahaan as acting ephorus in January 1993, some of Rev. Nababan's followers were arrested, because they refused to accept the appointment letter by the BAKORSTANASDA.[99] On May 12, three ministers and a youth mem-

---

[94] "Rival Church Groups Clash, 5 Injured," *Jakarta Post*, July 3, 1995, 3.

[95] "Ephorus HKBP Pdt P.W.T. Simanjuntak Mendukung Upaya Pemerintah Memberantas Premanisme" (Eng: "Ephorus HKBP Rev. P.W.T. Simanjuntak Supports Government Effort in Eradicating Street Gangs"), *Sinar Indonesia Baru,* March 28, 1995, 12.

[96] There was a letter with letterhead from the Foundation Boards of the HKBP University to Local Pemuda Pancasila (Pancasila Youth), asking for support to "empty the university's foundation house". Pemuda Pancasila is an organized youth gang that is notorious for asking "security money" in exchange for their services. Another letter dated November 5 and 6, 1993, from A.T. Sitio as security coordinator of HKBP to Pemuda Pancasila asking for their assistance in the taking over of the assets of HKBP Glugur Darat, Medan.

[97] The Pemuda Pancasila was hired for this occasion and the total budget Rev. Bakara proposed was for the expenses of the taking over of the district house dated on October 28, 1993.

[98] "Ulah Oknum Camat dan Koramil: Bibelvrouw Manur Boru Panjaitan dan Hutapea Dipukuli" (Eng: "The Head of Subdistrict and Chief of Subdistrict Local Military Office: The Beating of Bibelvrouw Manur boru Panjaitan and Hutapea"), *Sentana*, 3rd Week of March 1995, 3.

[99] "Menggugat Bakorstanasda, Menangkap Pendeta" (Eng: "Suing Bakorstanasda, Arresting Ministers"), *Forum Keadilan*, No. 21, February 4, 1993. Forum Keadilan is a magazine for law cases in Indonesia. The report indicated that 43 pro Nababan members and ministers of HKBP, among them Daulat Sitorus, Rev. J.A.U. Doloksaribu, Rev. W.T.P. Simarmata, were arrested.

ber of HKBP AP-SSA were arrested in Tarutung. They were beaten, had to be taken to a local hospital, and were then taken into custody without notifying the families about their whereabouts.[100] Similar treatment often happened to ministers or members of HKBP congregations that were loyal to Rev. Nababan. However, no arrest was made on Rev. Simanjuntak's followers.

The conflict in the Church caused families to be torn apart, supporting different sides. The Batak culture has a very close family structure. It extends to more than just the nuclear family. Many decisions are made not just by the nucleus family, but also with the involvement of the extended family. Because HKBP is a church that is very close to the Batak people with its tight extended family traditions, good family ties can be seen in the Church, as well as having influence the other way around. Thus, the conflict in the Church has triggered conflict in families too. One of the stories of family separations is about an old man with grandchildren who passed away in one of the traditional villages of North Sumatra. His descendants were divided into the two conflicting parties in the Church. A big argument arose on who should lead the funeral service for the late man. The conflict not only affected the life and unity of the Church, it also ruined the family's harmony.[101]

3.3 *Separation of Congregations*

Both conflicting sides were now in direct confrontation on every matter. Rev. Simanjuntak dismissed all the ministers that they claimed were on Rev. Nababan's side. In the HKBP District V East Sumatra meeting of ministers of HKBP SAI Tiara, December 16, 1994, it was decided that the ministerial office of Rev. Nababan was withdrawn from the Church. Therefore, HKBP SAI Tiara demanded that Rev. Nababan should not use the HKBP name on every occasion. Rev. Nababan clearly rejected this and managed to arrange the structure and the order of ministry of the congregations that were loyal to HKBP AP-SSA.

Separation also occurred in the institutions of the Church. As noted earlier, the HKBP Theological Seminary (STT HKBP) in Pematangsiantar was divided into two factions. Both sides ordained new ministers during the conflict and both refused to admit the other's new pastors. As a consequence, the number of ministers increased during the time of the conflict.

---

[100] These ministers were Rev. Ramlan Hutahean, Rev. Nelson Siregar, Rev. Juaksa Simangunsong, and Rev. Samuel Sitompul.

[101] Both sides agreed that this specific story did take place and accused the other party as the cause of the conflict.

Based on their statistical report of June 1, 1996, the AP-SSA group claimed to have 168 resorts out of a total of 273; 725 congregations out of a total of 2,533.[102] And, based on the added explanation in April 1997, they claimed to have 251 ministers, 96 teacher preachers, 61 bibelvrouws, and 60 deaconesses. The report also argued that there were approximately 789 congregations who clearly upheld the Church Order and by principle refused outside intervention but did not express their view openly. The reasons why they took this stance were:[103]

1. The concern of a negative impact on their members who worked as state employees.
2. The concern of outside pressure, extortion, rape, in their family's daily life.
3. To stay worshipping in the church building that they had built.

The conflict also had a huge impact on the Church as a whole as the report stated,

> Along these four years, hundreds of thousands of HKBP congregation members went to other churches that belong to members of PGI nearest to their homes. Some moved temporarily to avoid physical contact to the HKBP crisis. Some chose to stay away from the church and tried to maintain their faith by personal effort and hoped that the crisis would soon end. Small numbers openly declared that they had left HKBP, and some joined the Catholic Church.[104]

Some congregations and resorts were divided into two factions. Those who split had some options. They could choose to have a separate worship service but use the same building, or find another place of worship. Most of AP-SSA congregations that separated from the SAI Tiara group had to find another place of worship because they were not allowed to use the church building any longer. Many of Rev. Nababan followers then used houses and other buildings as their place of worship, showing in this way their resistance against HKBP SAI Tiara. They chose any place that they thought was safe for them to worship. Many buildings were then developed into an independent HKBP congregation outside their original HKBP church. In some churches the two conflicting sides managed to worship together with the arrangement that the preacher would be from the AP-SSA and the liturgist from SAI

---

[102] See the report written by Rev. SMP Hutasoit, Head of Congregation Bureau of HKBP, "Statistical Recapitulation of HKBP that Are Loyal to the Church Order", Tarutung: *not published*, June 1, 1996, and "Added Explanation on Statistical Recapitulation of HKBP that Are Loyal to the Church Order until April 1997".
[103] Hutasoit, "Statistical Recapitulation."
[104] Hutasoit, "Statistical Recapitulation."

Tiara side, as happened in HKBP Bakaran Batu in Tebing Tinggi region. They separated the seats in the church so that the collection plate would go to their own side.[105] There were some congregations that used the buildings of other churches as their place of worship as happened with the AP-SSA group led by Rev. J.A.U. Doloksaribu in the building of GBKP Kemenangan Tani Padang Bulan in Medan.[106] The position of GBKP (Gereja Batak Karo Protestan/ Protestant Karo Batak Church) leaders self were not really clear on this matter. However, the lending of the church was soon followed by an official objection by HKBP leaders against GKBP leaders.

We observe that it was impossible for the congregations to stay neutral during the time of conflict. Every congregation needed full time pastors to lead the service, and every resort needed a pastor. As a consequence, they had to ask for a minister who showed loyalty to one of the sides. Every congregation was also obliged to send one of the three collection plates to the central office, and so they had to choose which side they were on. As a result, the conflict really affected and separated the congregations.

4. Reconciliation Efforts

4.1 Reconciliation Effort within the Church

In September 1994, Rev. Simanjuntak attended the first Meeting of Ministers in Sipoholon Seminary, Tarutung, North Sumatera that was attended by 423 ministers. This Meeting of Ministers took the theme based on Ephesians 2:14, "For He Himself is our peace." Because this was the first major assembly after the Extraordinary General Synod in February 1993, the conflict was often mentioned during the meeting. They first decided to accept without condition the seventeen pastors who had been dismissed during Rev. Nababan's 1986-1992 leadership period because of the retreat case.[107]

---

[105] "Dari Gereja ke Gereja" (Eng: "From Church to Church"), *Sentana*, 3rd Week December 1993, 3.

[106] "GBKP Pinjamkan Gerejanya untuk Anggota-anggota HKBP yang Anti SAI" (Eng: GBKP/Batak Karo Protestant Church Lend Her Church to Anti SAI/Extraordinary General Synod HKBP Members), *Sinar Indonesia Baru*, March 22, 1994, 1, 11.

[107] HKBP, *Minutes of HKBP Meeting of Ministers 26–28 September 1994* (Tarutung: HKBP, 1995), 67. According to Rev. A.A. Sitompul's statement to the newspaper, there were 129 ministers from HKBP SSA side that did not attend the general Pastors Meeting, Front Page, "Hari Ini Rapat Pendeta HKBP Dimulai" (Eng: "The HKBP Meeting of

Rev. Dr. A.A. Sitompul was the Chairperson of the Meeting of Ministers during Rev. Nababan's leadership and continued until Rev. J.R. Hutauruk replaced him in 1994, which means he played a role during the period of the two ephoruses. He observed that the problem that the Church was facing mainly started with the appointment letter of the acting ephorus by BAKORSTANASDA. He also mentioned that the government's interference was driven by the will to maintain national stability before the People's Consultative Assembly General Assembly in May 1993. The transfer of ministers to new posts after the Extraordinary General Assembly in 1993 resulted in placements that did not go smoothly.[108] Rev. A. A. Sitompul also met with pastors from Rev. Nababan's side after the conflict broke out and he gave some input based on those meetings. He noticed four points of critique: 1) the Appointment Letter of the acting ephorus by BAKORSTANASDA was historically and ecclesiologically irresponsible; 2) the status of future church leaders especially those who have been sanctioned by the Church was unclear; 3) acts of violence ruined the Church's ministry and testimony; 4) the tendency to form other means of fellowship by those who call themselves Pro Constitution, AP-SSA.[109]

By expressing these critiques, Rev. Sitompul had rightly put the objections of Rev. Nababan's side in play. He was the only person who brought this point of view to the entire assembly. He did not see how the Church could answer the critique upon the appointment letter for the acting ephorus. He also criticized the policy of Rev. Simanjuntak on the congregation post's transfer of minister. This could be considered as a hard blow on Rev. Simanjuntak's leadership since Rev. Sitompul was supposed to be on his side. Eventually, Rev. Sitompul was not re-elected and was replaced by Rev. Dr. J.R. Hutauruk who later on became the next ephorus during the Reconciliation General Synod in 1998.

The 1994 Meeting of Ministers decided also to consider those who did not accept the authority of the extraordinary General synod in February 11-13, 1993, as to have withdrawn themselves as office bearers of HKBP. Moreover, the assembly refused to accommodate separate times of worship in a church because of the separation of the congregation. The ministers ordained in Rev. Nababan's group would no longer be considered to be ministers in HKBP. The assembly also expressed con-

---

Ministers Begins Today"), *Sinar Indonesia Baru,* September 27, 1994, 1 & 12.

[108] Rev. A.A. Sitompul, "Report of the Chairperson of the Meeting of Ministers" in *Minutes of HKBP Meeting of Ministers 26–28 September 1994* (Tarutung: HKBP, 1995), 76.

[109] Rev. A.A. Sitompul, "Report of the Chairperson of Meeting of Ministers", 79.

cern for retired ministers who were involved on the AP-SSA side. The assembly formed a special commission to approach the AP-SSA side to reconsider a return to the SAI Tiara side.[110] In short, the Meeting of Ministers decided to take a confrontational way in dealing with the AP-SSA side.

The 52nd General Synod by HKBP SAI Tiara formed a special commission on reconciliation with the local businessman D.L. Sitorus as acting chairperson. This commission tried to hold informal meetings through dinners with both sides.[111] The main task of the commission was to practice a "Christian-like approach (Col. 3:5) according to the theme of HKBP 52nd General Synod towards ministers, teacher preachers, bibelvrouws, deaconesses, elders and lay members who had not accepted the result of the Extraordinary General Synod so that they would return and unite under the leadership of the HKBP 1992-1998 leaders."[112] Sitorus said that even though Rev. Simanjuntak's side formed the commission, they would try to be neutral and not chose side in the reconciliation efforts.[113]

On November 17-22, 1996, Rev. Simanjuntak chaired another HKBP General Synod in Tarutung. The theme of the synod was "Do Not Feel Sorrow, for the Joy of the Lord is Your Strength (Neh. 8:11c), and the sub-theme was "The HKBP Preparation for the Starting and Reaching of the Future in the 21st Century in the Midst of Indonesia's Developing Process as a Nation and Country". It was attended by 600 voting participants. In this General Synod, the theme of reconciliation was not in the air anymore. The Annual Report of Rev. Simanjuntak as ephorus did not show that the reconciliation effort was a serious matter any longer. He only mentioned that the relation between HKBP and some

---

[110] An interesting remark was made on the comments of the recommendations made by Commission 7 who discussed the matter of the conflict, which was to ask the government to allow the SSA side to form a new church; see remarks on Commission 7, on Central Office of HKBP, Minutes, 32–33 commenting the recommendations on 180–181.

[111] This Special Commission has 14 members and was appointed by the Letter No. 186/II/PS-VII/SK/II/1994.

[112] Letter of Appointment, No. 200/II/PS-VII/SK/11/1994. The other tasks of the team was to handle special cases in some districts/resort/congregation whenever needed and to take back all church's assets that are still under the control of the people who do not admit the Extraordinary General Synod result.

[113] "Wakil Ketua Tim Khusus HKBP Raja D.L. Sitorus: Mujizat, Jika Sisa Kemelut Tuntas dalam Waktu Singkat" (Eng: "Vice Chairperson of Special Commission: It's A Miracle if the Conflict Can be Solved in a Short Period of Time), *Suara Indonesia Baru*, March 15, 1995.

national and international ecumenical bodies were resolved because of what had happened in the past.[114] One of the decisions of the General Synod was "on the attitude towards those who claim themselves as the "AP-SSA" (a small group of people who still refuse the current leadership of HKBP)."[115] They decided: (1) the delegates of the synod realized that there had been an improvement, based on reports from parishes and districts concerning the growing numbers of those who had come back to the HKBP; (2) the 53rd General Synod expected the rest of the group of AP-SSA to come back. Rev. Simanjuntak's side believed they had won the conflict. They did no longer consider the conflict a serious matter as the HKBP 1994 Meeting of Ministers had still done. They were convinced that the groups that went to Rev. Nababan's side would eventually return to their side. Rev. Nababan's side opted for a joint General Synod, attended by both parties that would elect a new leadership for the Church. HKBP SAI Tiara refused this idea because they expected the dismissed ministers to return. This time, reconciliation seemed far away.

4.2 Reconciliation Effort by Communion of Churches in Indonesia (PGI)

The ecumenical world was outraged to hear about the interference of government in the HKBP conflict. The Lutheran World Federation issued a letter to all its member churches in February 1993 informing them that they firmly rejected the Indonesian government decision to interfere in the HKBP conflict. They asked their global member churches to join a common protest against what they called "an act, which violates important principles of religious freedom." They also sent a formal letter to the Indonesian president on January 8, 1993, pleading the same case.[116] This letter was one among many letters from partner churches and churchly institutions from outside Indonesia that protested the decision of General Pramono to appoint Rev. Siahaan as acting ephorus.[117]

---

[114] P.W.T. Simanjuntak, "Barita Jujur Taon ni Ephorus HKBP 1994–1996" (Eng: "Annual Report of Ephorus HKBP 1994–1996"), *unpublished*.

[115] S.M. Siahaan, "Report on the 53rd General Synod of the HKBP," *unpublished*.

[116] The letter signed by Gunnar Staalsett said that "Aware of the fact of such an action would not be in harmony with the stated position of your government and would violate international guarantees for the free exercise of religion, I respectfully request that this situation be clarified."

[117] Among which are the letter from National Christian Council in Japan on February 25th 1993 to Indonesian Embassy in Tokyo, Evangelical Lutheran Church in Namibia, Presbyterian Church in Ireland, Council of Churches for Britain and Ireland, National Council of Churches in India, National Council of Churches in the USA, and many more.

Some international ecumenical organizations also took positions in the crisis. They not only rejected the interference of an outside party in the HKBP conflict, but also shown their support on Rev. Nababan. The Christian Conference in Asia (CCA) invited Rev. SAE Nababan's party and chose the director of the Department of Women in HKBP, Rev. Basa Hutabarat, as member of their Women Commission, and Rev. SAE Nababan as their financial advisor. The Vereinigte Evangelische Mission (VEM) based in Wuppertal, Germany, expressed their favour for Rev. Nababan's side by financing them. VEM also appointed Rev. Nababan as one of their Moderators during their General Assembly in Botswana, 1994.[118]

The Communion of Churches in Indonesia (PGI) gradually changed its position from being firmly against the government's decision to become the mediator between both conflicting sides. On December 28,1992, PGI sent a letter to Rev. Siahaan asking him to refuse the appointment letter from the military and warned him that they would refuse to accept his leadership if he accepted the appointment. On January 4, 1993, after the installation of Rev. Siahaan as the acting ephorus, the executive board of PGI published a statement that they only recognized HKBP under the leadership of Rev. Nababan, because the PGI refused to accept the sub-ordination of religions to the state.[119] After a meeting to discuss the HKBP problem from March 2-5, 1993, the PGI Executive Committee reconfirmed their acknowledgement of Rev. Nababan as the ephorus of HKBP in a letter of decision.

In a second stage, PGI formed a team to meet with the conflicting parties and maintained relations with them in order to work towards reconciliation within HKBP. The forming of the team was the outcome of the Annual Meeting of churches representatives of PGI in May 1993. The team was led by Rev. Dr. Ketut Waspada along with Rev. Karel Erari. They went to North Sumatra to get first hand information from the conflicting parties on the assumption that they were only trying to gather the facts and would try to become a catalyst towards the unity of the HKBP. They also choose a quiet method of investigation; they tried to avoid media contact. They met local PGI in North Sumatra, the Governor of North Sumatra, the Commander of the North Sumatra Provincial Military Office, the Regent of North Tapanuli (the region where HKBP has its central office), and both conflicting parties.[120]

---

[118] Also see Nadeak, *Krisis HKBP*, 130–132.

[119] PGI also sent a letter to the President of the Republic of Indonesia dated February 10, 1993, asking for the postponement of the HKBP Extraordinary General Synod that was going to be held on February 11–13, 1993.

[120] Tim PGI Untuk Konflik HKBP, "Laporan Tim PGI Maret 1994" (Eng: "PGI

Based on their investigations and interviews with both sides, they observed that both parties still insisted that they were right to bear the name HKBP. The SAI Tiara group explained that the problem had already started when Nababan was still the ephorus. They also said that Nababan's side was the first to start using military assistance to identify the participant's name tags for the 51st General Synod. When they were asked about reconciliation, Rev. Simanjuntak was sceptical, since there were too many victims. He mentioned that after some violent confrontations in Pangururan, Narumonda, and some other places he thought that the effort to gather the conflicting parties would not produce any positive outcome. He suggested a meeting of both parties on a lower level.[121]

Rev. Nababan's group suggested two options to solve the problem. It was either for the government along with Rev. Simanjuntak and Rev. Siahaan to abolish (they literally said "to kill") all HKBP congregations who had been loyal to the Church Order, or it was to obey the Church Order. We need to note that the people from Nababan's side who met the PGI team were the ones who had been physically hurt during the conflict; they therefore were really emotional about it. Rev. Nababan himself still hoped for one HKBP and said that he would not run for ephorus for the next period.

The Governor of North Sumatra, Raja Inal Siregar, and Major General Pranowo, as commander of North Sumatra Military Command, said that they only recognize the leadership of Rev. Simanjuntak. The team made a further note about the Governor's comments:

> Without any hesitation, the governor gave his account of the bringing together of some people to form the Committee for the Extraordinary General Synod. Siahaan (author: Rev. S.M. Siahaan) actually made a promise that he would not take any leadership position among the new elected office bearers. But he did not keep his words. This made things worse.[122]

This interesting remark shows that the government indeed intended the Extraordinary General Synod in Medan to take place. Both government representatives agreed to support any reconciliation effort sponsored by PGI.

Based on their observations, the PGI team concluded that the heart of the problem was the conflict among the leaders of the HKBP. Each party interpreted the Church Order according to its needs. Every-

---

Team Report March 1994") (Jakarta: PGI-report document), *not published*.
[121] Tim PGI, "Laporan Tim PGI", 4, 5, 25–27, 29–30.
[122] Tim PGI, "Laporan Tim PGI", 18.

one longed for reconciliation within the HKBP but also thought that it would require a miracle because of the escalated violence. The PGI team suggested that the next HKBP Meeting of Ministers could be a uniting tool long as both parties attended the meeting.

The PGI team worked discretely and did not want to focus on the past but on reconciliation in the future.[123] Their report did not analyze what had happened in the past, but was orientated towards what the Church should do for the future. Surprisingly, the PGI team did not mention the government's involvement in the conflict even when they visited the provincial officials. They even asked the support and advice of the government on the next steps needed for reconciliation within the HKBP. The PGI team report had no significant influence on the reconciliation process. PGI invited HKBP sides' representatives to attend the 12th PGI General Assembly in November 1994, and prepared one seat for both sides. The special meeting in the assembly decided to require the two delegates of HKBP to sit together and to become one delegate. Both sides did not accept this requirement and left the seat vacant. Rev. Simanjuntak's delegation left the Assembly because the General Assembly refused to call Rev. Simanjuntak the ephorus of HKBP.

Later on, PGI described their actions towards reconciliation within the HKBP in a report at a meeting of representatives of the World Council of Churches (WCC), the United Evangelical Mission (UEM/VEM), the United Evangelical Lutheran Church of Germany (VELKD), the Christian Conference of Asia (CCA), and the Lutheran World Federation (LWF) in March 1995 in Geneva. In it, they explained that the recognition of the HKBP leadership was one of the major causes of the conflict. PGI also recognized the casualties during the conflict, and observed, "Both ministers and members of congregations who rejected the leadership of the Rev. Dr. P.W.T. Simanjuntak went through a lot of pressure, terrors and obstacles in their ministry and in performing worship."[124]

---

[123] For instance in Tim PGI, "Laporan Tim PGI", 29. Rev. Sularso Sopater as PGI chairperson opened the meeting with Rev. Simanjuntak by stating that the content of their conversation should be on how we should move towards the future and not be about the past.

[124] J. M. Pattiasina, "To Proceed With the Efforts of the Reconciliation of HKBP" (A report presented at a meeting of representatives of the World Council of Churches (WCC), the United Evangelical Mission (UEM/VEM), the United Evangelical Lutheran Church of Germany (VELKD), the Christian Conference of Asia (CCA), and the Lutheran World Federation (LWF), Geneva, March 12, 1995. Pattiasina also said that "These were carried out by paid personnel who were recruited from the community as well as from the government circles." PGI also assumed that the government's intention was to maintain the *status quo* within the HKBP so that the HKBP would play a less

PGI noticed the difficulties of the reconciliation effort. PGI decided not to apply the term ephorus to either side. Rev. Simanjuntak's side rejected all participation in any reconciliation effort and consistently demanded to be recognized as the official leadership of HKBP.

PGI proposed that HKBP would organize a new General Synod according to the Order of the HKBP, with the PGI as facilitator. During the PGI Annual Committee Meeting in June 1995, a position paper proposed four things, mainly to ask both sides to face the conflict and to be willing to reconcile with each other. PGI asked that both sides should try to deal with the problem among them without involving any outside party. PGI then decided to temporarily withhold the involvement of the HKBP in its ecumenical work and movement until the conflict would be solved.[125] Rev. Nababan's side criticized this decision and felt that PGI had left the HKBP problem without any real solution.[126]

4.3 Reconciliation Effort by Government Representatives

The President asked Major General (ret.) T.B. Silalahi, the State Minister of State Administrative Empowerment to assist in resolving the crisis. After several quick meetings, he managed to bring Rev. Simanjuntak and Rev. Nababan together in one place to sign a joint statement with seven decisions on June 14, 1993. Rev. Nababan would support the government's decision, would acknowledge the leadership of Rev. Simanjuntak as ephorus, and would give him a chance to lead in peace and harmony. Rev Simanjuntak would postpone any movement of the minister's new posts, and would allow congregations that were in conflict to use the same building.[127] Surprisingly, Rev. Nababan signed the agreement with the conditions: a) all acts of violence had to be stopped; b) all HKBP members had to be allowed freely to worship in the church; and c) a General Synod should be held immediately to resolve the problems in the HKBP. This was a big event that was covered by national television and newspapers and witnessed by leaders of PGI.

The statement produced questions on both sides. Rev. Nababan's side refused to acknowledge Rev. Simanjuntak as ephorus, and Rev. Simanjuntak had to explain the postponing of the movement of ministers posts. This hasty agreement finally ended before it even started. The

---

prominent role in the Indonesian society and nation.
[125] PGI, "PGI Position Paper on the HKBP Problem" (paper presented during the PGI Annual Executive Committee Assembly, Kotamobagu, June 16, 1995), point G.17.a.
[126] Nadeak, *Krisis HKBP,* 147–148.
[127] Nadeak, *Krisis HKBP,* 136–139 and HKBP Information Bureau, *Building the Truth,* 23.

following day, Rev. Nababan still considered himself to be the ephorus of the HKBP at a service in HKBP Pabrik Tenun in Medan. Rev. Simanjuntak's side later on criticized this action as "embarrassing", and "such denials should not be done by a pastor."[128] Nadeak argues that the government and Simanjuntak's followers were very much against the postponing of the movement of pastors' posts and the fact that Rev. Simanjuntak had allowed the churches to worship separately. This effort failed not long after the agreement was signed. This was not only because of the hesitation to implement the decisions, but also due to the confusion about the nature of the agreement.

The Department of Religious Affairs of Indonesia suggested establishing a new church as a solution towards the HKBP conflict. They proposed that Nababan's side should become a new independent church outside the recognized HKBP. This idea originated from the observation that in the past, new denominations had developed out of HKBP congregations.[129] Rev. Nababan's side strongly rejected the separation and establishment of a new church in a letter to the secretary general of PGI on May 21, 1996.[130] They considered the idea as schismatic, undermining the unity of the church in Indonesia.

Until the Reconciliation General Synod in 1998, the government made no more effort to reconcile the HKBP. In the meantime, they stayed by their decision to recognize the legitimacy of the leadership of Rev. Siahaan and of Rev. Simanjuntak.

4.4 1998 Reconciliation General Synod

Before the Reconciliation General Synod happened, some developments within both parties and in the Indonesian political realm changed the context considerably. Within the HKBP SAI Tiara, an internal conflict between Rev. P.W.T. Simanjuntak as ephorus and Rev. S.M. Siahaan as secretary general came to the surface. The situation deteriorated and Rev. Simanjuntak was hardly present in the central office of HKBP in Tarutung. A statement without signature, but suspected

---

[128] HKBP Information Bureau, *Building the Truth*, 23.

[129] These new churches came out from the HKBP for different reasons, for instance Gereja Kristen Protestan Simalungun (GKPS/Simalungun Christian Protestant Church) that became independent from HKBP in September 1, 1963; the separation of GKPI (Indonesian Christian Protestant Church) in August 30, 1964 as a result of a conflict in the HKBP (see GKPI website http://www.gkpi.org/ accessed on January 2008). We will see this more clearly in the later part of this chapter.

[130] Letter Number 188/J/KD/V/1996, by Rev. S.A.E Nababan to Rev. J.M. Pattiasina as the secretary general of PGI.

to be written by the secretary general, with the title "My Complains during Working Together with Ephorus Rev. Dr. P.W.T. Simanjuntak" was published.[131] This author explained that Ephorus Rev. Simanjuntak had taken over the tasks of the secretary general, illustrated with specific examples. The author also did not support the reconciliation efforts with the AP-SSA side made by Rev. P.W.T. Simanjuntak. This conflict between the leaders created divisions within HKBP SAI Tiara. Rev. Simanjuntak referred to the internal conflict in his speech during the Extraordinary General Synod in July 1998, the one before the Reconciliation General Synod in December later that year. He said that, "we should be wise about the anonymous letter that has been spreading among us ... I feel sad because it is not only the AP-SSA group that we have to be careful about, but also friends from within have done such things using the office stamp."[132]

Within HKBP AP-SSA, tensions rose as well. *Forum Komunikasi Warga*, a forum formed to support communication between congregations, and to provide legal support for congregations that were still harassed by outsiders, sometimes used violence itself to make its point. Its intention to gradually take over church buildings, district offices and central office did not go unnoticed. Some ministers, critical towards the policy of Rev. Nababan, asked Rev. Nababan to prevent this violence. They regretted that Rev. Nababan after 1992 organized neither a General Synod nor a Meeting of Ministers. Nababan acted like this for strategic reasons. He did not want to have to replace some ministers with retiring age in leading positions such as praeses who supported him. And he himself would have to retire according to the Church Order, reaching the age of 65 in May 1998. Rev. Nababan tried to solve this by appointing these praeses to "General Praeses", a position that did not exist in the Church Order, and he appointed new acting praeses. These decisions resulted in conflict within HKBP AP-SSA. This can be

---

[131] Anonymous, "Angka na Pinarungkilhon di na Mangula Raphon Ephorus Pdt. Dr. P.W.T. Simanjuntak," June 1998. This was delivered with the purpose, "so that the participants of the General Synod will not only hear the good news and not easily accept the report of the ephorus". Rev. S.M. Siahaan was suspected of having written the report, because of the details mentioned in 41 points in 26 pages of report on the period of working with Rev. Simanjuntak.

[132] P.W.T. Simanjuntak, "Penjelasan dohot Pengarahan ni Ephorus ni HKBP Pdt. Dr. P.W.T. Simanjuntak Sinode Godang Istimewa, 09-12 Juli 1998" (Eng: "Explanation and Direction from Ephorus HKBP, Rev. P.W.T. Simanjuntak towards Extraordinary General Synod July 9-12, 1998") (Speech delivered during opening of Extraordinary General Synod July 9-12, 1998, 10.

observed by the publications of two versions of the HKBP AP-SSA Immanuel Bulletin for a couple of editions.

The situation in Indonesia's political sphere was even more chaotic at that time. Soeharto stepped down as President on May 23, 1998, after months of unrest and students demonstration all over Indonesia. Vice President B.J. Habibie succeeded Soeharto, and changed some policies. He allowed more press freedom and freedom of expression in general. He released some of the political prisoners, and dismissed subversive laws used by the previous administration for random arrests on security grounds. As a consequence, the military and the police brought less pressure on the AP-SSA group. So, two weeks after the resignation of Soeharto, neither police nor military interfered when leadership changed at HKBP Sudirman Medan, a move considered by SAI Tiara as a takeover of a HKBP AP-SSA group.[133]

In the meantime, the leadership of both HKBP factions started working together on the organization of a joint reconciliation synod. Both sides formed a team—Team Nine from Rev. Simanjuntak's, and Team Seven from Rev. Nababan's side—to discuss the possibility of reconciliation. Rev. Simanjuntak organized an Extraordinary General Synod in July 1998 as a preparation for the periodical General Synod later in October the same year. The Secretary General Rev. Siahaan along with 9 praeses did not attend the Extraordinary General Synod. Out of 25 Central Council members, 23 attended the session. The Synod was opened by the vice governor on behalf of the governor of North Sumatra accompanied by some high military officials.[134]

Early October 1998, before the General Synod of HKBP SAI Tiara and a couple of months before the Reconciliation General Synod was to take place, *Forum Komunikasi Warga*, the communication forum within the AP-SSA group, tried to take over the HKBP headquarter in Pearaja, so that they would be included in the organizing team for the reconciliation synod. Rev. S. M. Siahaan was threatened by a big scale invasion by his congregation members. This incident caused casualties. Rev. Mangontang Rajagukguk died because of the incident on October

---

[133] There was a report to PGI made by Rev. Halasson Silitonga with letterhead number 147/HKBP-RM/01/H-22/98, dated June 13, 1998, about the damage made to the church and minister's house by the SSA group. Silitonga wrote in his report that the police was acting out of the ordinary by not stopping the attack, neither by shooting a warning shot in the air, nor by using tear gas (point 7 on his report).

[134] Such as the Chief of North Sumatra Regional Command, Chief of North Sumatra Police Force, Major General Luhut Panjaitan (as the supporter and initiator of HKBP reconciliation), and some others.

9, 1998. By then, he was the fourth victim on the AP-SSA side, after the death of Willem Marpaung (76 years, in the Narumonda incident, August 1994); Leopold Sitompul (67 years, in the Binjai incident, June 1995); and Herbert Hutasoit (42 years, in the Banuahulu village incident, June 1994).[135] The police and army did not intervene. The new 23rd Regional Military Commander, Colonel Inf. Heryanto Rachman declared, "Since this is their internal problem, we can only make suggestions."[136] Those not in favour of the existence of the Forum within AP-SSA group, criticized the incident. Still after the incident, the AP-SSA group maintained its position at the central office in order to increase its bargaining position before the Reconciliation General Synod.

The 1998 General Synod in October chose Rev. J.R. Hutauruk, the chairperson of the Meeting of Ministers, as the new ephorus replacing Rev. P.W.T. Simanjuntak. His main task was to hold a Reconciliation General Synod together with the AP-SSA group. In November 17, Rev. Hutauruk signed an agreement with Rev. Nababan to hold a Reconciliation General Synod on December 18-20, 1998. They agreed that the Synod would choose the new leaders of HKBP for the period of 1998-2004 (ephorus, secretary general, central council, and praeses).

The Reconciliation General Synod in December 1998 was held in Pematangsiantar and took the theme from 2 Cor. 5:18 and John 17:21, "Christ reconciled us so we can be as one." The Synod chose Rev. J.R. Hutauruk as the new ephorus, and Rev. W.T.P. Simarmata as the new secretary general of the reconciled HKBP. Rev. Simarmata was a minister from Rev. Nababan's side who was part of the small group that opposed Rev. Nababan's policy on the retiring acting praeses. An agreement was reached about the numbers of people coming from each side to take the leadership positions in the new HKBP. This was considered as a *win-win* solution for the HKBP. However, a plan for a process of reconciliation was lacking. At that time, it seemed that leaving the con-

---

[135] This was noted in a statement written on flyers by FKW-HKBP Distrik VIII- Jawa (Member's Peace Forum—HKBP District VIII Java-Kalimantan), October 1998 edition. In this flyer they urge the members of HKBP to voice their opinion and demand for the dismissal of the appointment letter by BAKORSTANASDA of the acting ephorus in 1993.

[136] "Konflik di HKBP Kian Meruncing, Kerusuhan Massa Bisa Meletus" (Eng: "HKBP Conflict is Getting Worse, Mass Clash could Happen) *Republika* October 13, 1998, 3. The North Tapanuli Regional Police Chief, Lieutenant Colonel Try Utoyo also said that they had no reason to stop the SSA group of holding a praise and worship service inside the HKBP headquarter complex. See "Kapolres Taput: Tidak Ada Larangan Laksanakan KKR" (Eng: "Chief Police of North Tapanuli: No Prohibition to Celebrate Praise and Worship Service) *Waspada* October 13, 1998.

flict behind might be the best step to take in order to be able to talk to each other again.

4.5 After 1998 Reconciliation General Synod

During the period of the conflict (end 1992-beginning 1993) until November 1997, HKBP AP-SSA had ordained 65 ministers and accepted 42 vicars. The total number of ministers that HKBP AP-SSA had was 287. Total new ministers that were ordained from 1993 to 1998 are 319. This means that Rev. Simanjuntak's side ordained 254 new ministers. The following HKBP Meeting of Ministers finally acknowledged the new pastors from both sides.

The first Meeting of Ministers after the reconciliation opened in a spirit of reconciliation in April 1999 with the theme taken from Hosea 12:7 (verse 6 in NIV) "You must return to your God" and the sub-theme "In the midst of a nation's crisis entering the 21st century, HKBP is called to be a missionary congregation with the spirit of peace and unity." A first discussion group worked on the exploration of the theme. The group agreed that it was necessary to reach a common understanding on the root of the crisis if true reconciliation was to be reached.[137] However, disagreement arose on the way to reach this goal. Some argued that it was important to uphold justice.[138] Others warned that it could be risky.[139] Some wanted to let the problem of the past be changed by personal attitudes and argued that it was not necessary to make a statement of confession.[140] Others pleaded for an agreement so that it would not happen again in the future.[141] The Secretary General Rev. W.T.P. Simarmata suggested that the Meeting of Ministers to produce a statement containing a confession of sin, apologizing in front of God, the congregations, and society for the sin they have made over the last 6 years (1992-1998), and promising that such a thing would never happen again in the future.[142] The group decided to establish a Truth and Reconciliation Commission to find what really happened and to evalu-

---

[137] Group 1 Reaction to Theme and Sub-Theme, *Minutes of Meeting of Ministers* Pematangsiantar, 14–16 April 1999, (HKBP: not published, 1999), reaction no. 1.

[138] Group 1 Reaction, *Minutes of Meeting of Ministers 1999*, reaction no. 3.

[139] Group 1 Reaction, *Minutes of Meeting of Ministers 1999*, reaction no. 2.

[140] Group 1 Reaction, *Minutes of Meeting of Ministers 1999*, reaction no. 14, and there was another response saying the opposite that HKBP needs to make a letter of confession of sin in reaction no. 17.

[141] Group 1 Reaction, *Minutes of Meeting of Ministers 1999*, reaction no. 15.

[142] Group 1 Reaction, *Minutes of Meeting of Ministers 1999*, Suggestion from Chair of the Meeting.

ate what needed to be forgiven. In the end, the Meeting of Ministers recommended several decisions regarding the reconciliation process of the Church:

> Decisions Number 4.1 about the Theme and Sub-Theme
> 4.1.2 To perfect the peace and unity in HKBP, on the confession of sin and promise: The Pastors' Meeting realizes and regrets its sins, and promises that such sin that has caused the crisis in HKBP will never happen again. As a realization of peace, justice, and forgiveness, we must uphold the law, and the guilty ones should be held responsible.

The Meeting of Ministers seemed to agree that the conflict had to be completely dealt with and the guilty ones had to be held responsible for what they had done. It seemed that the HKBP was ready to let the past be investigated. This point was confirmed in another decision to establish a Truth and Reconciliation Commission,

> 4.1.7 The Leaders of the HKBP will establish a HKBP Truth and Reconciliation Commission, to handle the case that has sharpened the conflict in the last six years. The purpose of this commission is to strengthen the unity of the HKBP, and uphold justice and peace in the HKBP, based on the theme of the Meeting of Ministers.

However, some contradictions can be found in the same Meeting of Ministers decision that was pointing out to another direction, which is the rejection of the idea of investigating what had happened in the past. Decision number 4.1.4 said, "The intention 'To return to God' means that the HKBP pastors should look to the future without bringing back the sin that caused the HKBP conflict."[143] And in another passage it was stated that the Meeting of Ministers acknowledged a sharp difference between those who wanted to uphold the law on the guilty ones, and those who wanted to forgive them.[144] To conclude, the 1999 Meeting of Ministers was still in a dilemma on whether the investigation on the real source of the conflict should be done, and on what should be done once the guilty persons have been identified.

The truth and reconciliation commission was never formed. There was probably a dispute on the purpose of the establishment of such a team. The rejecting of such team was probably motivated by uncertainty what to do with the outcome of the inquiry. Would the HKBP have the courage, let alone the strength, to investigate who were the victims

---

[143] The meeting used the word "*mengungkit-ungkit*" taken from the original word "ungkit" in Indonesian, meaning to pry up, to dig back what was buried.
[144] Decisions, *Minutes of Meeting of Ministers 1999*, Decision Number 4.1.8.

76 *Chapter Two*

and who were the perpetrators when the conflict had been so complex in nature? Would the investigation bring justice to the HKBP or would it only bring back the pain of the past?

The report of the chair of the Meeting of Ministers, Rev. Bonar Napitupulu, in the following Meeting of Ministers in 2001 mentioned the conflict in this way,

> What we felt during the 1999 Meeting of Ministers was the lack of unity and sincerity in the fellowship. As if there was a bad energy that influenced the fellowship. Sometimes there was a tendency of being aware of other people's feeling. This has produced lack of brother and sisterhood feeling among fellow pastors. But now, do not worry, in time those feelings will have disappeared, the brother and sisterhood feelings have returned within those who are in the one ordination, as result of the work and leadership of our leaders of the Church especially the ephorus.[145]

The Chair of the Meeting of Ministers showed great optimism towards the reconciliation efforts in HKBP. There was only one among 39 reactions towards the report of the Chair that questioned the result of the reconciliation. The person expressed the opinion that the theme of the previous Meeting of Ministers had not been carried on that no real commitment had been made to change the HKBP.[146]

What happened with the congregations that were involved in the conflict? Some divided congregations refused to reunite and preferred to establish their own congregation—within the denomination. Many of the Church's assets were gone. Many members of the Church moved to another denomination and never came back even after the so-called reconciliation.

In January 2005, there was still conflict in one of the congregations in Jakarta between the two parties that separated themselves during the conflict. The conflict in HKBP Pondok Bambu, Jakarta started after the minister rejected to serve one of the groups, which still used the same church building to have their Sunday service. After a while, the congregation decided to appoint their own pastor.[147] In December 2007, the unification letter from the ephorus of the HKBP ordered HKBP

---

[145] Appendix 10, "Report of Chair of HKBP Meeting of Ministers" in *Minutes of HKBP Meeting of Ministers 20–24 August 2001* (Pematangsiantar: HKBP, 2001), point number 2.a.

[146] Reaction No. 29, "Reaction Towards the Chair of Meeting of Ministers Report" in *Minutes of HKBP Meeting of Ministers 2001*, 24. This research would suggest that this means there has been no real effort towards reconciliation because no real decision had been taken towards finding out what really happened in the past.

[147] See footnote 27.

Resort Bandung Riau and HKBP Resort Bandung to unite under the name of HKBP Resort Bandung Riau Martadinata. These two churches were originally one church before the 1992-1998 HKBP conflict, but separated during the conflict and decided to stay separated after the 1998 reconciliation. They still used the same church building, but were served by two pastors at two different times of worship. HKBP Resort Bandung Riau argued that it could only accept a decision by the General Synod, not one by the ephorus.[148]

5. Analysis of the Conflict

5.1 An Anthropological Analysis

Here we will take a bit of a turn by analysing the separation of congregations within HKBP from a non-theological analysis of the conflict. Bungaran A. Simanjuntak wrote his dissertation before and during the early years of the conflict. His anthropological research was on the status and power conflict among Batak Toba people.[149] Although he was not specifically speaking about the HKBP conflict, his anthropological analysis will be of use to have a clear picture of the HKBP conflict.

The churches that separate themselves during conflict seemed to be influenced by the Batak culture in solving conflict. Conflict stories within Batak churches mostly resulted in a birth of a new church. Simanjuntak somehow suggests that it probably has something to do with Batak culture.

Before coming to Bungaran Simanjuntak's analysis, let us first see briefly the situation of Batak churches. The 1992-1998 HKBP Conflict is not the only conflict that the churches that originated from North Sumatra have endured. The churches in North Sumatra have been growing in terms of denominations. Since the HKBP Church was first admitted as a member of the Lutheran World Federation in 1952, there are 11 more denominations that have been accepted—with the Christian

---

[148] The conflict between the two sides was not new and often happened. See "Konflik HKBP Bandung Terus Berlanjut," (Eng: "HKBP Bandung Conflict is Still Happening") http://www.suarakarya-online.com/news.html?id=184650, accessed on December 2007, and "Insiden Warnai Malam Natal HKBP Bandung," (Eng: "Disturbance in HKBP Bandung Christmas Celebration"), http://www.detiknews.com/index.php/detik.read/tahun/2007/bulan/12/tgl/24/time/224146/idnews/870419/idkanal/10, accessed December 2007.

[149] Bungaran Simanjuntak wanted to do a research on the conflict of Batak Toba people. He initially started his field research in 1986 and finished writing the dissertation in 1994.

Communion of Indonesia Church in Nias (Gereja AMIN) (Gereja Angowuloa Masehi Indonesia Nias) as its latest member joining in 2002.[150] While the growth in numbers can be seen as a positive development of Christianity in Indonesia, most of the new churches came as a result of separation from their old church.

Most of church separations in North Sumatra came because of language and culture bearing issues. Churches such as GKPS (Gereja Kristen Protestan Simalungun *or* Simalungun Protestant Christian Church), GKPA (Gereja Kristen Protestan Angkola *or* Christian Protestant Angkola Church), and GKPPD (Gereja Kristen Protestan Pakpak Dairi *or* Pakpak Dairi Christian Protestant Church) are the examples of the spreading out of the HKBP Church because it was too '*Toba*.'[151] These separation reasons are often intertwined with power and financial motives—which some have analyzed as also having roots in the varying cultural backgrounds.[152] These multi-layered causes contributing to church separations have sometimes resulted in differently shaped memories of what happened during the process of separation[153] between the originating church and the new church.

Bungaran Simanjuntak thinks that Batak culture also played a part in the case of these separations. His analysis states that Batak people tend to solve their conflicts by avoidance and going away and to begin a new life. This is what he called *mamungka huta* (Eng: to open a village).[154] Every time a conflict in the family surfaces, the losing side

---

[150] See http://www.lutheranworld.org/Directory/asi/Welcome-EN.html, accessed May 17, 2010. Just for comparison, Communion of Churches in Indonesia started from 21 members in 1950 (previously Council of Churches in Indonesia) and has grown to 88 church members in 2010. See http://pgi.or.id/home, accessed May 17, 2010. The issue of growing numbers of Christian communities is not limited only to church separations, but also international and national council/communion of churches.

[151] These churches are coming from the same Batak roots.

[152] See Bungaran Antonius Simanjuntak, *Konflik Status dan Kekuasaan Orang Batak Toba* (Eng: *Status and Power Conflict of Batak Toba People*), (Yogyakarta: Yayasan Obor, third edition, 2009).

[153] One of the examples of these conflicts is the separation of GKPS from HKBP. HKBP and GKPS apparently have two different versions of the break up. HKBP writes about the process as a peaceful one, while a recent book written by GKPS ministers Juandaha Raya P. Dasuha and Martin Lukito Sinaga tells a different version of the event. See *'Tole! Den Timorlanden das Evangelium!' Sejarah Seratus Tahun Pekabaran Injil di Simalungun*, 2 September 1903–2003 (Pematangsiantar: Kolportase GKPS dan Panitia Bolon 100 Tahun Injil di Simalungun, 2003).

[154] See Simanjuntak, *Konflik Status dan Kekuasaan*, 90–91. Simanjuntak explains that there are three reasons of opening a new village: 1) bad luck in the old village i.e., diseases or famine; 2) lack of new land; 3) conflict on the position of the village's leader.

will have to move away and start a new life in another place. Most of the expansions of Batak people to new territories were the result of a conflict within the family. Conflicts over land inheritance will usually force the losing side to move away and open up a new village somewhere else. This new village will usually have characteristics similar to the one that was left behind. Real reconciliation effort will not happen within families, at least not within the conflicting generation. The act of opening a new area will make conflicting parties grow apart. This separation solution seems to be the way of dealing with conflict within the Batak culture. Bungaran argues, by looking into the background of Batak churches, that the habit of separating oneself in time of conflict seemed to be frequently adopted.[155]

Adat also includes ways of resolving conflicts. They are 1) Traditional sayings, 2) Familial relations, 3) Social structure in *dalihan na tolu*, 4) Relation with elders, 5) Religious institutions, and 6) The market place.[156] Two of these six reconciling institutions that are seen within the church are the role of superiors or elders, and the role of the religious institution itself. After Christianity arrived, Christian religious institutions became the reconciling institution, with the role of elders being played by the religious leaders.[157] However, the unresolved conflicts in religious institutions have made the church lose its function as a reconciler, and the religious leaders lost their role as tribal elder. Simanjuntak argues that the present management system of church organizations has become the source of competition and conflict since the beginning of the 20th century until the time he wrote his disserta-

---

[155] See Simanjuntak, *Konflik Status dan Kekuasaan*, 376.

[156] See Simanjuntak, *Konflik Status dan Kekuasaan*, 122–129. He mentions six institutions that can prevent conflict in adat. 1) Traditional saying which often comes as a general agreement among the people, can help to prevent conflict in adat rituals. 2) Familial relations between parents and children, brothers and sisters, will help prevent moral conflict in families. 3) Social structure in dalihan na tolu, helps manage the conflict in the three group elements of the social structure. If there is a conflict in hulahula group, the boru becomes the mediator; if the conflict is in boru group, the hulahula becomes the mediator; if the conflict is in the dongan sabutuha group, then the boru and the hulahula become the mediator. Peace will be restored when one of the conflicting parties admits defeat. 4) Relation with superior. Batak system believes that the position of the raja (king/leaders, including ministers as leaders of congregation) have godly value. 5) Religious institutions. A religious institution has the potential of preventing or mediating social conflict within society. 6) The market institution. People will not be allowed to bring their conflict and war to the market, a place of trading that is established by the leaders of adat.

[157] See Simanjuntak, *Konflik Status dan Kekuasaan*, 127.

tion.[158] The fact that it is often the leaders of the church themselves who are involved in the conflict made it more difficult to find a reconciling institution outside them.

One other factor in the culture that also functions as a reconciling institution, Simanjuntak explains, is the new year's rite, *mangase taon*. It is a new year's celebration dated from the pre-Christian Batak era that functions to reconcile conflicting parties. In this rite, all participants will be asked to sit together, with the elders, and to forget their conflict, and move on to the future. It is a kind of new start in the new year for the conflicting sides.

The church has also adopted the rite *mangase taon* in the new year's family service, where all families are going to celebrate a service in their respective homes. The church will make a liturgy for families to use at home with order of the service and bible texts. At one point, the family will remember what happened in the previous year, apologize for the mistakes, and start a new year in prayer. It is a rite of a new beginning that is adopted by the church.

Further, Bungaran argues that Christian rites such as Christmas, Easter, or the Eucharist are not effective in solving conflict. He is of the opinion that the effect of religious rituals is not as strong as the effect of *adat*. The failure of religious rituals is caused by three factors: first, religious institutions do not have a strong foundation in giving sanctions to parties who do not obey the conflict solution that they offered; second, the advance in education system led people to trust the justice system; and third, the lack of authority of the church leaders caused by their own actions has ruined the trust of the people.[159]

It is understandable that Bungaran is of the opinion that religious institutions and rites in Batakland are not strong enough to function as reconciliation institution since the Church itself was in conflict; or in Simanjuntak's word, that the church's leaders were the source of conflict.[160] His analysis needs to be further explored in an anthropological research, but we will not do it here. However, we will give three responds to his analysis.

First, Simanjuntak could be right when he thinks that the *adat* of opening a new village might play a role in Batak churches conflict. Simanjuntak also offers his opinion that the better conflict solution for the church with the tradition of *mamungka huta* is by the split of the

---

[158] Simanjuntak, *Konflik Status dan Kekuasaan*, 127.
[159] Simanjuntak, *Konflik Status dan Kekuasaan*, 378.
[160] Simanjuntak, *Konflik Status dan Kekuasaan*, 372.

church.¹⁶¹ Looking at this particular culture, the decision of both conflicting sides in HKBP to return as one church can be seen as a positive move.

Our second response will ask if *adat* can also function as reconciling institute for the conflicts within Batak people. Can we really expect the *adat* to help people to stay together as a family? What often happened is that the conflict usually lasts to the next generation and families stayed apart. There is a particular folklore of the conflict within Simanjuntak family. The story is about the conflict between the first and second son of the Raja Marsundung Simanjuntak.¹⁶² This is a conflict story from the first Simanjuntak generation that is well known to at least the 17th generation at the moment. Some of the descendants of both sides still believe that the two sides should not live side by side. There are efforts made within *adat* to reconcile both sides, but the conflict was never fully reconciled.

Our last remark will be on the cultural way in the tradition of *mangase taon* of forgetting the past in order to move forward. There seems to be a contradiction in the culture. Batak people are asked to remember particularly the past to see the future and remember their history; yet they are also asked to forget the past conflict. We can say that the element of remembrance in Batak culture is stronger than the plea to forget the past conflict.

5.2 A Political-Theological Analysis

Rev. Fridz Sihombing wrote an in depth theological analysis of the conflict, with the focus on the relation of the church and the state. Especially in his second chapter, Sihombing described the policy of the administration of that time, the Soeharto administration.

Soeharto was the president of Indonesia for 32 years (1966-1998). He came to power after the "coup attempt"¹⁶³ by the Indonesian Communist Party (PKI), and was responsible for the killing of six army generals

---

[161] Simanjuntak, *Konflik Status dan Kekuasaan*, 379.

[162] For the story of the conflict, see "Cerita tentang Konflik Turunan Raja Marsundung Simanjuntak" at http://marsundung-simanjuntak.blogspot.com/2008/03/cerita-tentang-konflik-turunan-raja.html, accessed August 30, 2011.

[163] The quotation mark that we brought in indicates that there have been debates over the topic itself whether the communist party was really trying to topple Soekarno's administration at that time, or whether it really was an intervention from the outside world by those who did not like Soekarno's idea of accepting communists during the Cold War. See Robert Cribb, "Unresolved Problems in the Indonesian Killings of 1965-1966" in *Asian Survey* 42 (2002), 550-563.

and one senior officer, which ended in the great communist massacre in 1965. There have been many human rights violation cases under the Soeharto administration and many of them accumulated without further investigation. For instance, the Tanjung Priok killing of 1984, the attack on the headquarters of Megawati Soekarnoputri's Indonesian Democratic Party (PDI) in July 1996, the disappearance of activists and the rumored role of state forces in the destruction of some large areas in Jakarta during the May 13-15, 1998 riots.[164] Violent conflicts also erupted between communities, and religious groups in Indonesia—for instance the Muslim-Christian conflict in Ambon from 1999 until 2004; the Madura ethnic cleansing by the Dayak people in Kalimantan (1996-1997, 2001); the burning of churches in Surabaya, Situbondo, Tasikmalaya, and Rengasdengklok in 1996-1997—that have never been completely investigated.[165] Some of the problems that have not been completely solved have even led to separation movements such as the one in Aceh and Papua.[166] This was the background of the political situation in Indonesia at that time.

During Soeharto's administration, the military was a very powerful instrument of power with their dual role in society as a military as well as a civic force. It was common at that time for ex-generals to become governors, regents/mayors, and head of public organizations such as a

---

[164] For a short description of the cases, see R. E. Elson, "In fear of the people: Suharto and the justification of state-sponsored violence under the New Order", in Freek Colombijn & J. Thomas Lindblad (eds.), *Roots of Violence in Indonesia* (Leiden: KITLV Press, 2002), 173. Many consider that these acts of violence were carried out by the state. Recent efforts have been made to recall these past events, for instance the May Riot of 1998. See Headlines, "The May Riots: Remembering the Terror" in *Jakarta Post*, Monday May 16, 2005, 2.

[165] For a selection of communal conflict in Indonesia, see W.A.L. Stokhof et al. (eds.), *Konflik Komunal di Indonesia Saat Ini* (Eng: Communal Conflicts in Indonesia Nowadays) (Jakarta-Leiden: INIS & PBB, 2003), Mary S. Zurbuchen (ed.), *Beginning to Remember: The Past in the Indonesian Present* (Singapore: Singapore University Press, 2005), Kees van Dijk, *A Country in Despair: Indonesia between 1997 and 2000* (Leiden: KITLV Press, 2001), and Adam Schwarz, *A Nation in Waiting* (Australia: Allen & Ulwin, 1999).

[166] There have been many articles on this topic alone, for instance see Sayadi (ed.), *Aceh Jakarta Papua: Akar Permasalahan dan Alternatif Proses Penyelesaian Konflik* (Eng: Aceh, Jakarta, Papua: The Root of Problems and Conflict's Solving by an Alternative Process) (Jakarta: YAPPIKA, 2001). This book tries to analyze the root of the problem in Aceh and Papua. The problem in Aceh has roots in the first rebellion group of Hasan Tiro in 1976 as a reaction to the central administration's centralistic and militaristic point of view (see page 56 of the report). Now, despite the destructive effect of the Tsunami in December 2004, it is still considered a military operation area because of the separation movement of Aceh (GAM). On the other hand, the root of the problem in Papua started with the Papua's process of integration to Indonesia in 1969, where there have been strong voices to oppose this decision (see pages 86-87 of the report).

national sport organization, a national charity foundation, etc. In the context of this authoritarian political climate, Soeharto became interested in the HKBP with in 1991 some 1,6 million members scattered over 2,533 congregations all over Indonesia. According to the population census of 1990 Indonesia had 178 million inhabitants, which means the HKBP as an organization reached almost one percent of the total population.

According to Sihombing, Soeharto considered the HKBP as a potential threat to the stability of the nation's security for five reasons.[167] The first was the growing internal conflict within the HKBP after the election of Rev. Nababan as ephorus in 1986. His losing rival in the election was the incumbent Rev. P.M. Sihombing, the previous secretary general. Nababan as the ephorus candidate had status as the chairperson of the Communion of Churches in Indonesia at that time, after serving as its secretary general from 1967 to 1984. The supporters of Rev. P.M. Sihombing were the ones that criticized Nababan for bringing in the TEN team, which they accused of violating the Confession of the Church. The Church leadership answered by dismissing several ministers and elders. Because the case created unrest within the Church, the government interfered by setting up a reconciliation team, chaired by an ex-general who was a member of the Church. General (ret.) Maraden Panggabean, who was at that time acting as the Chairperson of Supreme Advisory Council (this body advised the President on matters in various sectors). He formed a "Peace Team" along with 7 other generals and business people all members of HKBP, based on a memo of the Minister of Religious Affair No. MA/132/1990 dated 6 September 1990.[168] Apparently, the ruling administration felt pressure to do something about the HKBP internal conflict.

The second issue that caught the government's attention was a seminar on the theme of "Justice, Peace, and the Unity of Creation" held at the HKBP Theological Seminary in Parapat, June 1990. The seminar concluded that the Church should raise its voice against injustice and if necessary should take actions in line with the Christian ways of life. The government understood this as an indication that the Church was entering the political domain.

The government was also irritated by a dispute about *tanah adat*

---

[167] For a complete description of these causes, see Sihombing, *Versöhnung*, 109–123. Sihombing differentiates the case within the HKBP such as *parritrit* case with the political issues cases.

[168] Also noted in Nadeak, Krisis HKBP, 69.

(cultural land). The Church was supporting a group of women who held a strike to fight for their land in Sugapa, a piece of traditional land in North Tapanuli region.

The fourth incident happened at the HKBP national youth conference that was held in Sipirok, in June-July 1990. The meeting discussed current political problems related to the industrialization of North Sumatra, an issue considered sensitive by authorities that kept a close on any mass gathering.

Sihombing's fifth observation referred to the Indorayon case, a pulp factory based near Lake Toba, in the region of Porsea, North Sumatra, that had caused severe ecological damage in the area, such as air pollution, a considerable declination of the water height at Lake Toba, deforestation, and landslides. Several important and powerful local persons supported the activities of the company. The protests against the company were not effective because the government openly support the running of its management. Soon, the Church was putting its weight behind the protests, supported by the study group KSPPM, a non-governmental organization that originated under the protection of the Church.[169] KSPPM was also inspired by Nababan's active social theology.[170] As a result of these social activities, KSPPM was officially banned in August 1990. Because the legal ground for the action was not clear they were able to reopen two months later.

According to Sihombing, all these factors contributed to the direct involvement of the government, because it felt threatened by the HKBP case. This interference was against the theological principles in the Barmen Declaration that had been adopted by the HKBP Confession in the article about the Church. Sihombing rightly showed that the critiques that were brought by HKBP, led by Rev. Nababan leadership towards the government at that time were not meant to lead to a political movement. It was part of the Church's commitment to society, including its social political life. However, the government was later on very much involved in HKBP social activities because they crossed some of their political interest, especially in the North Sumatra region.

---

[169] The acronym KSPPM stands for *Kelompok Studi Pengembangan dan Pemberdayaan Masyarakat*; Eng: Study Group of People Development and Empowerment. See Gerry van Klinken, "Battle for the Pews", in http://www.insideindonesia.org/edit49/hkbp.htm, accessed October 2007.

[170] This paper pulp company is still operating until now under another name Toba Pulp Lestari. It stopped operating during 1997–1999 when Soeharto resigned; the subsequent administration of Megawati gave way for the owners to operate again under another name.

5.3 A Church-Political Analysis

After gathering the above data, and looking at the analysis of Bungaran Simanjuntak and Fridz Sihombing, this section of the study will now present my own analysis of the conflict. The HKBP 1992-1998 conflict was the biggest conflict that the HKBP has ever experienced. It lasted over six years and damaged not only the trust among ministers but also among congregations. The conflict resulted in a substantial loss of membership, because many preferred to stay in their new church after the conflict. Some congregations that were separated during the conflict still refuse to unite with their original congregation until now.

As we have observed, we found that the conflict was the result of multiple interests, conflict of personalities, lack of ecclesiological clarity, supported by the national current political situation, all intertwined in one event. Thus, it was difficult to construct a history, let alone to find what really happened during the conflict in a simple manner. However, after analysing the case, there are some factors in the conflict that can be observed.

The conflict was the result of the strong personality, and the authoritarian and firm leadership style of Rev. Nababan, which clashed with national political interests supported by personal dislike against Nababan. The objection against Rev. Nababan first came from a group of people who disliked the way Nababan brought the TEN team into the region. The theological reason that was given by the group who rejected the TEN group was not proven to be legitimate when it was discussed in the Church's Meeting of Ministers, an institution that is suited to solve theological differences between pastors within the church. This dispute was made worse by economical interest about the establishment of new university by the owner of the local newspaper, who felt that rich Jakarta people who supported the TEN group competed against him. We can conclude that the objection of rejecting TEN group was not theologically based nor was it sound. However, the matter was made worse when 19 pastors were dismissed from their position. Thus, the strong and firm leadership style could not solve and make peace with the 19 pastors, one of them being the secretary general of the Church before Ephorus Nababan's leadership. This could be connected with Nababan's organisational profile: he never served fully in a congregation after his ordination, yet treated the other ministers as a subject matter of organization, and not as a fellow pastor.

The supporter of the group that objected to Nababan's leadership gained support from the clash between Ephorus Rev. Nababan and the Secretary General Rev. Simorangkir. This conflict was acerbated by the lack of clarity in the Church Order about the position and function of the ephorus and the secretary general in the Church. This uncertainty would later perpetuate tension in the relation between Rev. Simanjuntak as ephorus and Rev. Siahaan as secretary general.

Rev. Nababan's leadership changed the way HKBP reacted towards social problems in society, especially those that affected members of the Church. The new policy supported the lives of members of the HKBP and provided encouragement to fight injustices that happened in the society under the strong hand of the current administration on all levels. Rev. Nababan's decision to enter the political sphere and use the Church's bargaining power in order to improve the condition of the Church members—as in the Indorayon case, and the settlement of *tanah adat* case in Sugapa—caught the attention of the government. The HKBP deliberately helped the establishment of NGOs, such as KSSPPM, that were active in helping the society with legal cases against some of the government decisions. The government certainly did not like such an attitude coming from the leader of the biggest church in Indonesia. This would be seen as a threat.

Rev. Nababan made efforts to change the 1982—1992 Church Order, in order to make it possible to obtain a second term as ephorus. Secretary General Rev. Simorangkir and some members of the Central Council stated their objections and received support from some ministers who were dismissed during Rev. Nababan's leadership. The government observed this as an opportunity for interference in HKBP. The government's intention was to maintain national stability, which was obviously under threat in Rev. Nababan's era as leader of HKBP, because of his social protests. The government then decided to support Rev. Simorangkir's side and gave him permission to hold a General Synod with extra security forces in place. This was a great opportunity to stop Rev. Nababan from obtaining a second term.

Although the military involvement and presence during the 51st General Synod seemed awkward and out of place, Rev. Nababan also made use of their service by asking them to take care of the security problem when some participants were acting "badly". In a sense, both sides somehow had the idea that it was the task of the government to deal with security matters even in a problem that was actually an internal conflict of the Church. Both sides requested security help, which proves that Fridz's Sihombing analysis is right when he says that the church forgot about the part of the Confession that rejects government involvement in the church. At the same time, the presence of the military and the involvement of some government officials in HKBP problems prior to the General Synod illustrated the government's great interest in internal HKBP matters.

The HKBP 51st General Synod ended without any decision on the new leaders of the Church. The BAKORSTANASDA's decision to elect Rev. S.M. Siahaan as acting ephorus was a direct interference of the government in the internal affairs of the Church. Their "national stability" reason they used for appointing Rev. Siahaan was unacceptable, since the HKBP was never an actual threat to the stability of North Sumatra, let alone national security. Since the appointment of Rev. Siahaan the Church was, as a practical matter, divided between those who agreed with the government and those who were outraged with the decision.

The Extraordinary General Synod in Medan was fully supported by the government and it managed to elect Rev. PWT Simanjuntak as ephorus and Rev. S.M. Siahaan as secretary general. Waves of resistance came from those who supported Rev. Nababan's action to stand up against the new HKBP leaders who were elected with the support of the government. Conflict was inevitable. Legal and physical confrontations were the result of the conflict.

The conflict resulted in many victims at either side. Rev. Simanjuntak's faction had the advantage of government support and therefore was often helped by the military or police forces when they tried to take over church assets from Rev. Nababan's side. Third parties such as youth organizations were involved. People who were attacked fought back. The group of Rev. Nababan also received help from international and national pressure towards Rev. Simanjuntak's leadership. In order to defend themselves as well as driven by anger and revenge, Rev. Nababan's side also turned to violence and attacked Rev. Simanjuntak's side. Some people were injured, lost their possessions, or lost contact with family members because they were on different sides; some even were killed during the conflict. Both sides received help from outside the church, and both had become victims and perpetrators.

The conflict reached its climax during the years 1993-1995. Efforts that were made to reject the BAKORSTANASDA decision to elect an acting ephorus were soon changed into efforts to reconcile both sides. Many efforts were made to reconcile them, but all failed. Both sides claimed to be the party in the right.

After 1996, those on the Rev. Simanjuntak's side were satisfied with their situation and expected that followers loyal to the Rev. Nababan would soon return to their side. Rev. Nababan continued to look for justice outside the country and expressed the idea of a Joint General Synod as a reconciliation tool for both sides.

Between 1996 and the Reconciliation General Synod in 1998, the situation saw further developments at both sides. Because of the insufficient ecclesiological clarity of the Church Order about the position and task of ephorus and secretary general, Rev. Simanjuntak had in turn a personal conflict with Rev. Siahaan. This situation divided their own group. The followers of Rev. Nababan criticized him for not having decided unambiguously on the retiring resort's ministers and praeses on his side. Rev. Nababan himself was close to his retiring age of 65 in 1998. Rev. Simanjuntak and Rev. Siahaan were also facing their retiring age. When Soeharto resigned from his presidency and Indonesia faced new political reforms in 1998, a time of change was at hand.

The HKBP pastors and congregations who were tired of the conflict captured this mood of chance and reformation. Rev. J.R. Hutauruk replaced Rev. Simanjuntak. He agreed to hold a Reconciliation General Synod in December 1998 with Rev. Nababan's side. The Reconciliation General Synod managed to produce new leadership for the HKBP and somehow united the conflicting sides in a short time as was clear at the first Meeting of Ministers after the 1998 General Synod in April 1999.

We can conclude that the 1998 Reconciliation General Synod happened because of: 1.) The combination of political turmoil in Indonesia; 2.) The fact that the ephorus in both camps were entering their retirement age; plus 3.) The segregations that happened within each respective group. A willingness from both sides to reconcile hurts and grievances was left unexplored.

After the 1998 Reconciliation General Synod, suggestions were made to investigate what had happened during the conflict for the sake of true forgiveness and reconciliation, but such a process did not materialize. Separated congregations were automatically and pro forma asked to return to their previous churches without any official explanation from the Church about what had happened in the past. Indeed, some refused to return and instead established a new and separate congregation under the name of HKBP. Some members chose to stay outside the HKBP. Even so, some local congregations still have their conflict going on until today without a reconciliation.

5.4 Was the 1998 Reconciliation General Synod Enough?

The 1998 Reconciliation General Synod was the result of very many issues happening within the conflicting parties, together with the national political turbulence at that time. Efforts to reconcile failed, because both sides claimed to be the party in the right side.

However, after the Reconciliation General Synod, no one seemed to formally investigate what had happened in the past. How could both sides, who both claimed to be the right party for a long time, accept the opinion of the other in such a short time? Why was there hesitation when the idea of forming a Truth and Reconciliation Commission came to the surface? How could the opinion that the reconciliation was already going in the right direction be expressed at the Pastors' Meeting in 2001 without giving any basis or evidence of a deliberate process?

In December 2006, while finding and collecting data of the conflict, an employee in the bookshop of the mission body of the Church in Pematangsiantar was interviewed. When she was asked about the data of the conflict, she started crying and said that she had burned all the documents because she did not want to remember the pain anymore. She claimed that by burning them she would burn away the pain because she was also one of the victims of the conflict. Her reaction is exactly what the Church at large seems to be doing. The Church might be trying to bury the pain by forgetting the past and trying to move on based on a new future. In 2011, the Church has not yet taken any decision to formally investigate or even gain discernment about what happened during the conflict.

Has the Church made the right decision by letting go of the past and move forward to the future without any process of closure to the case? Since there was no further effort for reconciliation that was made afterwards, are the proceedings of the 1998 Reconciliation General Synod sufficient enough for the Church to move on? If the Church claims to have settled the unity among conflicting parties then why is there hesitation to find out what really happened in the past and learn from it? If the Church decided not to remember the past because it is too painful—just what made the deaconess librarian act in the way she did—is that not a sign that the Church cannot yet accept and make peace with the past? Precisely because the Church is not ready to investigate what has happened why and how, indicates that the Church has not been fully reconciled within herself.

Based on the explorations of this chapter, we can conclude that the 1998 Reconciliation General Synod was, and still is not enough for a true reconciliation of the Church.

6. Conclusion

Even if we grant that a reconciliation of sorts has been made within the Church, the Church clearly still hesitates to further investigate what really happened in the past because it could ruin the present ambiguous order. The question is "Are the people truly reconciled to one another?"—especially since "there are still some congregations which have not yet been in full harmony"? Has forgiveness taken place? How does the Church deal with this? What will happen if the Church refuses to talk about it? How important is it for the Church to remember and deal with the conflict thoroughly?

Some may think that the Church's decision not to talk about the past traumas anymore makes some common sense because nothing positive seems to be gained from telling and thus passing on this story. It is too painful to tell through generation upon generation. The retelling and remembrance of the painful past could stir up hidden anger among those who hear it for the first time, and also the people who have experienced the conflict. Indeed, remembrance can be a form of vengeance. People fear that the remembrance of the case will lead to yet another dispute on whom to blame for the conflict, and this could possibly lead to a juridical matter in which both winners and losers can only lose more than gain. Such considerations can be explanations of why the Church has become silent about the past internal conflict.

However, the story might be too important to be silenced. The conflict has stayed deep in the heart of the congregations and their members. Would it not be better to talk and share the stories of both conflicting sides in a spirit of reconciliation instead of forgetting it? How should the Church react to the past conflict? Is it better to be silent about it or, on the contrary, is an act of remembering and sharing the story between the conflicting sides to be preferred as the route to true reconciliation?

Before we can answer these questions, we will now turn to the basic source and guide of theology which is the Bible, the Scriptures that tell the stories of God and God's creatures. It is crucially important to look for the biblical theological aspects of remembrance in the context of communal conflict, forgiveness and reconciliation. What is the biblical foundation of practicing remembrance? These are the questions that will be explored further in the next chapter.

Chapter Three

Biblical Meaning of Remembrance

Before we continue our exploration any further, let us refresh the fundamental question of the whole research. The main question is, "How can the current culture of remembrance be informed by a deeper understanding of remembrance in biblical, theological, and liturgical resources of the Christian tradition in order to deepen reconciliation after the 1992–98 conflict in the HKBP?"

What have we found so far? Remembrance is indeed a new culture that is being applied in communal conflict in order to remember the victims. The remembrance of the past is important for several reasons. First, it may prevent a similar atrocity to take place in the future. Second, it offers a release of pain for the victim or victims so that their voice can be heard. Third, it is a way of exercising justice for the victim. Fourth, it helps victims give a new meaning to the painful past. Lastly, it is a way of going into the future and living with each other by learning from the past and having faced it. We can definitely add some more considerations to this list but these are the factors that we have encountered so far. However, remembrance of a negative form or process can lead to revenge and to perpetual cycles of violence. This is why we need to look for an adequate foundation of doing the work of the remembrance of the past hurt.

Many churches like the HKBP have their own conflicts as well. In the previous chapter, we have seen that instead of dealing with her past conflict, the HKBP seemed to opt for a way of forgetting and moving forward to the future. We want to question the way that the HKBP took in dealing with its past. We want to suggest a helpful way of remembrance to the church and this is why we will need a good theological and biblical basis of doing such remembrance.

In looking for the foundation of remembrance in theology, it is important to go back to the primary source of doing theology which is the Bible. What is the biblical basis of remembrance in relation with forgiveness and reconciliation? In order to answer this question, we shall explore the biblical aspects of remembrance. What does remembrance mean in biblical terms? We will explore the questions further in this chapter using the methods of biblical theology. Here we will try to look for the biblical foundations of remembrance in the Old Testament and New Testament, by looking into the words and what they mean, and how society creates and perceives their memory in the Bible. The theme of remembrance will by and large be connected with the theme of community, forgiveness and reconciliation.

The Bible is in itself a book of remembrance. It is a book that consists of the memories of people who encountered God in their life experiences, and who were inspired to tell their stories and write them down to pass them on to the next generations. Precisely because of this, our exploration on the theme of remembrance wants to find out if the theme of remembrance in the Bible provides a more complex understanding than a mere recalling of something back into the mind of the individual or the group. If the Scripture does this, we would like to understand how biblical communities perceived remembrance and how they treated their memory, especially when it is connected with a past conflict and their relationship with God.

To go further, we will divide what the idea of remembrance means in the Old and New Testament into two different parts. First, we will utilize the recent social memory theory—a term we will explain later—in understanding the context of how remembrance is used in Old and New Testament. This theory will speak about what memory means to the context, not as an historical event, but rather as narrative of memory. Secondly, we will look at the meaning of remembrance in both Old and New Testament from a linguistic analysis of the terms that are used for it. At some point, we will also use exegetical analysis of selected texts that are connected with remembrance in society, especially in the context of forgiveness and reconciliation. By using two different methods, we are hopeful that we can establish the biblical understanding of remembrance.

1. Social Memory in Biblical Context

Biblical scholars are now appreciating the new researches in other fields of studies such as sociological, philosophical and anthropological research in memory, and use this new awareness in their own researches. The concept of "social memory" in biblical analysis tries to analyze the Bible as a web of stories, delivered by different storytellers that are coming from different societies that have different views on how memory should be delivered and preserved. The study of social memory started as a philosophical and social analysis research method that tried to look at how the social groups in which the story teller or writer lived shaped the memories that became included in the texts.[1]

Phillip Davies, an Old Testament biblical scholar, acknowledges the recent interest in cultural or collective memory. He recognizes the contribution of the research of Maurice Halbwach, Jan Assmann, and of Paul Ricoeur research—the latter of whom we have reviewed briefly in the first chapter—in the field of biblical social memory.[2] For him, social memory as a method, is not intended to find out what really happened in the past, but "rather at a narrative of the past that makes sense of (and in) the present and for the future. Hence, it is a constitutive function of ethnicity, the *ethnos* being in this case the group bonded by the shared "memory" of the past."[3]

Holly Hearon, a New Testament scholar who is actively engaged in the discussion of social memory states her understanding of social memory as follows. "...in the study of the Second Testament, we are inclined to view texts as the production of individuals belonging to groups whose identity is shaped in part by their perception of the extent to which they are able to exercise social power, and the real ways in which they are able, or not able, to do so."[4] In other words, the concept of social memory in biblical research analyzes how groups influence the writer in delivering the memory that was later passed on in the form of narratives, texts, images, or even rituals. This is why the study of social memory particularly encourages us to move away from a mere historical approach of finding out what truly happened in the story, by moving to the approaches of what we remember and

---

[1] See Mark S. Smiths, *The Memoirs of God: History, Memory, and the Experience of the Divine in Ancient Israel* (Minneapolis: Fortress Press, 2004), 133. He argues that most of biblical scholars have been putting their attention towards the social power in the production of the texts. For a short history of the social memory process in biblical society, see Dennis C. Dulling, "Social Memory and Biblical Studies: Theory, Method, and Application," in *Biblical Theology Bulletin* 36 (2006).

[2] See Maurice Halbwachs, *On Collective Memory* ed. and trans. Lewis A. Coser (Chicago: University of Chicago Press, 1992); Jan Assman, *Religion and Cutural Memory: Ten Studies* transl. Rodney Livingstone (Stanford, California: Stanford University Press, 2006); and Paul Ricoeur, *Memory, History, Forgetting*. Davies acknowledges all of them in Philip R. Davies, *The Origins of Biblical Israel* (New York: T & T Clark, 2007), 31.

[3] Davies, *The Origins of Biblical Israel*, 32.

[4] Holly Hearon, "The Construction of Social Memory in Biblical Interpretation," in *Encounter* 67 no. 4 (2006), 348. See also Holly Hearon, "The Art of Biblical Reinterpretation: Re-Membering the Past into the Present" in *Encounter* 66 no. 3 (2005). Hearon is one of the scholars who is involved in the theme of feminist theology.

how we remember it.⁵ Social memory emphasizes "the importance of history for understanding and interpreting the context that gives shape to social memory as it is encountered in literary texts. Material remains, diaries, letters, and the like."⁶

Hearon found that stories of the past can indeed become the group's social memory if it speaks to the people, and is being emphasized by the storyteller. Most of the time, the story of God's saving power in the past is being transferred as hope that God will intervene in the present and the future. Hope gives certain stories their power and durability in social memory. Stories can also function as acts of resistance towards the present and foster hope for the future. Hearon concludes, "This is where social memory parts with the past and turns towards the future. At the same time that it offers an interpretive framework for the present through continuity with the past, it points the ways that lie open before us as we ponder how to negotiate the future."⁷

In other words, in order to understand what the writer of a specific book in the Bible writes, we also have to understand what is happening in the surrounding place and time, and how others viewed and understood the event. If we want to understand the meaning of written history, we have to know the understanding of the writer who functioned as the deliverer of the story to a certain reader, in a certain time and cultural understanding.

Social memory theory in biblical researches wants to see the context in which the story was produced, and what the social powers in the society are that could influence the writer of the story in the way the writer remembered and delivered the story. When we apply this new method to our research of what remembrance means in the understanding of biblical theology, or how communities in the Bible did understand the terms "memory" and "remembrance" and what they meant for them, we have to first understand how memory and context shaped the society, and how important their cultural memory was in order to have the biblical understanding of memory. Only then, we can have the right understanding of memory. Thus, what we are doing is trying to find out what it means to remember in a biblical context, and how far remembering did influence the forming of the memory and identity of the people at the time the text was written and in the future.

---

⁵ See Hearon, "The Construction of Social Memory", 348.
⁶ Hearon, "The Construction of Social Memory", 349.
⁷ Hearon, "The Construction of Social Memory", 355.

Precisely because of this reasoning, we should also be sensitive to the problem in the context of social memory that arises from the fact that certain memories are being preserved, while others are not being preserved, with special reasons and purposes. Usually, such traditions of memories have already travelled far, from an oral tradition to a written tradition. To understand the complexities of social memory in the biblical context means that we will try to perceive the narratives within the horizon in which they were written or remembered.[8] Remembering as well as forgetting in biblical context is a social action of hearing a story and also choosing it in its details and form so that it becomes the defining story and the identity of the community in the biblical time.

If we want to combine the social memory theory with our exploration of what remembrance means in biblical understanding, then we have to find out what it means to remember in the context of Israel, how it shaped the concept of remembrance of the biblical writer, and how it represents the feeling of the context where remembrance was asked. If we are doing it this way we, hopefully, can find out what remembrance really means in the Old Testament and the New Testament, and how it contributes to our research.

Despite the different contexts and the great span of time in which the Bible was written, the written narratives in the Bible have the same common ground. One thing that we will see in the theory of social memory in biblical researches is that the basic memory that underlies the whole remembrance in Israel, and later in Jesus' time, is the purpose of remembering God's saving action. Different context have their way of remembering and defining the moments when and where God saved God's people. Nevertheless, the purpose is always the same, never to forget how great God's saving action is to the people of the covenant. This command to remember is then being translated in the written form of narratives about what to remember.

---

[8] For an argument that defended the visibility of understanding the story of the past, despite the different contexts and understanding in looking at the context, See Philip Francis Esler, *New Testament Theology: Communion and Community* (Minneapolis: Augsburg Fortress, 2005), 67–87. He uses intercultural communication arguments to understand how specific contexts understand their narratives, and how we can use those findings in understanding that context from a distant time span. He thinks that by using four factors, culture, groups and social roles, the individual, and the environment, we can interpret a document in its context or in its social memory.

2. Remembrance in the Old Testament

2.1 The Role of Memory in the Old Testament Community

> In the Old Testament, "Remember!" and "Behold!" are two of its great commands. Craig Dykstra, a practical theologian, says that Israel is constantly told to remember the day of their freedom from Egypt, to remember that they were once slaves, to remember how God has led them through the wilderness and into the land of Canaan.
> Israel is told to remember the entire law God has commanded them. They are told to remember the covenants and to remember how God has judged and has been merciful. Above all, they are to remember God as God remembers them in steadfast love. And often, they do remember. They remember in times of trouble and affliction. They remember as they seek understanding and a way to live. They remember in the midst of judgment, and they remember while in bondage. They remember in order to interpret what is going on in the world and what it means, and they remember in giving thanks and praise.[9]

The order to remember is lived out by the Israelites. Israel remembers what God has done for them in their life. Remembrance is an important thing for Israel, whether for their covenant with the Lord, or for their identity as well. God commands Israel to teach and remember the knowledge of faith "when you sit at home and when you walk along the road, when you lie down and when you get up (Deut. 11:19)." The remembrance that Israel is told to practice is to live by them obediently every day. Memory is the foundation in the forming of Israel as a nation. They preserve the memory as God's chosen people and the covenant that they have with God. Israel has preserved its social memory mostly in the form of an oral tradition. The whole community acts as a web of memories.

Joseph Blenkinsopp, a biblical scholar on social memory in the Old Testament, compares Israel's way of preserving its identity to our time. He says, "…social memory functions like biological memory, the genetic code in the individual. In most societies, even today, the primary vehicle for memory transmission at the local level is the kinship network and, along with this, its many analogous – affinity associations of different kinds, such as churches, synagogues, religious congregations, parties, and sects."[10] Social memory in the context of the Old Testament is

---

[9] See Dykstra, "Memory and Truth" in *Theology Today* Vol. 44, No.2 (July 1987), 159.
[10] Joseph Blenkinsopp, *Treasures Old and New: Essays in the Theology of the Pentateuch* (Grand Rapids, Michigan: Wm. B. Eerdmans Publishing Co., 2004), 3.

basically the genetic code that defines the identity of the nation, which was preserved in a big web of institutions of remembrance.

What makes Israel keen to preserve the memory is the way in which the narrative was being told to them. They realize that in their narrating of their origin as a nation, Israel has endured so many trials. Apparently, the consciousness of preserving identity as survivor, or victim is much stronger than those who do lack such experiences. Blenkinsopp explains, "The collective consciousness of societies that have experienced disaster, the Irish and Poles, for example, is more profoundly shaped by memory than those whose experience of disaster is more episodic or, a fortiori, those who have acquired a reputation for inflicting disaster on others."[11] The narrative of history, with such trials, played an important role in how strong the urge for Israel to remember.

The transmission of oral traditions in such a long span of time will make it difficult to maintain its originality, or in this sense, its original story. This is why, the most important story that needed to be preserved in Israel's story is the covenant between God and Israel as God's people, and how Israel should observe the laws. The core of the story was being preserved through an oral tradition in the social memory of the Old Testament community. The theme of God's saving action, and Israel as God's chosen people, was being transmitted in the oral tradition through rituals, commemorative ceremonies, and sharing of memories through storytelling.

One of the factors that could explain Israel's strong appeal to the remembrance of their identity in the form of narratives and memory is the difficulty in determining what the real Israel is.[12] Philip Davies distinguishes three different Israels: "one is literally (the biblical), one is historical (the inhabitants of the northern Palestinian highlands during part of the Iron Age) and the third, "ancient Israel", in what scholars have constructed out of an amalgamation of the two others."[13] We will not go in length into discussing the real identity of historical or biblical Israel, because that is not the intention of our research. What we want to say is that Israel perceives herself by the construction of a society that created the identity of biblical Israel. The identity construction of

---

[11] Blenkinsopp, *Treasures Old and New*, 3. He uses the theory of Paul Fussell, *The Great War in Modern Memory* 25th anniversary edition (1975) (New York: Oxford University Press, 2000).

[12] See the complexities of defining a historical or even biblical Israel account in Philip R. Davies, *In Search of "Ancient Israel"* (Sheffield: Sheffield Academic Press, 1992), 23–59.

[13] Davies, *In Search of "Ancient Israel"*, 11.

biblical Israel could only be preserved when the act of passing on the narratives through remembrance was strong within the community. The remembrance of the narratives strengthens the sense of identity of a society and connects it to the present, while at the same time giving it hope for the future.

Davies believes that the narratives that the people of Israel shared in the exodus from Egypt, the revelation in Sinai, the wanderings in the wilderness, and the passage as a unified people into the Promised Land, became the basis for the identity of the people. He says, "Even if some or many of these formative events did not really happen in the way that they are told, they were—and still are—felt and to be understood to be a shared memory of a collective past."[14] While we do not want to argue Davies' theory about the historicity of Israel as a nation—because our research is not the place of doing this—we can conclude that memory and narratives played a central role in the forming of Israel's identity.

As we have mentioned earlier, the remembrance of the narratives was open to revisions and reinterpretations. Davies gives an example of how open the narratives are to interpretation in the story of Abraham. He says that the remembrance of Abraham serves "to motivate the remembering agent to take appropriate actions, to give solace, and to activate social, religious, or political ideals."[15] The remembrance of Abraham and his covenant with God is open to reinterpretation, depending on the context of the reader and the subject of the story. Davies explains,

> To the Israelites in exile, the memory of Abraham gives new hope for a return to the Promised Land, with the exiles resuming Abraham's original journey from Babylon to the Promised Land. To God in the stories of Exodus and Sinai, the memory of Abraham reawakens his original commitment to Israel, which had wavered in the interim. God's promise of future memory ensures that this original commitment will never be extinguished, even when all seems hopeless. To both God and humans, Abraham's memory restores a link between the past, present, and future, providing a catalyst for reflection and action.[16]

Different subjects in different times and places give different meaning to the narrative of the covenant between God and Abraham. We can conclude that memory is an active form, where it is not only accepted as a narrative of identity; it is also open for reinterpretation.

---

[14] Davies, *In Search of "Ancient Israel"*, 8.
[15] Davies, *In Search of "Ancient Israel"*, 31.
[16] Davies, *In Search of "Ancient Israel"*, 32.

Biblical Meaning of Remembrance

The reinterpretation of the narratives in how Israel recognized what identity is was also renewed and reinterpreted in the later written story of Israel. A biblical scholar of social memory in the Old Testament, Ronald Hendel, thinks that the book of Chronicles is a good example of the re-telling of the stories of the books of Samuels and Kings. He says, "The book Chronicles revises the presentation of the past in the books of Samuel and Kings by recombining and interpreting these texts to bring them into line with current understandings – embellishing events that are important, omitting episodes that are irrelevant or problematic, and harmonizing divergent presentations in the source texts."[17] In short, the Old Testament itself has already given us an example of how remembrance of the past event was emphasized by the writer's interpretations of the event.

Hence, we can say now that memory is actively reinterpreted and re-experienced in the social memory of the community. What Davies means by saying that memory is active in the social memory of Israel is,

> In the Hebrew Bible, the memories of the past exert powerful claims on the present. In many aspects, the religious culture of ancient Israel is characterized by a perpetual negotiation with its memories and representations of the past. The effects of the past are changeable and multifaceted, since memories can refigure earlier memories, and representations of the past can express clashing interest.[18]

His view on active memory also gains support from fellow Old Testament scholars. Joseph Blenkinsopp also shows that he is in the line with Davies—and as we will see in the following part of this chapter with Brevard Childs—on the idea of the active meaning of remembrance in the Old Testament. He says,

> In biblical usage, likewise, remembering is rarely a simple psychological act. Joseph in prison asks the Pharaoh's butler to remember him when he gets out, which is a tantamount to requesting that he mention his name and intervene on his behalf with the Pharaoh, which the butler promptly forgets or neglects to do (Gen 40:14, 23). The same is true, it seems, for the deity. God remembers Hannah, with the result that she beats the odds and conceives (1 Sam 1:19-20). The common prayer formula of the

---

[17] Ronald Hendel, *Remembering Abraham: Culture, Memory, and History in the Hebrew Bible* (New York: Oxford University Press, 2005), 97. See also the authors to whom Hendel refers: S. Japhet, "Postexilic Historiography: How and Why?" in *Israel Constructs its History: Deuteronomistic Historiography in Recent Research*, eds. A. de Pury, et al., 155–166, and M.Z. Brettler, *The Creation of History in Ancient Israel* (London: Routledge, 1995), 20–47.

[18] Davies, *In Search of "Ancient Israel"*, 33.

"remember me"(*zokrâ-lî*) type, addressed to a deity, is, equally clearly, a request for divine intervention on the petitioner's behalf, whether addressed to Yahveh by Nehemiah or by a pious individual who puts up the money for a mosaic in the local synagogue.[19]

Collective memory of the covenant is not only re-called back into the mind, it is also re-experienced. Passover is one of the examples of a collective remembrance through the means of rituals. In the Passover, Israel remembers and re-enacts the past. The past must be internalized by individuals as if the story happened to themselves.

It is also important to note that the subject of remembrance is not only Israel as a nation, God is considered as a subject too. Blenkinsopp says, "In the Old Testament God also remembers, and occasionally forgets, and one of the goals of cultic performance, including common prayer, whether in the family circle or the state shrine, is to activate God's memory."[20] Thus, one of the goals of remembering and re-experiencing the past in the form of ritual actions is to ask God to remember the covenant. "To speak of God remembering is therefore a way of spanning the gap between the past and the present."[21] The meaning of God's remembrance in the Old Testament is also the same as the Greek *anamnesis* in the New Testament. We will discuss this point later in the linguistic analysis of biblical term for remembrance.

2.2 "Zākhar" as the Central Expression for Remembrance in the Old Testament

After exploring how social memory was perceived in the Old Testament community, we shall now do a linguistic analysis of the root of words in Hebrew. Afterwards, the use of remembrance will be seen through some exegetical analysis of the connection of remembrance with sin and guilt. We will see how the terms are employed in those texts and discern what the idea behind them is.

With regard to the Hebrew word analysis, we will use Brevard Childs as the main source for the understanding of the word *zakhar*.[22] Although

---

[19] Blenkinsopp, *Treasures Old and New*, 8.
[20] Blenkinsopp, *Treasures Old and New*, 9.
[21] Blenkinsopp, *Treasures Old and New*, 9. See the connection later on with Brevard S. Childs on active remembrance in the Old Testament.
[22] Brevard S. Childs, *Memory and Tradition in Israel* (London: SCM Press, 1962). We will also use the work of Yosef Hayim Yerushalmi, *Zakhor: Jewish History and Jewish Memory* (Seattle and London: University of Washington Press, 1982). Yerushalmi wrote his book for the understanding of "remember" among Jewish people then and now.

Biblical Meaning of Remembrance 101

Childs' work is not the most updated research in recent development in biblical studies, we will argue and establish that his word examination of remembrance in the Old Testament proved to be consistent with the more recent understanding of social memory. For him, memory in Old Testament cannot be seen only from the word itself, but also from the context. If we are going to look at the meaning of remembrance in the context of the word, we will find that remembrance has a more active understanding than just re-calling something of the past back in to one's mind. For this section, we will also get help from biblical dictionaries on the term, especially on the topic of remembrance in the Old Testament.

Childs wrote his book following a general attack on the book of Josh Pedersen by James Barr. Child studied the use of the verb "remember" in the setting of the cult, the law court, the prophecy narrative, etc. in the methods of form-criticism. However, the book of Childs only focused on the word "remember". As Barr has warned us, we must be careful of the complexity of the use of an isolated word-use in languages for they can have different meaning. Childs performed his research as (1) an attempt to find the scope of meaning and understanding of memory in the Old Testament; (2) to discover the meaning of memory through a form-critical analysis of the context within Israel's life in which memory plays a significant role; (3) to discuss the theological problem of memory and its relation to tradition.

2.3 *Etymology, Occurrences, Contexts, and Usages*

In the Old Testament, the word that is translated as "remember" comes from the root זכר (*zkr*) which is a verb of common masculine singular construct, and means "to think" (about), meditate (upon), pay attention (to); remember, recollect; mention, declare, recite, proclaim, invoke, commemorate, accuse, confess.[23] An important differentiation has to be made before we observe the understanding of memory in the Old Testament. Childs distinguishes the meaning of the root *zkr* in the qal and in the hiphil forms. He says, "the lexicographical analysis is significant in revealing the complexity of the root *zkr* and the danger of confusing fundamentally divergent meanings. Two basic meanings

---

[23] In Georg Fohrer & Hans W. Hoffmann, *Hebrew and Aramaic Dictionary of The Old Testament* (New York: Walter de Gruyter, (1973) 1993), 70, זכר is translated as *q.* recall, think of, remember; *ni.* be remembered, mentioned; *hi.* remind, mention, confess and praise. With vocals, it is translated as memory, mentioning, naming, and invocation. It is interesting to note that Zechariah is also named after the same root of *zkr*.

can be distinguished: *a.* to remember, in the qal, *b.* to utter, in the hiphil. The latter can either be a cultic naming of the name or a juridical accusation of sin."[24]

In six passages, *zākhar* expresses the active intellectual engagement of a person with himself (e.g. Hab. 3:2 prays to God that he will remember to have mercy; see also Lam. 3:20; Job 4:7; 7:7; 21:6; Ps. 22:28). The instances in those passages are showing an intellectual activity. The fact that *zākhar* often expresses the idea of the past does not automatically means to limit the meaning only to the basic meaning of the word, which is to remember in the sense of "to recall." Easing explains that, "it would be more accurate to say that the nuance of "recollection" springs from intellectual activity with reference to the past."[25] For instances, Shimei's plea to David (2 Sam. 19:19) and Abigail's request that the king will remember her with favor (1 Sam. 23:31) likewise refer to the past experienced by the person being asked to remember or forget (see Est. 2:1 and 2 Kings 9:25). In Lam. 1:7, 9, recollection of the glorious past is a repeating "motif" that works to accentuate the affliction of the present. The future can also be the subject of intellectual activity expressed by *zākhar* (Isa. 47:7).[26]

The verb *zkr* often appears in combination with other verbs such as forget. Such parallelism shows that *zkr* denotes the presence and acceptance of something in the mind. What is remembered is "taken to heart", where the heart to be taken as an expression for the personality as a whole.[27] When *zkr* is combined with *pāqadh*, "act with visible results", an element of concrete performance is added (see Ps. 103:18). An interesting sequence can be seen in Numbers 15:39 when Israel sees the tassels in their clothing, they will remember that they are connected with God's law. This will confirm their obligation, to act accordingly with the Law. *Zkr* often implies an action or appears in combination with verbs of action. In the observation of the context of *zkr*, it is clear that the verbs used in parallel do not refer to the past only. The interpretation of *zkr* as "remember" in the sense of recall can hardly represent its basic meaning.[28] We will treat the discussion on this in the next part of this chapter.

---

[24] Childs, *Memory*, 16.

[25] Eising, "Zākhar, Zēkher, Zikkārôn, "Azkārāh" in *Theological Dictionary of the Old Testament Vol. IV*, eds. G. Johannes Botterweck & Helmer Ringgren (Grand Rapids: Wm. B. Eerdmans, 1980), 66.

[26] Eising, "Zākhar", 67.

[27] See Eising, "Zākhar", 65. We will explore the connection of heart, soul, and remembrance later on in this chapter.

[28] See Eising, "Zākhar", 66.

Biblical Meaning of Remembrance 103

The word remembrance shows a complex usage in Hebrew of the root form *zkr*. This verb occurs in all branches of Semitic languages. It appears absolutely, or with a verb as complement, only in a few passages; in most cases it is combined with the object of the intellectual activity, with (39 occurrences) or without (52 occurrences) the use of *'eth*.[29] It occurs 168 times in the qal form and 20 times in the niphal. The hiphil (31 occurrences), with the causative meaning "bring to remembrance," exhibits extended usage, as does the noun *zēkher* (33 occurrences), and *zikkārôn* (24 times) as a memorial, and the cultic term *'azkārāh* (7 occurrences).

There are some derivations from the root *zkr*. Eising notes that the niphal form, *nizkar* functions as a passive of the qal, but a few of its occurrences exhibit characteristic supplementary elements belonging to the meaning of *zākhar*. Childs says that the verb should be translated "mention" (see Isa. 23:16; 65:17).[30] Meanwhile, the proper causative meaning of the hiphil *hizkir* should be conceived as "bring to remembrance", "make someone remember" or "be mindful of" something (see Gen 41:9).

Allen notes that the noun *zēkher* (23 occurrences) refers to remembrance when it is associated with death. Evildoers and Israel's enemies suffer the fate of not being remembered at the time of death (see. Ex. 17:14; Deut. 25:19; 32:26; Ps. 9:6), while on the other hand, wisdom teaching promises that the righteous will always be remembered (Ps. 112:6; Prov. 10:7).[31] God has his remembrance because of the way he reveals his name *yhvh* (Ex. 3:15). The "memory" of God is often praised just as God's name (Ps. 30:5). The late psalms also show that the *zēkher* of God's name involves an element of proclamation (Ps. 111:4; 145:7). Eising notes, "The fact that there is no remembrance of God in Sheol (Ps. 6:5) can even be the motif for a lament in which the worshippers pray that God will remember and will let them live. The human lives because God remembers him/her and is obligated to remember God's wonder with praise."[32]

The nom. *zikkārôn* has at least three meanings. First, it can mean remembrance (Eccl. 1:11; 2:16); second, it is a memorandum, record,

---

[29] See Eising, "Zākhar", 64–65.
[30] See Childs, *Memory*, 16; and Eising "Zākhar", 72.
[31] Leslie C. Allen, "זכר", in *New International Dictionary of Old Testament Theology and Exegesis Vol. 1,* ed. Willem A. van Gemeren (Grand Rapids: Zondervan Publishing House, 1996), 1104.
[32] Eising "Zākhar", 77.

or "something to be remembered" in itself (Ex. 17:14), such as the scroll of remembrance in Mal. 3:16. The most common sense meaning is "a memorial" or "reminder of something else".[33] In the Pentateuch, *zikkārôn* occurs only in P; to the notion of remembering it adds the element of a sign that evokes remembrance.[34] God or human could institute a "memorial" to remind either God or human. The regulations concerning the Passover in Ex. 12:1-20 includes an '*ôth* for God (v. 13) and a *zikkārôn* for man (v. 14). The blood of the Passover lamb is to be a "sign", while the day of the Passover is explained as a memorial. Jeremiah 17:2 could also bear witness that the sins of Judah were written upon the horns of the altar "as a momento" against them.

The next derivation from the root *zkr* is '*azkārāh* which is translated as sign-offering or memorial portion.[35] The noun '*azkārāh* which is often translated as *anamnesis* in the LXX,[36] occurs 7 times in the Old Testament. Averbeck analyzes that the noun refers to the part of the regular grain offering that the officiating priest would normally offer to the Lord on the burnt offering altar as a "memorial (portion)" to the Lord (Lev. 2:2, 9, 16; 5:12; 6:15), the "shrewbread" or "bread of the Presence" (Lev. 24:7; cf. Ex.. 25:30), and the grain offering for the suspected adulteress ritual (Num. 5:26).[37] It is generally held that the meaning of '*azkārāh* does not move beyond the realm of concept: pronounce, make known, proclaim.[38]

---

[33] Allen, "זכר", 1105. Compare to Schottroff who distinguishes several meanings of *zikkārôn*: "record book" (Est. 6:1; Mal. 3:16; Ex. 17:14; Ezr. 4:15; 6:2); "remembrance" or favorable "consideration" on the part of God (Ex. 30:16; Nu. 31:54; Zec. 6:14; also Ex. 28:12, 29; 39:7; Nu. 10:10); "remembrance on the part of men as a religious and cultic act (Ex. 12:14; 13:9; Lev. 23:24; Nu. 17:5 [16:40]; Josh. 4:7; Isa. 57:8; Neh. 2:20); and "miscellaneous meanings" such as "statements" (Job 13:12) and "the (lasting) remembrance among men that men seek in vain" (Eccl. 1:11; 2:16). See W. Schottroff, „Gedenken" *im Alten Orient und im Alten Testament* "Gedenken" *im Alten Orient und im „Alten Testament"* (Neukirchener: Verl. Unbekannter Einband, 1967), 337, as in Eising "Zākhar", 79.

[34] See Schottroff, *Gedenken,* 299–328, as in Eising "Zākhar", 77.

[35] Richard E. Averbeck, "Azkārāh" in *New International Dictionary of Old Testament Theology and Exegesis Vol. 1*, ed. Willem A. van Gemeren (Grand Rapids: Zondervan Publishing House, 1996), 335.

[36] See C. Brown "Remember, Remembrance" in *The New International Dictionary of New Testament Theology*, ed. Colin Brown (Grand Rapids, Zondervan Publishing House, 1981), 239.

[37] Averbeck, "Azkārāh", 260.

[38] Eising "Zākhar", 80. See Schottroff, *Gedenken,* 335ff. who put the Akkadian parallels as his basis demonstrates that '*azkārāh* is best rendered "invocation (by name), because the sacrificial portion set aside for Yahweh was concentrated by having his name pronounced over it

2.4 Hebrew Psychology of Memory

In his research, Josh Pedersen has stimulated further research on the topic of memory within the Old Testament.[39] The essence of man is fragile, but through the breath of God, a *nepheš*, it was transformed into a soul. Man in his total essence is a soul. The soul is the totality of the whole will and volition. Therefore, the relationship between thought and action differs radically from that conceived of by modern thought. There is no such thing as objective and theoretical thinking that is divorced from the soul as a whole. Childs summarizes this theory of Pedersen as "the Hebrew understands as thought the process by which an image enters the heart and immediately influences the will. Thought which does not lead to action is a meaningless flash."[40]

The Israelites consider the heart as the soul, "being the organ which at the same time feels and acts."[41] The relation between the *nepheš* (soul) and *lēbh* (heart) is that the heart is the totality of the soul as a character and operating power. Some particular stress is being laid upon its capacity; "*nepheš* is the soul in the sum of its totality such as it appears; the heart is the soul in its inner value." What about the *rūah* (spirit)? Pedersen explains that the heart is the soul as an operating force, and the same time holds good of the spirit. The spirit is more particularly the motive power of the soul, it is the strength emanating from the soul and reacting upon it. He concludes, "man in his totality is a *nepheš*, but he has *lēbh* and *rūah*. The heart and the spirit act upon the center and urge it in certain direction, which is towards an action."[42]

This is when Pedersen turns his attention to *zākhar* (זכר). Pedersen translates this word into: "to remember, call to mind, commemorate". What Pedersen understands by "remember" is this: "when the soul remembers something, it does not mean that it has an objective memory image of something or an event, but that this image is called forth

---

[39] Josh Pedersen, *Israel: Its Life and Culture I-II* (London: Oxford University Press, first published 1926, reprinted 1946), 99ff.
[40] Childs, *Memory*, 17.
[41] Pedersen, *Israel*, 104.
[42] Pedersen, *Israel*, 104. Pedersen uses the verse Exodus 35:21 as an example where the heart moved the totality into an action; "and everyone who was willing and whose *heart moved* him came and brought an offering to the Lord for the work on the Tent of Meeting, for all its service, and for the sacred garments." In this case, the translation of NIV is not appropriate, in comparing it to the KJV translation, "And they came, every one whose *heart stirred* him up, and every one whom his *spirit made willing*, and they brought the Lord's offering to the work of the tabernacle of the congregation, and for all his service, and for the holy garments."

in the soul and assists in determining its direction, its action... The peculiarity about the Israelite is that he cannot at all imagine memory, unless at the same time an effect on the totality and its direction of will is taken for granted."[43]

There are four basic ideas in his method that were explored by Childs.[44] In the first place, Pedersen finds that the verb *zkr* appears frequently in direct parallelism with verbs denoting an action, for instance: to bless (Ps. 115:12), to set free (Ps. 136:23), to show favor (Ps. 136:23; 106:4), to punish (Jer. 14:10). In passages where there seems to be no direct parallelism, the act of remembering is closely linked with action of some kind. The second idea is that synonyms, which a modern reader might classify as expressing merely a mental process, are often regarded in the Old Testament as affecting an external event (e.g. for *hgh* [mutter] which is parallel to *zkr* in Ps. 63:7, cf. Ps. 115:7).[45]

The third idea Childs proposed has a connection with the antonym of the verb *zkr*, which is *škh* (forget), that appears over 10 times in connection with *zkr*. He says that forgetting "is not a psychological act of having a thought pass from one's consciousness, but an outward act of worshipping other gods (Deut. 8:19), of forsaking someone (Isa. 49:14), of not keeping the commandments (Deut. 8:11)."[46] However, Childs continues, "The frequent identification of the verb with an action does not eliminate the process of thought which is involved in the act." The thought and act is often fused because the thought inevitably leads to an act. Lastly, Childs develops Pedersen's idea and considers that the most important idiom for revealing the psychology of memory is formed with verbs that are connected with the heart.

The idea of "forget" is very interesting because it is considered as an act of sin and guilt. Forgetting God, others, and the commandments are considered as sin. This has something to do with the idea of the soul as a whole. A thought arises and enters upon the heart, and it immediately effects the action. These components are seen as one totality. To remember or to forget means an action has already happened. One cannot be told that he has forgotten something unless he has done something. One is told that he has forgotten God because he has worshiped other gods.

Pedersen noticed that the word *zkr* is used in various contexts and often suggests far more than to recall something or to call to mind. To

---

[43] Pedersen, *Israel*, 106–107. See also in Childs, *Memory*, 17.
[44] See Childs, *Memory*, 18–19.
[45] Childs, *Memory*, 18.
[46] Childs, *Memory*, 18.

"remember" often has a meaning that we would describe as an action. Childs says that this discovery only reveals that the Hebrew use of the word "remember" is more inclusive than that of English.

However, Pedersen's ideas were attacked in the work of James Barr.[47] Pedersen suggested that because the verb can mean both to think and to act, these two processes are not distinguished in Hebrew mentality.[48] Barr criticizes this idea by stating that no conclusions can be drawn from this use of words regarding different mentalities.

In principle, Childs support Pedersen's method and at the same time agrees with Barr who thinks that Pedersen's evidence for *zkr* has not been conclusive. The verb does stand for both a process of thought and an action, however, there is no real evidence that demands a semantic identification. Childs agrees with Barr that Pedersen has not been able to show that there is a different mental relationship between memory and action that sets the Old Testament from the modern. However, Pedersen has shown us that the verb *zkr* has a wider semantic range in which thought and action are both included.[49] In the Theological Dictionary of The Old Testament, Eising says that from the context, *zkr* reveals that the term used in parallel does not refer to the past only, so that the interpretation of *zkr* as "remember" in the sense of "recall" can hardly represent its basic meaning.[50] The future can also be the subject of the intellectual activity expressed by *zkr*. In Isaiah 47:7, it is said that Babylon should have remembered its end. We can see that the

---

[47] See James Barr, *The Semantics of Biblical Language* (London: SCM Press, first published 1961 – third impression 1991). In his preface, he says that "One of the greatest dangers to sound and adequate interpretation of the Bible comes from the prevailing procedure which, while claiming to rest upon the knowledge of the Israelite and Greek ways of thinking, constantly mishandled and distort the linguistic evidence of the Hebrew and Greek languages as they are used in the Bible. The increasing sense of dependence upon the Bible in the modern church only makes this danger more serious. The fact that these procedures have never to my knowledge been collected, analyzed and criticized in detail was the chief stimulus to my understanding of this task myself."

[48] See Childs, *Memory*, 20. There are three main objections from Barr to Pedersen ideas. They are: (1) Pedersen attempts to see in the structure of the Hebrew language a reflection of a Hebrew mentality that failed to recognize the arbitrary character of words which is a fundamental law of synchronistic linguistics. It also fails to recognize the complexity of establishing a simple connection because of the historical factor. (2) Pedersen fails to examine the Hebrew language as a whole, and treats it in isolation from other relevant linguistic material. (3) Pedersen tries to reconstruct from the Old Testament certain unique categories, which he calls "primitive" on the basis of a theory of pre-logical mentality. However, these categories do not arise from the material itself, but are imposed upon it.

[49] See Childs, *Memory*, 23ff.

[50] Eising, "Zākhar", 66.

intellectual object of *zkr* constitutes a more comprehensive knowledge than the past. It also implies the consequences for the future. Therefore, the meaning of the word *zkr* seems to be more than just a psychological act of recalling something from the past to the mind, as it is understood nowadays.[51]

Childs' research has been proven visionary for his time. His research on the understanding the word and the command to remember in the Old Testament is in line with the more recent research on social memory. Based on the argumentations above, this research agrees that in the Old Testament, "remember" means something more than just an activity of the mind, or a recollection of the memory. It is an active term in which action and thought cannot be separated.\

3. Aspects of Remembrance in the Old Testament

3.1 God Remembers People

The word *zkr* is used with God as subject at least 73 times in the qal. They are widely distributed in the Old Testament; mostly it is found in the prophets except Hosea and Jeremiah who seldom use it. The largest use of the word is in Psalms and Nehemiah.[52] The word is often used as in: He "remembers" his covenant and the covenant people, that is, He will "keep" it and them (see Gen. 9:15-16).[53]

Childs says, "By and large, the preposition maintains its basic meaning of aiming toward a goal. The emphasis falls on remembrance

---

[51] Blair also agrees that remember in the Hebrew understanding of the word is more than just an action in one's mind to recall something from the past. He says, "In the Bible, memory is rarely simply psychological recall. If one remembers in the biblical sense, the past is brought into the present with compelling power. Action in the present is conditioned by what is remembered." He gives several examples when "memory" means activity. When Shimei entreats King David not to remember his rebellious insults (2 Sam. 19:19), he obviously wants the King to forgive him. When God "remembered" Hannah (1 Sam. 1:19), God gave her a son. Blair says, "conversely, to forget someone or something, is to let the past fall out of dynamic, conditioning relation to the present." To forget means to forsake (Isa. 49: 14, Hos. 4:6). See Edward P. Blair, "An Appeal to Remembrance: The Memory Motif in Deuteronomy," *Interpretation*, Vol. XV, (January 1961), 43.

[52] See Childs, *Memory*, 31–32. Childs puts Nehemiah 5:19 as the request of Nehemiah for God to remember him for good (Compare to the NIV translation which puts "remember me with favor").

[53] Childs, *Memory*, 43. To remember is in the perfect tense; the action of the verb continues. Likewise, the psalmist may ask God in his lament to "remember" His covenant. He expects God to do more than thinking about him, for he anticipates God to save him from the foe, as God has promised and has done in the past.

as an action directed toward someone rather than the psychological experience of the subject. Moreover, the preposition has strong forensic overtones which appear both in a positive and negative sense."[54] When the verb *zkr* is used with God as subject, then it is not the same with the general sense of remember. It is a technical term that bears a specific juridical meaning: to credit to one's account. When God remembers it is not merely a psychological experience, it is actually an action.

As a response to prayer, God's remembrance often results in an action. Because God remembered, Rachel (Gen. 30:22) and Hannah (1 Sam. 1:11,19) were given children; Samson was given his strength back (Judges 16:28). God does not forget to avenge the supplicant (Ps. 9:12) and remembers the afflicted (Lam. 3:19). Psalm 89:50 beseeches God to remember how his people are scorned, and Ps. 136:23 can give thanks that God remembered the humiliation of his people. God's remembrances mentioned above are followed by an action.

God will not forget those who have been faithful to God. People will call on God to remember both themselves and their good works. Jeremiah 2:2 speaks of how Israel loves God in its youth, and asks God to remember and reward it. David is remembered for his hardships he endured for the sanctuary (Ps. 132:1 cf. also Ps. 20:3). King Hezekiah is remembered because he is wailing in faithfulness before God (2 Kings 20:3; Isa. 38:3). Jeremiah asks God to remember his intercession on behalf of his enemies (Jer. 18:20).

There are some passages where God's remembrance can be punitive as well (Hos. 7:2; 9:9; 8:13; Jer. 14:10), in which God remembers iniquities and punishes them. When iniquity is threatened by God's punitive remembrance, the worshippers pray that God will not remember iniquity. Isaiah 64:9 contains the prayer, "do not remember our sins forever." The fact that iniquity can continue to affect future generations (third and fourth generations: Ex. 34:7) explains why the prayer asks for God not to remember their sins.

In accordance with the remembrance of sin and forgiveness, there are several texts where the idioms that are used to carry the same

---

[54] Childs, *Memory*, 31–32. Childs gives several examples of these forensic overtones. Nehemiah requests that God "remember for good" all that he has done (Neh. 5:15). The psalmist pleads that God credits to David's account all his suffering (Ps. 132:1). Similarly, Yahweh remembers in Israel's favor the devotion of her youth (Jer. 2:2). These are not a nostalgic reflection of Yahweh's but rather a reckoning of this earlier loyalty to Israel's account. Childs says that God can also remember in a negative forensic way. It is done against Edom that is participated in the destruction of Jerusalem (Ps. 137:7). The psalmist also prays that the sins of the forefathers be not placed upon his account.

strong forensic meaning without the use of the preposition. In these texts, one disfavor is presupposed. We will see some of these texts in a deeper exploration later in this chapter; however, we shall take a brief look at them.

Isaiah 43:25 connotes the connection of remembering and forgiveness, where God says that God is the one who "remembers your sin no more". It seems that when God is not remembering Israel's sins it means that they are removed. Eising notes that this corresponds to the article of faith that Yahweh is "…the compassionate and gracious God, slow to anger, abounding in love and faithfulness" (Ex.. 34:6).[55] Because of God's own nature, the people ask God not to remember their sins for it is already a punishment to them. In Isaiah 63:9, the people ask God "not to remember our sins forever" because "we are all your people". God's remembrance cannot be understood as a psychological term because it is already an action that makes the people afraid of the consequences.

Isaiah 43:18 seems to be the direct antithesis of remembering when it says, "Forget the former things: do not dwell on the past." However, here the prophet warns Israel to seek continuity and meaning in its existence and not to turn to former things. God is doing something new that is great enough to overshadow the past completely. Israel must look to the future and experience God's redemption rather than look to the former action God has done.[56]

The prophet stresses both the continuity and discontinuity in Israel's history. God is the main connection of the past and the future. The discontinuity lies in Israel's failure to remember. Childs is right when he says, "Israel's memory is an active response in faith that links her to redemptive action of God's entrance into history."[57]

When Jeremiah prayed for Israel concerning the drought and famine, the LORD says that "the LORD does not accept them; now God will remember their wickedness and punish them for their sins."[58] Jeremiah 14 presents one of the most striking examples of prophetic reaction to the tradition of complaint psalms. As we can see, here, God's remembrance is already a punishment for Israel because they have sinned against God. Verses 2-6 describe the disastrous effect of a drought that calls forth a fast. Then the communal complaints

---

[55] Eising, "Zākhar", 72.
[56] See also Isaiah 65:17 where the similar contrast occurs in terms of new heavens.
[57] Childs, *Memory*, 59.
[58] Jeremiah 14:10

were outspoken in vv. 7-9. Yahweh is addressed in the vocative, and implored to intervene the disaster with intense pleas. They confess their guilt. Then, as any other complaint, the cries of "why" arise. Reasons are advanced why Yahweh should help. Israel is the covenant people, "we are called by thy name" (v. 9). Yahweh has redeemed his people in the past, within a series of saving events: "redeemer in time of trouble" (v. 8). Yahweh dwells in Israel's midst (v. 9). The complaints ends with a last passionate cry "Leave us not!"

The divine answer comes in the form of an invective and threat (v. 10). Israel's prayer is not accepted. Her people can only expect judgment, because "Yahweh remembers their iniquity". A younger hand has elaborated on the judgment (vv. 11-12). The time of fasting and offering is over. The prophet must no longer intermediate for them, because Israel now faces total destruction.

Hosea 7:2 notes that God "remembers all their (i.e. *God's people*) evil deeds. Their sin engulfs them, they are always before me." This is when the Lord says that every time God restores the communion with Israel, God will always remember their sins. Even when Israel gives sacrifices as an offering for their sins, God will "remember their wickedness and punish their sins".[59] Again, God's act of remembrance is followed by a forensic action, a punishment.

Psalm 25:6-7 shows us a bipolar motive of God's remembrance.[60] "Remember, O LORD, your great mercy and love, for they are from of old. Remember not the sins of my youth and my rebellious ways; according to your love remember me, for you are good, O Lord." Instead, he asks God to "remember O LORD, your great mercy and love," and to remember the psalmist according to the Lord's love for the Lord is good. We will explore these verses further later in this chapter. In fact, the psalmist expects God to do more than thinking about him, for he anticipates God to save him from the foe, as God has promised and has done in the past. In the praise psalm, he thanks Yahweh that "He remembered". In the hymns of worship, God is God who keeps his covenant forever (Ps. 105:8; 111:5).

The idea of a forensic and specific juridical meaning is obvious. When God remembers, it is not merely a psychological action in one's brain, as we understand it in our modern language of memory. Childs says, "frequently the psychological processes involved in remembering

---

[59] Hosea 8:13; 9:9
[60] See Clark Hyde, "The Remembrance of the Exodus in the Psalms," in *Worship* vol. 62, (Sept. 1988), 404–414.

are included along with the pure action toward someone. God remembers and forgets and this process stands parallel to a series of psychological descriptions (Jer. 31:20; 44:21)." To remember is already an action which is either to bless or punish the people of God. Further he explains, "God's remembering has not only a psychological effect, but an ontological as well."[61] God's act of remembering is so important that the people that God does not remember have no existence at all.[62] It is important to be remembered by God for it will show us his act of love, and at the same time it is important to ask for forgiveness of our sin because God also remembers our sin.

Childs concludes that God's act of remembering has an implication of a movement, an active movement towards the object of God's memory. He says,

> God's remembering always implies his movement toward the object of his memory. The action varies in nature, can be physical or forensic. The objective side of memory is accompanied, in differing degrees, by an internal reaction in God's part. The essence of God's remembering lies in his acting toward someone because of a previous commitment.[63]

The idea of an active remembrance of God is clearly shown. God already remembers the object in an action, not merely a psychological act of the mind.

However, God's memory is not always related to a past event. In the relation with "remembering the covenant", God's great act continue to meet Israel in their present situation. Israel put her center of praises in God's faithfulness in remembering the covenant. "He has remembered His covenant forever."[64] Psalm 111:5 notes that God remembers his covenant forever. We can find a similar expression in Psalm 105:8. Therefore, God's remembering is "not conceived of as an actualization of a past event in history; rather, every event stems from the eternal purpose of God...God's memory is not a re-creating the past, but a continuation of a selfsame purpose." Further, "God's memory encompasses his entire relationship with his people. His memory includes both the great deeds of the past as well as his continued concern for his people in the future."[65]

---

[61] Childs, *Memory*, 33. He also says that memory is not identical with action, but it is never divorced from it. It is very important to note that Childs suggests, "There can be no dichotomy between God's thought and action", 34.

[62] See Psalm 88:5. The psalmist says that he is like the slain who lie in the grave because he is "remembered no more" and "cut off from God's care".

[63] Childs, *Memory*, 34.

[64] See Childs, *Memory*, 41–44. See Psalm 105:8 cf.; 106:45; 111:5; 1 Chron. 16:15.

[65] Childs, *Memory*, 42. In accordance with the covenant, the object of God's

Biblical Meaning of Remembrance

The heart of remembering when it is used as God's action is more than a re-collection, to call something from memory, or repeating something from the past; it is actually a complex psychological and ontological action. Therefore, to be remembered by God is an important condition to be able to receive his ongoing action and love. Remembrance is already about God's action.

To conclude, remembrance is about a God who remembers; not only in a passive meaning of remembering, but also in an active continuous manner by which God still can create our remembrance. Child states,

> God's memory is not a re-creating of the past, but a continuation of the selfsame purpose… The Old Testament witnesses a series of historical events by which God brought up the people of Israel into existence. These events were placed in a chronological order within the tradition, and never recurred in Israel's history… Redemptive history continues. What does this mean? It means more than that later generations wrestled with the meaning of redemptive events, although this is certainly true. It means more than the influence of a past event continues to be felt in successive generations, which obvious fact no one could possibly deny. Rather, there was an immediate encounter, an actual participation in the great acts of redemption. The Old Testament maintained the dynamic, continuing character of past events without sacrificing their historical character as did the myth.[66]

God has brought Israel into existence and Israel took it as her history. How does Israel remember this covenant and identity? We shall see how Israel remembers in the following section.

3.2 People Remember God

When the word *zkr* in the qal form is used with Israel as the subject, it occurs 94 times. The distribution of its use is significant because of the concentration of the word in certain areas.[67] The objects of the verb falls into different categories, and the most important groups includes the act of God (22 times), God himself (17 times), the commandments (9 times), sins (7 times), special days (3 times).

When "remember" is used with Israel as subject, in most of the times, the subject denotes a basic human psychological act: to recall a past event. This verb appears in narratives in this basic psychological meaning,

---

remembering the covenant is either the recipient of the covenant or the covenant itself. The basic of the covenant is God's promise to Abraham of a people and a land.

[66] Childs, *Memory*, 83–84.
[67] See Childs, *Memory*, 45. Israel here can be translated as a people or as a member of a group. The first really significant concentration falls in Deuteronomy with 13 examples. The most frequent use is in the Psalms with 17 examples.

and in the legal material of the Pentateuch to remember to do the commandments. The verb plays a role within two closely allied forms, the trial and the disputation. It also appears in the hymn calling forth Israel's thankful remembrance acts of the past. It is important to note that Israel's disobedience and rebelliousness was often connected because they often did not remember the great acts of God.[68] In the book of the Prophets, the verb is used for different meanings.[69] However, the varied uses of the verb suggest that, as Childs interprets, "a new and highly theological usage of *zkr* emerged from Israel's attempt to reinterpret the significance of her tradition."[70] The understanding of the verb is, again, more than a psychological meaning.

In reading the Old Testament, we find that there are themes that are brought up again throughout the history of Israel with their own characteristics and purpose. These themes are used extensively in one book and mentioned again in the later books. For instance we can find the theme of Exodus mentioned again in the Book of Hosea (Hos. 11:1), Amos (Am. 9:7), Psalms (Ps. 78:12-16; 105:23-42; 106:6-12); and in different context of Nehemiah (Neh. 9:9ff.). The theme of the Davidic kingdom can be found not only in the Deuteronomistic history books, but also in Psalms. The metaphor of husband-wife in the book of the prophets is used in different ways, elaborations, and for different purposes.[71] The history of Israel is being told again in different ways and with different purpose. Remembrance has become an important element in Israelites' lives and history.

What Israel remembers is not the same as what modern human understand as history. Israel is bound to her history in a completely different way. Von Rad says, "For Israel that interest was not a thirst for knowledge that happened to be concentrated in history; for in history, as nearly every page of the Old Testament affirms, Israel encountered her God."[72] The calling Israel received is not a one-time encounter rather it comes about to every generation of Israel. Von Rad concludes the Old Testament to a great extent as, "nothing but the literary record of a

---

[68] We will see them in Psalm 78; 106; Isa. 63:7; Neh. 9:16 ff.

[69] See Childs, *Memory*, 49–50. He also notes there are 8 functions of remembrance in the book of prophets. They are as warning, invective, taunt, disputation, trial, salvation oracle, promise, and threat.

[70] Childs, *Memory*, 50.

[71] For more information on the extensive use of the theme of Exodus in the Old Testament, see C. R. North, *The Old Testament Interpretation of History* (London: Epworth Press, 1946).

[72] Gerhard von Rad, *God at Work in Israel* (Nashville: Abingdon, 1980), 13.

people's passionate millennium-long conversation about the meaning of its history."[73] Therefore, the command to "remember" for Israel is always related with her encounter with God; that it always changes and renewed through the generations. The Old Testament is Israel's testimony of their encounter with God. It is committed to talk about this "remembrance" in no particular method or manner. Remembrance is within the theology of Israel.

The sharing of past events does not mean that they will remain in the past. Each event becomes actual for each subsequent generation. Von Rad says, "This is not just in the sense of furnishing the imagination with a vivid present picture of the past events – no, it was only the community assembled for a festival that by recitation and ritual brought Israel in the full sense of the world into being: in her own person she really and truly entered into the historic situation to which the festival in question was related."[74] The celebrated ritual was actually an actual event of the saving God who encounters Israel through generations. The past events are taken and experienced as her history through time.

What is the idea of history in Israel? Israel sees history as the time when God accompanied her. God establishes the continuity between the various separate events and is the One who ordained their direction as they followed one another in time.[75] Israel's understanding of history is centered in God saving action. Thus, Israel always renews its history through generations in the sense of experiencing the past event in a new meaning. Each event becomes history because Israel feels the saving action of God on its own terms in each subsequent generation.

The Deuteronomy editor had often pointed out Israel's history of disobedience in her failing to remember (Deut. 9:7), and used it as a framework of history (Judges 8:34). The failure to remember could already be called apostasy because it was not a mere absentmindedness; rather it was unfaithfulness to the covenant. Therefore, the use of the verb in Deuteronomy goes beyond the general psychological term. The role of memory is also to link the present commandments as events with the covenant history of the past. It establishes the continuity between the past covenantal history and the present.[76]

---

[73] von Rad, *God at Work*, 13.
[74] Gerhard von Rad, *Old Testament Theology Vol. II: The Theology of Israel's Prophetic Traditions* (Edinburgh: Oliver and Boyd, 1967), 104.
[75] See von Rad, *Old Testament Theology*, 110.
[76] See Deut. 7:18; 9:7; 24:9; 25:17.

While dealing with the complaint psalms, Childs concludes,

> The use of memory arises often in terms of separation from God felt by an individual or the community…In intense struggle to relate to the tradition, Israel encounters again through the medium of her memory the God of the past. Her attention no longer focuses on specific historical events, but on the divine reality who imprinted her history. The vocabulary used to describe the wrestling process indicates the tremendous internalization which has transpired. To remember is to grasp after, to meditate upon, indeed, to pray to God.[77]

Through the historical events in the past, the psalmist remembers God and all his grace towards Israel. The memory of the past is shared over again as the experience of the new generations having grace and love of God. This remembrance is already a prayer to God.

In accordance with the remembrance of sin, Israel prefers God not to remember their sins. They already have the idea that punishment will follow when God remembers their iniquities. Israel knows that they as a people have sinned, they remember their sins, but they did not want God to remember their sins. Pedersen says, "The Israelite constantly asks his God to remember him, but just as often he begs him not to remember his sins; the sins are to pass out of Yahweh's soul and are not to influence his actions."[78] The failure to remember already meant to forsake the covenant (see Isa 17:10 where forgetting means to forsake God for alien gods).[79]

One of the instances where Israel remembers their sins is when Ezekiel focuses his attention on the problem of Israel's remembering her sins. The phrase of "days of her youth" is used to refer to an early condition of Israel so that they who did not remember are ungrateful (16:22). Or the early days can be sinful days that are not to be remembered (23:19, 27). When Israel remembers her sinful ways, she despises herself (16:61; 20:43; 36:31). Likewise, the effect of Israel's remembering God is to loathe the sin into which she has fallen (6:9; 16:63).

When Israel tried to find her identity after the exile, her quest involves a search for signs of God. They acknowledge their sin when they recall the memory of the past. With this remembrance, they experience a new encounter with the God of their forebears. Here, memory as the recalling of the past, has made Israel repent. Through remembrance,

---

[77] Childs, *Memory*, 64–65.
[78] Pedersen, *Israel*, 107.
[79] For other texts where it shows God's judgment being connected with Israel's forgetfulness see Jer. 3:21; 13:25; 18:15; Ezek. 22:12; 23:35; Hos. 2:13; 4:6; Ps. 78:42; 106:7; Neh. 9:17.

the distant past is shared again in the new encounter with God. The theme of remembrance is important to remind Israel of its sin and make Israel regret its sin and eventually cry for forgiveness.

Memory also plays an important role in linking Israel to the future. In the post-exilic period, Israel has to establish herself by remembering her history and tradition in order to be able to move to the future. The people try to connect themselves to the former covenant history by remembering what happened to their forefathers. By relating and remembering the past in memory, Israel becomes part of the future, because past and future is one in God's purpose. Therefore, the order to remember is very important in Israel's life.

3.3 The Cultic Representation of the Past

Because "remember" is one of the great commandments for Israel, the feasts, ceremonies, and memorial objects of Israel were designed to help the people "remember". Creation in the Sabbath, exodus in the Passover, and other feasts are examples of celebrations meant for Israel to remember the good act of God. Remembrance is embedded in the religion of Israel. Simon J. de Vries says that "Hebrew theology is both concerned with remembrance and expectation, with both origin and eschatology, with beginning and end…Her past and future were indispensable for an understanding of her abiding covenant relationship with God."[80]

The remembrance of Israel and God has a very important place in the cultic act of Israel's life. Remembrance is not only mere information about the past; it is an act that deals with the present and even the future. The question then is, how can the past saving event be made present by the later generation? This is the role of cultic memorials (*zikkārôn*) in Israel's life, to bring them constantly to God's attention, which would result in God's gracious aid.[81] Allen Verhey notes that through great festivals and rituals, the people of Israel participated in both remembering and establishing the meaningful history of Israel and thus understood themselves better in the light of that meaningful

---

[80] Simon J. de Vries, "Remembrance in Ezekiel," *Interpretation* vol. XVI (1962), 58–64. We will see later that Ezekiel is a good example of the linkage with the future, because the book ends with a vision of the new temple.

[81] Childs, *Memory*, 74. However Childs notes that, "It is important to recognize that this cultic understanding of God's memory is not an actualization of the past. The problem of making a past reality contemporary is not involved in God's memory.…The question at the issue in the cult is whether God will continue to act on Israel's behalf as he did in the past or withdraw his aid because of her disobedience."

past.⁸² This is what Blair also says, "Israel's worship was centered in dramatic re-enactment of the past, which were designed to supply meaning and direction to the present."⁸³ After the Exodus, Israelite families must remember the time in which God saved them and entered the covenant. Further, "by remembering, a family was made conscious of belonging, and by a sense of belonging it was constrained to be faithful and obedient to the terms of the covenant."⁸⁴ This is the context of the remembrance motive in Deuteronomy. Remembering brings the new nation back to the mountain that they never saw. We may even say that the remembrance of the mountain is brought again into the present for those who never saw the mountain, and for those who never feared the voice of the Lord to hear the voice of the Lord again. Israel was asked to be obedient to the commandments in order to remember the redemptive act of God. Childs concludes, "the concept of memory served a significant role in Deuteronomy's theology in meeting the crisis brought by a reinterpretation of the cult."⁸⁵

Allen notes that the Passover was a memorial or commemoration of the Exodus (12:14), keeping the memory of it renewed in each generation. It is a remembrance of God's deliverance of them from Egypt, and it made that story fresh to the new generations through rituals and celebration.⁸⁶ The feast of Unleavened Bread was celebrated to "remember" the Exodus (13:9), to function in the same way as phylacteries, reminding God's people to obey the Torah. According to Childs, even the observance of the Sabbath is also a cultic remembrance of the Exodus.⁸⁷

---

⁸² Allen Verhey, "Remember, Remembrance" in *The Anchor Bible Dictionary Vol. 5*, ed. David Noel Freedman (New York: Doubleday, 1992), 668.

⁸³ Blair, "An Appeal", 44. Von Rad says that when doing and celebrating the festivities, Israel was manifestly doing more than merely remembering the Exodus or any other events in the past; she was actually entering into the saving event of the Exodus itself and participating in it in a quite "actual" way. See von Rad, *Old Testament Theology*, 104–105.

⁸⁴ Blair, "An Appeal", 44. Blair also divided the terms remembrance in Deuteronomy in 7 parts in p. (45: 1) The fact of servitude in Egypt (16:12; 24:22); 2) The deliverance from Egyptian servitude (often with some reference to the wonders and judgment of God) (5:15; 6:12; 7:18–19; 8:14; 15:15; 16:3; 24:18); 3) The giving of the covenant at Horeb (4:9–13,23); 4) Yahweh himself – his unity, his commandments (4:39–40; 6:6; 8:11, 14, 18, 19; 11:18; 26:13); 5) The experiences in the wilderness – Israel's rebelliousness, God's providence and discipline (8:2, 14–16; 9:7; 24:9); (6) What the Amalek did (25:17–19); (7) The days of old (32:7).

⁸⁵ Childs, *Memory*, 79.

⁸⁶ See Allen, "זכר", 1105.

⁸⁷ Childs, *Memory*, 52 f.

Biblical Meaning of Remembrance 119

Child argues that the festivals celebrated by Israel were to actualize the redemptive acts of the past both to renew the tradition and to participate in its power. In connection with the term used, he says,

> According to the Priestly idiom, the *zikkārôn* is a "memorial for the children of Israel before Yahweh". One has only to recall the role of the cult for the Priestly writer to recognize the full significance of the phrase. God has established a covenantal relationship with Israel which expresses itself in his eternal ordinances (*huqqath 'ôlām*, Num. 10:8). Signs and memorials serve within this dispensation of grace both to guarantee and maintain for each generation this eternal relationship. The cultic acts of Israel continually remind God of this eternal covenantal order. The cultic objects and rites act to guarantee that the covenant is not forgotten.[88]

However, Eising rejects the assumption that the feast of Unleavened Bread and the Sabbath were celebrated to remember the Exodus. He says, "For the feast of the Unleavened Bread, too, its annual observance is important as a remembrance of the original event (Ex. 13:8 f.; Deut. 16:3). The same God who brought the event to pass also ordained its memorial."[89] While Schottroff is of the opinion that any cultic celebration does not assume any realization of the past, instead, he finds the message to be a moral motivation for obedience to the commandments based on recollection of God's blessing in the past.[90] Both Eising and Schottroff rejected Child's opinion that the Sabbath and the feast of Unleavened Bread were celebrated to remember the Exodus; in fact Schottroff rejected the very idea of re-experienced events that was suggested by Child. Nevertheless all three scholars accepted the idea that the celebration of the feast is still an event of remembrance. Israel remembers her past event and God's salvific action through the cultic representation of the past.

The cult was an important context for remembering for Israel. Memory plays the role of being a means of actualizing the past in Israel's cult.

---

[88] Childs, *Memory*, 67.
[89] See the discussion in Eising, "Zākhar", 81. He rejects Child's opinion that considers the cultic realization has developed in Deuteronomy into moral motivation from the past for observance of the law. Easing thinks that this idea is not clearly enough attested. In Deut. 24:18, 22; however, the purpose of the reference is to motivate certain conduct toward slaves, not to account for observance of the Sabbath as a memorial of the Exodus. It is also important to note the rejection of the concept cultic actualization in the Old Testament by Fritz Chenderlin, *Do This as My Memorial* (Rome: Biblical Institute Press, 1982), who denies that there was ever a cult in the Old Testament. Chenderlin goes to great lengths in proving that there was no "cult" in the Bible. His main argument is that there is no cultic actualization, thus Israel was never really actualizing its remembrance in a cultic way, see 246–250.
[90] See Schottroff, *Gedenken*, 123–126, 339, as in Eising "Zākhar", 81.

Childs says that in time of crisis, when the role of the cult was threatened, Israel's memory assumed a new significance in renewing her tradition.[91] The point of the actualization of the cult is not just some mysterious way of calling it back to the mind of Israel; rather, it was a continuity of the tradition, the covenant's identity and fidelity in a new situation.

After his exploration of the verb, Childs concludes his study on the word *zkr* by saying that, the act of remembrance is not a simple inner reflection, but involves an action, an encounter with historical events. Each successive generation in Israel witnessed in faith to a reality which it encountered when remembering the tradition."[92] We can also conclude from Childs' analysis that remembering is not static, but it always moves forward in sequence with the past to get a hold on the future. Further he concludes that, "the same verb is used to describe God's redemptive action toward Israel as well as Israel's responses in faith to this action…redemptive history is conceived of as resulting from God's action and Israel's response."[93] Throughout the ups and downs, Israel's history never ceased to be without God's redemptive action. It takes both sides to create her history, God's action and Israel's reaction. The remembrance of the covenant is the bond between the two that creates Israel's history.

4. Remembrance in Connection with Forgiveness and Reconciliation

In the next part, we will do exegetical analysis on some main texts where remembrance is connected with remembrance of sins and guilt, and forgiveness. Because our research is intended to look for the meaning of remembrance in a communal context, the following texts are taken this consideration. Four main texts are selected from other possible texts. Thus these passages do not mean that there are no other texts that are in connection with forgiveness of sins beside the ones that are being scrutinized. They have been selected as fitting in the cycles of Israel's apostasy, affliction, repentance and deliverance in the time of the exile.

We will look at Hosea and several texts within the book of Hosea where it is clearly stated that God remember sins. Hosea grounded his whole preaching in the saving history of God. We can say that Hosea only feels secure when he can base his arguments in history.[94] Therefore, Hosea has a prevalent theme of remembrance in his preaching, and this makes him interesting for us to observe in light of the remembrance

---

[91] Childs, *Memory*, 80.
[92] Childs, *Memory*, 88.
[93] Childs, *Memory*, 89.
[94] See von Rad, *Old Testament Theology II*, 140.

of sins. After this prophet, the book of Malachi will be investigated, especially verse 3:16 where God is said to put the records of his people in the book of remembrance. Malachi is exclusively concerned with abuses practiced by his community during the completion of the rebuilding of the temple. Malachi sends a warning to Israel in his eschatological message in two of his oracles that God will bring judgment to those who are godless, but that God will save those who feared God.[95] Next we will take a look at Nehemiah 9 where Israel remembers and acknowledges their sins. Israel was rebuked for not remembering the redemptive action of God in the past. After the warning by the prophet, Israel confessed its sin and remembers all her iniquities. This is a text of repentance where an example of remembrance of sins is shown by the perpetrator. The last text we will look at is the text where God promises forgiveness for those who truly repent. The text of Jeremiah 31:34 is an often noted text on the topic of forgiveness of sins, where forgiveness is connected with remembrance. As mentioned earlier, these texts were selected because they have their own uniqueness; however, they are not intended to exclude other texts.

4.1 *Hosea: God Remembers Sins*

Hosea was active in the third quarter of the 8th century B.C. His prophecy began when King Jeroboam II (786-746) was still in charge. His time stretched from times of prosperity and comparative stability through to the instability of toppling dynasties, social unrest, warfare, vacillating leadership, and partial subjugation to humiliation and the shadow of final disaster.[96] Hosea makes a major contribution to the message of hope and comfort. The book functions as an entrance into the Book of the Twelve, telling the unforgettable imagery of God's love which will not let God's people go.

---

[95] See von Rad, *Old Testament Theology II*, 288-289.
[96] See H.D. Beeby, *International Theological Commentary: Hosea, Grace Abounding* (Grand Rapids: Wm. B. Eerdmans, 1987), 1-2. For the interpretation of Hosea, this research also used James Limburg, *Interpretation: A Bible Commentary for Teaching and Preaching, Hosea-Micah* (Atlanta: John Knox Press, 1988); Henry MacKeating, *The Cambridge Bible Commentary: The Books of Amos, Hosea and Micah* (London: Cambridge University Press, 1971); David Allan Hubbard, *Tyndale Old Testament Commentaries: Hosea, An Introduction and Commentary* (Leicester: Inter-Varsity Press, 1973); Douglas Stuart, *World Biblical Commentary: Hosea-Jonah* (Waco, Texas: World Books, 1984); Gale A. Yee, "The Book of Hosea: Introduction, Commentary, Reflections" in *The New Interpreter's Bible: A Commentary in Twelve Volumes: Volume VII, Introduction To Apocalyptic Literature, Daniel, The Twelve Prophets*, ed. Leander E. Keck (Nashville: Abingdon Press, 1996).

Because of God's command, Hosea married a prostitute. This symbolizes God who chooses Israel, that is a rebellious and unfaithful wife,[97] and shows God's love towards Israel even though "they turn to other Gods and love the sacred raisin cakes (3:1)." The theme in Hosea is that God chose Israel and gave her grace and love. Yet, her response was rebellion and more sin. This unfaithful act of Israel made God punish her. However, Israel was unable to learn from her history and repeated the same cycle and again deserved the punishment. However, God is gracious and full of love, who remembers the covenant and is faithful to his promise. It means, God remembers the covenant while the other partner forgot to do so. Israel needed to be reminded about the covenant. Thus, Hosea's message pointed to the falling of Israel and to remind them of their sins and God's love.

In at least four passages in Hosea God is said to remember the evil deeds of Israel. Hosea 7:2 says, "but they do not realize that I remember all their evil deeds. Their sins engulf them; they are always before me." What does it means that God remembered the evil deeds that Israel has done? This could mean that Ephraim's guilt is not hidden; God watched it all. When Israel did not remember the covenant, God remembered their sin. Beeby puts it like this in his comments, "God remembers all their evil words in the past and their present villainy is even now before his face…as for Israel they do not realize this even though their sins engulf them. They do not remember, and they cannot see…yet it is God who remembers not them."[98] God set eyes on all our sins and misdeeds and remembers them. However, Israel was still not aware of their sins and totally content with what they were doing then.

Further, God did not only remember the sins of Israel, but God also punished them. "They offer sacrifices to me and they eat the meat, but the LORD is not pleased with them. Now he will remember their wickedness and punish their sins (8:13)." The evil acts of Israel were not only remembered, they were even written down in a record. This act of remembrance can soon be connected with punishment. The sacrifices offered were done with a wrong motivation. The worshippers ate the meat

---

[97] For modern readers, these explanations could become an interpretative problem. In the first place, the story tells us about the divine as the human's husband. God is considered as an all-forgiving male, and sometimes people concluded that the male becomes the divine. Second, the sinful is embodied in the image of an unfaithful wife. As it was typical in Israel culture, women become the primary offenders in adulterous affairs. Third, the metaphor comes close to sanctioning a husband's domestic violence against his wife. For further discussion on this read Yee, "The Book of Hosea", 210 ff.

[98] Beeby, *Hosea: Grace Abounding*, 84.

for the glory of the Lord, or they could do it for their own satisfaction. The people love to eat the offered flesh because they assumed that by eating the meat they will be forgiven from all their sins and restored to full fellowship. The sacrificial system did not reach its intended purpose; rather it became a kind of barbecue party, while it allowed Israel to continue sinning. The verdict is obvious: God remembers their iniquities and will punish their sins. The act of remembering here again affects both present and future. God's act of remembering Israel's iniquity includes the inevitable future punishment.

Hosea 9:9 notes that "They have sunk into deep corruption, as in the days of Gibeah. God will remember their wickedness and punish them for their sins." Two possible answers can be given about which event is "the days of Gibeah". The first event points to the starting of the monarchy which produced so much corruption. The second, and more likely answer, is the horrifyingly shameless episode narrated in Judges 19-21.[99] God remembers the days when Israel has sinned. God then remembered and punished Israel. The remembrance of the Israel past sins are not deleted. We can see a stronger emphasis on the remembrance of Israel's record of sins in the verse "their sins are kept in a record" (13:12). It is evidence that Israel's record of sins are being preserved and kept as a written reminder.

This part of the Old Testament indeed has interesting passages about how God remember Israel's sin. Hosea reminded Israel that they have been unfaithful to the covenant and have not remembered that they have sinned. God remembered all the wrong deeds of Israel and punished them for it. Because of their sins, Israel will go back to Egypt, which symbolizes the time of the slavery. However, God is gracious and compassionate. God did not let Israel fall forever. He asks for Israel's repentance (Hosea 14), and when Israel repents, they will receive God's blessing again.

4.2 Malachi 3:16: The Book of Remembrance

The book of Malachi is written anonymously but uses the name Malachi, which means the messenger. It is difficult to set up a specific time line of its writing, however the common time of writing is taken to be after the religious revival under Haggai and Zechariah and the completion of the rebuilding of the temple,[100] and before the final breakdown

---

[99] See Beeby, *Hosea: Grace Abounding*, 118. See Yee, *Hosea*, 269.
[100] See Gerhard von Rad, *The Message of the Prophet* (New York: Harper & Row

of Persian rule in Palestine.[101] The portion of Malachi is similar in some places to Ezra, Haggai, Obadiah, and the late material in Isaiah. The problem within Malachi's community is about having Israel return to their homeland.

What is fundamental in Malachi's teaching is the concept of the covenant. It can be seen through his opening theme, which is the Lord's love for Israel (1:2-5).[102] The book also ends with a call to fulfill the obligations of the covenant as expressed in the law (4:4). The covenant is threatened by Israel's sin: they corrupted the covenant of Levi (2:8) and the people as a whole profaned the covenant of their fathers (2:10). Israel has despised their Lord (1:6). Their failure to protect the covenant also occurs in their broken relationship in the society: intermarriages and divorce are the examples. The family relationship illustrates love and loyalty towards the covenant, while divorce typifies broken faith and a severed relationship. One of the problems in Malachi's days was also the blurring of moral and theological values. No one seemed to be able to distinguish right from wrong, or the righteous from the wicked.

Malachi mentions God's eschatological action in two of his six oracles (Mal. 2:17-3:5; 3:13-21 [3:13-4:3]). Malachi 3:16 is generally included as the part of 3:13-4:3 with the heading of "God's judgment will be final."[103] Malachi begins with God's accusation in verse 13 by saying that Israel has spoken harsh words against God. This accusation was answered by what seems to be an ignorant answer, "What have we said against you?"

Publishers, 1965), 254–255. Von Rad says that it is remarkable that this prophet's message contains practically no clues which might determine the tradition to which he belongs. While Eileen M. Schuller, "The Book of Malachi" in *The New Interpreter's Bible: A Commentary in Twelve Volumes: Volume VII, Introduction To Apocalyptic Literature, Daniel, The Twelve Prophets*, ed. Leander E. Keck (Nashville: Abingdon Press, 1996), 847, also suggest that the book of Malachi has no references to specific persons or events that would enable us to situate these words on a larger stage of the world history, and many of the abuses the prophets condemns are generic to almost any period of biblical – or human history. In other words, the book of Malachi is curiously showing no sign of any time-bound characteristic.

[101] See Graham S. Ogden & Richard R. Deutsch, *International Theological Commentary: Joel & Malachi, a Promise of Hope – A Call to Obedience* (Grand Rapids: Wm. B. Eerdmans, 1987), 67–68. Their prove to the timeline of the writing of Malachi was in Hag. 1:1,14; Ezra 8:36; Neh. 2:7; Est. 3:12; 8:9.

[102] See Joyce G. Baldwin, *Tyndale Old Testament Commentaries: Haggai, Zechariah, Malachi, an Introduction and Commentary*, (Leicester: Inter-Varsity Press, 1973), 216.

[103] Most of the commentaries divide this book in the same parts except the title. Schuller, "The Book of Malachi", divides this part under the heading "The Righteous and the Wicked." Ralph L. Smith, *World Biblical Commentary: Micah – Malachi* (Waco, Texas: World Books, 1984), calls this "A Dispute about Speaking against God."

Israel's answer has shown their lack of understanding of their own mistakes. The question posed by Israel was, how could God's people suffer while the evildoers prosper? However, this is not a reason to be ignorant of the covenant. Justice will occur in the future, on the day that God will act. There is no promise of a sudden transformation, the ultimate judgment will eventually happen sometime in the future.

The message is that God will come unexpectedly, and he will bring judgment to those who do not fear him. The "scroll of remembrance" will be read upon God's presence. The names of those who feared the Lord and his name will be written. In this part, the prophet returns to the subject of judgment. He shows that there is a fundamental difference between the people who remember God and the covenant and those who are not. Innocence and guilt will be exposed in the day of the final judgment.

> In verse 16, the divine reward of one's faithfulness toward God is mentioned. "Then those who feared the LORD talked with each other, and the LORD listened and heard. A scroll of remembrance was written in his presence concerning those who feared the LORD and honored his name."[104] This verse has two scenes, one set in the community, and one outside the human sphere. The reward was that their names, those who had been faithful to the Lord, shall be written in the book of remembrance. When it says, "Book of remembrance," it means that God will not fail to remember those who are faithful to him (Ex. 32:32–33; Ps. 69:28; Isa. 4:3; Dan. 12:1; Rev. 20:12). People who are faithful are witnesses to God's love and care. The faithful ones will be rewarded and noted in God's book of memory. This verse, however, suggests that "the fulfillment of this hope may now have been thought to have been deferred to another time, or even to the world to come."[105] The remembrance now can also mean that the event is not forgotten but that the reward will come later on. This has been an apocalyptic message of the prophet: God will remember those who have been faithful to the Lord. The righteous and the wicked shall be separated before the face of the Lord. It is the people's assurance of God's act towards those who are in favor of him. God will forget not one of the believers.

Interestingly, some comments note that "those who feared the Lord are not necessarily a different group from those who had been complain-

---

[104] Malachi 3:16, NIV. Notice the difference translation between the NIV that uses "a scroll of remembrance" and the NRSV who uses "a book of remembrance".

[105] Ogden, *International Theological*, 109. Further, they say that the idea of a "book of remembrance", a record of the faithful, appears to have been an important topic in so-called apocalyptic writings (beside Dan. 12:1 see 7:10; 10:21; Rev. 3:5; 17:8; 20:12). Perhaps the "tablet of fate" (ANET, 541), or the "book of memorable deeds" (Est. 6:1) gave rise to the idea of a "book of life" (cf. also Ps. 139:16).

ing, but they are the ones who have taken the rebuke to heart and begin to encourage each other to renewed faith."[106] However, it seems to be unlikely that the people who feared God are the same people who have been complaining. Smith suggests that it is better to take both groups separately because it is not possible to identify the God-fearing persons of verse 16 with the persons who gave expression to their doubt in the language of verses 14 and 15; thus, in this reading of the text two distinct classes exist. If we are thinking that the people who complained and those who feared the Lord are one and the same, then we must think that repentance has already happened. With this interpretation, we are saying that to be written in the book of remembrance means to remember one's guilt and to repent. To be written in the book of remembrance is the consequence of the act of repentance.

We can conclude that Malachi 3:16 is an apocalyptic message about God who will not leave those who have been faithful and remember the covenant. A book of remembrance means that those who have not felt justice will receive it in front of God, or we can also say that God will remember those who have sinned against the Holy One. Righteous and wicked deeds indeed stay in God's memory. However, God's remembrance, as mentioned earlier, is not a merely psychological act. God's act of remembering those who feared him is already a reward for them, and a punishment towards those who have done him wrong.

4.3 Nehemiah 9:1–37: The Great Confession of Sins

Nehemiah is written in the post-exilic period. The nation must find its own identity after being exiled in Babylon. During this period, the sacred tradition of the forefathers must be re-adapted and re-actualized. In other words, they must remember what their forefathers have done in order to be able to grasp their new identity. They must be able to do this without the city, the temple, and the Davidic leader. This is the setting that Nehemiah, Haggai, Zechariah, Malachi, and Ezra must face.

There is a strong emphasis in the book of Nehemiah on the covenant by which God has bound himself to Israel in this way. God's choice of Abraham, God's rescue of Israel from Egypt and God's patience under their provocations dominate the great confession of Nehemiah 9 and, less broadly, of Ezra 9; and the same faithful love had sent God's Spirit among them, however little heeded, in the wilderness and in the preaching of the prophets (Neh. 9:20, 30).

---

[106] Smith, *World Biblical Commentary*, 338.

Nehemiah 9 tells the story of the time when the Israelites confess their sins. It is a chapter where Israel celebrated the remembrance of her sins. On the twenty-fourth day of the month they gathered together, fasting, wearing sackcloth and having dust on their heads (v. 1). Their actions could be seen as a symbol of mourning, nakedness and death. Israelites felt that their sins have made them mourners. They also separated themselves from all foreigners.[107] This is interesting because Israel did not blame anyone else for their sins. They confessed that they have sinned. For the next six hours, the Torah was read and Israel confessed their sins. The reading of the Torah was to remind Israel what they had done against it.

Like some of the Psalms (see Ps. 78; 105; 106), Israel's prayer in Nehemiah 9 is an example of confession in both senses of the word: 1) a confession of God's glory and grace, and 2) a confession of Israel's ingratitude. What Israelites did in delivering their confession was in the context of worship and not merely a wallowing in self-reproach.[108] The theme of the worship was about promise and fulfillment; and the subject is God (vv. 6-15).

The prayer is opened by mentioning Israel's history, which runs from the time of Abraham to the present context of Nehemiah 9. In these events, God is remembered with praise, even in times of bondage in Egypt, the journey in the desert, and Israel's survival. Here, the law is viewed not as some obligation, but as a gift for Israel.[109]

The later part of the confession consists of recalling how generous and patient God is towards the ungrateful Israel (vv 16-25). In spite of the rebellious act of Israel, God continues to bless Israel. Israel confessed their times in the period of Judges where the cycle of sin, decline, appeal, and rescue continued to happen. Neither preaching nor experience could hold back Israel from living the same pattern repeatedly (vv. 26-31). Although Israel persistently broke the covenant, God considered

---

[107] See Fredrick Carlson Holmgren, *International Theological Commentary: Ezra and Nehemiah, Israel Alive Again* (Grand Rapids: Wm. B. Eerdmans, 1987), 130. Holmgren suggests that this separation did not mean that Israel wants to protect her selves from the other, it means that Israel felt responsible for its own sins. Only those who were in the covenant with Yahweh were responsible when this covenant was broken. Foreigners (who could have been the people that were married to Israelites or their servants) could hardly expect to confess their sins before God for breaking the covenant because foreigners did not receive the covenant.

[108] See Derek Kidner, *Tyndale Old Testament Commentaries: Ezra & Nehemiah, an Introduction and Commentary* (Leicester: Inter-Varsity Press, 1973), 111.

[109] See D. J. Clines, *The New Century Bible Commentary: Ezra, Nehemiah, Esther* (Grand Rapids: Wm. B. Eerdmans, 1984), 194.

himself to be bound to it. Israel confessed their rebelliousness "in your great mercy you did not put an end to them or abandon them, for you are gracious and merciful God (v. 31)." This is the covenant that God and Israel have to remember.

There is a difference between self-pity and self-knowledge. Israel recognizes herself in her sins. The painful admission, "you have acted faithfully (v. 33)", would open the door to God's mercy. Israel puts her hopes in God who continues to keep the covenant faithfully. The prayer calls this gracious God to look on the suffering that Israel has experienced during the exile.

Israel soon takes the experience of their forefathers as their own experience. Their encounter with God has been renewed through the remembrance of their sins. The new generation took over the sins because they experienced it as their own. The great distress, which ends the prayer, is a sign of life and of a vision that has not been tamely given up.[110]

What is the point of this confession and prayer from Israel? Clines ends his commentary in this chapter by saying that the meaning is,

> that there is more than one way of telling the history of Israel. It can be recited as a story of salvation or of apostasy; it can be recounted with praise or with penitence. God needs no reminder of the tragic history; but the congregation in praying thus is confessing how it understands itself. Prayer is here shown to be not simply a matter of speaking to God, but also of critical self-reflection in the lights of God's demands and his grace. Hence, this prayer cannot conclude with a superficial appeal for deliverance from misery, but must end simply on a note of confession (vv. 33ff) and distress (vv. 36f).[111]

In other words, self-knowledge is needed to be able to confess sins before God. A true confession demands an act of remembrance from the confessor, of how one betrayed the covenant with God. Israel, in this part of the prayer, is able to show her self-knowledge and repent. A note of confession and distress closes the prayer.

To conclude, Nehemiah 9 is an example of who Israel confessed their sins. Israel's plea for forgiveness was put forward after they put their cards on the table. First, they remembered their sins, and not only their own, but also the sins of their forebears. They remembered that God has been a gracious God who keeps the covenant faithfully, and it is Israel who keeps breaking it. God does not need any reminder of our history;

---

[110] See Kidner, *Tyndale Old Testament Commentaries*, 113.
[111] Clines, *The New Century Bible Commentary*, 199.

rather, he would like to hear how we understand ourselves. Israel needed forgiveness from God. To be forgiven means to repent the sins Israel has done. A critical self-reflection is needed towards a true repentance. Therefore, a remembrance of sins and guilt of the past is needed to be able to step forward towards the future, which is God's forgiveness. Israel lived through its history and learns their remembrance of it as an encounter with God. Israel took over its past and experienced it as a new story with the grace of a God who is able to forgive sins by being faithful to the covenant. A clear story of remembrance of sin in connection with forgiveness is shown in this passage. To remember sin is important as recognition of oneself to be able to ask for forgiveness from the victim – as in the story of Israel with God.

4.4 Jeremiah 31:34: God Remembers Sins No More

Jeremiah was not a systematic writer; rather he was a preacher whose preaching came from life's experiences and from what he had learned from Israel's tradition. [112] His writing was reflective and responsive to the historical crisis of the last days of Judah, culminating in the destruction of Jerusalem and the temple in 587 B.C. His writing engages in poetic reflection and didactic prose explanation about the cause of Israel's end and the destiny of those departed to Babylon. The governing paradigm for the tradition of Jeremiah is Israel's covenant with Yahweh, rooted in the memories and mandates of the Sinai tradition. Disobedience to the covenant will bring heavy sanctions that would be experienced as death or displacement. The destruction of Jerusalem is caused by Judah's refusal to adhere covenantal requirements.

In the famous passage of 31:31–34 that describes the new covenant, Jeremiah reached the apex of his thinking on the new hope. He envisioned that one day God's law will be written on people's heart and give his people a new covenant, not like the one that they had broken during the centuries, but it will be the time when Israel will remember the covenant. For Jeremiah, restoration will take place in the land under a wise and good government, with the king and the people being

---

[112] For the commentary on Jeremiah, this research uses Gerald L. Keown, Pamela J. Scalise & Thomas G. Smothers, *World Biblical Commentary: Jeremiah 26–52* (Waco, Texas: World Books, 1984), R. K. Harrison, *Tyndale Old Testament Commentaries: Jeremiah & Lamentations* (Leicester: Inter-Varsity Press, 1973); R. E. Clements, *Interpretation: A Bible commentary for Teaching and Preaching, Jeremiah* (Atlanta: John Knox Press, 1988); J. A. Thompson, *The New International Commentary on the Old Testament: The Book of Jeremiah* (Grand Rapids: Eerdmans, 1980).

renewed in heart, so that all people will avow Yahweh and obey him by nature. Verse 31:34 is one of the passages that most churches use as the absolution part in liturgy. This is the promise when God will not remember our sins.

What does it mean that God remembers sins no more? Actually, to be forgiven means to know *(yada')* Yahweh. Here, the verb "know" probably carries its most profound connotation, the intimate personal knowledge which arises between two persons who are committed wholly to one another in a relationship that touches mind, emotion, and will. In such relation the past is forgiven and forgotten. According to Hosea 8:1–2, the opposite of knowing the Lord is breaking the covenant and transgressing the law. "No longer will a man teach his neighbor, or a man his brother saying, "Know the Lord," because they will all know me, from the least of them to the greatest," declares the Lord, "For I will forgive their wickedness and will remember their sins no more."

Israel has survived because God has pardoned their sins. Through Jeremiah's ministry, the Lord had invited Israel to repent and be forgiven (5:1; 36:3), but his contemporaries had refused the pardon. The final promise in this verse will put an end to the threat in Jeremiah 14:10 when the Lord remembers sin and punishment follows (see 44:21). The Lord's promise not to remember their sins anymore means an end to divine wrath. The people of the new covenant will not bear the guilt of their ancestor's sin or their own. They will be free to make a fresh start, under no lingering threats, because of God's gracious gift and pardon. The Lord will write the Torah on a heart polished smooth by forgiveness (50:22). The heart and mind inscribed with the revelation of God cannot turn sin again. Therefore, faithfulness to the new covenant will be a gift of divine mercy and not of human achievement.[113] The new covenant will be successful because God will put his love upon his people's hearts. This new covenant will be recalled as grace, and the power will come along with forgiveness of sins because God remembers sins no more.

5. Remembrance in the New Testament

5.1 The Role of Memory in the Early Communities in Jesus' Time

We have seen what remembrance means in the Old Testament, in its social memory context, and through linguistic approaches and exegetical

---

[113] See Keown, *World Biblical Commentary*, 135.

analysis. Remembrance is not only to recall something back to mind, but it is an active term that sometimes requires or has already involved action. In the following part, we will shift our attention to what remembrance means in the New Testament and what part memory plays in the New Testament community.

Early Christian communities were preserving their memory of Jesus in the form of oral tradition. Werner Kelber, a New Testament scholar who is engaged in the subject of social memory in biblical studies, said that Jesus teaching was represented subsequently through storytelling for present needs. Kelber is of the opinion that memory was understood as "a continual process of commemorating activities, intent on remembering the past while simultaneously addressing social identity in the present."[114] This tradition of preserving the past is done through repeated patterns of oral transmissions. The problem that comes from this tradition is that the repetition of the message by the second storyteller is perceived as if the story was told for the first time. The audience regarded the stories that were told to them as original; while the storyteller always tried to keep the structural core of the story original.[115] Thus, the preservation of memory is being done under the repetitive mode of memory transmission in the form of its structural core.

Oral tradition was then changed to early scribal tradition. A few years after Jesus, early communities realized the need of preserving the best form of the stories for the next generations, especially after the growing distance in time between them and the actual events. The fluidity of oral traditions also influenced the written tradition. There were many differences on the various account of a single memory. Thus finding a single original saying of Jesus was a difficult task, if not an impossible one. The tradition of remembering Jesus' words was kept alive by continuous reflection and interpretation.[116] This is why Kelber thinks that, "We will best understand the early tradition's proclivity

---

[114] Werner H. Kelber, "The Generative Force of Memory: Early Christian Traditions as Processes of Remembering" *Biblical Theology Bulletin* 36 (2006), 15. See also Werner H. Kelber, "The Works of Memory: Christian Origins as Mnemohistory" in *Memory, Tradition and Text, Semeia 52*, eds. Alan Kirk & Tom Thatcher (Atlanta: Society of Biblical Literature, 2005), 221–248.

[115] Kelber uses John Dominic Crossan's theory of *ipsissima structura* (structural core) in *In Fragments: The Aphorisms of Jesus* (San Francisco: Harper and Row, 1983). So, the community in Jesus time preserved the tradition through a repetition of structural core of Jesus story.

[116] See also David C. Parker, *The Living Text of the Gospels* (Cambridge: Cambridge University Press, 1997), 93, as in Kelber, "The Generative Force of Memory", 20.

toward variable renditions if we view them not as variations on or transmissions of a given text, but rather as authentic re-performances."[117]

The action of preserving memory of the past was motivated by the urge to keep the message alive for the present context. Tradition is based on the stories and the actions to preserve those memories in the communities. The traditions are not accepted as it is, rather, as Hendel says, "tradition can—and must be—revised in order to retain its truth,"[118] because what matters most is interpretation and revision of the past instead of truth or fiction. The re-membered and re-interpreted social memory in the tradition will then form the identity of the new communities that received it. The purpose of remembering is "as a functioning social memory, e.g., as a continual process of commemorative activities, intent on commitment to the past and serving social relevance and identity in the present."[119] Precisely because of this mode and purpose of transmitting social memory, it is no surprise that memory was also a strong force in the forming of the early Christian communities.

Here we can conclude once again that memory is acting as a strong force in the preservation of the tradition in the early communities after Jesus' time. Memory is again not considered as a mere recalling of something back from the past, but it was remembered precisely to re-live and re-experience the teachings of Jesus and to make it actual to the present context. We can say that memory and the order to remember in the social context of the early communities is an essential essence in the continuation of the tradition.

James D.G. Dunn, who wrote extensively on the new perspective on Paul, has recently published his work on the rise of Christianity. His work, *Jesus Remembered*,[120] discusses the impact of Jesus tradition through historical and theological assessment. His main goal was to find out how Jesus was remembered and why. He sums up his idea in the book as follows:

> (1) The only realistic objective for any "quest of the historical Jesus" is Jesus *remembered*. (2) The Jesus tradition of the Gospels confirms *that* there was a concern within earliest Christianity to remember Jesus. (3)

---

[117] Kelber, "The Generative Force of Memory", 21.
[118] Hendel, *Remembering Abraham*, 98.
[119] Kelber, "The Generative Force of Memory", 21, He continues, "At this point, one can agree with the observations of Kirk and Thatcher that "every act of tradition is an act of remembering" (39) so that " 'tradition' is in fact the substance of 'memory' " (40).
[120] James D.G. Dunn, *Jesus Remembered* (Grand Rapids: Wm. B. Eerdmans. 2003).

The Jesus tradition shows us *how* Jesus was remembered; its character strongly suggests again and again a tradition given its essential shape by regular use and reuse in oral mode. (4) This suggests in turn that that essential shape was given by the original and immediate *impact made by Jesus* as that was first put into words by and among those involved as eyewitnesses of what Jesus said and did. In that key sense, the Jesus tradition *is* Jesus remembered.[121]

Dunn is convinced that the remembrance in the oral tradition in Jesus' time was so strong, that his teachings stayed strong in the disciples and passed on to the others as if the memory of Jesus is Jesus himself.[122] The memory of the past Jesus' teachings, which was being passed on through oral traditions, was considered as valid as Jesus teaching. Dunn agrees with Kelber in saying that memory transmission especially through oral tradition is intended more to transmit the message rather than to know what really happened. He also says, "In oral transmission a tradition is performed, not edited."[123] The essence of the memory lies in the core of the story and not the details.

However, the free interpretation of Jesus' story does not mean that it is entirely free to be interpreted in any manner whatsoever. Dunn says that in the New Testament, Jesus' earliest community and followers were passing on the tradition in a controlled manner.[124] Dunn uses the argument of Kenneth E. Bailey, a New Testament scholar that is specialized in Middle Eastern life who mentions three types of oral tradition in the Middle East: formal controlled, informal controlled, and informal uncontrolled.[125] These three models were available from the time of Jesus until now.

Informal, uncontrolled oral tradition, is the transmission of tradition where the community does not express interest in preserving or controlling the tradition. The example of this type of oral tradition is like the spreading of gossip. He argues that Rudolf Bultmann's view on the Synoptic tradition belongs to this type. He says, "Bultmann does not deny that there is a tradition stemming from Jesus, but asserts that it has, for the most part,

---

[121] Dunn, *Jesus Remembered*, 882, 335. See also an analysis on the book by Samuel Byrskog, "A New Perspective on the Jesus Tradition Reflections on James D.G. Dunn's *Jesus Remembered*," *Journal for the Study of the New Testament* 26.4 (2004), 459–471.
[122] See also Byrskog, "A New Perspective on the Jesus Tradition", 461.
[123] Dunn, *Jesus Remembered*, 248–249.
[124] Dunn, *Jesus Remembered*, 180, 186.
[125] See Kenneth E. Bailey, "Informal Controlled Oral Tradition and the Synoptic Gospels", *Asian Journal of Theology* (April, 1991), 34–54; and "Middle Eastern Oral Tradition and the Synoptic Gospels" in *Expository Times* 106 no. 12 S (1995), 363–367. See also Dennis Ingolfsland, "Jesus Remembered: James Dunn and the Synoptic Problem" in *Trinity Journal* 27 NS No. 2 (Fall 2006), 187–197.

faded out. The community, he feels, was not interested in either preserving or controlling the tradition. Furthermore, the tradition is always open to new community creations that are rapidly attributed to the community's founder."[126] Bailey gives an example of this kind of tradition with a story that happened in Beirut, Lebanon. The story of three people killed in a bread line in front of a bakery by random shell in 1975, becomes a story of 300 people massacred in cold blood when it was told by angry compatriots of the victims in 1984.[127]

The second model is the formal controlled oral tradition which means that "It is *formal* in the sense that there is a clearly identified teacher, a clearly identified student, and a clearly identified block of traditional material that is being passed on from one to the other. It is *controlled* in the sense that the material is memorized (and/or written), identified as "tradition" and thus preserved intact."[128] The defender of this model is the Scandinavian school of Riesenfeld and Gerhardson.[129] The example of this tradition is the memorization of the Bible, hymns, or the Qur'an as a way to preserve the content. Jesus' message was using the mnemonic techniques of preserving the Torah. Jesus taught his disciples by using this method. The church also recited Jesus' teachings under the guidance of the apostles. This tradition lives on until now in the Middle East where people recite and memorize the Qur'an, or the Bible.

Bailey argues that the oral tradition in preserving the story of Jesus could come from neither model. His argument is that the Gospels are too similar to each other to be the result of uncontrolled oral tradition, but since they are not exactly the same, it shows that this tradition is not fully formally controlled.

The third model was then suggested, which Bailey calls the informal controlled type, which he thinks is the most likely used model of oral tradition during Jesus' time. The retelling of Jesus' story was informal in the sense that there was no "one correct story", but they were controlled

---

[126] Bailey, "Informal Controlled Oral Tradition", 38. Bailey quoted Bultmann to show his argument when Bultmann wrote, "I do indeed think that we can now know almost nothing concerning the life and personality of Jesus, since the early Christian sources show no interest in either, are moreover fragmentary and often legendary, and other sources about Jesus do not exist." See Rudolf Bultmann, *Jesus and the World* (New York: Charles Scribner's Sons, (1934) 1958), 8.

[127] Bailey, "Informal Controlled Oral Tradition", 38.

[128] Bailey, "Informal Controlled Oral Tradition", 38.

[129] See Birger Gerhardsson, *Memory and Manuscript: Oral Tradition and Written Transmission in Rabbinic Judaism and Early Christianity* (Copenhagen: Ejnar Munksgaard, 1961); and *Tradition and Transmission in Early Christianity: Coniectanea Neotestamentica XX* (Copenhagen: Ejnar Munksgaard, 1964).

in the sense that the stories had to be within certain more or less strict limits. What is important is that the core of the memory remains the same, while the performance and the way that the stories were told can be different. The most important thing in the transmission of memory is the main content and not the details.

An example of this model that still happens in the Middle East until today is a gathering called *haflat samara* (a party for preservation), that usually takes place in isolated communities. The stories told in the form of *haflat samra* involve three levels of flexibility. The first level, which is included in the form of poems and proverbs, is very strict where not even a single word is subject to change. The public will correct the reciter should the person make any mistake. The correction involves a sense of honor and competence of the person who recites, for no one wants to publically recite some poems or proverbs unless he or she is sure that the entire passages have been accurately memorized. The second level is where the core of the story must not be changed but the way it is being told is subject to the storyteller's style. This level of flexibility can be found in historical stories and parables that are important to the identity of the community. The last forms of storytelling that can be told with great flexibility are jokes, casual news of the day, and inter-communal violence.[130]

The stories about Jesus, according to Bailey, at some point had to be preserved accurately. Yet the different accounts of the story show that the informal controlled tradition is the best explanation for the oral tradition in preserving Jesus' teachings. James Dunn uses the third model from Bailey and concludes that Jesus followers were careful to preserve and pass on Jesus tradition, but because of the nature of oral tradition in storytelling, the dialogue and oral interpretation may change slightly, but the core remains essentially the same.[131]

Different stories and performances in transmitting Jesus teachings have convinced Dunn to object the idea that we can find a true account of Jesus in historical reality. He says, "The idea that we can get back to an objective historical reality, which we can wholly separate and disentangle from the disciples' memories and then use as a check and control over the way the tradition was developed during the oral and earliest written transmission, is simply unrealistic."[132] Thus, the only

---

[130] See Bailey, "Informal Controlled Oral Tradition", 40–42; "Middle Eastern Oral Tradition", 364, 366.
[131] Dunn, *Jesus Remembered*, 212–221.
[132] Dunn, *Jesus Remembered*, 131.

realistic way in understanding Jesus is in understanding the way Jesus is being remembered.

Although Dunn did not describe exactly how Jesus was being remembered, or what remembrance means for the society in the time of the storytelling, we can assume that what he was describing is how collective memory or social memory works in the time of early New Testament communities. There are some important elements that Dunn misses to explain such as the relation between collective and individual memory, the role of society in choosing what to remember, and that performances of a story can also change the meaning of a story. However, assuming that his analysis is correct, what he has found shows a very important element on how social memory is formed or being passed on in early communities.

The stories of Jesus are being remembered and enacted as though done by Jesus himself. We still sense the strong element of remembrance from the Old Testament society in Jesus' communities, since the apostles were also very familiar with this tradition. The call to remember is also connected with a sense of identity in an active way. Memory in the New Testament community was being preserved through an oral tradition, to remember, to recognize, and to give a sense of communal identity.

5.2 Linguistic Analysis of Memory in the New Testament

After looking at what the role of memory is in the context of New Testament community, we will now turn to linguistic analysis of the word "memory" and "remembrance" in the New Testament, and try to find what they really mean in their respective contexts of the words. We will mainly use the help of theological dictionaries and some scholarly research on the words.

The main word that is used for remembrance is ἀνάμνησις (anamnesis) which means "remembrance" or "recollection". The synonym of the word is ὑπόμνησις. Anamnesis is distinguished from μνήμη (memory) as the "re-living of vanished impressions by a definite act or will". There is an active element within the word, it can lead to the signification of: a. "recollection in the consciousness" to that of b. "recollection by word or commemoration" and c. "recollection by act," i.e. "an action whereby the object is represented in memory."[133]

---

[133] Behm, "ἀνάμνησις" in Gerhard Kittel (ed.), *Theological Dictionary of the New Testament Volume I* (Grand Rapids, Wm. B. Eerdmans, 1972), 348. Compare to J. H. Thayer, *A Greek English Lexicon of the New Testament* (Edinburgh, 1986), 40. Compare to Max Thurian, The Eucharistic Memorial I: The Old Testament (London: Lutterworth

In the New Testament, the words μιμνῄσκομαι, μνημονεύω and μνείαν ἔχειν or μνείαν ποιεῖσθαι are closely connected and have the same characteristic as the Jewish *zkr* where it contains a certain action.[134] God remembers certain persons and turns to them in grace and mercy. In the New Testament, this word has more meaning than just a mental process of bringing something back into the mind. In some usage, recollection can also strike someone (Matt. 5:23), or it may constantly accompany him (1 Cor. 11:2). The book of Hebrews also notes that God who thinks on man means that God is with the person, but can also withdraw from him (Heb. 2:5-8). *The Theological Dictionary of the New Testament* notes, "Every event on earth has its effect on God. His remembrance is concealed in His acts of grace and judgment. The fact that God remembers is revealed by the word of His messengers."[135]

The remembrance of Jesus' words lives through even when Jesus was already resurrected. Johannine remembrance suggests that Jesus' words and teachings were only remembered, perceived and believed by the disciples after the resurrection (John 2:22; 12:16). The apostolic teaching also demands recollection. Paul for instance demanded Timothy to carry on the tradition of remembrance in the way Paul teaches them in every congregation (1 Cor. 4:17). We can also connect this tradition to how society perceives memory and passed it on in an oral tradition community, like was discussed earlier.

In the observation of the word, the *New International Dictionary of the New Testament Theology* says that 72% of all the passages in New Testament reflect the normal Greek usage.[136] We will look at the usage of the words that are being used as remembrance in the following part.

  a. To remember, call to mind, to be mindful of (i.e. Matt. 26:75, Mark 14:72; Luke 22:61);
  b. To consider (i.e. Luke 17:32, 2 Pet. 2:7, Heb. 10:31);
  c. To remember for good, to remember in a way which will benefit the person concerned in some way or other (i.e. Luke 1:54; Heb. 8:12);
  d. To be mindful of, to affect one's behavior (i.e. Heb. 11:15; 2 Pet. 3:2; Jude 5, 17; Acts 11:16);
  e. To mention (i.e. 2 Cor. 7:15; Rev. 16:19; 18:5).

Press, 1968), 20, where he decided to translate ἀνάμνησις as memorial.

[134] Michel, "μιμνῄσκομαι, μνείαν, μνήμη, μνῆμα, μνημεῖον, μνημονεύω" in *Theological Dictionary of the New Testament* Vol. 3, ed. Gerhard Kittel (Grand Rapids: William B. Eerdmans, 1979), 675–683.

[135] Michel, "μιμνῄσκομαι", 677.

[136] See K.H. Bartels, "Remember" in Colin Brown (ed.), *The New International Dictionary of New Testament Theology* (Grand Rapids: Zondervan Publishing House, 1981), 240–241.

In these instances, the use of "remember" is within the normal Greek usage that is to remember, to call to mind. Looking at the percentage of the use, it seems that Greek understood "remember" in a more direct way of its literal meaning which is an action taken by the mind.

The specifically biblical use of the word occurs only 28% in the New Testament. They bear the following meanings:[137]

(a) To mention in prayer, to remember in prayer. The two phrases *mneian poiumenoi* "mentioning" and *mnēmoneuontes* "remembering" in 1 Thes. 1:2 f. both mean to intercede. In Acts 10:4, Cornelius the centurion is told by an angel of God, "Your prayers and gifts to the poor have come up as a memorial offering before God." The meaning here is simply that the prayers and gifts are remembered before God, and that the prayer has been heard.

(b) To proclaim. The reminder in 2 Pet. 1:12 f. says, "So I will always remind (*hypomimnēskein*) you of these things, even though you know them and are firmly established in the truth you now have. I think it is right to refresh your memory (Bartels use the translation as "by way of reminder," *hypomnēsei*) "as long as I live in the tent of this body." Here, it is understood in terms of presenting again the known truth of the Gospel.

(c) To believe. In 2 Tim. 2:8 Paul wrote, "Remember Jesus Christ (*mnēmoneue Iēsoun Christon*), rose from the dead, descended from David, this is my Gospel." What to remember here is a short creedal statement, to confess the proclamation. It may be compared with the longer form in Rom. 1:3 f., where the order is chronological. Stress is laid on the fact that these truths are integral to the apostolic gospel.

(d) To confess, referring to the sacrifices under the old covenant (i.e. Heb 10:3). In the context the remembrance of sins, Behm presents Hebrew 10:3 as an example, where "those sacrifices are an annual "reminder of sins" (*anamnēsis hamartiōn*)." The annual sin offerings made on the day of the atonement are inadequate to remove sins, but serve rather to remind of them by the very fact that they are offered. To the members of the community, the sacrifices make sins present *in actu* as a hindrance to fellowship with God.[138]

The other instance of the use of the verb in the New Testament occurs in the Pauline and Lukan accounts of the Eucharist. In 1 Corinthians 11:24 when Jesus broke the bread, he says "…do this in remembrance of me" and in the same way also the cup, after supper, verse 25 saying, "…whenever you drink it, in remembrance of me", Christians are to enact the whole

---

[137] Bartels, "Remember", 242–243.
[138] See Behm, "μιμνῄσκομαι", 348–349.

action of the Eucharist. This is done in the recollection of Jesus, and this is not merely in such manner that they simply remember, but rather, in accordance with the active sense of anamnesis and the explanation in verse 26, in such a way that they actively fulfill the anamnesis.[139]

It is worth to note here what anamnesis means in the liturgy, since anamnesis is used variedly in worship. In the Dictionary of Worship, anamnesis is considered untranslatable. Words such as memorial, commemoration, and remembrance suggest that the person or deed commemorated is past and absent, whereas anamnesis means exactly the *opposite*: "it is an objective act, in and by which the person or event commemorated is actually made present, is brought into the realm of the here and now."[140] In connection with it, "the Eucharist is the recalling before God of the one sacrifice of Christ in all its accomplished fullness so that it is here and now operative by its effects in the souls of the redeemed."[141] Anamnesis means that the event of the past celebrated is actually re-lived and re-experienced in a new realm. Just like most of the use of *zkr* in the Old Testament, the meaning of anamnesis contains an active action of remembrance. It is not merely a recall of something back into the mind, rather it expresses the past event in a present reality.

As a liturgical term, the anamnesis signifies the part of the anaphora in which it is explicitly stated that the church is offering the bread and the cup with this meaning and for this purpose, in obedience to Christ's commandment to do so. A statement of the memorial and a statement of the offering are comprised in the normal form of the anamnesis.[142]

The use of *anamnesis* in the New Testament has a different employment from that in the Old Testament. If the Old Testament rarely translates *zkr* as a mere remembering as psychological act of recalling something from the mind, the New Testament uses *anamnesis* more in its normal Greek use.[143]

5.3 Anamnesis in Hebrew 10:3: The Memorial of Sins

The first part of Hebrews 10 points out that there is a theme of memorial of sins in connection with God's forgiveness. The memorial of sins used

---

[139] See Behm, "μιμνῄσκομαι", 349.

[140] W. Jardine Grisbrooke, "Anamnesis", in *The Westminster Dictionary of Worship*, ed. J. G. Davies (Philadelphia: The Westminster Press, 1979), 15.

[141] Davies, *Dictionary of Worship*, 15.

[142] Grisbrooke, "Anamnesis", 15.

[143] In our opinion, this could be connected with the psychological dimension and the development of the language itself, and also the environment where the language is used. However, this would need a further exploration.

here comes from the term anamnesis and the synonym of the word. In the letter to the Hebrews, it is said that the sacrifices are not effective anymore for the worshippers to ask for God's forgiveness. Nevertheless, the sacrifices are used as a reminder of sins. The sacrifices and offerings for sins mean that the people are being reminded to confess before God and repent. God shall consider this an act of repentance.

There is a kind of similarity between this letter and Numbers 5:15 where a reminder must be made to draw attention to guilt. Fred B. Craddock notes that a key term in the discussions of the subjective side of Christ sacrifice for sin is conscience. At Hebrews 9:14, it is clear that the benefit of Christ's self-sacrifice is the purifying of the conscience from the dead works in order that worship of God may follow. Further, he explains, "the major inadequacy of the system of animal offerings was not only the inability to remove the "consciousness of sins" (NIV: felt guilty of their sins), but also a reminder, by the fact of constant repetition, of the very sin that could not be erased by the process (vv 2–3)."[144]

Max Thurian, connects this calling with remembrance of sins. His opinion will help us to understand more about the ritual part of the text. He understands these verses as a calling upon God regarding the guilt and sins of the people so God would not punish the people for it. The word anamnesis in Hebrews 10:3 means that there is an element of the memorial of sins before God to receive God's forgiveness.[145] There is a difference between the memorial action of sins through sacrifices and offerings in the Old Testament and the New Testament. In the Old Testament, sacrifices are to remind Israel of their sins before God, while in the letter of Hebrews, offerings are made to remember God's compassion through Christ. The sayings of Jeremiah were quoted in Hebrews, "This is the covenant I will make with them after that time, says the Lord. I will put my laws in their hearts, and I will write them on their minds.... Their sins and lawless acts I will remember no more."[146] The remembrance of God's compassion can also be seen in the Song of Mary and the benediction of Zechariah (Luke 1:54, 72).

---

[144] Fred B. Craddock, "The Letter to the Hebrews" in Leander E. Keck (eds.), *The New Interpreter's Bible Volume XII* (Nashville, Abingdon Press, 1998), 114.

[145] Max Thurian, *The Eucharistic Memorial II* (London: Lutterworth Press, 1963), 5–14. See also Jusen Boangmanalu, *Anamnesis: Study on the Anamnetic Meaning of the Communion Compared with The Ancestors Memorial Activities in the Batak Traditional Religion* (Jakarta: Thesis presented to the Faculty of the South East Asia Graduate School of Theology, 1992), 49–55.

[146] Heb. 10:16–17; see Jeremiah 31:33–34. Jeremiah 31:34 is quoted two times in the letter of Hebrews, see Heb 8:12. Compare with Revelation 18:5, "for her sins are piled up to heaven, and God has remembered her crimes."

There is a unique character of Jesus' act of sacrifice on the cross. Thurian considers that Jesus is "a priest forever, in the order of Melchizedek (7:17, 21)." The status of Jesus as the priest, once and for all, is absolute. Jesus' act of sacrifice as a priest has replaced the animal's offerings (see 10:12). Other priests cannot replace Jesus' status as the sacrifice on the cross. The sacrifice of the cross is above all sacrifices, the time is once and for all, and it carries all of human's offerings, prayers and actions. This means that in the letter of Hebrews, Christ's fulfillment is done within the consecration of faith.[147]

However, there is an important note that we need to mention here about the time of the writing of the book of Hebrews. The book, "…represents in many ways a hybrid blending of traditional Christian theology, the ideological perspectives and concerns of a particular Jewish Christian community, and an anonymous author's own highly individualized exegesis of the Old Testament."[148] While most authors agree with regard to the author of the book, they could not find an agreement about the time of writing. There are two different opinions as to when the book of Hebrews was actually written. The first group says that the writing was prior to the destruction of the Temple in Jerusalem in A.D. 70.[149] The argument of those who support this opinion is that the destruction of the temple was so traumatic to the Jewish community, that it is hard to imagine a Jewish writing after the event with no reference to it. This view on the time of writing will give a stronger testimony to Jesus' sacrificial act as replacement of animal's offering as a prophetic message. The second group concludes that the book of Hebrews was written after the destruction of the temple.[150] The reason to support this theory is the fact that Clement of Rome quoted from the book, which means the date of its writing could not have been later than A.D. 96. This particular view on the time of writing will

---

[147] See Thurian, *The Eucharistic Memorial II*, 9–10. Compare with F. F. Bruce, *The Epistle To The Hebrews* (Michigan: Wm. B. Eerdmans, 1964), 104–106, 160.

[148] Richard N. Longenecker, *Biblical Exegesis in the Apostolic Period* (Grand Rapids: Eerdmans, 1999), 140.

[149] One of the supporters of this view is Llyod Kim, *Polemic in the Book of Hebrews: Anti-Judaism, Anti-Semitism, Supersessionism?* (Orlando: Pickwick Publications, 2006). The thesis of the book is that the book of Hebrews was written to an audience of Jewish Christ-believers while the temple cult was still active.

[150] A supporter of this view is Charles B. Puskas, *The Letters of Paul: an Introduction* (Minnesota: The Liturgical Press, 1993). Because of the difficulty of deciding the actual time of writing, Fred B. Craddock, "*Hebrews,*" in *The New Interpreter's Bible: A Commentary in Twelve Volumes: Volume XII*, ed. Leander E. Keck (Nashville: Abingdon Press, 1996), 8 says that the time of writing is between 65–95 A.D.

weaken the argument of Jesus' sacrificial act because it can be seen as an argument to replace the act of offering in the Temple to Jesus' status as the ultimate sacrifice. For our study we decided that the writing of the book of Hebrews could not be later than the year 70 A.D. because of the use of the present tense for the cultic activity, thus giving a prophetic meaning to Jesus' sacrificial act.[151]

The offerings and sacrifices in the Temple have been completed by the sacrificial act of Jesus. There will be no more offerings because the perfect offering has completed it all (Heb. 10:8). Nevertheless, the offerings made by Israel are considered as a memorial of sins to receive God's forgiveness. The repeated offerings are an objective memorial of the proclamation of sin.[152]

6. Anamnesis in the Eucharist

The only other New Testament instances of anamnesis occur in Pauline and Lucan accounts of the Eucharist. The Eucharist is the account that Jesus institutes himself in ordering a remembrance of him. We will look at what anamnesis means in the Eucharist from the mutual understanding that Christ gave his life as a sacrifice and that we are to recognize the communion as a remembrance of him. We shall see and explore the meaning of remembrance in the Eucharist and the connection of it with the forgiveness of sins and reconciliation.[153]

6.1 The Four Texts

Anamnesis is the heart of the Eucharist. The act of remembrance is being told in and through it and is repeatedly celebrated by the church. However, the account of the Eucharist is written in four sections in the New Testament. There is no exact match between the stories. Matthew, Mark, Luke, and Paul are telling about the same story with different emphasis on what they consider important to convey to their readers. According to the time of writing, we should first go and look at the account of the Eucharist in Paul's letter to the Corinthians. Paul wrote,

---

[151] See William L. Lane, *Word Biblical Commentary* Vol. 47: *Hebrews 1–8* (Dallas, Texas: Word Books Publisher, 1991), lxiii. He considers both facts and conjectures, and concludes that the writing date could not be later than 70 A.D. because the writer refers to cultic activity in the present tense.

[152] See Thurian, *The Eucharistic Memorial II*, 10–11.

[153] The discussion about the presence of the Lord in the Eucharist will be presented in the fifth chapter of this research.

And when he had given thanks, he broke it and said, "This is my body, which is for you; do this in remembrance of me." (*touto poieite eis tēn emēn anamnēsin*) In the same way, after supper he took the cup, saying, "This cup is the new covenant in my blood; do this, whenever you drink it, in remembrance of me (*touto poieite, hosakis ean pinete, eis tēn emēn anamnēsin*) (1 Cor. 11:23–25).

In the account of Mark, which is the oldest of the synoptic gospels, the chapter on the Eucharist is very essential in the whole teaching of Jesus' suffering. It is important to note that the last supper Jesus had with his disciples is similar to the Passover meal (Mark 14:12).[154]

> While they were eating, Jesus took bread, gave thanks and broke it, and gave it to his disciples saying, "Take it; this is my body." Then he took the cup and gave thanks and offered it to them, and they all drank from it. "This is my blood of the covenant, which is poured out for many," he said to them. "I tell you the truth, I will not drink again of the fruit of the vine until that day when I drink it anew in the kingdom of God (Mark 14:22–25).

The Gospel of Matthew is fully connected with the Gospel of Mark and places the order in the same context.

> While they were eating, Jesus took bread, gave thanks and broke it, and gave it to his disciples, saying, "Take and eat; this is my body." Then he took the cup, gave thanks and offered it to them, saying, "Drink from it, all of you. This is my blood of the covenant, which is poured out for many for the forgiveness of sins. I tell you, I will not drink of this fruit of the vine from now on until that day when I drink it anew with you in my Father's Kingdom (Matt. 26:26–29)."

Luke, the third writer in the Synoptic Gospels, is not fully different from the other gospels, but has a noticeably long entrance before the order of the Supper.

> When the hour came, Jesus and his apostles reclined at the table. And he said to them, "I have eagerly desired to eat this Passover with you before I suffer. For I tell you, I will not eat it again until it finds fulfillment in the kingdom of God. After taking the cup, he gave thanks and said, "Take this and divide it among you. For I tell you I will not drink again of the fruit of the vine until the Kingdom of God comes." He took the bread, broke it, and gave it to them, saying, "This is my body given for you; do

---

[154] See C. J. den Heyer, *De Maaltijd van de Heer: Exegetische en Bijbeltheologische Studie over Pascha en Avondmaal* (Kampen: J.H. Kok, 1990), 12. Discussions continue whether the Last Supper that Jesus had with his disciples is the same as the Passover meal in the Jewish tradition. We will further discuss the connection of the Eucharist and the Passover meal in the last part of this chapter.

this in remembrance of me." In the same way after the supper he took the cup saying, "This cup is the new covenant in my blood, which is poured out for you (Luke 22:14-20).

Similarities between the Mark and Matthew account clearly show. Even so, in fact, it seems that Matthew is in line with Mark, while Luke seems to follow the Pauline tradition of the institution. It is notable that the account where Jesus instructed his disciples to do the same communion as a remembrance of him is only stated in Luke and the letter to the Corinthians. Mark, without much doubt is the oldest tradition and Matthew is using it as his source. Having both accounts at his disposal, which are Mark and Pauline tradition, Luke chooses to use Paul's version that notes the instruction to do the same rite again as a remembrance of Jesus. Luke realizes that there are two instances where Paul urges the people of Corinth to do the communion. Luke took the tradition and the instruction, used it only once, and put an eschatological emphasis instead of the second instruction.

Another thing that is important to note here is the aspect of the communion in the literal meaning of the word. Luke puts stress on the importance of the talk after dinner. He noted that Jesus and his disciples did not leave right after the meal. They had a conversation. The table is not only a place for eating and drinking, it is a place where people meet and tell stories (see Luke 7:36-50; 10:38-42; 11:37-54; 14:1-24).[155] Luke sees the connection between the institution of the communion and the talks after the meal which places Jesus as the servant.

The Eucharist is considered as an event that establishes and confirms the remembrance of Jesus. Anamnesis here means not only the subjective representation of something in the consciousness, and as an act of the remembering mind, it is also the objective effectiveness and presence of the salvific actions of God.[156] The words Jesus said signify a declaration that the bread and wine are Jesus' body and blood, and are a command to do the same celebration as the memorial of Jesus.

---

[155] See den Heyer, *De Maaltijd van de Heer*, 98–99; 106.

[156] See Josef Andreas Jungmann, "Eucharist" in *Encyclopedia of Theology*, ed. Karl Rahner (London: Burns & Oates, 1981), 448. See also Michael Welker, *What Happens in Holy Communion?* (Grand Rapids, Wm. B. Eerdmans, 2000), 126, who states that this remembrance, this act of memory, includes firmly established and living memories, experiences, and expectations of the saving presence of Christ. It draws the human beings who establish and confirm this remembrance into the fullness of Christ's life. The remembrance of Christ is an effect of the Holy Spirit.

6.2 The Eucharist and the God who Remembers

Over the years, the meaning of Jesus' words, "do this in remembrance of me" has been battled about and have been deeply and widely examined. Some modern scholars have suggested that instead of the interpretation that this was an Israelites memorial of what God has done for them, it actually enables Israelites to remind God of what he had done for them in the past with a plea that he will act for them again.[157] We will see what exactly this interpretation means, since it is not the same as the general opinion of the meaning of the institution.

Joachim Jeremias, a New Testament scholar claims that in passages such Mark 14:9 (par. Matt. 26:13); Acts 10:4; and in the Palestinian and Old Testament memorial formula, it is almost always God who remembers.[158] In the feast of the Passover, God is spoken about as the one who has given to his people festal seasons and *lezzikārōn* – as the whole festal of the Passover and is a festal of remembrance, and the Passover meal is a meal of remembrance. He says,

> This *zikhrōnōth* are prayers which enclose Bible passages entreating of "remembrance", exclusively God's remembrance of His covenant promises both in the past and in the future. The closing prayer of the *zikhrōnōth* ends with a doxology: "Praised be thou, O Lord, that rememberest the covenant. Of the special importance is the old Passover prayer which beseeches God for "the remembrance of the Messiah."[159]

The same process could be happening in the Eucharist. Paul's explanation of the verse in 1 Cor. 11:26 (For whenever you eat this bread and drink this cup, you proclaim the Lord's death until he comes) is translated by Jeremias by "As often as the death of the Lord is proclaimed at the Eucharist, and the maranatha rises upward, God is reminded of the unfulfilled climax of the work of salvation until (the goal is reached, that) he comes."[160] Briefly, his thesis is that Jesus instituted the celebration of the Eucharist to remind God; God is therefore being asked to remember the messiah by bringing the kingdom through the parousia (because when God remembers, God acts).[161]

---

[157] See Donald Bridge and David Phypers, *Communion: The Meal That Unites?* (Illinois: Harold Shaw Publishers, 1981), 21. Among those scholars are Joachim Jeremias, *The Eucharistic Words of Jesus* (New York: The Macmillan Company, 1955), 159–165; and Paul Tihon, "The Theology of the Eucharistic Prayer" in *The New Liturgy*, ed. Lancelot Sheppard (London: Darton, Longman & Todd, 1970), 178–179.

[158] Jeremias, *The Eucharistic Words*, 162–163.

[159] Jeremias, *The Eucharistic Words*, 161.

[160] Jeremias, *The Eucharistic Words*, 164, see Bartels' comments, "Remember", 244–245.

[161] See the discussion on Jeremias interpretation in Geoffrey Wainwright, *Eucharist*

Jeremias is making quite a different point when he says that there is nothing in his argument which suggests a doctrine of a real presence of Christ or a eucharistic sacrifice which either repeats or extends that of Christ on the cross. His emphasis is eschatological. God's remembrance would point back to the Messiah, Christ himself. This is because "God's remembrance ... never means a mere recollection on the part of God; but when God remembers somebody, he acts, he does something, he sits in judgment and grants his grace, he fulfills his promise." The eschatological message in Jeremias' understanding is quite definite in his idea of the way God is expected to remember when the Messianic community meets and prays to him, that "God remembers the Messiah by bringing his kingdom in the parousia."[162]

Up to this point we can agree on Jeremias' idea that God will always remember. However, this idea of God's remembrance and the referral to the Old Testament for the idea of God remembering does not rule out other interpretations. Bartels suggests that *touto poieite* (this do) may be regarded as a summary of the procedure to be followed by participants in the Eucharist. The participant act as Jesus did just like what Jesus had done in the institution of the Eucharist, as being told in the Synoptic Gospels. The comparison made between the Old Testament and Heb. 10:3 can be paraphrased as follows, "Do this, by eating the bread and drinking the cup (i.e. by participating in my life and death), by the preaching of the word (1 Cor. 11:26) and the singing of praise."[163] The words "until he comes" denote a meaning that is more than "waiting for the end of the day until the second coming of Christ", it is actively reaching out action towards it, a prayer, *maranatha*. Bartels concludes that the word *anamnesis* covers all these ideas.

6.3 The Eucharist and Passover

The Eucharist can only be understood in its most profound sense against the background of the liturgical tradition of the Old Testament. The Eucharist is not a new and independent act of Jesus. It is actually very important to interpret the Eucharist in the light of Jewish liturgy and in particular the paschal liturgy, and to see the importance of the link between the Passover and the Eucharist.

---

and Eschatology (London: Epworth Press, 1971), 64–65.

[162] Jeremias, *The Eucharistic Words,* 163, see Bartels' comments, "Remember", 245.

[163] Bartels, "Remember", 245.

There is also a possibility that the last supper that Jesus had with the disciples was a common practice of *eranos*, or "potluck dinner" which is a common social meal in the Greek-Roman culture in which the first Christians participated.[164] There are some ideas that the established relationship between the last supper and the Passover is a later re-interpretation. Before we can connect the relation between the Eucharist and Passover meal, we have to address the question first. Panayotis Coutsoumpos, a New Testament scholar, addresses this question and says, "1 Corinthians 8, 10, and 11 clearly shows that there was disagreement and factiousness (σχίσμα) among the church members because of gluttony, drunkenness, and the lack of tolerance in understanding one another's social and religious differences."[165] The cause of the problem, which was shown in Paul's letter to Corinth is that it was normal to begin to eat first before the others arrived in Graeco-Roman potluck custom. There was also the problem of the meat that was sacrificed to the idols. The distinction between the haves and have-nots were that the rich would not hesitate to eat first and not wait or share food with the less fortunate (1 Cor. 11:22–23). That is why Paul advised them to eat at home instead.

What happened was that the Corinthians were influenced by the custom of eating *eranos* dinners, and considered the Lord's Supper to be a dinner. Since they misunderstood the supper because of what was customary to them, Paul tried to correct their false behaviours. Paul was trying to "show the Corinthians the correct practice of the Lord's Supper as a united body with one purpose in mind, to build up the body of Christ and to eradicate the divisive elements in the congregation at the eucharistic meal."[166] He was doing this in his own words and their own terminology for the sake of argumentation.[167] The explanation that Paul gives the congregation in Corinthians thus does not show that the Lord's Supper is the *eranos* potluck dinner.

What Jesus did in the Last Supper was actually a celebration of the Passover which itself in turn was also a celebration of remembering the exodus. The Passover is an act of remembering God's salvific action, and Jesus used this tradition as a remembrance of him. Therefore we

---

[164] This was the problem that Panayotis Coutsoumpos wants to raise in his research, *Paul and the Lord's Supper: A Socio-Historical Investigation* (New York: Peter Lang Publishing, 2005).
[165] Coutsoumpos, *Paul and the Lord's Supper*, 3.
[166] Coutsoumpos, *Paul and the Lord's Supper*, 103.
[167] Coutsoumpos, *Paul and the Lord's Supper*, 131.

should see the link between those two events; what it actually means for God's people at that time and how Jesus used the tradition and even added a new meaning to it. However there is a problem in interpreting the Last Supper within the framework of the paschal celebration. Not all the facts in the Passover can be entirely reconciled with the Eucharist. We thus will investigate whether the Eucharist is actually a celebration of Passover or even a continuation of the Passover festival.

There are several indications that the Last Supper was indeed a Passover meal.[168] First, the Supper took place in the evening and extended into the night,[169] which is similar to the obligation that the Passover meal should be eaten at night. Second, Jesus and his disciples reclined at their last meal together (Mark 14:18; Matt. 26:20; Luke 22:14), where it was a Passover ordinance that Israel should recline as a symbol of their liberty.[170] Third, a dish precedes the breaking of bread, which only happens at the Passover. This is shown where the meal is already in progress when Jesus takes the bread and offers a blessing and breaks the bread (Mark. 14:18; Matt. 26:21). Fourth, wine as an obligatory drink at the Passover and was drunk at the Last Supper. The specific wine in the Passover was red wine, and this is proven by the comparison of it with the blood of Jesus.[171] Fifth, the supper ended with the singing of a hymn (Mark 14:26; Matt. 26:30), which likely would have been the second part of the Hallel that closes the Passover meal (Ps. 114, 115, 118). Sixth, Jesus did not return to Bethany after the meal because, according to the Passover regulation, one should spend the night in a larger area after the Passover had been eaten. Seventh, Higgins argued that the very fact that Jesus spoke of his body and blood in connection with the bread and wine is an indication of the Passover character of the Eucharist, because in the Passover Haggadah the person presiding explained the various elements in the meal, which what exactly Jesus has done. Based on the words of Jesus during the last supper, Jeremias has no more doubt that the Last Supper was indeed a Passover. The word of institution over the bread, which was commonly done before

---

[168] See A. J. B. Higgins, *The Lord's Supper in the New Testament* (London: SCM Press, 1956), 20–21.

[169] See Mark 14:7,30; Matt. 26:20; 1 Cor. 11:23. It seems that the synoptic gospels and Paul agree on this point. Luke's explicitly draws the description that the meal is a Passover meal.

[170] See Jerusalem Talmud, *Pesahim* 10.1, as in Higgins, *The Lord's Supper*, 20, footnote 5.

[171] See Mishnah, *Pesahim* 10.I, and for a cross-reference see Jeremias, *The Eucharistic Words*, 106–107.

the Passover meal, was spoken by Jesus in connection with the grace at the beginning of the main meal.[172]

However, there are also different notes found in the Gospel of John that do not place the Passover in relation with the last supper. Jesus has the evening meal with his disciples, afterwards he is arrested and brought before Annas and Caiaphas and the following morning before Pilate. Here, John 18:28 note that, "Then the Jews led Jesus from Caiaphas to the palace of the Roman governor. By now, it was early morning, and to avoid ceremonial uncleanness the Jews did not enter the palace; they wanted to be able to eat the Passover."[173] Kilpatrick, a scholar in Bible exegesis, argues that the time of the last supper John gives makes it most probable that the last supper was not done as part of a Passover meal, for it would not have been possible for conservative Sadducee and Pharisee alike to take part in the arrest, trial, and crucifixion of Jesus during the Passover. Therefore he concludes that John has the most possible account of the time of the last supper… it happened before the Passover.[174]

Den Heyer admits that the problem of interpretation between the Synoptic Gospel and the fourth Gospel on the exact date of the Last Supper has been debated for centuries. He suggests that the fourth Gospel is not defining the exact date of the Last Supper, instead, the writer wants to stress his theological point of view by showing the real Paschal lamb died outside of Jerusalem when thousands of other lambs are ready to be sacrificed (see John 19:36, compare with Ex. 12:46).[175] In other words, den Heyer wants to state his position on trying to reconcile the two conflicting exact dates of the Eucharist by saying that he is with the date given by the Synoptic Gospels and at the same time not underestimating the theological value of John's chronology.

Given the fact that the connection between the Eucharist and the Passover has been widely debated, we should take a brief look at the meaning of the Passover itself, as promised. The Passover is the most

---

[172] See Jeremias, *The Eucharistic Words*, 58–60.

[173] See the note of G. D. Kilpatrick, *The Eucharist in Bible and Liturgy* (Cambridge: Cambridge University Press, 1983), 43–58. Notice that John 19:14 says that it was the day of the preparation of the Passover Week, about the sixth hour. In John 19:31 it was noted that the Sabbath and the Passover fell together on the following day after Jesus was put on the cross.

[174] See Kilpatrick, *The Eucharist*, 58. He also suggests that Jesus did not plan to hold the Passover. He says that family plays an important role in the Passover meal, and it cannot be substituted with disciples.

[175] Den Heyer, *De Maaltijd van de Heer*, 38–40.

widely celebrated of all the Jewish festivals. It celebrates a turning point in the history of the Jews, the time when they emerged as a free people after years of slavery in Egypt. It is a stirring festival of freedom, commemorating the birth of a community. [176] The day of the Passover was to be celebrated from generation to generation as a memorial. Exodus 12:14 told Israel to "commemorate; for the generations to come you shall celebrate it as a festival to the Lord." This feast is a recalling of the Lord's act of deliverance that can be relived in liturgy, and also as a thanksgiving to God. Jeremias thinks that Jesus already referred to himself as the paschal lamb that has to be sacrificed. This is shown by the fact that the words of interpretation refer the bread and wine to Jesus himself. Jesus' parable only announces that no matter how, his vicarious death will happen, and that he foresees a violent death.[177] This could strengthen the thesis that Jesus and his disciples are celebrating the paschal meal during the Last Supper.

Now we are going to get a little help from a liturgical point of view that also deals with the aspect of the Eucharist and its relation with Passover meal. Max Thurian, a liturgist and systematic theologian in liturgy who has been investigating the relation of the eucharistic memorial in the Old and New Testament, says, "The Passover is not just a didactic recalling to or edification of the people, it is a praising of God; the third cup of the paschal meal, in particular, emphasizes this thanksgiving."[178] There is a triple memorial, or a triple anamnesis within the paschal meal: of a past deliverance regarded as typical, of a present deliverance through the sacramental action of the paschal meal and of a coming

---

[176] See Howard Greenfeld, *Passover* (New York: Holt, Rinehart and Winston, 1978), James C. Vanderkam, *An Introduction to Early Judaism* (Grand Rapids: W. B. Eerdmans, 2001), 204–205. Much of the biblical legislation of the celebration can be found in Exodus 12: a one-year old lamb or goat without blemish was to be selected for each household on the tenth day of the month; it was to be kept until the fourteenth, when it was to be slaughtered and its blood sprinkled on the doorpost of a dwelling so that the Lord would see it and pass over that house when he came through Egypt at night. This event is celebrated every year on the fourteenth day of the first month.

[177] Jeremias, *The Eucharistic Words*, 144–146. For a comparison, see Léon-Dufour's comments of the theses of Jeremias of the connection between the Eucharist and the Passover. Léon-Dufour concludes that the only datum that tips the balance in favor of a Passover meal is the fact that the synoptics seem to say that the Supper was in fact a Passover meal; but the question is do they not tell how Jesus sent disciples to "prepare the Passover" which he is to celebrate? Therefore, he proposes that the way the Supper is presented is not in the Passover of the Jews but in fact the Passover of Jesus, *Sharing The Eucharistic Bread*, 306–308.

[178] Max Thurian, *The Eucharistic Memorial I: The Old Testament* (London: Lutterworth Press, 1968), 27.

Biblical Meaning of Remembrance

salvation in the day of the Messiah.[179] This is an interesting sequence of time in celebrating one event. The past deliverance is celebrated and then taken into the present time by the sacramental act, and God was asked to fulfill it by sending the Messiah. The night of the Passover becomes the night when Messiah is awaited – a way to celebrate the past event to live for the future. Thurian says,

> The paschal meal is the memorial (*zikkaron*) *par excellence* in which the people of God actualize the historical deliverance, in a liturgy, and remind God what he once did, so that he may continue it today: "Our God, and God of our fathers!" says the Jewish paschal prayer, "May our remembrance (*zikkaron*, memorial) of our fathers…of Messiah … Remember us …" How many liturgical acts of the Old Testament are called in this way because they are a symbolic way of saying to God: "Remember us because of thy fidelity shown in former times by deliverance from slavery and by covenant with thy people.[180]

Thurian thinks that the liturgical celebration of the Passover makes concrete the mutual covenant of God and man; it recalls to God his promise of salvation and to the faithful the protection of his God; it is an act of witness to the faithfulness of God before the world. Four aspects of the paschal meal are to be found in the eucharistic liturgy: the affirmation of the presence of God in the covenant; the communication of salvation; the effective intercession by means of the memorial, and finally the proclamation of the word of God.[181]

Therefore, Thurian concludes that the manner in which Jesus celebrated the Holy Supper within the Jewish liturgy of the Passover makes us understand that the Eucharist is a blessing for the wonderful deeds of God, a sacrifice of praise and thanksgiving, a memorial. It is an actualization of the passion, resurrection and intercession of Christ, a memorial which rises before the Father as the Church's offering of prayer, recalling to God's remembrance all the needs of the people… "Remember, Lord, thy Church and all those for whom we present to thee the sacrifice."[182]

Whether or not that last supper was actually a Passover meal, its proximity both to the Jewish feast and to Jesus crucifixion gave it both paschal and sacrificial connotations which Christians utilized to

---

[179] See Thurian, *The Eucharistic Memorial I*, 28.

[180] Max Thurian, "The Eucharistic Memorial, Sacrifice of Praise and Supplication" in Max Thurian (ed.), *Ecumenical Perspectives on Baptism, Eucharist and Ministry* (Geneva: World Council of Churches, 1993), 94.

[181] See Thurian, *The Eucharistic Memorial I*, 39.

[182] See Max Thurian, "The Eucharistic Memorial, Sacrifice of Praise and Supplication", 95.

interpret the meaning of the event.[183] Jesus has used the tradition and gives it a new meaning. This is the connection between the Eucharist and the Old Testament tradition, that it is actually rooted in the Jewish tradition of the Passover. Jesus remembers this tradition as a celebration of memory and uses this as a remembrance of him.

6.4 The Eucharist and Sacrificial Act

The next part is to connect Jesus' sacrificial act with the Eucharist. What we understand from Jesus' sacrificial act is that the blood of Jesus acts as the last sacrificial lamb that closes the relation with other sacrificial rituals. However, this is the common understanding that we have received. What we would like to know is, "How did Jesus understand his role in the Eucharist?" And moreover, what is Jesus' understanding of sacrifice?

There are three accounts in the synoptic Gospels that recorded the prediction of Jesus' death in Mark 8:31 (compare with Matt. 16:21 and Luke 9:22); Mark 9:30-32 (compare with Matt. 17:22-23 and Luke 9:43-45); and Mark 10:33-34 (compare with Matt. 20:18-19 and Luke 18:31-33). Jesus' prediction even provides some details about how it took place, and even the condemnation that he will receive, that "the Son of Man will be delivered over to the chief priests and the teachers of the law. They will condemn him to death and will hand him over to the Gentiles, who will mock him and spit on him, flog him and kill him. Three days later he will rise (Mark 10:33-34; see also Matt. 20:19; Luke 18:32-33)." There was also the parable of the wicked tenants who murder not only the vineyard-owners' messengers but also his son, that offers a parable of Jesus' death (see Mark 12:7-8; Luke 20:14-15; Matthew 21:38-39). We can say that Jesus did predict or speak about his passion and death, and his resurrection.

In the talk before the supper, Jesus also associates the bread and wine as his body and blood respectively. In the previous part we have seen that this act has shown that Jesus realized that his sacrifice would be for forgiveness of sins. Jesus understood himself as the sacrifice paschal lamb in the Last Supper.

However, it is important to note that what was understood as sacrifice in his days is not the same as what modern people think about sacrifice.

---

[183] See J. Martos, "Eucharistic Theology" in *A New Dictionary of Christian Theology*, eds. Alan Richardson & John Bowden (London: SCM Press, first published 1983, 11th edition 2002).

Scholars have speculated about the meaning of sacrifice. The key verse is held to be Leviticus 17:11, "For the life of a creature is in the blood, and I have given it to you to make the atonement for yourselves on the altar; it is the blood that makes the atonement for one's life." Bridge notes that there are two main opposing understandings of sacrifice resulting from this passage. Some scholars think that the worshipper is releasing the life of the sacrificed animal and offering it to God. However, other scholars think that in sacrifice the animal is a replacement of the worshipper and the violent offering of life is important rather than the continued presence of life for some new purpose.[184]

Kilpatrick suggested that the meaning of sacrifice has been developed from an understanding of the ancient world concerning this word.[185] There are three types of sacrifice: communion sacrifice, gift sacrifice, and atonement sacrifice; they mean a releasing and a conferring of life and power (2 Kings 3); to strengthen a material object (Exodus 12); reinforcing action (Numbers 22-24). In the story of Balaam, sacrifice can also reinforce a curse as well as a blessing.

Paul understood the Eucharist as sacrifice, and understood that it could bring a blessing or curse. That is why he wrote,

> Therefore, whoever eats the bread or drinks the cup of the Lord in an unworthy manner will be guilty of sinning against the body and the blood of the Lord. A man ought to examine himself before he eats of the bread and drinks of the cup. For anyone who eats and drinks without recognizing the body of the Lord eats and drinks judgment on himself. That is why many among you are weak and sick, and a number of you have fallen asleep (1 Cor. 11:27–30).

F.F. Bruce explain the context of this examination of oneself as a self-examination to ascertaining whether or not one is living and acting "in the love and charity" with his/her neighbor. Certain members of the church, who do not think about their poorer fellow Christians, were considered guilty and should incur divine judgement.[186] This account of Paul must have the stories of Korah and his company and King Uzziah in mind, where the virtue of a sacrifice which should have been for the sake of their benefit turns back against them because they are unworthy of it.[187]

---

[184] Bridge, *Communion: The Meal*, 32–33.
[185] Kilpatrick, *The Eucharist*, 45. For further information about this topic, see F.C.N. Hicks, *The Fullness of Sacrifice* (Macmillan, 1930).
[186] F. F. Bruce, *The New Century Bible Commentary: I & II Corinthians* (London: Marshall, Morgan & Scott, 1980), 114–116. This judgment took the form of sickness and death which were rife in the community.
[187] Kilpatrick, *The Eucharist*, 53.

Therefore, the meaning of sacrifice is basically the meeting or exchange between God and men, where it arises out of God's initiative. Kilpatrick says,

> Sacrifices like them [all kind of sacrifices from the basic ideas to the more developed forms of it] assumes the primacy of God, and obviously they arise out of God's initiative. Thus God forms the divine society and calls man into it, he inspires the prophets and speaks through the Scripture. Man is involved in these institutions, but while he co-operates with God, he does so in response to the divine initiative sacrifice on the other hand does involve both God and man, but at first sight, at any rate, the initiative seems to rest with man; he offers to God, who receives and gives again.[188]

Sacrifice is an exchange between the human and God, where God takes the initiative and inspires the people to a response in an initiative of an offering. Kilpatrick suggests that the Eucharist must also be seen through this lens. This is a reaction not only to the presence of God but to God's manifestation of himself in the saving act of the Lord. This manifestation calls for a response, which has been determined by what Jesus did. Jesus is the pioneer of the Eucharist where he first offers himself in love and worship to the Father, and in him and through him we continue this offering.[189]

The tradition of offering in the Old Testament is fulfilled by Jesus' unique act of sacrifice, the once-for-all offering. To understand what Jesus did on the cross means to understand the tradition of offering and sacrifices in the Old Testament. The blood of the paschal lamb that was shed on the cross is perfecting the animal offering.

7. Conclusion

We have seen that the idea of remembrance indeed has a biblical foundation. The previous part on the Old Testament has shown us the aspects of remembrance in Old Testament theology as a memorial which not only serves to remind men of the past mercies of God as a ground for their present obedience but also enables man to recall God's past promises and deeds in thanksgiving and prayer for new blessings.

Israel, as the chosen people of God, shares their identity in their remembrance of God. Israel's social memory is being passed on through oral traditions and it was open to interpretation. Israel believes that they

---

[188] Kilpatrick, *The Eucharist*, 98. Compare to Bridge, *Communion*, 32–45.
[189] Kilpatrick, *The Eucharist*, 98.

should actively re-experience and re-actualize those memories as their identity and not just as an act of calling something into mind. Thus, the memory of God's saving action is very important for Israel to create their identity, and it shapes the present and future Israelites' tradition.

In connection with sins and forgiveness, the theme of remembrance in the Old Testament is in line with God who remembers Israel's sins and Israel who remembers their own sins. The idea of remembrance has a very strong root in the Old Testament, and it is also a way towards forgiveness of sins. The theology of remembrance for the forgiveness of sins has likewise shown a very strong biblical grounding in the Old Testament. The remembrance the covenant people have with God is the basis of all their remembrances.

The use of some words that can be translated into memory in New Testament also shows the active sense of the term "remember". Communities in the New Testament time preserved their social memory on Jesus' teachings through storytelling and continuous reinterpretation, and understood the story as active as Jesus himself had told them the story. Although storytellers might have different details from what really had happened, the core remains the same. The purpose of what we called informal controlled type of oral tradition is that they want to keep the message alive to their own context. Memory is still acting as a strong force in the preservation of the tradition of the New Testament communities. It is not considered as a mere recalling of something back from the past. It is kept to re-live and re-experience the teachings of Jesus and to make it actual to the present context.

The idea of remembrance in the New Testament leads us to the institution of the Eucharist which was celebrated to remember Jesus. Jesus himself institutes the command "to remember" in the Eucharist. Anamnesis is the heart of the Eucharist in which Jesus is present in the hearts and minds of the participants. We will further explore the importance of remembrance in the liturgy of the Eucharist in the fifth chapter.

The Eucharist is not a whole new tradition that Jesus created; it is indeed a continuation of remembrance expressed in the Passover meal. The past deliverance of Israel is retrieved for the present moment by making present the redemptive act by Christ, and they are to be remembered for the future. Jesus is the paschal lamb that is to be sacrificed on the cross, and his sacrifice is a unique one-time event that works forever.

In summary, we can say that the idea of remembrance in biblical understanding is always more than just a passive psychological understanding of recalling something back into the mind. The term "remember" is often followed by an action, both by God or Israel. The order to remember is a strong theme in the Old and the New Testament to remember the core of the tradition which is God's saving action towards God's people. In connection with the sin and guilt, God also remembers what happened in the past. When God remembers, it is usually connected with consequences. When past wrongs are not remembered anymore, it means that Israel is not being punished any longer and does not necessarily mean that God does not remember them.

Chapter Four

Towards a Theology of Remembrance

After analyzing the biblical foundation of remembrance, we will now see how theologians have used this term or idea in their theological explorations. We will investigate some theologians that might be able to answer our question on the role and understanding of remembrance in Christian theology and its relation with forgiveness and reconciliation. How do Christian theologians do their theology in relation to remembrance and forgiveness? What can they contribute to our current research?

In the light of the main question, this research will investigate three theologians that have contributed their theological analysis on the notion of remembrance and memory. These theologians are from different denominations and contexts. They will also have different approaches on looking at our main question. Despite their differences, they have something in common which is to find the meaning of memory and remembrance, mostly in the memory of Christ, for the life of the church, for forgiveness, and for healing. Their distinctive approaches will enrich our discussion on the topic.

Johan Baptist Metz, a Roman Catholic theologian, explores the notion of dangerous memory and its relation with the memory of Christ. Second, we will look at Alexander Schmemann, an Orthodox theologian who approaches the issue of communal memory from a liturgical perspective. Our third theologian is Miroslav Volf, a Protestant theologian who connects the ideas of memory and forgiveness and reconciliation. These are the theologians whose idea on memory and remembrance which we are going to analyze. After taking note of them individually, we will put them in a dialogue and evaluate how they can contribute to our own research question.

1. *Johann Baptist Metz: Memoria Passionis as Dangerous Memory*

Johan Baptist Metz, born in Auerbach, in Bayern, Germany on August 5, 1928, is a German Catholic theologian who is among the foremost of Post World War II theologians. He experienced the war when he was drafted into Hitler's Army in 1944 and was captured in 1945 and imprisoned in the United States. He then returned to Germany and studied philosophy and theology in his Roman Catholic tradition. He then became a student and colleague of Karl Rahner, one of the leading theologians of the twentieth century. He is also a good friend and colleague of Jürgen Moltmann, a leading German Protestant theologian who wrote the Theology of Hope, who later became the teacher of Miroslav Volf. Metz became a professor of Fundamental Theology at Westphalian Wilhelms University in Muenster, Germany, where he enjoys emeritus status.

What is the real issue in Metz's thinking and how can it contribute to our research? Metz raised an issue of "dangerous memory" in the wake of political theology. Metz's idea on "dangerous memory" has made an impact on the development of political theology because he thinks that theology should opt for remembering the suffering. The elaboration of dangerous memory, which we will explore later on, is an important part in our effort of building the foundation of remembering the suffering of the past. He thinks that theology should be sensitive to the questions of the world's suffering and thus be governed by "a *memoria passionis* which includes and emphasizes the suffering of the stranger-other, thereby taking them into consideration in determining one's own behavior."[1] Because the remembrance of the suffering of others is fundamental in Metz's theology, his work seems likely to make an important contribution to our research. However, before we begin the investigation on Metz's theology, we will first briefly look at his context and history because they also play an important role in his future ideas.

As a German-Catholic theologian, Metz's war experience and the story of the Holocaust[2] in German history have a major influence in

---

[1] Johann Baptist Metz and Jürgen Moltmann, *Faith and Future: Essays on Theology, Solidarity, and Modernity* (Maryknoll, New York: Orbis Books, 1995), viii.

[2] Metz prefers the use of the term Auschwitz instead of Holocaust because of the semantic confusion of the word. He says, "Today the word *holocaust* is very often mentioned in German newspapers, more or less every day, but no one would think of Auschwitz when he hears the word *holocaust*. They all think of the nuclear holocaust. What I tell them is that it is much easier to talk about the possible future catastrophe in which we are the victims, than to talk about a past catastrophe in which we were the actors." Johann Baptist Metz, "Communicating a Dangerous Memory" in *Love's Strategy: The Political Theology of Johann-Baptist Metz (Selection of Writings)*, ed. John K. Downing (Harrisburg: Trinity Press, LTD., 1999), 140. However for the purpose of continuity of this research we will still use the term Holocaust while bearing Metz' Auschwitz in mind.

his theological thinking. One of the experiences that shapes his life and theological experience happened during this time. In his own words he remembers,

> Toward the end of the Second World War, when I was sixteen years old, I was taken out of school and forced into the army. After a brief period of training at a base in Würzburg, I arrived at the front, which by that time had already crossed the Rhine into Germany. There were well over a hundred in my company, all of whom were very young. One evening the company commander sent me with a message to battalion headquarters. I wandered all night long through destroyed, burning villages and farms, and when in the morning I returned to my company I found only the dead, nothing but the dead, overrun by a combined bomber and tank assault. I could see only dead and empty faces, where the day before I had shared childhood fears and youthful laughter, I remember nothing but a wordless cry. Thus I see myself to this very day, and behind this memory all my childhood dreams crumble away.[3]

This particular experience has been central to Metz's theology of memory and God's role in suffering. The experience of suffering brought him to the search of justice and peace. In introducing Metz, Francis Schussler Fiorenza says, "The German experience with National Socialism, the Holocaust, and World War II provided the stimulus for their theology (speaking of Jürgen Moltmann and Metz) which proclaimed that the passion *for* God and *of* God is a passion for justice and peace."[4] This is the drive that encouraged Metz to propose his idea on political theology.

As a student and friend, Metz had a fruitful relationship with Karl Rahner. Metz sees Rahner's work as "the mystical biography of the ordinary, the average Christian person…in short it is the biographical theology of an expressly anti-biographical type."[5] He was very much influenced by Rahner in building his arguments based on fundamental theology and he continues one of Rahner's basis views on the correlation between human history and the history of salvation.[6] He also has a drive towards finding a more pastoral-focused theology. Metz attempts

---

[3] Johann Baptist Metz, *A Passion for God: The Mystical-Political Dimension of Christianity* trans. J. Matthew Ashley (New Jersey: Paulist Press, 1998), 2–3.
[4] Metz, *Faith and the Future*, foreword by Fiorenza, xi.
[5] Metz, *A Passion for God*, 103. Gaspar Martinez paraphrases Metz opinion on Rahner's theological life as "a conceptually summarized and condensed narrative of a life-story before God." in *Confronting the Mystery of God: Political, Liberation, and Public Theologies* (New York: Continuum, 2001), 5.
[6] See the part of Martinez' introduction of Metz theology in connection with Rahner, *Confronting the Mystery of God*, 21–24.

to give an answer to the emphasis on the spiritual nature of man of Rahner's theology.[7]

Almost every analysis made of the connection between the two theologians understands that Metz seemed to have developed further away from Rahner's transcendental approach in his later years. This progress comes as a result of the continuity in Rahner's view on the meaning of faith and the role of theology in context. Metz decided to go further when he found that Rahner's theology did not satisfy his quest for the place of theology in suffering. Ashley made an analysis of why Metz moves away from Rahner, "Metz is convinced that Rahner's transcendental theology was incapable of answering the question of suffering, that it could not overcome the strangling constraints of privatization that modernity had placed upon Christian faith and theology, that it could not give an account of the hope in the future that sustains Christian praxis, that, for all its talk of historicity it was, in the final analysis, ahistorical, idealist, even Gnostic. He left the transcendental paradigm because of its constitutional inability to meet the challenges of doing theology in a still (or post)modern world."[8] In Metz own words, he thinks that "Rahner's hesitation, indeed his refusal, to talk of a suffering God has something to do with his fundamental theological respect for the suffering and the history of suffering of humanity."[9] Metz understands this hesitation and decided to take Rahner's fundamental legacy as his own drive forward. He says, "Suffering unto God: for me this is the key phrase that summarizes Rahner's theological existence, in which he became, for me and for many others, not only a teacher but also a father in faith."[10] Metz then steps forward and uses the social and historical context as a basis in his theology.

One of Metz own writings that precisely describes his passion in doing theology is clearly stated in *Faith in History and Society*. He says,

> At the center of my theological interest in Christianity is the questionable religious-political treatment of the so-called 'theodicy question', the

---

[7] For a complete reading of how Metz develops his theology away from Karl Rahner, read Roger Dick Johns, *Man in the World: The Theology of Johannes Baptist Metz* (Missoula, Montana: American Academy of Religion, 1976). See also James Matthew Ashley, *Interruptions: Mysticism, Politics, and Theology in the Work of Johann Baptist Metz* (Notre Dame, Indiana: University of Notre Dame Press, 1998). Since Metz goes further in developing his theology in later years, the analysis of Ashley on Metz is more up-to-date than Johns'.

[8] Ashley, *Interruptions*, viii.

[9] Metz, *A Passion for God*, 116.

[10] Metz, *A Passion for God*, 119.

question of God in light of the experience of suffering. Autobiographically, this is all of a piece with the very drastic experiences of the war in my youth so that I slowly became aware of my Christian theological situation as a 'post Auschwitz' one and finally increasingly realized that the condition of suffering and oppression in the world poses a decisive question to us Christians. For me, Christianity deals with the foundation capable of supporting a universal solidarity and unconditional justice, i.e. a solidarity and justice even in the face of the victims and victors of history, for those burdened ones for whom we live and build our paradise but whose fate no passionate struggle of the living can raise a finger to change. The Christian belief in a God, before whom past suffering does not disappear subjectless into the abyss of an anonymous evolution, in my estimate vouches for the fixed standard of a universal liberation, of the ability-to-be-a subject of all humanity, in the midst of unceasing conflict. Where our socially accepted wisdom lets itself be led exclusively by the imaginary totality of an unjust evolution, not only does 'God' become unthinkable, but consequently every selfless interest in a universal liberation also disappears. All dialectics of the emancipation of humanity in the end proves itself to be a trick of an indifferent evolution if there does not exist a God who interrupts the faceless and apathy producing continuity in nature and before whom even the past is not fixed. This God is, for me, the trustworthy foundation of any universal solidarity and justice—not just now, by the decree of the spirit of the age, but throughout the history of humanity.[11]

We see that Metz's central concerns are the question of suffering; his own context; the question of justice, solidarity, and liberation; the place of victims and perpetrators; the history and future; and the place of God in the history of humanity. These questions can be answered by challenging them in the real historical situation. We will follow these discussions later on as we try to understand Metz's idea of dangerous memories.

Metz's approach of fundamental practical theology gives an important role for memory in theology. We have to keep in mind that Metz's first intention is not to serve the world, but to find answers to why suffering happened and what the right response towards it is as Christians. He sees this, especially, coming from his experience of Auschwitz. This one event has influenced him, along with the influence of his dialogue

---

[11] Johann Baptist Metz, *Faith in History and Society: Toward a Practical Fundamental Theology*, trans. David Smith (New York: The Seabury Press, 1980), 51. Many would agree that this book is continuous with his earlier work *Theology of the World*, trans. William Glen-Doepel (New York: Seabury Press, 1969). *Theology of the World* however is also a collection of Metz's essays concerning the issue of Christian identity and relevance in the world with crisis of faith and belief.

with his teacher, and later on with some of the philosophers and other German theologians. He was also influenced by the process of the second Vatican council in which he was very engaged as a participant. Thus, our analysis on Metz cannot move far from these experiences. It is not surprising that Metz thinks also that some of the criticisms Marxist shared are true for Christians.

However, we have to be aware of the difficulties in reading Metz, since he never intended to build a systematical approach towards his own questions, let alone our specific question in this research. In reading Metz, one cannot expect to find ready answers to the questions he raised. His intention is to build awareness in theology by asking important issues rather than to setting up a systematical political theological system. In investigating Metz's theological development James Matthew Ashley says, "Metz's thought has been driven and "interrupted" at key junctures by a deep and disturbing consciousness of God's presence to the world of late modernity."[12] Therefore, Metz is building his theology as a kind of interruption towards the stability of the present, or in Metz's words, that he is "teaching fundamental theology and seeks to explicate the faith in a manner corresponding to the present historical modes of human understanding."[13]

We will also find it difficult to trace Metz's consistency in building his arguments because his works are scattered in collections of essays and articles which were dedicated to specific audiences. He did not provide a clear systematic approach on one specific issue for the sake of a specific reader. This is the main difficulty in constructing a so-called 'Metz's theology'.[14] All Metz writings are scattered and has taken so many different forms for different audiences and purposes—or as J.A. Colombo calls it as "a sort of theological guerilla."[15] Therefore we have to be really careful in reading Metz's works before drawing to any conclusion.

We will mainly base our investigation with Metz on his major work *Faith, History and Society* with the help of some selected essays and some researches that have been made on Metz. This means we will not

---

[12] Ashley, *Interruptions*, xii.
[13] Metz, *Love's Strategy*, 13.
[14] For more explanation on his style see Ashley, *Interruptions, xii*. Ashley says, "He intends to interrupt social norms and ideals (progress, efficiency, quantification of the norms that define what the Frankfurt School thinkers called "instrumental reason") that could operate quite well—indeed better—without concrete, living human subjects."
[15] J. A. Colombo, *An Essay on Theology and History: Studies in Pannenberg, Metz, and the Frankfurt School* (Atlanta: Georgia: American Academy of Religion, 1990), 157.

investigate the historical development of Metz's theology before he wrote the particular book; rather, we will try to understand the main ideas in it. In this part we will first try to understand his view on the Church, and his political theology as a consequence of it. Subsequently, his thoughts on *memoria passionis* will be explored more intensively. This section will look into what Metz's idea is concerning 'dangerous memory' and the implementation of memory of the suffering. In the section that will follow next, bearing our research question in mind, we will try to connect him to Bruce Morrill's analysis who tried to communicate Metz's idea of dangerous memory through Alexander Schmemann's liturgical theology.

1.1 The Bourgeois Church, Middle Class Religion, and Post-Bourgeois World

Metz's theology is very close to the history of humanity and the challenges in it. In other words, his theology was never far from his own culture and society. He is a citizen of a developed society in Western Europe, yet was raised in a rural small Catholic town in Bavaria.[16] He thinks that the Church has lost its messianic meaning in this privatistic society of Western Europe. He made this point after reflecting on his own context which includes not only his own Catholic Church, but all the churches of the middle class citizens in what was then West Germany.

He sees that the Church in his own context has become the place for people with a stable economical condition. This condition allows people to become content with their life and future because they already have a secure future in terms of financial capability, thus leaving no reason for a strong hope for a better future. Metz is building his questions as a kind of interruption for people who get too comfortable in their own lives to look at the suffering around them. He wants the Church in a middle class society, which does not lack in material things, to be aware of, and attentive towards, the story of the suffering around it.

The privatized middle class society tends to claim that it has understood the teaching of the Church about love by interpreting solidarity towards others by mere donation without being emotionally attached. Therefore, he poses the question, "Do we share the sufferings

---

[16] Martinez made an interesting short historical introduction on Metz's context which is Bundesrepublik Deutschland/BRD (and later The Republic of Germany), *Confronting the Mystery of God*, 25–38.

of others, or do we just believe in sharing with them and remain, under the cloak of a belief in 'sympathy' as apathetic as ever?"[17] He thinks that the Church—and theology—in his part of the world should have a change of heart, especially in putting more attention towards suffering in other parts of the world.[18] These are the characteristics of a bourgeois community and Church that has lost its messianic significance. However, Metz thinks that the reason why the Church has lost its messianic meaning lies deeper than merely the economical surface.

Metz looks at the Enlightenment as the source of the reduction that brought theology in the modern age into a crisis. There are five central elements of the middle class religion that were initiated by the Enlightenment that he criticized. The first one is a privatistic reduction that tends to put religion into the private sector. The privatization triggered by the Enlightenment has played a main role in the existence of a private middle class citizen that increased individual freedom. One of the dangers of this situation according to Metz is, "everything that does not conform to calculating reason and the laws of profit and success is left to individual and private choice."[19] Second, when people consider religion as a private individual matter and tend to see things from their exchange values, then the traditional values such as friendliness, thankfulness, attention to the dead, mourning, and so on will be losing its power for they do not offer economical return.[20] The third is the crisis of authority; when tradition is challenged, then the authority of the Church on freedom, justice and suffering, all of which have no exchange value, will be lost.

The fourth element is the crisis of (metaphysical) reason, since reasoning becomes the property of the people that have education and property. A new elite has emerged that developed "a praxis of control of nature in the interest of the market."[21] Fifth, the crisis of metaphysical reason will bring religion in a state of crisis. Metz thinks, "If metaphysical reason, which is divorced from the subject, loses its

---

[17] Metz, *Love Strategy*, 19.

[18] Metz says, "The crisis (or sickness) of life in the Church is not just that the change of heart is not taking place or not taking place quickly enough, but that the absence of this change of heart is being further concealed under the appearance of a merely believed-in faith....Do we show real love, or do we just believe in love and under the cloak of belief in love remain the same egoists and conformists we have always been?" in Johann Baptist Metz, *The Emergent Church* (New York: Crossroad, 1981), 3.

[19] Metz, *Faith in History and Society*, 37.

[20] Metz, *Faith in History and Society*, 38.

[21] Metz, *Faith in History and Society*, 43.

(political) innocence in the light of Enlightenment, then religion, which also makes use of this abstract metaphysical reason to justify its universal claim to validity, at once becomes suspect."²² At the end of his description of the effect of the Enlightenment, Metz thinks that this specific stance in the world has brought religion in the private sphere of the middle-class. Thus, a political theology as Metz proposes, should establish the true values of the subject within the actual social circumstances of its day.

In later years Metz develops this thinking further and is of the opinion that this middle class society is now standing at the edge of history and that we are now entering a post-bourgeois, post-capitalistic society. He thinks that the transition of Western Europe and Western Christianity from being the center of the big story of modernity towards a postmodern world has created confusion and a conflict of ideas. Metz thinks that this is the time for a second Enlightenment after the Enlightenment. This is where he introduces his idea about the change of heart of the Church and again puts out the question that Martin Luther once asked: "…where feelings and forebodings emerge of one age passing away and being replaced by another age marked by radical change, there breaks through again in a new way the original Reformation question: How can we attain to grace?"²³ Metz is again trying to challenge the middle class religion when entering the post-bourgeois society.

Metz sees a chance for Christianity to play a role in the situation caused by a post-bourgeois society. Christianity has to move beyond the bourgeois order with the help of its resources. In order to do this, the Church should be able to give voice suffering by whatever name as an interruption to the world that surrounds her. Doing this will lay the foundation of a practical theology. Theology should be linked to the context where it is at and at the same time should be based on Scripture. This is where Metz develops his idea of political theology.

1.2 *Political Theology*

We have to 'remember' that Metz's main question is to find out what the place of suffering in theology is. He thinks that the Church should

---

²² Metz, *Faith in History and Society*, 44.
²³ Johann Baptist Metz, "Toward the Second Reformation the Future of Christianity in a Postbourgeois World" in *Cross Currents* (Springs 1981), 86. See also the comparison of how Metz and Küng deal with the problem of post-bourgeois society in Rudolf J. Siebert, "Towards a Critical Catholicism: Küng and Metz part II" in *Anglican Theological Review* (January 1983), 1–13.

not be a place that gives further comfort for those who are already comfortable in their middle class society. The Church should be able to stimulate people of faith to be more sensitive to the suffering around them. Metz understands politics in a very wide sense of the word which includes both the situational context and the historical realm. As such, he thinks that the Church should be more aware of the political realm around her.

Such a political awareness is very close to faith and theology. Metz thinks that theology cannot remain objective and be uninvolved in real life situations. The Church needs to give reflection and to raise her voice to bringing God's will in the world. This idea comes from Metz's understanding of what faith is all about. He says,

> The faith of Christians is a praxis in history and society which is understood as solidaristic hope in the God of Jesus as the God of the living and the dead, who calls all to be subjects in God's presence. In this thoroughly apocalyptically expectant praxis (of discipleship) Christians prove themselves in historical struggle for men and women: they commit themselves to a reality in which all persons become subjects in solidarity, and in this praxis they resist the danger of a creeping evolutionary dissolution of the history of men and women as subjects, as well as the danger of a negation of the individual in view of a new, as it were, post-bourgeois image of the person.[24]

This means that Metz believes that faith is about a praxis that brings solidaristic hope to a society with individualistic trends and premises. Faith is never far from historical reality, and yet should be able to give hope and spread God's voice in the world as it is. This has a consequence for theology. He says, "If it is not to remain at the level of a pure assertion that is suspected of ideology, theology must be able to define and call upon a *praxis* in which Christians can break through the complex social, historical and psychological conditions governing history and society. What is needed, then, is a praxis of faith in mystical and political imitation."[25] What Metz means is that the praxis of Christian life lies in mystical (read: prayer) and political (read: action) imitation of Christ life. Theology should be able to support this praxis of faith. Thus, what Metz says by *imitatio Christi* means the remembrance of Christ, not only by recalling his story and action into our mind, but by remembering him in such a way that it shapes our life and actions.

---

[24] Metz, Faith in History and Society, 73.
[25] Metz, Faith in History and Society, 76, 77.

So what then *is* political theology?[26] Metz thinks that political theology is "a critical corrective to contemporary theology's tendency to concentrate on the private individual, and at the same time as a positive attempt to formulate the eschatological message in the circumstances of our present society."[27] Political theology, as fundamental theology, is aimed to "reassess the relation between religion and society, between the Church and public society, between eschatological faith and social life, not in a pre-critical sense, in view of identifying these two realities, but in a post-critical sense, the sense of 'second thoughts.'"[28] Thus political theology functions as critical attitude towards society. It is a practical fundamental theology, which means that it is related with the concrete human history of the Church and society; and also because it is guided by the Christian message through biblical narrative, and thus always takes the side of the oppressed and the suffering persons and people. Political theology is needed to bring God's hope in the midst of suffering in the world.

This is also why Metz is very much in support of liberation theology. He thinks that a theology of liberation is dealing with real issues that bring hope in the midst of crisis. It is a theology that comes out of real contexts and shows how dynamic theology is. For him, theology of liberation does not deal with the effort to free us from poverty, disease or powerlessness, rather it targets the opposite: it frees us from greed and the will to power. This is where the Church can take part in the process of a change of heart. When the Church acts as a community with a change of heart, they can be re-enforced and regain their freshness and not getting sucked into the post-bourgeois society.

What Metz has brought to the fore may not be new to some Protestant thinkers, but it opened up a possible future for further developments in Catholic theology. Roger Dick Johns calls Metz's early writings a breakthrough and says that Metz "attempts to move the center of consideration in Catholic theology from abstract metaphysical epistemology and ontology to the socio-political reality

---

[26] Dorothee Sölle defines political theology as "a theological hermeneutic, which, in distinction from a theology that interprets reality from an ontological or existentialist point of view, holds open a horizon of interpretation in which politics is understood as the comprehensive and decisive sphere in which Christian truth should become praxis." in *Political Theology*, trans. John Shelley (Philadelphia: Fortress Press, 1974), 59. Political theology was not a new idea in theology when Metz came into the field, but he is one of the theologians that give a strong systematic foundation for it.

[27] Metz, *Love's Strategy*, 24.

[28] Metz, *Love's Strategy*, 29.

of man's incarnate existence in the world."[29] Metz has given a critique of his church towards a greater engagement with the social political world.

In the years after *Faith in History and Society*, Metz showed that his view on political theology further developed. It started as a "sort of corrective, as a corrective to situation-less theologies, to all theologies that are idealistically closed-off systems or that continually barricade themselves behind theological systems."[30] Metz wanted theology to be sensitive to the context and formulated a theological reflection on it. The development of political theology has since developed and now must face three new situations: the influence of social and practical questions in systematic theology; the awareness of theology after Auschwitz; and the development of theology outside Europe. Metz shows that theology has to develop and cope with whatever contexts it is in.

However, this seemingly always changing political theology leads us to the question what is the basis of political theology? Should theology always cope and adapt to its context? What is the foundation that gives certainty to this sort of contextual-practical theology? How can we be sure that the Church is not voicing a mere reactive message but a truly meaningful message?

Metz believes that Christians should be aware of the social-political surroundings where they belong so that they would be able to put their faith into praxis and raise their voice wherever they see suffering. Theology should be present in the historical world and it should always bring the Christian message into modern world by becoming a public witness of a dangerous memory. The basis for doing this is the memory of Christ's love and this is why memory is dangerous as well as liberating. The Church's engagement in social political contexts should always be based on the memory of God's liberating power and unconditional love in Jesus Christ. This is our entry point in the investigation towards Metz's exploration of 'dangerous memory'.

1.3 *Memory and Time*

Memory is an important category in theology. One of Metz's main concerns about this private and bourgeois church is the loss of the sense of memory and history. It is lost because private society tends only to remember those things that bring meaning for themselves. The conse-

---

[29] Johns, *Man in the World*, 2. Johns correctly analyzes Metz's early theological development as a result of relating Thomas Aquinas' idea of transcendental view of human to contemporary social development.

[30] Metz, *A Passion for God*, 23. Metz wrote this in an opening article of the book in 1991.

quence of this kind of society is the forgetfulness of human suffering, the past misery and the voiceless victims. Metz rejects religion that also falls into this modern concept of time and history.[31] The way to avoid this narcissistic-self-centered religion that is characterized by forgetfulness is by having memory available that brings the narrative and solidarity with those who suffer to the fore.

Metz builds his concept of memory on three basic elements:[32] 1) memory as a way of knowing God; 2) memory that demands your action (dangerous); and 3) memory as rooted in the Christian memory of the life of Jesus. These three basic elements are supported by the two notions of 'narrative' as a way of preserving the memories and of 'solidarity' as a result of the memories that are being shared.[33] When these elements are combined, memory is a strong resource for doing theology. In fact Metz says that Christian theology becomes theological because "it tries to preserve the dangerous memory of the messianic God, the God of the resurrection of the dead and judgment."[34]

Christianity has a memory that is shaped by a historical remembrance and yet still gives the truth and solidarity with those who suffer. This is a memory that gives hope through remembrance and narrative. Metz explains this memory and gives the theological foundation for it,

> The Church must understand and justify itself as the public witness and bearer of the tradition of a dangerous memory of freedom in the 'systems' of our emancipative society. This thesis is based on memory as the fundamental form of expression of Christian faith and on the central and special importance of freedom in that faith. In faith, Christians accomplish the *memoria passionis, mortis et ressurectionis Jesu Christi*. In faith, they remember the testament of Christ's love, in which the Kingdom of God appeared among men by initially establishing that kingdom between

---

[31] See Metz, "God Against the Myth of the Eternity of Time," in *The End of Time: The Provocation Talking about God*, eds. Tiemo Rainer Peters and Claus Urban, trans. J. Matthew Ashley (New Jersey: Paulist Press, 2004), 26–27. Although this article was written in much later stage of Metz work (1998), in it he briefly describes the recent challenges on the concept of dangerous memory.

[32] Michon Marie Matthiesen, "Narrative of Suffering: Complementary Reflections of Theological Anthropology in Johann Metz and Elie Wiesel," *Religion & Literature* Vol. 18, No. 2 (Summer, 1986), 47–63. Matthiesen compares Metz's ideas with Wiesel and found similarities in their ideas of memory.

[33] See Metz, *Faith in History and Society*, 229–230. He says, "It is in this solidarity that memory and narrative (of salvation) acquire their specific mystical and political praxis. Without solidarity, memory and narrative cannot become practical categories of theology. In the same way, without memory and narrative, solidarity cannot express its practical humanizing form."

[34] Metz, *Love's Strategy*, 52.

> men, by Jesus' confession of himself as the one who was on the side of the oppressed and rejected and by his proclamation of the coming kingdom of God as the liberating power of unconditional love… It is therefore a dangerous and at the same time liberating memory that oppresses and questions the present because it reminds us not of some open future, but precisely this future and because it compels Christians constantly to change themselves so that they are able to take this future into account.[35]

There are several key items that we can grasp from Metz's statement. First, the Church is a community of remembrance by acting as public witness in a historical context and at the same time it is also the bearer of the remembrance of Jesus. Faith also has an important role in keeping the memory of Christ—and in Metz's term it is always connected with praxis. This memory of Christ can be liberating and dangerous at the same time. What does it really mean? What is dangerous memory exactly; and what does 'dangerous' refer to?

Before we can answer this, we have to first explore what Metz thinks about memory. Metz divides memory into two parts. *The first one* is the common memory of the past that is not seriously dealt with if and when people only remember positive things from the past. This kind of memory has become the primary model of memory since the Enlightenment. In the logic of the Enlightenment, our history has no beginning and no end because everything goes as it is. He sees that the Enlightenment tries to demythologize the story of God by seeking help from modern sciences to be critical about God. This in the end could lessen the sense of mystery in God and even detach God from it.

Metz understands Nietzsche's criticism in the term 'death of God' as a message about time. He criticizes Nietzsche's idea of 'god is dead', because that implies that the world is a world without a beginning or an end, no memory, no identity, and no subject. When there is no God, there will be no beginning and no end; time has becomes boundless and without a goal or purpose.[36] As a result of this kind of evolutionary thinking, history has no subject. In this evolution history will keep on developing without a subject.[37] In this way time has been regarded as something that runs its own course without a subject. Thus time runs its course because it simply is as it is; no one can interfere and it does not have any specific purpose. If modern humans continue to live with

---

[35] Metz, *Faith in History and Society*, 89–90.
[36] See Metz, *Faith in History and Society*, 109–110, and how Metz explains Nietzsche in Peters, *The End of Time*, 29–31. See also Metz, *Faith and Future*, 75.
[37] Metz, *Love's Strategy*, 75.

the idea of time without a final end, then everything will be relative, and even subjects will have no more meaning. "No finale could be ever as bad as no finale at all."[38] Humanity's biggest fear is not that the end is coming, but that it should have no end at all.[39]

The danger of enlightenment rationality in evolution is that everything can be explained and yet does not necessarily have an origin. When time has no subject, time only serves as a process; it is continuous, with no end and no beginning. If religion also falls into this view, then God will have no place anymore. When this happens technology will become a master of itself, therefore no subject is needed. Time will continue without a subject. Because it has no subject, a cultural amnesia will be inevitable.

This crisis attacks the subject of history which is God. "It is…clear from this that the so-called historical crisis of the identity of Christianity is not a crisis of the contents of faith, but rather a crisis of the Christian subjects and institutions which deny themselves the practical meaning of those contents, the imitation of Christ."[40]

Metz thinks that modern humans only have future and success oriented lives. Combined with a subject-less history, the past suffering will soon be forgotten because it has no place anymore in history. This kind of selective memory will create a "false consciousness of our past and opiate for our present."[41] The voice of suffering and the victims will be forgotten. This is the danger of the first type of memory.

The second type of memory is a kind of memory that is not passive, but one that makes demands on us.[42] This understanding of memory is the basis of faith praxis. It connects Jesus' love in *memoria passionis* to the reality of suffering in our own context. Memory in this sense will have a transformative power that supports the voice of the suffering. This memory reminds us of the reality of suffering in human history because it interrupts and makes us realize the danger of the first memory.

In Metz's thoughts therefore, the story of Jesus is the dangerous memory in Christianity. It is a story about the death and resurrection of Jesus Christ which means a story of suffering and triumph. The Church has been a public witness of this memory in history. This kind of memory becomes dangerous because it demands our response based

---

[38] Metz, *Faith and the Future*, 86.
[39] Metz, *Love's Strategy*, 146.
[40] Metz, *Faith and the Future*, 165.
[41] Metz, *Faith in History and Society*, 109.
[42] Metz, *Love's Strategy*, 7–8.

on Christ's love. In the following section we will see how Metz develops his theology of memory and how it becomes fruitful for our research of remembrance as a way towards forgiveness and reconciliation.

1.4 Dangerous Memory: Memoria Passionis

Dangerous memory is the memory that asks us to remember suffering and act upon it. Christianity's dangerous memory plays an important role in the development of Metz's theology. He thinks that this kind of memory "can have a very decisive ecclesiological importance in defining the Church as the public vehicle transmitting a dangerous memory in the systems of social life; memory is of importance in our dynamic understanding of dogmatic faith; it is the basic concept in a theological theory of history and society as such and at the same time the basic concept of a theology in the age of criticism as a category of the salvation of identity."[43] This concept of dangerous memory also provides us with an ecclesiological basis for the Church.

Dangerous memory is a significant foundation in political theology as fundamental theology. However, the memory will not become involved directly in a socio-political sense. The memory suffering that Metz uses will serve as a basis of theological action. Metz says, "Memory of suffering in the Christian sense, does not merge with the darkness of social and political arbitraries, but creates a social and political conscience in the interest of another's suffering. It prevents the privatization and internalization of suffering and the reduction of its social and political dimension."[44] Its memory of suffering will not be used as a political agenda; rather it is used as a guideline of the heart for political actions.

Now the question is, exactly why is it dangerous, and what makes it dangerous? Metz was never really clear about the term except that he gives examples of what it is. However here is a quote that he uses might be able to explain the term 'dangerous,'

> Remembering the past can let dangerous thoughts arise and established society appears to be afraid of the subversive content of these memories. Remembering is one way to become detached from the 'given facts', a way which, for a brief moment, breaks through the almighty power of things as they are. Memory summons back to mind past screams as well as past hopes.[45]

---

[43] Metz, *Faith in History and Society*, 184.
[44] Metz, *Love's Strategy*, 13.
[45] Metz, "Politische Theologie", 287, as quoted by Colombo, *An Essay on Theology*

Memory can be dangerous because we are disconnected from the history of the winners and we are enabled to think about the past experiences and reflect on it. It is a sort of self-realization of the present by looking at the past and it is to decide what step to take for the future. It is a chance of stepping back from stability of the society and looking into what happened in the broader picture. This action could lead to a revolt against what is happening in the present. It could evoke a feeling of discomfort and thus it is dangerous for the stability of the present.

The fundamental dangerous memory of Christianity is based on the *memoria passionis*. Through the *memoria passionis* we can remember the life, suffering, death, and resurrection of Christ, that God promises redemption of all suffering. God is the subject of history; there is hope for the suffering. This is why Metz thinks that theology should defend hope (1 Pet. 3:15). What kind of hope should be defended by theology? He says, "It is the solidarity of hope in the God of the living and the dead, who calls all men to be his subjects."[46]

Metz believes that there should be no *memoria resurrectionis* that is separated from *memoria passionis*. Therefore the memory of suffering is not a solution, rather "The Christian memory of suffering is in its theological implications an anticipatory memory: it intends the anticipation of a particular future of man as a future for the suffering, the hopeless, the oppressed, the injured and the useless of the earth."[47] In analyzing Metz on his idea of dangerous memory, Flora Keshkegian says that remembering serves as a reminder of suffering. It is not itself the solution, but it serves as a resource towards it. She understands Metz's memories as to "provide support for resistance and hope."[48] These memories will be preserved by the Church as community of believers, and it could be the basis of their faith in praxis of solidarity.

This kind of spirituality, one that holds dangerous memory of human sufferings, will result in demands of action. The praxis of faith will make theology to be in solidarity with the victims. After memory and narrative, solidarity is an important category of the Christian message. Martinez rightly sums up Metz's understanding of solidarity as "the affirmation and support of the subject as such under historical circumstances, especially under the threat of suffering and destruction

---

and History, 187.

[46] Metz, *Faith in History and Society*, 80.

[47] Metz, *Faith in History and Society*, 117.

[48] Flora A. Keshkegian, *Redeeming Memories: A Theology of Healing and Transformation* (Nashville: Abingdon Press, 2000), 137.

of that subject. It is a practical category, a category that affirms its truth in action and that, in doing so, brings into existence the power of memory and narrative through mystical political praxis."[49] This solidarity is for everyone and it "...extends to those who have been overcome and left behind in the march of progress. It includes the dead. Indeed, the theological category of solidarity reveals its mystical and universal aspect above all in its memory of solidarity with the dead."[50] It is an extension of hope for everyone.

This solidarity that brings hope is also about remembering God. Metz says, "The stories of setting out and hope, stories of suffering and persecution, stories of resistance and resignation, are at the center of the Christian understanding of God. *Remembering* and *telling* are, therefore, not just for entertainment; they are basic forms of Christian language about God."[51] Thus, solidarity that is coming from the memory of God is also an action of telling the story about God.

Our eschatological hope and solidarity in God will not allow us to be individualistic. We have to be one with the others in the memory of suffering. In later years, Metz also stresses the importance of remembrance of suffering of others. This means that we have to emphasize the remembrance of other's suffering and not those of ours alone.

One of the major events that influenced Metz in his thinking about the life of the Church as a community of remembrance is the event of the Holocaust. He says that "Christian theology after Auschwitz must—at long last—be guided by the insight that Christians can form, and sufficiently understand, their identity only in the face of the Jews."[52] Like many other German theologians that lived during the Second World War, Metz is distraught by the fact that so many people in Germany did not realize that the suffering was taken place. He thinks that this event changed the life of the Church and that theology should always be connected with Auschwitz. It "directs theology away from the singular of 'history' to the plural of 'histories of sufferings' which cannot be idealistically explained but rather can only be remembered with a practical intention."[53] This could also be a strong point and a weak point of Metz that we will again touch on later. He thinks that because of this event, Germany have no more right to criticize Israel.[54]

---

[49] Martinez, *Confronting the Mystery*, 67.
[50] Metz, *Faith in History and Society*, 231.
[51] Metz, *Faith and the Future*, 52.
[52] Metz, *Faith and the Future*, 38.
[53] Metz, *Faith and the Future*, 139.
[54] Metz, *Faith and the Future*, 48.

Metz also talks about eschatology in his theology of time. Metz wants to avoid the being of time with neither a subject nor an end. He wants to show that God is the subject of time, and that history has an end when God wills it. In the end, God will bring justice to all. God is the ultimate justice. However, this does not mean that we become a passive being because when we are talking of God we are also talking about justice, and we are called to implement it.

When God is the subject of history, then time also has an expiration date. There is a biblical message about the end of time, and God is the author. Time has a finale.[55] Metz stresses that in the end God will end time. However, this does not mean a passive remembering and waiting for God and do nothing on the suffering because God will take care of it in the end; instead, we have to be active because there is limited time. There is an end to this time, thus we have to go on and move forward.

Christianity believes that God is the subject of world history. He says, "Christian theology recalls the God of Jesus' passion as the subject of the universal history of suffering, and in the same movement refuses to give political shape to this subject and enthrone it politically."[56] Whenever a world ruler, a certain class, a group, or a race tries to become the subject, Christian memory must oppose that and unmask its political idolatry.

But when it comes to remembering, what should we do? How can people remember? Metz believes that the task of remembering should be done on the communal level. In explaining how dogma can be theologically responsible, he is of the opinion that the church congregation has to take up the task. He says, "The process of remembering…cannot exclusively or even primarily take place in the individual. As formulations of the collective memory, dogmas may therefore have an entirely new part to play here. They can, as it were, compel me to recollect in the present something that I cannot grasp or realize in the narrow basis of my own personal experience."[57] It is also clear that for him the Church is the ideal community of remembrance. He calls the Church "an individual institution of social-critical freedom", "the bearer of dangerous memory within modernization process", "a community of memory and narrative in discipleship of Jesus, who

---

[55] Metz, *Faith and the Future*, 79–86.
[56] Metz, *Faith and the Future*, 15.
[57] Metz, *Faith in History and Society*, 202. Metz was not specifically speaking about remembering the suffering here, he was actually talking about dogma. However, he suggests that society as a whole and not as individuals has the responsibility to remember.

focused first on other people's suffering, and speaks of a Church of compassion."[58] This means that the Church holds an important role in preserving the memory of suffering. It is the main player in Metz's theology as a whole; the one that will keep the *memoria passionis* as the main drive of the political theology.

1.5 Memory of Suffering?

Metz's theology serves as causing interruptions towards a stability that only benefits the winner of history. He wants to maximize the function of the Church as God's mediator to the world, the preserver of the narrative of *memoria passionis*. He wants to challenge the development of knowledge of time that has no end. He wants to put God back in the big picture of history. Time does have an end, and it brings hope for the suffering.

What Metz has done here has contributed to our own search for the question of memory of the past suffering. The memory of the past is remembered in such a way that it encourages us to take action. He emphasizes the importance of the Church as a community of remembrance. This provided invaluable support for our research.

However, we have some questions and worries that we need to address to his thought. One of our critiques towards Metz is with regard to his explanation of how political theology can enter the political realm without entering practical politics. Theology should indeed be political but we have to be careful that it is not the first intention of doing theology. We do have memories of how Church tends to become corruptible with political power.

Metz did not seem to come to any specific conclusion. His remembrance came as a message towards a forgetful society. He wants to interrupt the life of the Church which he considered to be a bourgeois church. Thus, we suspect that the real intention of Metz was actually the awareness of the Church to the context around her. Metz wants the Church to be more sensitive towards the cry of the suffering and act accordingly. However, due to the nature of his essays and papers, he did not clarify his ideas into an elaborate systematic theological system.

The memory of Jesus is not *only* about suffering. What we remember in Jesus is his life, teaching, death and resurrection. The demand to remember the suffering alone is not complete when it is not being accompanied by the *memoria ressurectionis*. How can we remember the

---

[58] Metz, "God against the Myth", 36.

suffering and at the same time remember the glory of Christ? Metz did not provide satisfactory answers to this question.

We also did not find any sufficient explanation concerning the role of forgiveness in the context of suffering. It seems that Metz missed the point of victims and perpetrators in the context of suffering, and this is also why Metz is of the opinion that Germany has no right to tell Israel what to do because of what happened in the past during the Holocaust. However, how far do we have to go with the memory of suffering? Does it have an end? Does dangerous memory have reconciliative power? When we speak about dangerous memory, do we have a specific role of perpetrators and victims or does suffering happen without actors? These are important questions for our research because when dangerous memory encourages praxis of faith, who are the ones that get encouraged? Are victims and perpetrators being called by the same memory and produce the same action? Does dangerous memory play any role or function for them? Is there a chance that this *memoria passionis* is also a *memoria reconciliatio*? These are the questions that we bring to the next part of this chapter.

1.6 *Flora Keshkegian: Redeeming Memories for Healing and Transformation*

Before we come to Schmemann, there is one theologian that will be able to bridge Metz's ideas and function as an interlude before we analyze our next theologian, which is Alexander Schmemann. One of the theologians who has developed Metz's idea of memory of suffering is a feminist theologian Flora A Keshkegian.[59] Keshkegian contributes to Metz's demand to remember because she is developing her theology from the perspective of the victims. Her contribution in our research is the idea that the act of remembering should be done for the healing and transformation of the victims. She thinks that remembrance is intended for healing. Her idea of redeeming memory contributes to

---

[59] Flora A. Keshkegian, *Redeeming Memories*. The author is a feminist theologian who is now a Faculty Ombudsperson at Brown University and an ordained Episcopal Church minister. She was once assistant professor of theology at the Episcopal Theological Seminary of the Southwest. Keshkegian comes from an Armenian genocide survivor family. She connects her personal experience with the quest of looking for a redeeming place for victims in memory. Her latest work is *Time for Hope: Practices for Living in Today's World* (New York: Continuum, 2006). Here she sees the problem of hope as located in the dominant western Jewish and Christian narrative of linear time. It focuses on an eschatological aspect and is the continuation of her first book. *Time for Hope* sees God as the subject, which also connected with Metz's idea of God as subject of time.

our research in moving forward from Metz's theology. She points out what is lacking in Metz and suggests that we should see memory as a resource of liberating power.

Keshkegian comes from an Armenian American family. She was taught to remember the identity of suffering that Armenian people had experienced during the administration of Sultan Abdul Hamid in the 19th century and the genocide perpetrated by the Turkish government during World War I. She felt that the obligation to remember is becoming more complicated and wanted to find out what it means to remember. She wanted to know how this memory of past hurt could become a redemptive memory. Her personal experience led her writing in search of "the centrality of remembering for Christian witness, practice, and identity, and seeks to reformulate what is meant by remembering."[60] She is determined to do this from the perspective of the victims with "a Christian feminist political theology"[61] approach.

A question we are left with after Metz is: can the memory of suffering be healed in the memory of Christ's suffering? Metz did not answer this. Metz was trying to remind people who are ignorant about the suffering of others to do something about it. Metz was acting as an interpreter for his church and his context. The real message that Metz wants to bring is that he wants people to be more critical about their own context. He wants the Church, especially, to be actively engaged in the real life situation whenever suffering is happening. The Church should not be silenced, and should raise her voice against injustice and suffering. But the question remains, how can the memory of suffering help heal the wounds of past hurt? Is it really the answer for healing suffering?

Keshkegian tries to answer this question by stepping beyond Metz's argument. She thinks that Metz's idea of *memoria passionis* is not sufficient. Remembering Jesus means to remember the whole story of the life of Jesus. The cross is an event that should be remembered from the perspective of Jesus' life, death, and resurrection. This is why she has some sort of uneasiness about Metz because he tends to remember and re-enforce the memory of suffering without having the intention of solving it as such. The memory of Jesus and the story of the cross

---

[60] Keshkegian, *Redeeming Memories*, 26.

[61] Keshkegian, *Redeeming Memories*, 17. This approach can be seen throughout the book which she argues would be able to support that "redeeming memories lead to remembering the truth and practice of Christianity, especially in relation to histories of domination." She also analyzes some feminist theologians that are doing their work in witness to the victimization and oppression of women such as Elizabeth Johnson, Elisabeth Schüssler Fiorenza, Sharon Welch, and Rita Nakashima Brock.

can only be remembered rightly when it is viewed from the perspective of the whole story. Keshkegian says, "In the end, the term "dangerous memory" is not adequate for the complex processes of remembering that we saw emerging from the experiences of the victimized."[62] She thinks that remembering the past pain is not helping the victims to overcome their painful past. There are further steps that need to be taken for the sake of hope and healing.

Keshkegian thinks, and we agree with her, that Christians should not immediately introduce forgiveness into the process of remembrance. Although not against it, she proposes that "Christians prescind from moving too quickly to talk about forgiveness until we learn better the practices of remembering for re-membering."[63] The purpose of the remembrance of the past hurt is not to reinforce the feeling of hurt and trauma; rather it is for healing and transformation.

The reason for remembering is the "desire for life."[64] This kind of remembrance needs a different story, one that shows the passion of life outside the history of victimization. It "seeks birth and actualization; relationships of intimacy and mutuality; embodied structure of justice; fruitfulness, and joy—not only as imagined, but as realized, in however partial form."[65] Someone who needs to carry on after a story of suffering happened to his/her life needs help from different stories about the event, or as Keshkegian puts it, from "multiple remembrance". This multiple memorative practice that Keshkegian proposed includes: remembering as preserving; remembering as resisting; and remembering as life connecting.

The remembering of the past requires stories and narratives of what had happened in the past. She argues that there is no single narrative

---

[62] Keshkegian, *Redeeming Memories*, 151. She elaborates this objection into six reasons why Metz's approach is not sufficient for the victims, see 140–143. Keshkegian's different point of view can be seen as a product of a different context and purpose of remembrance. Metz thinks that his context did not have a sufficient memory of suffering which seemingly is driving him to advocate especially the memory of such suffering in his post-war context. Some important points that Keshkegian proposed, hold out possibilities that would be useful for our research.

[63] Keshkegian, *Redeeming Memories*, 195. She mentions the work of Pamela Dickey Young, "Beyond Moral Influence to an Atoning Life," *Theology Today* 52 (1995), 351–354 to support her statement. She says further on that reconciliation does not necessarily have to entail forgiveness. The term reconciliation is mentioned here without any proper explanation of what she meant by her statement. Our research disagrees with her explanation and we will elaborate on the reason later.

[64] Keshkegian, *Redeeming Memories*, 152.

[65] Keshkegian, *Redeeming Memories*, 153.

that can hold the full story of true remembrance. She says, "Narrative adequacy and effectiveness are to be measured by a narrative's ability to communicate multiple and even conflicting remembrances; and to do so in the face of threats, psychological, social, and political challenges."[66] The question then, what kind of memory can hold such multiple remembrances?

This multiple memory practice that she proposes can give the answer to our questions. The purpose is to enlarge "the multiple narrative repertoire of what it means to remember suffering."[67] She wants to find the redeeming memory that "honors the suffering, yet makes life possible".[68] This is why she wants to remember the whole story of Jesus and not just the story of the suffering on the cross. This story is just part of the whole story of God's redeeming action.

We need to remember the whole story of Jesus' incarnation and not merely focus on the story of the cross in order to bring hope to the victims. When the community of believers remembers Jesus, they remember Christ for the sake of salvation and hope. It is a re-experienced history which incarnates in the present.[69] How can this memory of the past be transformed so that it brings hope to those who suffer?

The memory of the cross is indeed the memory of suffering. It is a narrative that bears the stories of people who have suffered unjustly. It can be seen as an act of solidarity: that God is "taking responsibility of the degradation and tragedy of the human condition."[70] However it does not stop here. The story of the resurrection is a story of hope. There is hope over death. This is why Keshkegian sees resurrection as being "about the power of life to persist and to prevail. The affirmation of life, even when death seems more powerful."[71] The memory of the cross and resurrection are the redemptive memories that can bring life and hope for the victims.

---

[66] Keshkegian, *Redeeming Memories*, 154.
[67] Keshkegian, *Redeeming Memories*, 158.
[68] Keshkegian, *Redeeming Memories*, 158.
[69] For her, incarnation is "an ongoing process and experience of divine presence," Keshkegian, *Redeeming*, 165. Keshkegian is not really consistent in her understanding of incarnation, as she suggests that incarnation is also a historical process (192). Then she also suggests that "the way we know the power of God is through incarnation, through God's presence with us, among us, in us" (193). It seems that she understands incarnation as divine historical events in the past that continuously influence us in the present.
[70] Keshkegian, *Redeeming Memories*, 174. Keshkegian puts a reference to Isabel Carter Heyward, *The Redemption God* (Lanham: University Press of America, 1982) as feminist theologian who gave a similar argument.
[71] Keshkegian, *Redeeming Memories*, 179.

The healing memory is the redemptive memory. This memory is intended to help the victims to overcome their past pain. In order to do so, Keshkegian thinks that Christianity needs to reaffirm the promise of incarnation. This can be achieved when the remembrance of Christ is done with guiding principles which,

> (1) affirm our being human as the site of redemption; (2) declare God to be on the side of redemption in and through humanity; (3) see the goal of redemption as wholeness and integrity, right relation and full humanity; and (4) recognize redemption as political, meaning it is in history and involves community and relationships, as well as the exercise of power.[72]

Keshkegian does not really explain these guiding principles that should be used for remembering God's saving action in Christ. However, we can see that the 'humanity factor' is playing an important role in these principles. This is probably caused by the purpose that has been established in the beginning of the research which is to voice the narrative and support the victims. We will see shortly whether these principles, or these kinds of approaches, are suitable for our research.

The choice of taking side with the victims requires witness that shares the memory of the unjust. This task of being a witness to the suffering comes from God because "bearing witness reflects God's presence as life and breath of the universe. When we bear witness, we image the divine, whose power is for life, whose power is not finally reducible to good and evil."[73] The accounts of the witness will build a strong network of stories thus enabling the multiple redemptive remembrances to exist. The role of witness is crucial because they are the agents of the narrative. Just as Christians are witnesses of the narrative of the cross, so we are asked to be a witness of other's suffering.

The Church is a fitting place because it is already a community of remembrance and witness. The church has always acted as witness and memory bearer of God's saving action especially through the story of Christ. The church has kept the memory of Jesus Christ in teaching and practice. The church's calling is to be "a community of remembering/re-membering for redemption, formed and reformed in hope."[74] This calling influences several aspects. First, it influences the identity of the church as a community of believers; second, it shapes

---

[72] Keshkegian, *Redeeming Memories*, 190. She based this principle on Paul Lehman, *Ethics in a Christian Context* (New York: Harper and Bros., 1963). Further she says that the Church has not always remembered these principles.
[73] Keshkegian, *Redeeming Memories*, 194.
[74] Keshkegian, *Redeeming Memories*, 201.

our understanding of God; third, it gives us the relevance of the past into our present; and lastly, it mediates salvation. These are indeed the significant elements of the church's calling to remember.

This calling to remember lives in the dynamic of the three dimensions of the church: divine mystery, community, and institution. Thus memory will always be dynamic yet in check with the confines of the given community. Of course there is the tendency of using selective memory as a result of the interaction of the three dimensions of the church. Such selective memory should be avoided.[75] This can be achieved by opting for healing and transformation when it comes to interpreting the church as divine mystery. Keshkegian is talking about divine mystery as a process of "coming to be again and again, in history and time, embodied and transitory, yet persistent."[76] This relation is a witnessing relation that brings love and life because the church is constituted through the remembrance for the sake of redemption. She says, "It is to this complex and conflictual universe that the church as divine mystery bears witness. The divine mystery is a process of remembering and re-membering amid all these dynamics."[77] Therefore this interpretation of memory should be done actively and holistically.

The complex process of remembering in the story of Jesus helps Christians to focus on the multiple commemorative practices that she proposes. First, memory of the suffering serves as a challenge to history. Second, memory of resistance is important as a counter narrative to the suffering. And the third practice is the memory of life experiences beyond or alongside victimization and resistance that moves beyond opposition of the first two and creates a different memory of life.[78] These multiple memory practices are based on the life and work of Jesus Christ.

How can we do this in the life of the church? Keshkegian comes right to the point where she writes that worship and ritual of the church are "in some way about remembering, about being reminded of who God is,

---

[75] She thinks that selective memory is the result of power interplay. When the "ecclesial traditionalist"—a term she uses for people who opted to become in line with status quo and traditionalist (see *Redeeming Memories*, 205–206), is still in charge, The church will still act as community of remembrance only in favor to those in power. When this happens, the memory will be interpreted not in a dynamic and active way so that it can transform our present, rather nostalgia of the past glory will be kept and everything that does not go along with it will be set aside or kept hidden. This situation will preserve the memory and the status quo of the past and will fight change in any form.

[76] Keshkegian, *Redeeming Memories*, 215.
[77] Keshkegian, *Redeeming Memories*, 215.
[78] See Keshkegian, *Redeeming Memories*, 28–29.

who we are, and what God calls us to."[79] She correctly comes to the idea that this transformative and redeeming remembrance can be found in the space and time of worship and ritual. Thus, she rightly asks the following important questions that are also useful for our research, "To what does the church bear witness in its worship? What does the church remember, memorialize, and commemorate in and through its rituals? Does that witness contribute to a process of redeeming memories?"[80] These very questions are important in dealing with the focus of this research.

How does Keshkegian deal with them, and does her answer provide enough answer for this research? Keshkegian does not provide a clear answer about this and only mentions some of the factors that are needed in the rites of "healing and remembrance, as well as rites of reconciliation and integration."[81] She also leaves an open space for further exploration when she mentions the Eucharist as the heart of Christian worship. She sees the eucharistic liturgy as "the recalling of traumatic events of suffering, degradation, and death."[82] By doing this we can bring the sufferings of the victims to the table and remember them through the Eucharist. "The Eucharist must be reenacted as the memory of Jesus' life and resurrection, as well as his crucifixion."[83] However, she does not explore how this remembrance is made possible in liturgy.

---

[79] Keshkegian, *Redeeming Memories*, 218.
[80] Keshkegian, *Redeeming Memories*, 218.
[81] Keshkegian, *Redeeming Memories*, 220. In order to achieve that she thinks that the Church must "incorporate multiple memorative practices into its prayers and rituals," and "providing rites of mourning, healing and integration." She also mentions the work of Rebecca, Lea Nicoll Kramer, and Susan A. Lukey, "Spirit Song: The Use of Christian Healing Rites in Trauma Recovery," *Treating Abuse Today* 5 and 6 (1995/1996), 39–47. This is an article that describes the role of rituals in the journey of Rebecca (the victim) based on traditional Christian rituals. Rebecca is a survivor of sexual abuse and had suicidal thoughts (40). She experienced sexual abuse during her childhood and was made to believe that she was the child of Satan. Susan Lukey (the minister) performed the rituals with the supervision of Lea Kramer (the therapist). Keshkegian understands this not only to restored Rebecca's relationship with God, but also between Rebecca and herself. For a perspective by a psychologist, see Janice Haaken, *Pillars of Salt: Gender, Memory, and the Perils of Looking Back* (New Brunswick, NJ and London: Rutgers University Press, 1998), 235–237. Haaken was rather skeptical about the process by saying, "the therapist seems to be blind to the hostility towards religion implicit in this material." Further, she said that the healing rituals may have provided some measure of relief from frantic acts of self-destructiveness but at considerable costs which are relapses and "rebellious impulses incompatible with the ideal state of virtuous believer (237)."
[82] Keshkegian, *Redeeming Memories*, 224.
[83] Keshkegian, *Redeeming Memories*, 224.

Keshkegian mentions some of the rituals that can be used for the commemorative practice without giving or explaining the theological foundation for them. She says,

> Lament is one obvious form of prayer that attends to suffering. We can lament for ourselves or on behalf of others. Intercession and confession also afford opportunities for the community to bear witness, lend support, acknowledge, and take responsibility for complicity. Prayers of thanksgiving and praise can be occasions for celebrating healing and transformation. Rites of healing are powerful occasions of remembrance and transformation. Certain elements of the Christian story may also be expanded to include the remembrance of the victims. The symbol of Christ's descent to the dead before his resurrection and ascension is a powerful reminder that no one is forgotten by God. It may also symbolize that hidden parts can be retrieved and are accessible to God. Rituals of cleansing and renewal, often associated with baptism, are another way to symbolize and enact remembrance and transformation.[84]

These are the rituals and forms of prayer that could provide the means for the implementation of redemptive memory. However, she did not provide further explanation about these rites.

Liturgy is not the only source of redemptive memories for the church. Keshkegian thinks that the church must also bear witness in the church's preaching and teaching as well as in its pastoral practices and its programs of social and political action.[85] These are the means that the church can use as witness of memory of suffering.

Keshkegian has lent us her voice by saying that the story of the cross is not only about the memory of suffering. She is taking us forward from Metz's idea by saying that the story of the cross cannot be understood without the story of the life of Jesus and the resurrection. Remembrance is way of offering space for the story of hope for the victims. We will take this idea further by saying that it is not only the victims that need to be healed; perpetrators also need to be embraced. We cannot exclude the perpetrators. Everyone should be included in the story and narrative of the suffering.

She is also correct in connecting remembrance with the church as community of remembrance. As such, the church must play an important role in the remembrance of the past, and act as witness

---

[84] Keshkegian, *Redeeming Memories*, 225. She also says that "The language, structure, and forms used in worship need to be evaluated and changed to respond to these challenges and to become sites of healing, rather than of further injury," 226.

[85] See Keshkegian, *Redeeming Memories*, 226–230. We will return to Keshkegian's idea of remembrance through preaching and explore it further in the next chapter.

of suffering. The church can also bring an important element in redemptive memory which is to offer the story of life through the story of resurrection. These are all points that has been taken from Keshkegian for our further research.

What we see lacking in Keshkegian's exploration is that she does not provide a sound theological explanation about how remembrance can be celebrated in the church. She offers no biblical argument to support her idea and she does not explain how the Eucharist can serve as the center of Christian worship.

What is Christian worship and liturgy and what is the connection between worship and remembrance? What is the role of the Eucharist? What is the real meaning of *anamnesis* in the Eucharist when it is applied in the liturgy? What transformation does the Eucharist bring to the church as a community of remembrance? These questions are the basis for our further exploration of the remembrance in the Eucharist as the central act of Christian liturgy.

2. Alexander Schmemann: The Eucharist and Liturgical Memory

One of the influential theologians in the field of liturgy, who will become our subject of investigation, is of the opinion that theology and liturgy should not be separated and thus came up with the idea of liturgical theology. His main contribution towards our research is that he brought back the Eucharist as the center of liturgy and the celebration of remembrance of the church. Coming from an Orthodox background, Alexander Schmemann's idea on the Eucharist as a sacrament of remembrance will give an important basis for the understanding of meaning of communal remembrance in the liturgy.

Alexander Schmemann was born in a refugee family in Tallin, Estonia in 1921.[86] His father was an officer of the Russian imperial cavalry who fought during the First World War and also fought on the side of the White Army (the loosely-allied anti-Bolshevik forces) during the Civil War of 1917–1920. His mother came from a clergy family. After the war, his parents escaped and lived as refugees abroad, where Schmemann was born. His family moved to Yugoslavia and then to France. He grew up in Paris and went to a private secular school

---

[86] He is a Protopresbyter in the Orthodox Church, which is the highest title for a married Eastern Orthodox priest. Orthodox Church commonly referred to as the Eastern Orthodox Church. The Orthodox Church is composed of several self-governing ecclesial bodies, each geographically and nationally distinct but theologically unified.

and then to private military school established by emigrant Russian military officers. He received his theological education at the Orthodox Theological Institute of St. Sergius in Paris and became an Orthodox priest. France has always influenced Schmemann and he loved reading French besides Russian poems.

He was ordained a priest in 1946 and taught at St. Sergius until 1951. Afterwards, he moved to New York City where he taught in St. Vladimir Seminary (the seminary moved to Crestwood in 1962) and became the dean until he passed away in 1983. He was also teaching as adjunct professor at Columbia University, New York University, Union Theological Seminary and General Theological Seminary in New York. Much of his focus at St. Vladimir's was on liturgical theology, which we will explore shortly.

Paul Meyendorff, Schmemann's successor as dean of St. Vladimir's, writes that Schmemann's theology was shaped during his Paris years under the influence of French Roman Catholic thinkers such as Jean Daniélou and Louis Bouyer. Meyendorff writes, "It is from that existing milieu that Fr. Schmemann really learned "liturgical theology", a "philosophy of time" and the true meaning of the "paschal mystery".[87] Meyendorff believes that Schmemann holds the legacy of the post-conciliar Roman Catholic liturgical reform of 1969, in which the issue of the Eucharist was at stake.[88]

Schmemann became widely acknowledged as a prominent Orthodox liturgical theologian and was invited as Orthodox observer to the Second Vatican Council from 1962–1965. His main theological contribution is his work on giving a systematic theological foundation for liturgy. *For the Life of the World*, Schmemann's popular volume on Christian faith as reflected in liturgy that we are about to explore, has been translated into eleven languages. It was originally prepared as a study guide for the National Student Christian Federation in 1963, which was then translated anonymously into Russian. His final book *The Eucharist* was finished in Russian just before his death. This and several collections of his writings were published posthumously.

The main purpose of his explorations in liturgy originated from his own question about his Church, "...the question of the destiny

---

[87] Paul Meyendorff, "Protopresbyter Alexander Schmemann: A Life Worth Living" *St. Vladimir's Theological Quarterly* Vol. 28, No. 1 (1984), 6.

[88] For a more a concise reading on the issue read Geoffrey Hull, "The Proto-History of the Roman Liturgical Reform" on http://pagesperso-orange.fr/civitas.dei/hull.htm, accessed January 2010.

of the Orthodox Church in this second half of the twentieth century, in a world radically different from that which shaped our mentality our thought-forms, indeed our whole life as Orthodox, in a world moreover deeply marked by a spiritual crisis which acquires with each passing year truly universal dimensions..."[89] Thus his main concern is on how the Orthodox Church faces the spiritual crisis in the midst of his context. His contribution towards this question is not only that he tried to investigate the importance of liturgy and its basic meaning, but also his reminder of returning to the Eucharist as the source of liturgy and theology. His idea on the Eucharist will give clarity on our further investigation on the place of remembrance in liturgy. His main intention in building his theology was to bridge the separation between liturgy and theology that has caused a sort of crisis in the Orthodox Church. He says,

> It must be clear by now that the tragedy which I denounce and deplore consists not in any particular 'defect' of the liturgy—and God knows that there have been many such defects at all times—but in something much deeper: the *divorce between liturgy, theology, and piety*, a divorce which characterizes the post-patristic period of the history of our Church and which has altered–not the faith and not too much the liturgy–theology and piety. In other terms, the crisis which I try to analyze is the crisis not of liturgy but of its *understanding*—be it in the 'key' of post-patristic theology or in that of rather recent, but assumed to be traditional, liturgical piety. And precisely because the roots of the crisis are theological and spiritual rather than liturgical, no liturgical reform can by itself and in itself solve it.[90]

He thinks that the crisis happens because the Church did not put her theology on its very fundamental source which is the liturgy. The dualism and separation between liturgy and theology have altered the action of faith; or in Schmemann's term—piety. Schmemann brings this idea as a departing point and builds his arguments consistently around this topic.

2.1 *Crisis in the Church*

As mentioned earlier, Schmemann's concern is always on the Church. He wants to challenge the church's reaction on what he called as a crisis of spirituality in the Orthodox Church. This crisis is caused by the

---

[89] Alexander Schmemann, *Church, World, Mission* (New York: St. Vladimir's Seminary Press, 1979), 7–8.
[90] Alexander Schmemann, "Liturgical Theology, Theology of Liturgy, and Liturgical Reform," in *St Vladimir's Theological Quarterly* 13 no. 4 (1969), 219.

context that has challenged the Church "in her every senses, and being, a world trying consciously or unconsciously to reduce her to values, philosophies of life and world-views profoundly different from, if not totally opposed to, her vision and experience of God, man and life."[91] The encounter of the Church and her context has not been very fruitful because of the fact that the Church is still living in the past. The Church has not fully aware of the changes in her surrounding while she continues to live as if this is still in the early time of the Church.

The Orthodox Church cannot change its past easily to adapt to its context because its tradition is a continuity of theology and identity of the Church. The task that should be dealt with is how to correctly understand the tradition and its relation with knowledge of the past, and how theology can cope with this issue. He then argues that theology, the *lex credendi*, has been isolated from the Church. He suspected that theology of the Church has been separated from the Church because it has not been able to deliver the message of the past and reveal the tradition and to relate them contextually. It fails to do so because of a double reduction, which is historical and intellectual. He explains "historical" as the limitation of theology to mere texts without the understanding of the experience and testimony of the church behind it; and "intellectual" as if the Fathers of the Churches have their own presuppositions of theology based on their context and influence without being connected to the Church.[92] Schmemann wants to put back the importance of connecting theology with the Church and her experience.

Because of the historical and intellectual reduction, contemporary problems have become the source of theology for the Church. He thinks that "issues relating to economics, politics and psychology have replaced a Christian vision of the world at the service of God. Theologians, clergy and other professional "religious" run busily around the world defending—from God?—this or that "right", however perverse, and all this in the name of peace, unity and brotherhood."[93]

---

[91] Schmemann, *Church, World, Mission*, 9.
[92] Schmemann, *Church, World, Mission*, 17. *Lex Credendi* is the law of belief (what we believe) and *Lex Orandi* is the law of prayer (the way we worship).
[93] Alexander Schmemann, *The Eucharist: Sacrament of the Kingdom* trans. Paul Kachur (New York: St. Vladimir's Seminary Press, 1987), 10. It took him several years to write "Eucharist" in his native Russian, and he died before seeing the final version of its English translation. While his earlier book *For the Life of the World* (New York: St. Vladimir's Seminary Press, 1973) was written in English and was then translated into Russian. In the preface which he wrote in November, 1983 he said, "This book

Thus, we can see that Schmemann does not agree if the Church uses contextual tools for her contextual problems. He wants to bring the Church back to its original source of theology which is the experience of the words of God.

This is why he insisted that in order to understand the meaning of tradition and experience, the Church should return to its *lex orandi* which is the liturgical experience "which alone therefore transcends the past, the present and the future, which alone actualizes Tradition into life, fullness and power."[94] Liturgy is the place where the Church can find again her true experience of living the words of God. *Leitourgia* is "an all-embracing vision of life, a power meant to judge, inform and transform the whole of existence, a 'philosophy of life' shaping and challenging all our ideas, attitudes and actions."[95] It is a representation of the Church's existence. It brings our context and challenges and renews the old life. Liturgy will provide the continuity and renewal that the Church has been looking for.

However the situation in liturgy is not much better than that in theology. There has been a growing number of liturgical practices that hardly express the genuine *lex orandi* of the Church.[96] Further, he notices that liturgy has suffered a kind of erosion by "the growing discrepancy between the demands of tradition on the one hand, and the nominalism and minimalism of the liturgical piety and practice on the other hand."[97] This way, the purpose of liturgy "to inform, shape and guide the ecclesiastical consciousness as well as the "worldview" of the Christian community"[98] has ceased to happen. According to Schmemann, the lack of proper theology and liturgy are the source of the crisis in the Orthodox Church.

Schmemann's main concern in the relation of theology and liturgy was that there has been no sufficient theological foundation in the exploration of the liturgy of the Church in general. He thinks that most assessment on liturgics is on the question *how* (to perform) instead of *what* (is *leitourgia* for the Church). This is the liturgical crisis in how people understood and used liturgy.

---

represents a series of reflections on the Eucharist. These reflections, however, do not come from a scientific analysis, but from my own experience, limited though it may be."
[94] Schmemann, *Church, World, Mission*, 22.
[95] Schmemann, *Church, World, Mission*, 121.
[96] Alexander Schmemann, "Liturgy and Theology," *The Greek Orthodox Theological Review* No. 17 (1972), 87.
[97] Schmemann, "Liturgy and Theology", 87.
[98] Schmemann, "Liturgy and Theology", 88.

This crisis on liturgy has influenced the worship in the Church. He thinks that "Worship is no longer understood as the function of the Church, but on the contrary, the Church is thought of as being a function of worship."[99] This is the result of separation between theology, church and faith. These three elements are the main sources of the Church and therefore they should not be understood separately. The question then for Schmemann is how we can use those three basic elements in providing the source for the Church to face her context and yet still be true to her tradition.

2.2 *Liturgical Theology*

In giving answer to this need, Schmemann feels that liturgy should be restored to its theological meaning and theology to its liturgical dimension, or in other words, a liturgical theology. Thus,

> The task of liturgical theology consists in giving a theological basis to the explanation of worship and the whole liturgical tradition of the Church. This means, first, to find and define the concepts and categories which are capable of expressing as fully as possible the essential nature of the liturgical experience of the Church; second, to connect these ideas with that system of concepts which theology uses to expound the faith and doctrine of the Church; and third, to present the separate data of liturgical experience as a connected whole, as, in the last analysis, the rule of prayer; dwelling within the Church and determining her 'rule of faith.'[100]

This basically means that liturgical theology gives the systematic foundation for the theology of liturgy. Liturgical theology is not theology of liturgy; it is not a part of a theological system or a theological subject, rather it is the essence and manifestation of theology.

Liturgical theology then functions as "slow and patient bringing together of that which was for too long a time and because of many factors broken and isolated-liturgy, theology and piety, their reintegration within one fundamental vision."[101] In other words, the task of liturgical theology then is to combine and elaborate liturgy and theology and to explain the connection between worship as the

---

[99] Alexander Schmemann, "Liturgical Theology: Its Task and Methods," *St. Vladimir's Seminary Quarterly* no. 1 no 40 (1957), 24.

[100] Alexander Schmemann, *Introduction to Liturgical Theology* trans. Asheleigh E. Moorhouse (Portland, Maine: The Faith Press Ltd., 1966), 14. See also his argument in defending liturgical theology in Alexander Schmemann, "Liturgical Theology, Theology of Liturgy, and Liturgical Reform," *St Vladimir's Theological Quarterly* 13 no. 4 (1969), 223.

[101] Schmemann, "Liturgical Theology", 223. Schmemann even calls liturgical theology the illegitimate child of a broken relationship between theology and liturgy.

public act of the Church and the Church itself. Liturgical theology stands in between worship as a fact and its use in dogmatics,[102] and is also an independent theological discipline that is very important in completing the understanding of the Church's faith and doctrine. This means worship will take the center stage in the Church's life.

Liturgical theology has since emerged as a distinct discipline especially among the Orthodox and Protestant who put more interest in liturgical reform in Christian traditions. Some key concepts in liturgical theology include the notions: remembering (anamnesis), invocation (epiclesis), thanksgiving (eucharistia), blessing and praise (berakah), offering (oblation), and sacrifice.[103]

Schmemann understands worship as "a whole, within which everything, the words of prayer, lections, chanting, ceremonies, the relationship of all these things in a 'sequence' or 'order' and, finally, what can be defined as the 'liturgical coefficient' of each of these elements."[104] Worship is essential for the life of the Church. "It is in worship that she partakes of the Kingdom of God, contemplates the mysteries of the world to come, and enters into the communion of the Holy Spirit."[105]

Worship is not a private matter because Christian worship is always the public act of the Church. Thus, worship is about publicly expressing the Church's response to the remembrance of Eucharist as the center of liturgy which eventually brings the rhythm of liturgy in the people's lives through prayer and experience. Schmemann says, "The purpose of worship is to constitute the Church, precisely to bring what is 'private' into the new life, transform it into what belongs to the Church, i.e. shared with all in Christ. In addition its purpose is always to express the Church as the unity of that Body who's Head is Christ. And finally, its purpose is that we should always 'with one mouth and one heart' serve God since it was only such worship which God commanded the Church to offer."[106] Schmemann is right by stressing that worship is a communal matter and it should always serve the purpose of unity.

This unity should not be mistaken with uniformity. The Church has never had or believed in the complete uniformity of the worship. Worship has also developed and changed from time to time. The

---

[102] Schmemann, *Introduction*, 15.
[103] See D.E. Saliers, "Liturgical Theology," in *The New Dictionary of Christian Theology*, eds. Alan Richardson, and John Bowden (London : SCM Press Ltd., 1983), 336–337.
[104] Schmemann, *Introduction*, 15.
[105] Schmemann, "Liturgical Theology: Its Task and Methods", 25.
[106] Schmemann, *Introduction*, 19–20.

historical study of liturgy has shown that the Church has adapted the forms of worship to meet the need of the people. These changes of forms has expressed that liturgical practice is full with historical perspective which could also be distorted by its context.

Schmemann sees the danger when liturgy is being separated from theology in two ways. First, the Church can become a cultic liturgical institution which directs all her activities to the liturgical needs. It falls into an institutional cultic celebration. The other extreme is the danger that liturgy will become an institution that fulfills the religious needs of her members, which makes liturgy changeable, transformable, according to the needs of the users. These are the dangers when liturgy and theology are not incorporated. Thus, he wants to warn that the liturgy is not for the satisfaction of individuals, or clergy, in the Church; it is the expression of faith and at the same time the shape-giver of the faith of the Church. While at the same time, he thinks that theology should come from its natural resource, which is faith on which the Church is based and by which she lives is her liturgical relationship to certain events: the life, death, resurrection, and glorification of Jesus Christ, his ascension to heaven, the descent of the Holy Spirit on 'the last and great day of Pentecost.'[107] Thus what he wants to say is that the Church cannot be free from the experience that is given and received in the Church's *lex orandi*, which is the *leitourgia*; the Church is formed in them.

One thing that Schmemann wants to argue is that the basic root of liturgy is "the rhythm of the Lord's Day as the day of the eucharistic commemoration of the death and resurrection of Christ."[108] This should be the source and center of the life and liturgy of the Church. When this event becomes the center of the Church's life, liturgy should encourage the congregation into entering this rhythm of worship in their lives through experience and prayer. He also insists that the Eucharist as a sacrament of life must be preceded by the study of Baptism and Holy Chrism.[109]

This is the point when Schmemann starts focusing his attention on the eucharistic commemoration of the death and resurrection on Christ. The Eucharist should be the heart of worship. Thus it takes the center stage of both liturgy and theology. It is the source and purpose of the Church's very existence, because it is "the act, which ever makes the

---

[107] Schmemann, *Church, World, Mission*, 134.
[108] Schmemann, *Introduction*, 18.
[109] Schmemann, "Liturgical Theology: Its Task and Methods", 24.

Church to be what she is—the People of God, the Temple of the Holy Spirit, the Body of Christ, the gift and manifestation of the new life and the new age."[110]

Schmemann thinks that the Church can face this crisis by looking back to her own tradition. He believes that the problem is not the lack of strength and depth of the tradition, rather it is how we interpret it and bring it to our own context. He says, "Nothing has changed in the tradition, what has changed is the perception of its very essence. This crisis consists in a lack of connection and cohesion between what is accomplished in the Eucharist and how it is perceived, understood, and lived."[111] In this instance, we can see the common crisis that Schmemann and Metz were facing. They are dealing with the secular world. While Metz opted for looking at the world of suffering as the context of the Church's theology, Schmemann wants us to return to the Eucharist as the living experience of the words of God.

This latter desire is where his theology would be fruitful for our research. His approach to the Eucharist—and the remembrance constituted in it—is important for our own investigation. We will now look at how Schmemann understands the Eucharist and question whether it has a reconciliative factor in the remembrance that was constituted in it.

2.3 *The Central Place of the Eucharist*

For Schmemann, the Eucharist is very important for both liturgy and theology, in fact it is the center of the life of the Church. He continues to use the idea of his predecessors in France and Russia and tries to place the Eucharist at the center of both the Church and the liturgy. For Schmemann, the Eucharist functions as the main unifying idea of his theology and liturgy. It is, according to Schmemman, the "entrance," and "ascension" into the Kingdom of God,[112] and it is done in joy. He says, "The Eucharist is the entrance of the Church into the joy of its Lord. And to enter into that joy, so as to be a witness to it in the world, is indeed the very calling of the Church, its essential *leitourgia*, the sacrament by which it "becomes what it is."[113] It is a meeting place between

---

[110] Schmemann, "Theology and Eucharist," *St. Vladimir's Seminary Quarterly* no. 5 (1961), 12.
[111] Schmemann, *The Eucharist*, 9.
[112] Schmemann, *For the Life of the World*, 102.
[113] Alexander Schmemann, "The Proclamation of Joy: An Orthodox View," *Living Pulpit* 5, no. 4 (1986), 8.

the divine and human[114] where all lives will be transformed through bread and wine as God's food and drink for the life of the world.[115]

Schmemann also argues that the Eucharist is the central sacrament that brings together all individual members of the Church as a community. "For all the sacraments, except the Eucharist, deal with individual members of the Church and their purpose is to integrate the individual—his life, his particular *'leitourgia'* or calling—into the Church. But the Church is fulfilled in the Eucharist, and each sacrament, therefore, finds its natural end, its fulfillment in the Eucharist."[116] This is a very strong argument that gives the highest appreciation to the Eucharist as the communal act of the Church. The Eucharist is the sacrament that—while others function as the acceptance or integration of individuals to the community—brings the community together as one and acts as the communal sacrament; it is the fulfillment of other sacraments.

We have to understand the difference between what Protestant, Catholic, and Orthodox called sacrament. The Catholic Church has seven sacraments: Baptism, Confirmation, Ordination, Eucharist, Reconciliation, Anointing the Sick, and Matrimony. Most Protestant churches only have Baptism and Eucharist as their sacrament. The Orthodox Church however, does not limit the number of their sacraments. When Schmemann speaks about sacrament, he understands it as 'sacred actions' which also include blessing of holy water, fasting, praying for God's blessing, etc. Schmemann defines sacrament as an act of "embracing the entire mystery of the salvation of the world and mankind by Christ and in essence the entire content of the Christian faith."[117]

---

[114] Schmemann, *Church, World, Mission*, 211–214.

[115] Schmemann, *The Eucharist*, 36–48. Michael Plekon rightly indicates that Schmemann, in his view of the Eucharist, was influenced by the Russian theologian and philosopher Alexis Khomiakov, whom he quoted in his book *Church, World, Mission*, 183–184.

[116] Schmemann, "Theology and Eucharist", 18. The Eucharist is indeed very special for Schmemann, not only in his theological but also personal life. He wrote in his journal, which was later published, "The Eucharist reveals the Church as community--love for Christ, love in Christ--as a mission to turn each and all to Christ. The Church has no other purpose, no 'religious life' separate from the world. Otherwise the Church would become an idol... Only this presence can give meaning and value to everything in life, can refer everything to that experience and make it full." See Alexander Schmemann, *The Journals of Father Alexander Schmemann 1973-1983*, trans. Juliana Schmemann (New York: St. Vladimir's Seminary Press, 2000), notes of December 17, 1973.

[117] Schmemann, *The Eucharist*, 217.

Schmemann understands the Eucharist as the communal sacrament. When he was preparing the statement of confession and communion for the Holy Synod of the Orthodox Church in America in February 1972, Schmemann stressed the importance of the communal act in the Eucharist. He says,

> It is a well-known and undisputed fact that in the early Church the communion of all the faithful, of the entire *ecclesia* at each Liturgy was a self-evident norm. What must be stressed, however, is that this corporate communion was understood not only as an act of personal piety and personal sanctification but, first of all, as an act stemming precisely from one's very membership in the Church, as the fulfillment and actualization of that membership. The Eucharist was both defined and experienced as the "sacrament of the Church", the "sacrament of the assembly", the "sacrament of unity." "He mixed Himself with us," writes St. John Chrysostom, "and dissolved His body in us so that we may constitute a wholeness, be a body united to the Head."[118]

It is a central sacrament in the life of the Church from the beginning. It connects to Baptism as the entrance into the Church, and becomes the only uniting act for the whole congregation. And as a consequence the Eucharist is also connected to the community. As a result, the Eucharist is tightly connected with the life of a person as a member of the Church community. "The excommunication from the Church was the excommunication from the eucharistic assembly in which the Church fulfilled and manifested herself as the Body of Christ…This understanding of communion, as fulfilling membership in the Church, can be termed *ecclesiological*. However obscured or complicated it became later, it has never been discarded; it remains forever the essential norm of Tradition."[119] The community factor is essential in the Eucharist.

One of Schmemann's goals in theology is to "recover its (read: the Eucharist) ecclesiological and eschatological 'fullness' to know it again as the Sacrament of the Church."[120] The purpose is "partaking of Christ, who has become our food, our life, our manifestation as the body of Christ" (Schmemann: 1987, 226). For him, the Eucharist is at the heart of worship and liturgy, the place where the Church should reflect on her theology and be connected with the mystery of God. The Eucharist is

---

[118] Alexander Schmemann, "Confession and Communion," http://www.schmemann.org/byhim/confessionandcommunion.html, accessed October, 2009.
[119] Schmemann, "Confession and Communion". This is also why Schmemann agrees with the term eucharistic ecclesiology. This means "the return to the Church through the Eucharist and to the Eucharist through the Church", "Theology and Eucharist", 23.
[120] Schmemann, "Theology and Eucharist", 22.

both a personal and communal experience which reminds the Church of God's given hope and joy. And it is through the Eucharist the Church can come to the Kingdom of God, "For the Eucharist, we have said, is a *passage,* a procession leading the Church into "heaven," into her fulfillment as the Kingdom of God."[121]

Schmemann's discernments have put the Eucharist (again, fully) at the center of Christian faith. He rightly puts the Eucharist back at the core of Christianity as a communal act that gathers the community under the body of Christ. This is the strong finding that we would like to take as a resource from Schmemann as it might give us a place for a communal remembrance both for victims and perpetrators gathered in the same body of Christ.

The close connection between the Eucharist as the center of theology and its uniting role gives us the opportunity and hope for finding a place of common remembrance for every member of the Church, and this includes remembering the past conflicts for both victims and perpetrators. The Eucharist is the table of remembrance that is God's doing, where we can have the opportunity to be reunited in joy as a community of believers. The question now is how can we get to that point? Although Schmemann did not intend to answer our specific question, we will further investigate how the Eucharist serves as a place of remembrance for the community of believers.

2.4 *Liturgy of Time*

In searching for the real meaning of the Eucharist, Schmemann took the direction of looking back to the text and to how the Eucharist was originally perceived in the early Christian communities. He wants to "return to the Bible, return to the Fathers."[122] This means he tries to find the real meaning of the Eucharist through the texts and tradition.

He sees that there is a connection between Christian liturgy and the concept of time in the liturgical tradition of Judaism.[123] There is a similarity in the liturgical elements of the worship in synagogue and early Christian services, albeit with a crucial difference on the eschatological point of view. The difference between them was shown

---

[121] Schmemann, "Theology and Eucharist", 19.
[122] Schmemman, "Theology and Eucharist", 23.
[123] See more about the relation between Judaism liturgy and Christian worship. See R.T. Beckwith, "The Jewish Background to Christian Worship" in *The Study of Liturgy,* eds. Cheslyn Jones et al., revised edition (New York: Oxford University Press, 1992) 68–80.

through new elements in Baptism and the Eucharistic tradition of breaking the bread and sharing the cup. These two new traditions of Christian worship can nevertheless be traced to Jewish worship. Their novelty when they were connected with their eschatological content, is "the fact of the coming of the Messiah and the events of His messianic ministry, that is, his preaching, his death and his resurrection."[124] The Jews celebrate them in the expectant waiting for the Messiah, while the Christians are doing it in the joyful affirmation of Jesus coming. The Eucharist, especially, is "the affirmation and 'actualization' of the coming of the Messiah as an accomplished fact—the actualization of the beginning—in Him—of salvation and new life."[125] And since Jesus instituted the Great Thanksgiving at the Table of the Lord, therefore the Eucharist is a celebration of the presence of Christ. Through it they "proclaimed the death of the Lord and confessed His resurrection."[126]

In the biblical concept, Hebrew understands time as linear, meaning that time has a beginning and an end. Time is always connected to a creator God. Worship is a waiting and a response to that moment of God's salvation. The cycle of time is seen with this particular idea in mind. Therefore the 'liturgy of time' in Judaism is connected with the expectation of the day of the Lord which will come in time. The whole life of a person is connected with a life cycle of rites that strengthen the identity in anticipating the Day of the Lord.[127]

This concept is also taken up in Christianity, except for the fact that the Messiah has already come and that here the liturgy revolves around the Messiah who has come and will return again. Schmemann says, "The difference between Christianity and Judaism is not in their understanding or theology of time, but in their conception of the events by which this time is spiritually measured."[128] Again, time is seen as something with a beginning and an end. Christianity has a central event in this journey of time which is the coming of the Messiah. This event is what makes time receive a new intensity, "It becomes the time of the Church: the time in which the salvation given by the Messiah is

---

[124] Schmemann, *Introduction*, 49.
[125] Schmemann, *Introduction*, 49.
[126] Schmemann, *Introduction*, 50.
[127] For further explanation on the connection of the cycle of liturgy in Christianity and Jewish life and tradition, see Lawrence A. Hoffman & Paul F. Bradshaw (eds.), *Life Cycles in Jewish and Christian Worship*, Vol. 4 (Notre Dame, Indiana: University of Notre Dame Press, 1998). Here, scholars are writing essays on models of human life in Judaism and Christianity by looking at their life-cycle liturgies.
[128] Schmemann, *Introduction*, 56.

now accomplished."[129] Because of this view, the Eucharist is then seen as actualization and manifestation of the Church as the new *aeon*.[130] Through this understanding of time and eschatology, we can have a clearer view of Schmemann's idea on liturgy and the Eucharist,

> This messianic Kingdom, or life in the new *aeon*, is 'actualized'—becomes real—in the assembly of the Church, in the *ekklesia*, when believers come together to have communion in the Lord's body. The Eucharist is therefore the manifestation of the Church as the new *aeon*; it is participation in the Kingdom as the *parousia*, as the presence of the Resurrected and Resurrecting Lord.[131]

Schmemann sees that the Church is connected with eschatology because she is the representation of the Kingdom of God in Christ. The Eucharist then functions as "the presence and the manifestation of Christ, who is 'the same to-day, yesterday, and forever' (Heb. 13:8)."[132] This means that by partaking in the Eucharist, Christians accept the new life which is already in the Church. The Church that already has an eschatological fullness in Christ is now set in the world to bear witness in word and deed of Christ's death and resurrection. The *parousia* of the Lord is, "this world will pass away and the Lord will reign in glory." All told, the Jewish's liturgy of time is indeed preserved in Christian liturgy but renewed in the light of the Eucharist.

The Jewish liturgy of time, especially the weekly cycle, is built around the Sabbath. The Sabbath day was essential in Jewish tradition as the commemoration of how God created the world and rested on the seventh day. "The Sabbath sanctions the whole natural life of the world unfolding through the cycles of time, because it is the divinely instituted sign of the correspondence of the world to God's will and purpose."[133] Thus, the flow of time revolves around the Sabbath.

The Eucharist is connected with the Sabbath because of "the real nature and significance of this new day was defined in relation to the Sabbath and to the concept of time connected with it."[134] The Eucharist is therefore not a substitute for the Sabbath day but rather it is the Messianic fulfillment of God's promise and becomes the

---

[129] Schmemann, *Introduction*, 57.

[130] *Aeon* here can be translated as eternal life, a long age before the second coming. Schmemann says, "The Church belongs to the new aeon, the Kingdom of the Messiah, which in relation to this world is the Kingdom of the age to come." *Introduction*, 57.

[131] Schmemann, *Introduction*, 57.

[132] Schmemann, *Introduction*, 58.

[133] Schmemann, *Introduction*, 60.

[134] Schmemann, *Introduction*, 60.

eighth day, which is the Lord's Day. As the first day of the week, the day of the resurrection became the Christian day of rest, and is thus the marker of the revolving of time in liturgy. The Eucharist is performed as a remembrance of this eighth day. And it is, as Michael Pomazansky rightly summarizes Schmemann's thought, "an expression of the ecclesiological union in an assembly of the faithful, the joyful banquet of the Lord. Its whole meaning was directed to the future, to eschatology, and therefore it presented itself as a 'worship outside of time,' not bound to history or remembrances, as eschatological worship that made it sharply distinct from the simple forms of worship, which are called in the book the 'worship in time.'"[135] This demonstrates the significance of the eschatological nature of the Eucharist. Nothing besides the Eucharist could therefore be the central point of Christian liturgy.

The relevance of the cycle of time in Christian liturgy is important in building the life of the Church as the new *aeon*. With the Eucharist at the center, liturgy will bring back the energy for the renewal of all believers who partake. Morrill rightly sums up this important element by saying, "The renewal of time and, thus, the world, is precisely a renewal from within: This, to my reading, is crucial to what Schmemann is claiming about the transformative power of Christian liturgy and sacramentally and, more foundationally, about Christ."[136] By experiencing liturgy with its tracing of time, and the Eucharist at the heart of it all, we will experience the presence of the Lord and thus be renewed.

If liturgy that centered in the Eucharist can renew and transform the Church, and more specifically for our present study, that it can also bring joy beyond our suffering, the question then is how does the Eucharist renew and transform the Church? What conditions and aspects does the Eucharist have that enables it to bring back the joy in the community of believers who know of fear, failure and fissures? These important questions will have direct implication for our own research that has brought us to discern the Eucharist as a place of communal remembrance that invites us to come and see that God's presence in broken bread and poured-out cup is able to bring renewal and transformation of the past wounds.

---

[135] See Michael Pomazansky, *Selected Essays* (Jordanville, NY: Holy Trinity Monastery, 1996), 82–102.

[136] Bruce T. Morrill, *Anamnesis as Dangerous Memory: Political and Liturgical Theology in Dialogue* (Collegeville, Minnesota: The Liturgical Press, 2000), 99.

2.5 Sacrament of Remembrance

In trying to find answers for these questions, we will look into Schmemann's latest work *The Eucharist*. This book was not written in a systematical way to explain what the Eucharist is, but it is rather the result of his reflections. Here he speaks about the mystery and relation of the Eucharist to the liturgy of the Church. There is one part that is particular significant for our quest, namely when he sees the Eucharist as sacrament of remembrance.

He thinks that the eucharistic remembrance is important because it is about the remembrance of the kingdom of God that comes with the memory of the cross. He says, "The Eucharistic remembrance is the remembrance of the kingdom of God which was manifested and appointed at the Last Supper. But the remembrance of the cross, the body of Christ broken for us, the blood of Christ poured out for us, is inseparable from it."[137] He does in fact distinguish the remembrance in the Supper from the remembrance of the cross, but sees them as two elements that are inseparable. Further he says, "This is why it is only through the cross that the gift of the Kingdom of God is transformed into its reception, its manifestation at the Eucharist—in our ascent to heaven, in our partaking at the table of Christ in his kingdom."[138] This distinction enables Schmemann to focus on what he thinks the meaning of remembrance in the Eucharist to be.

Schmemann links remembrance in the feast of the last Supper with liturgy. He says,

> Being the sacrament of Christ's presence, the Eucharist is the feast of the Church, or even more, the Eucharist is the Church as Feast, and consequently the measure and the context of all feasts. For a feast is not a mere "remembrance" of such or such an event of the earthly life of Christ, but precisely the reality of His presence in the Church by the Holy Spirit. And therefore whatever event or person are commemorated in a feast, this commemoration necessarily finds its fulfillment in the Eucharist, in the "mysterion" which transforms remembrance into presence. The Eucharist manifests the link between all particular events, all the saints, all the theological affirmations with the saving work of Christ. Whatever we commemorate, whatever we celebrate, we always discover—and this discovery is made in the Divine Liturgy—that in the Church everything has its beginning in Jesus Christ and everything has in Him its end, its fulfillment. We can note here that the Orthodox Church has never accepted the principle of a non-festive Eucharist, similar to the Roman "low

---

[137] Schmemann, *The Eucharist*, 210.
[138] Schmemann, *The Eucharist*, 210.

Mass." For a long period, the Eucharist was an essentially dominical cult because it is always Paschal by its very nature, it always announces the death of Christ and confesses or bears witness to His Resurrection.[139]

By saying this, Schmemann is pointing out that the Eucharist is the feast that brings celebration in the mystery of liturgy. With the remembrance of this celebration in liturgy, we are linked with the events of the past and transform them into the present. Schmemann always sees the remembrance of the Eucharist as a remembrance of the past which transforms the future.

He argues that the institution of remembrance in the Eucharist has more mystical elements and is not only, neither a mere, historical remembrance of what Jesus has done. The ritual historical remembrance was actually a later development in theology. He says, "In the early Eucharist there was no idea of a ritual symbolization of the life of Christ and His Sacrifice. This is a theme which will appear later…under the influence of one theology and as the point of departure for another. The remembrance of Christ which He instituted (*This do in remembrance of Me*) is the affirmation of His 'Parousia,' of His presence; it is the actualization of His Kingdom… One may say without exaggeration that the early Church consciously and openly set herself in opposition to mysteriological piety and cults of the mysteries."[140] Schmemann is again stressing the importance of the mystical element in the remembrance of the Eucharist.

There are two reductions that reduce the understanding of mystery in the Eucharist as the sacrament of remembrance. The first one is the idea that the remembrance only refers to the establishment of the event and what had happened that night; that "The remembrance is the 'cause' of the actuality of the sacrament, just as the institution of the Eucharist as the last supper is the cause of actuality of the commemoration itself."[141] The second reduction is Schmemann's critique against Protestant theology that tend to focus on the question "of *how* the institution at the Last Supper 'operates' in the Eucharist, but not on *what* Christ accomplished through this last act of his earthly ministry before his betrayal, cross, and death."[142] He thinks that Christian theology should free themselves from these kinds of reductions.

---

[139] Schmemann, "Fast and Liturgy: Notes in Liturgical Theology," *St. Vladimir's Seminary Quarterly* ns 3 no. 1 (1959), 5.
[140] Schmemann, *Introduction*, 85–86.
[141] Schmemann, *The Eucharist*, 193.
[142] Schmemann, *The Eucharist*, 194.

One of the warnings that Schmemann addresses is the tendency of Christians using and performing the Eucharist for *their* own purpose. The Eucharist cannot be celebrated in order to achieve an agenda but the agenda can only come later as a result of the mystery of the remembrance in the Eucharist. The other warning that he gives is directed towards his own Orthodox Church that tends to sacralize everything. In that case the requirements of performing the Eucharist become more important than its content. However, by focusing on the mystery of its rituals and remembrance, the Eucharist will be the right resource for the Church as a community committed to change. Or, as Morrill sums up this thought, it is "giving oneself over to the radical otherness, the transcendent, messianic, and eschatological content of the liturgy, changes the way one perceives and prioritizes all aspects of life—interpersonal, economic, familial, political."[143]

Schmemann suggests that we can find the real meaning of the Eucharist in the Eucharist itself. This means, "in the continuity, in the identity of that *experience*, not personal, not subjective, but precisely *ecclesial*, which is incarnated in the eucharistic celebration and is fulfilled each time the Eucharist is celebrated."[144] Although he thinks that we cannot answer what the real meaning of the mystery in remembrance is in full, the experience in liturgical remembrance of the Eucharist can grant us the participation in such mystery.

The mystery can be seen through the relation of the Eucharist with the concept of time and the Church. Through the Eucharist we are invited to experience the transformation of time in the Great Thanksgiving as a remembrance of how Jesus opens the door to the Father. This experience is not only a remembering of a past experience, but is also a present one because we are experiencing it at the moment we are celebrating, and it is a future one because we are thankful for the future that Christ will give us. Through it we are also invited to the fulfillment of Christ's love. Schmemann says that "the last supper is the *Telos*, the completion, the fulfillment of the end, for it is the manifestation of that kingdom of love, for the sake of which the world was created and in which it has its *Telos*, its fulfillment."[145] Schmemann also sees that the institution of the Eucharist is connected with the institution of the Church. It can only

---

[143] Morrill, *Anamnesis*, 106. This is the obvious difference between Schmemann and Metz who seem to have a different agenda with the Eucharist. We will address this issue further in the next part of this chapter.

[144] Schmemann, *The Eucharist*, 198.

[145] Schmemann, *The Eucharist*, 200–201.

be understood when it is connected with the Church. Thus, Schmemann concludes, "only in relation to this link, to its fulfillment, its actuality, is the genuine meaning of the most profound and joyous mystery of our faith—the transformation in the Eucharist of our gifts into the body and blood of Christ—revealed to us."[146] The experience of the mystery will transform the Church and make the past relevant to the present and future.

The transformation that the Eucharist brings is a joyous one. Schmemann considers that joy is fundamental in liturgical transforming power. Christianity has always been a proclamation of joy where Jesus rose victorious over sin, which can be seen through the remembrance in the Eucharist. It is "the entrance of the Church into the joy of its Lord."[147] Further he explains, "This joy is pure joy because it does not depend on anything in this world, and is not the reward of anything in us. It is totally and absolutely a *gift*, the *'charis'*, the grace. And being pure gift, this joy has a transforming power, *the only really transforming power in this world.*"[148] Thus this joy is not only a psychological state of one's mind; it is a transformation of the whole that can spread outside the Church.

This transformation of joy does not exclude the suffering that the cross displays. However the remembrance of the cross should not always be understood as suffering because an act of self-sacrifice is also linked with love. This is the perfect love that Jesus has shown for the sake of the salvation of humans. Thus, the joy experienced in the Eucharist is also connected with the act of self-sacrifice. Schmemann says, "The cross is suffering. But through love and self-sacrifice this same tribulation is transformed into joy. It is experienced as being crucified with him, as accepting his cross and hence taking part in his victory."[149] What Schmemann suggested is to see the remembrance of the cross not only as suffering but also as self-sacrifice of suffering which in turn will bring joy for those who remember it.

Further he stresses again the importance of this memory of Christ and the transformation it brings to the Church. The memory of the cross as sacrament of offering is a transformed memory of suffering

---

[146] Schmemann, *The Eucharist*, 202. Besides these, Schmemann also mentions the *mystery of sin* which is symbolized in Judas who was in the last supper but nevertheless walked away from the kingdom and betrayed Jesus; and *mystery of victory* in Christ that gave his self-sacrifice, condemned himself and achieved victory over the death, Schmemann, *The Eucharist*, 206. It is through the cross that Jesus achieved victory over sin, thus giving the joy of resurrection.
[147] Schmemann, *For the Life of the World*, 26.
[148] Schmemann, *For the Life of the World*, 55.
[149] Schmemann, *The Eucharist*, 210. See John 16:33 and John 16:22.

into joy. He says, "From the very beginning, the faith of Christians was memory and remembrance… this new memory is a joyous recognition of the one who was resurrected, who lives and therefore is present and abides."[150] Christianity was built on this joyous remembrance of Christ. It is not a remembrance of the past, it is the remembrance of Christ, "and this remembrance becomes our entry into his victory over time."[151] Thus, it is not a passive act of the mind, but this is an active remembrance that transforms the lives of people who are remembering Christ. The past and the future are "*living* in us, as given to us, as transformed into our *life* and making it life in God."[152]

Schmemann was not very clear on how this remembrance in liturgical experience can be applied to practical daily life. However, he gave a suggestion that this commemoration demands us to be together with our fellow neighbors. This remembrance is a communal remembrance, where we are not only aware of how God remembers us and how we remember God, but also how we remember the others. Because of Christ offering we are united in the past memory of self-sacrifice, we remember it in the present, and act in love for one another. "Therefore, in bringing his sacrifice to the altar, we *create the memory of each other*, we identify each other as living in Christ and being united with each other in him."[153] This memory of each other is the identity of the members of the Church.

2.6 *Joyous Communal Memory*

Why is Schmemann important in our research? Schmemann has been among the first theologians who gave the Eucharist its proper place back in Christian theology. He wants worship and theology to be centered in the Eucharist, which is the story of God's love and work through Christ. When this happens, then the acts of faith will be done accordingly. What we can also highlight from him is his insistence on rejecting the use of worship for specific goals. He thinks that worship should remain as a place of togetherness with God without any hidden agenda.

Schmemann's idea gives two important things in our research. First, Schmemann's exploration on the communal and eschatological remembrance in the Eucharist provides the ground for a communal remembrance. This communal remembrance gives an opportunity

---

[150] Schmemann, *The Eucharist,* 129
[151] Schmemann, *The Eucharist,* 129.
[152] Schmemann, *The Eucharist,* 130.
[153] Schmemann, *The Eucharist,* 130.

for communal memory of the past. This communal commemoration could be the place for victims and perpetrators to come and celebrate the table of the Lord together; to re-membering the community of Christ. The Eucharist is the place where people will be brought one by one into one.

Second, it gives opportunity for a transformation in the Church as a community. The eucharistic commemoration can transform the memory of community. The memory of the past is being transformed in mystery to become the communal memory and identity. This memorial is done in a joyous celebration, at a feast of bread and wine, which reminds us that the remembrance of the life of Jesus is a joyous communal remembrance. The joyous remembrance gives space for transformation and redemption for victims who seek to release their memory of pain in the community.

One of the strong points, and at the same time his weakness, is Schmemann's idea on the mystery of the Eucharist that can transform the Church into being active in its context. As we pointed out earlier, he did not really explain how this mystery can lead the Church into action except that we should be open to the Spirit. He warned us about the use of a specific goal in liturgy and rightly does so. This seems contradictory to Metz's idea of *memoria passionis* that tried to bring the memory of the suffering into the Church.

2.7 Liturgical Theology and Political Theology in Dialogue

Bruce Morrill, a Catholic liturgist, has done research on the dialogue between Schmemann and Metz. He thinks that a dialogue between Metz's political theology and Schmemann's liturgical theology will be fruitful and that they can complete each other. Morrill's research, although not directly connected with the purpose of this chapter, tries to put the two opinions into a fruitful discussion by focusing on the two theologians' starting point which is anamnesis. The two seemingly different ideas of Metz and Schmemann will be fruitful for our research in looking at the theological foundation on the remembrance of the past.

Morrill appreciates Metz's *memoria passionis* and thinks that Schmemann's idea of liturgical theology can help implement this idea by giving a foundation for it. He thinks that Schmemann does not give a clear answer on how liturgical theology can answer the practical problems of history. Morrill thinks that Schmemann "offers a vague, abstract mission for Christians."[154] This is why he offers Metz's idea of remembrance of suffering as the mission of the Church.

He directly criticizes Schmemann's objection to liberation theology. His argument is, and we agree with him, Schmemann should not reject liberation theology if it comes as a result of liturgical commemoration. He says,

> Schmemann's error lies in identifying the signs of the kingdom *only* in liturgy, where they are glorious. But is that the case? Are the signs of the kingdom only evident in liturgy? No, signs of the kingdom, while only fragmentary now in the time of history of this world, are nonetheless powerfully real for people who see with the eyes of faith. The liturgy must enable Christians to perceive the poor and suffering as the special object of God's favor, as well as kenotic deeds of service as signs of the Christ who "came in the form of a servant and reigned only through the cross.[155]

This is why Morrill says that Schmemann misses the point that mystery can also lead to action. Morrill rightly challenges Schmemann that when the Eucharist as the center of liturgy is indeed the one that influences the action of the Church, then Schmemann cannot be against liberation theology if it indeed came as a result of the liturgy and memory of suffering.

Morrill even thinks that Schmemann's idea could support the type of bourgeois church that Metz was addressing. He criticizes Schmemann by saying,

> Schmemann's theology is a stellar confirmation of Metz's prediction. Schmemann's diatribes against theological and practical concern for social justice, and the efforts of liberation theologies, are borne out of (1) the ideological shortcomings in his critical analysis of contemporary religious piety and (2) the heavy theoretical reliance on classical metaphysics in his sacramental-liturgical theology.[156]

He thinks that Schmemann came to this idea because of his eschatological view of the Eucharist that sees God as the ultimate judge of time. Such view could encourage the Church into an exclusive type of church that only takes care of itself.

The core of Christian theology, for Metz, must be found by the reflection of the context. He suggests that this source of theology can be traced to the history of liturgical remembrance. Unfortunately Metz did not explore this further, for "Metz does not, however, elaborate in detail the history and theology of the Jewish and Christian practices

---

[154] Morrill, *Anamnesis*, 123.
[155] Morrill, *Anamnesis*, 134.
[156] Morrill, *Anamnesis*, 137.

of liturgical remembrance, which could provide fuller elaboration on how this fundamental category of memory practically functions in Christian faith."[157] Schmemann on the other hand provided the concept of memory in Christian faith through liturgy. However, Morrill is skeptical about Schmemann's idea. For him, Schmemann was being too theoretical and did not give a clear explanation of how this memory could be interpreted in practical life. He says that the Church "has long failed in what Schmemann would consider an adequate recognition of this essential role of memory in the profession and practice of faith."[158]

Despite the fact that Metz is advocating praxis for Christian faith in social issues, he seems "predominantly to serve the political aspect of his definition of Christian praxis. Narrative memory breaks into prevailing social consciousness and goads action."[159] While on the other side, Schmemann is putting his work at the mystical point of Christian faith.

In the end, Morrill is of the opinion that both Metz and Schmemann have failed to fully draw the picture of "Christian tradition of memory and its capacity as the dynamic, mediating force in the dialectic between mysticism and politics." Further he says, "What is needed is a framework for explaining the function of memory in the praxis of Christian faith, a framework which takes into account the elements of worship (mysticism) and ethics (politics)."[160] Further, Morrill develops his idea that "the 'anamnestic' character of eucharistic liturgy, as well as other elements in Christian tradition, are capable of forming the *ekklesia* in the memory of, concern for, and solidarity with others in their suffering."[161]

One of the strong points of Schmemann's liturgical theology is that he brings back the Eucharist as a celebration of joy. The memory of Christ is a memory of joy that is celebrated in the feast. On the other hand,

> Metz, however, seems to have difficulty bringing the joyously liberating potential of sacramental ritual together with his descriptions of prayer as both a passionate search for the loving God, of Jesus and an urgent lament to God in the face of human suffering, catastrophe, and crisis.

---

[157] Morrill, *Anamnesis*, 141.
[158] Morrill, *Anamnesis*, 142
[159] Morrill, *Anamnesis*, 146.
[160] Morrill, *Anamnesis*, 146.
[161] Morrill, *Anamnesis*, 132. Morrill then analyzes the meaning of anamnesis in biblical usage. He mainly uses Nils Alstrup Dahl's analysis on the meaning of Anamnesis in early Christianity, *Jesus in the Memory of the Early Church* (Minneapolis: Augsburg, 1976). We have discussed the biblical meaning of remembrance in the previous chapter.

Schmemann's emphasis upon the joyous realization of the kingdom of heaven on earth in the Eucharistic liturgy clearly provides support for much of what Metz seeks in sacramental practice. I am arguing, however, that we can expect more from the liturgy as the performative knowing and appropriation of the Christian faith in an "anticipatory memory" of both crisis and consolation.[162]

Liturgy can provide the healing and redemptive memory for the victims, especially in the commemoration of the Eucharist. The joyous remembrance of the past suffering of Jesus, and also the resurrection will make victims realize that there is a different ending to a *memoria passionis*. This is the space of remembrance that supports healing for victims and transforms the memory of suffering into joyous celebration. The question now is how is this transformation possible?

It seems that Schmemann and Metz have important points that we can use to answer our question on the place of a common place for victims and perpetrators to share their memory of the past hurt. Our question now is how can we do this? Metz and Schmemann have different ideas that we somehow need to reconcile. Can we see the Eucharist as the proper place of remembering suffering? Can we change this memory of suffering through the memory of Jesus into a joyous commemoration of the past hurt? We will now try to look at these questions by exploring the most recent analysis of the notion of remembrance and memory in the light of forgiveness and reconciliation by a Protestant theologian, Miroslav Volf.

3. *Miroslav Volf: The End of Memory*

We will now look at the third major theologian in this chapter, a Protestant theologian, Miroslav Volf. Volf is one of the recent theologians that explore the possibility of forgiveness and its relation with memory. His theological exploration on forgiveness has brought him to the issue of memory and its important role within the context of reconciliation. This is why this chapter chooses to explore his idea on forgiveness and its relation with remembrance as an important part of our research.

Volf's theological ideas were developed from his background and life experience. He was born in Osijek, Croatia in 1956 in the midst of the war that divided the former Yugoslavia. Volf lived in Serbia in a family with a Pentecostal background.[163] Volf's father was half-German

---

[162] Morrill, *Anamnesis*, 201.
[163] Mark Oppenheimer, "Embracing Theology: Miroslav Volf Spans Conflicting Worlds," *Christian Century* 120 (January 2003), 18. Peter Kuzmic suggested that Croatia

and his mother was part of the Czech minority. His multi-ethnic background, the division of churches by ethnic groups in his homeland, the war that divided the former Yugoslavia, and his discussions with modernism and post-modernism thinkers brought him to his theological exploration on the matter of identity and otherness, and forgiveness and reconciliation.

In this part we shall explore the meaning of forgiveness for Volf and its relation with remembrance and reconciliation.[164] The topic of forgiveness is central in Volf's theology which cannot be separated from his eschatology and ecclesiology.[165] We sum up Volf's fundamental basis in his writings as a Trinitarian theologian that embraces everybody— whether they are victims or perpetrators, or whatever ethnic groups or religion backgrounds they are coming from—in the communion of God's love; and gives hope that in the end God's justice will be fulfilled. This is Volf's underlying assumption in developing his theology.

Taking his departure from this primary, basal idea, Volf's understanding of the difficult task of forgiveness is well described in his preface of *Exclusion and Embrace*,

> It was a difficult book to write. My thought was pulled in two different directions by the blood of the innocent crying out to God and by the blood of God's Lamb offered for the guilty. How does one remain loyal both to the demand of the oppressed for justice and to the gift of forgiveness that the Crucified offered to the perpetrators? I felt caught between two betrayals—the betrayal of the suffering, exploited, and excluded, and the betrayal of the very core of my faith. In a sense even more disturb-

---

evangelical Christianity was different from the American model of Pentecostals as they offered a refuge from communist mind control and ethno-religious ideology. See Volf's own description on the different denomination in Eastern Europe in "Fishing in the Neighbor's Pond: Mission and Proselytism in Eastern Europe," *International Bulletin of Missionary Research* 20 No. 1, January 1996, 25–31.

[164] We will largely use three books by Miroslav Volf's on forgiveness: *Exclusion and Embrace: A Theological Exploration of Identity, Otherness, and Reconciliation* (Nashville: Abingdon Press, 1996), *Free of Charge: Giving and Forgiving in a Culture Stripped of Grace* (Grand Rapids, Zondervan: 2006), *The End of Memory: Remembering Rightly in a Violent World* (Grand Rapids: William B. Eerdmans Publishing Co., 2006).

[165] Volf describes his Free Church ecclesiology in his book, *After Our Likeness: The Church as the Image of the Trinity* (Grand Rapids, Michigan: Williams B. Eerdmans, 1998). In this book he was trying to build on ecclesiology that is based on faith and communion while being grounded in tradition, ecumenical, and catholic. He also based his ecclesiology on the Trinitarian theology which is connected with his whole theology that we shall see later on in this section of the present chapter. See also a catholic response by Ralph Del Colle, "Communion and the Trinity: The Free Church Ecclesiology of Miroslav Volf—A Catholic Response," *Pneuma: The Journal of the Society for Pentecostal Studies* Volume 22, No. 2 (Fall 2000), 303–327.

ingly, I felt that my very faith was at odds with itself, divided between the God who delivers the needy and the God who abandons the Crucified, between the demand to bring about justice for the victims and the call to embrace the perpetrators.[166]

Volf sees the tension between opting for the victims' voice and God's gift of forgiveness for the perpetrators. He struggles with the questions: how can one opt for the oppressed and yet carry an offer of forgiveness; how can one carry out justice yet share God's love for everyone—even for the perpetrators? These tensions can be seen throughout Volf's elaboration of forgiveness, which eventually carries us into the use of remembrance in the dialogue of forgiveness.

Volf then offers a theology of embrace, where victims and perpetrators are ready to accept and embrace each other. Theology of embrace is Volf's exploration of Jesus' command to love your enemies. Embrace is a picture of the relation of the Trinity in which different people are inhabited by the other, recognizing multiple identities, and recognizing the self because of the other.[167] Embracing the enemy does not put justice aside; in fact it "cannot take place until justice is attended to."[168] Volf stresses the importance of justice that precedes embrace, and "forgiveness is the boundary between exclusion and embrace."[169] Thus, justice is connected with forgiveness and eventually leads to embrace, the true act of reconciliation.

The best way to see Volf's argument within his context is by looking at his dialogue with postmodern philosophy's critique towards modernism's "grand-narrative" theory.[170] Postmodern theory suggested that Western

---

[166] Volf, *Exclusion and Embrace*, 9.

[167] See Volf's own description of embrace in Mark Oppenheimer, "Embracing Theology", 19–21. Celestine Mukesura also gives useful information about Volf's theology of forgiveness in his dissertation, *An Assessment of a Contemporary Model of Forgiveness* (PhD diss.: Dallas Theological Seminary, 2007), 108–120.

[168] Miroslav Volf, "Forgiveness, Reconciliation, and Justice: A Christian Contribution to a More Peaceful Social Environment," in *Forgiveness and Reconciliation: Religion, Public Policy, and Conflict Transformation*, eds. Raymond G. Helmick and Rodney L. Petersen (Radnor: Templeton Foundation Press, 2001), 43. We will see what Volf's understanding of justice is somewhat later.

[169] Miroslav Volf, "Exclusion and Embrace: Theological Reflections in the Wake of 'Ethnic Cleansing,'" *Journal of Ecumenical Studies* vol. 29 (1992), 247.

[170] David Ingram, "Postmodernism," in *Encyclopedia of Philosophy 2nd Edition Vol.7*, ed. Donald M. Borchert (Michigan: Thomson Gale, 2006), mentions that the term "postmodernism" emerged in 1950s to describe new architectural and literary movements that opposed commonly accepted canons regarding the unity and coherence of narratives and artistic styles. This term has been used by mainly French and German philosophers to "designate a criticism of reason regarded as a universal and certain foundation for knowledge and morality, and of modern culture, understood

society has been operating under a few notions of grand-narratives that were considered as the way that the whole world should behave. Jean-François Lyotard says that narratives are "the stories that communities tell themselves to explain their present existence, their history and ambitions for the future."[171] Lyotard sees that there are two types of meta-narrative. The first type is the speculative grand-narrative where all truth and values are based on a single rule, which is determined by its relation to the whole of knowledge. The second type is the grand-narrative of emancipation where knowledge is valuable because it is the basis of human freedom and the basis of truth is morality, where "knowledge is no longer the subject, but in the service of the subject."[172] Although the two meta-narratives have different purposes and seem to be in contrast with each other, they tend to act as 'the grand-narrative' that forces everyone to follow their main story.

Volf thinks that the idea of a grand narrative can lead to endless rejection from other stories that are excluded from the picture. The division can cause exclusion that separates "we" from "they".[173] The question then should be how can we reconcile different cultures and languages while not creating another set of rules that can lead into another grand narrative. Picking up Jean-Francois Lyotard's rejection of the intention of universality of a grand narrative to reach the "final reconciliation based on systematic totalization", Volf is asking, "what resources we need to live in peace in the absence of the final reconciliation?"[174]

---

as a progressive unfolding of knowledge and morality", 729. One of the main objections of postmodernism is whether there will ever be a complete and coherent system of thought based on reason. The creation of 'the grand story' will have to exclude other stories that do not fit the scheme of the big story. Zygmunt Bauman rightly compares this forming of the grand story as a gardener picking what should be included and excluded to form a beautiful garden, see *Modernity and the Holocaust* (New York: Cornell University Press, 2000), 65–66.

[171] Simon Malpas, *Jean-François Lyotard* (London: Routledge, 2003), 21. Malpas summarizes Lyotard's idea of narrative in his phenomenal work of Jean-François Lyotard, *The Postmodern Condition: A Report on Knowledge*, trans. Geoff Bennington and Brian Massumi (Minneapolis: University of Minnesota Press, cop. 1984), 7. This book is Lyotard's masterpiece that tries to answer how the lives and identities of people are constructed by contemporary structures of knowing. He realizes that the driving force of knowledge has changed from its use for humanity to efficiency and profit. According to him this modern ultimate driving force of knowledge is not sustainable, thus we need to respect the different languages and different roles of different system of organizations instead of creating a new grand narrative.

[172] Lyotard, *The Postmodern Condition*, 34.

[173] According to Volf, exclusion can be either by separating oneself from the other and seeing the other as enemy or by assimilating the other to oneself and make them like the self, Volf, *Exclusion and Embrace*, 67.

[174] Volf, *Exclusion and Embrace*, 109.

This is the moment where Volf parted with postmodern thinkers who he thought are hesitant to grasp on to a story of final reconciliation. For Volf reconciliation always has a social meaning. It should not be stressed on only the personal reconciliation of a person to God nor the pursuit for justice. Declining the first two meanings, Volf says that reconciliation's ultimate goal is "community of love."[175] He believes that the hope for the final reconciliation in Christian faith must not be put aside in order to accommodate the "non-final reconciliation" that modern projects of emancipation and its deconstructive critique suggest. Volf argues that, "First, the final reconciliation is not a work of human beings but the triune God. Second, it is not an apocalyptic end of the world but the eschatological new beginning of this world. Third, the final reconciliation is not a self-enclosed "totality" because it rests on a God who is nothing but a perfect love."[176] Because the triune God is the only author of the final reconciliation, theology can only offer a "nonfinal reconciliation based on a vision of reconciliation that cannot be undone."[177] This view provides a strong foundation for Volf's offer of embrace. By reflecting on the relation of the triune God, one will be able to receive the other into oneself and thereby be challenged and changed into a new identity through the other's alterity.

3.1 Volf's View on Forgiveness

The act of embracing demands forgiveness to take place. Volf views forgiveness as an echo of God's love towards humanity. It is something that is given. Because God forgives, humans too must forgive. Humans have the power and right to forgive because God has already forgiven the sinful humanity. Forgiveness is not only the reflection of God's forgiveness, but it also intends to make God's forgiveness our own, and it is actually Christ who forgives through us. This is the foundation of forgiveness and thus answers the question whether human has the ability and right to forgive one another.

Forgiveness is also a tool to break the cycle of vengeance. It "breaks the power of the remembered past and transcends the claims of the affirmed justice and so makes the spiral of vengeance grind to a

---

[175] Miroslav Volf, "The Social Meaning of Reconciliation," a paper given as the Henry Martyn Lecture at the 1997 EMA annual conference. The text can be viewed at http://www.globalconnections.co.uk/pdfs/ reconciliation.pdf, accessed September, 2008.

[176] Volf, *Exclusion and Embrace*, 110.

[177] Volf, *Exclusion and Embrace*, 110.

halt."[178] Even though it breaks the cycle of vengeance, forgiveness is not a substitute for justice. Volf is of the opinion that people who have been forgiven and are willing to forgive are the very ones who will be capable of pursuing justice without turning the role in reverse, since it will change in restorative justice. In fact, according to Volf, embrace is part of the definition of justice. Volf sums up the position of the two by saying, "to agree on justice you need to make space in yourself for the perspective of the other, and in order to make space, you need to want to embrace the other…The knowledge of justice depends on the will to embrace."[179] With his opinion on justice, which is depending on the will to embrace the other, Volf has refused the position of hesitant post-modern thinkers who set up a rule of justice. He also rejects a single notion of justice because humans are different from one another. The will to embrace becomes universal in terms of being applicable to everyone, and it is not singular because it depends on the will itself.

Forgiveness also demands genuine repentance from perpetrators and victims. To repent means to "simply take our wrongdoing upon ourselves."[180] It does not mean that we can find excuses for our past misbehaviors or blaming someone or something else. Repentance is an act of self-realization and humility.

What is the relation between forgiveness and repentance? Can one forgive or being forgiven without repentance? This is where Volf describes forgiveness as a social affair, as it does not demand the participation of one party but of both the perpetrators and victims. Here we can agree with Volf when he points out that forgiveness must be sent and received in order to work fully. The forgiveness that is sent contains both an accusation and a release from guilt and punishment. When victims offer forgiveness, it means that they are saying that the offensive action is real and that they feel the pain but are willing to release the perpetrators from guilt and punishment. To forgive means "to accuse wrongdoers while at the same time freeing them of charges against them, releasing them from guilt, and eventually letting the wrongdoing slip into oblivion."[181] If the perpetrators do not accept this offer, then it

---

[178] Volf, *Exclusion and Embrace*, 121. Volf agrees with Hannah Arendt that Jesus fought injustice and oppression of the Lamech's logic with a creative 'injustice' of forgiveness by telling people to forgive seventy-seven times (Matthew 18:21–22). See Hannah Arendt, *The Human Condition: A Study of the Central Dilemmas Facing Modern Man* (Garden City: Doubleday, 1959), 212–214.

[179] Volf, *Exclusion and Embrace*, 220.

[180] Volf, *Exclusion and Embrace*, 119.

[181] Volf, *Free of Charge*, 195.

means the gift of forgiveness was sent but not received, so it is not fully working as it was intended.[182]

Volf is of the opinion that repentance is not a condition of forgiveness, but it is the consequence. God offers forgiveness but if the perpetrators do not take it then they stay untouched by it. God's forgiveness is not conditioned by repentance, but the perpetrators' being forgiven is conditioned by repentance. The perpetrator will repent if he/she knows that he/she was offered forgiveness that consist accusation and release of guilt at the same time. Volf says, "We are able to genuinely repent only when forgiveness has first been extended to us."[183] However, Volf also says, "Forgiveness does not cause repentance, but it does help make repentance possible."[184] In his view, forgiveness can be offered without repentance but eventually true forgiveness will drive repentance to be in place.

Volf says that repentance is the consequence of forgiveness and to repent means to realize what we have done and feel remorse for it. These actions require an inquiry into memory. We need to remember what we have done to be able to realize what we have done. The question then is: what is the role of memory in forgiveness and how can it be useful in the dialogue of forgiveness and repentance? Here, Volf describes the path of forgiveness and its relation with remembrance if it "starts with remembering truthfully, condemning wrong deeds, healing inner wounds, releasing wrongdoers from punishment and guilt, repentance by and transformation of wrongdoers, and reconciliation between the wronged and their wrongdoers; and it ends with the letting go of the memory of wrongdoing."[185] Based on this premise, Volf elaborates his thinking on the issue. He has two premises that he wants to argue concerning how we should deal with our memories of wrongdoing. The premises that he rejects are, "We should remember wrongs solely out of the concern for victims"; and "We should forever remember wrongs suffered."[186] This is where Volf takes an important turn in his view on forgiveness and connects it with the role of memory and remembrance.

---

[182] Volf, *Free of Charge*, 181–183.
[183] Volf, *Free of Charge*, 185.
[184] Volf, *Free of Charge*, 186.
[185] Volf, *The End of Memory*, 151.
[186] Volf, *The End of Memory*, 231. Even though he describes his rejection on these two notions in his 'Afterword' chapter, he already had made them clear throughout the entire book.

3.2 The Role of Memory

The End of Memory is a collection of the revised version of the annual Stob lectures that were presented in 2002 by Volf at the campus of Calvin College and Calvin Theological Seminary in honour of Henry J. Stob.[187] His lectures were originally subdivided into three parts: *Quick Forgetting, Obligatory Remembering*; *Truthfulness, Integration, Exemplarity*; and *Memory of Liberation, Memory of Reconciliation*. However, Volf changed his mind and presented a revised three parts of his *Love's Memory* lectures: *Dante's Strange Vision, Three Great Defenders of Forgetting, Eschatological Non Remembrance: Meaning, Identity, and Final Consummation*. Later in his book, Volf divides his idea again into three parts: *Remember; How Should We Remember;* and *How Long Should We Remember*.

Volf writes *The End of Memory* as he comes to terms with the recent explorations on the importance of memories in the contemporary cultural situation. In the world's history of violence and conflict, there is a feeling of the necessity to remember evils committed and suffered. In an interview, he says that memory is important because,

> we live in such a fast-paced culture, in which we have a hard time remembering what's transpired only a few days or a month ago. We're glued to this ever-shifting and changing present, so we feel that memory is slipping away from us. We want to hold onto memories, because we rightly believe that part of our identity is what we remember about ourselves and our interactions with others. Part of our identity as a nation depends on what has happened to us in the past.[188]

Memory is important because the fast-paced culture makes us aware that we need to have a grasp of memories in order to have a sense of identity. Thus, we are trying to get a hold of some memories that can relate us to our identity. This also happens with traumatic memories where victims and perpetrators relate their identity with their role. However, these memories are—as Volf explained—not innocent. Therefore, holding on to painful memories of the past can easily turn into a weapon if we do not remember rightly. Memories can be as dangerous as they can be helpful to heal past suffering.

At the end of the 20th and the early 21st century, we see the need of the term "memory and remembrance" within social, psychological, and

---

[187] Miroslav Volf's lectures are available at http://www.calvinseminary.edu/continuingEd/stob/pastLectures.php, accessed August, 2008.

[188] Collin Hansen, "Redeeming Bitterness: Miroslav Volf Tells How to Stop the 'Shield of Memory' from Turning into a Sword," *Christianity Today* 51 no. 5 (May 2007), 50.

philosophical studies. Volf thinks that this memory boom—as he calls it—was caused by two things. The first one is because the fast paced, forward moving culture, paradoxically makes us try to grasp recent memory and memorialize certain events without even having enough time to reflect on the meaning of those events. Therefore, "the memory boom tries to compensate for an actual memory bust."[189] The second cause is the consensus to remember major catastrophes of the world in honor of the victims so that our world's violent past will not happen again in the future.

Volf explains that, if used rightly, memory is an important factor in forgiveness. Nevertheless, memory can also be used as reason to commit violence in return towards people who hurt us because the memory of the painful past can turn into making the victims become the perpetrators themselves. The question that Volf poses is how we can remember in a constructive way that memory becomes a bridge between adversaries instead of a tool of vengeance. Volf tries to answer this question by exploring his own memory of pain when he was interrogated by Captain G. during his compulsory military service in the then Communist-Yugoslavia in 1984. Volf felt so threatened and abused by those interrogations that he could not forget this experience. Volf raises the question,

> How then should I relate to Captain G. in my imagination now that his wrongdoing was repeating itself only in my memory? How should I, a victim of his abuse, *remember* him and what he had done to me? Like the people of God throughout the ages, I often prayed the words of the psalmist: "Do not remember the sins of my youth or my transgressions; according to your steadfast love remember me, for your goodness' sake, O Lord" (Ps. 25:7). What would it mean for me to remember Captain G. and his wrongdoing the way I prayed for God to remember me and my wrongdoing? How should the one who loves remember the wrongdoer and the wrongdoing?[190]

However we should not start our exploration in memory without a clear purpose, or already even to have revenge as our goal. In exploring his memory, Volf is committed to the final goal, which is embracing everybody in the love of God, and this includes Captain G. the perpetrator. Volf beautifully phrases his purpose on exploring memory in relation with forgiveness as, "It is to remember the wrongdoing suffered *as a person committed to loving the wrongdoer.*"[191] Thus, in line with his

---

[189] Volf, *The End of Memory*, 40.
[190] Miroslav Volf, "God Forgiveness and Ours: Memory of Interrogations, Interrogations of Memory," *Anglican Theological Review* (2007), 218–219.
[191] Volf, "God Forgiveness and Ours", 219.

goal in forgiveness and embrace, his remembrance is always in the light of embracing the other.

If being used rightly, the final process of reconciliation according to Volf is the act of forgetting the past hurt. This final step assumes that, "the matters of "truth" and "justice" have been taken care of, that perpetrators have been named, judged, and (hopefully) transformed, that victims are safe and their wounds healed, a forgetting that can therefore ultimately take place only together with the creation of "all things new."[192] The idea of forgetting in Volf's theology of forgiveness can only take place when all the steps needed have been fulfilled; the steps which are truth and justice.

Therefore, for Volf, memory has always been a central part in the relation of forgiveness and reconciliation. The challenge is not about whether or not we should remember the past hurt, but rather on how we should remember the past rightly. This question takes us to his idea or remembering truthfully.

3.3 Remember Truthfully

To be able to speak about the past, to celebrate it as a social event between the perpetrators and victims, means that it should resonate on both sides and thus be accepted by them. Volf gave three reasons why this remembrance should be truthful not only for the victims but also for the perpetrators. First, this should be a social affair because the victims' memory will influence their future behavior towards their environment. Second this remembrance can be used as a tool or a lesson to reject any similar treatment in the future. Third, to remember rightly also means to do justice to the perpetrators; this is done by not accusing them for something than they did not do, nor by freeing them from their wrongdoing.

Because of those reasons, remembering truthfully is a very important step in recognizing the past. In doing so, he suggests one rule, "Be truthful in telling what you remember no less than in telling what you experience or intend to do."[193] He realizes the difficulty and challenge in the perception of the truth in one's memory and that the other party might well have different memory. Volf says that to remember truthfully demands a good intention with no intentional lying and to "render the past event truthfully to the best of our knowledge."[194] The

---

[192] Volf, *Exclusion and Embrace*, 131.
[193] Volf, *The End of Memory*, 45. Volf connects this idea of speaking truthfully with the ninth commandment of "Thou shall not bear false witness" (Exodus 20:16).
[194] Volf, *The End of Memory*, 49.

truthfulness of the story lies in the "indication that it is pleasing, or that it offers a window into a desirable way of being in the world, or that it has succeeded as a move in the struggle of power—a struggle in which all human beings are involved, not only as possessors of things but as speakers of language."[195] Volf tries to show that even someone's perception of the truth, when it is done in a good intention, could be considered as truthful memories. He says that "when we claim to remember, we are claiming that, to the best of our knowledge, our memory is true in the sense that it corresponds in some way to events as they occurred."[196] Therefore truth cannot be forced with violence to make others accept this truth. He says, "Commitment to non-violence must accompany commitment to truth otherwise commitment to truth will generate violence."[197] Thus, remembering truthfully demands a good intention and the will to embrace.

The next question is: How can we know what the truth is? There are difficulties in deciding the truth among different memories. Volf agrees with this assumption but still insists that "the will to embrace cannot be sustained and will not result in an actual embrace if truth does not reign."[198] Even when seeking the truth is a difficult task to do, Volf stresses that we need to embrace for truth. Here, Volf parts again with post-modern hesitance of seeking the truth or the common truth.

We notice that Volf uses memories in the plural form instead of memory as a single entity. This means that he admits that there could be more than one truthful memory. This delivers the question, how can we know that the memory that one perceives is truthful, even when one is saying the utmost best account from one's true memory? Isn't it true that even our memory can play tricks on our perception of truth, as we have seen earlier? This is where Volf suggests that to remember truthfully is a moral obligation even when it is limited in nature. Based on the biblical dimension in Exodus 20:16 and James 5:12, Volf says that one may not be culpable if he/she misremembers unintentionally; but one is responsible to remember correctly.[199]

To remember truthfully has roots in doing justice. When connected to an event where there are perpetrators and victims, to remember truthfully is seen as doing justice to the story. If victims decide to

---

[195] Volf, *The End of Memory*, 49.
[196] Volf, *The End of Memory*, 51.
[197] Volf, *Exclusion and Embrace*, 272.
[198] Volf, *Exclusion and Embrace*, 258.
[199] Volf, *The End of Memory*, 52.

remember fewer atrocities than really happened, it means that he/she is not being just to him/herself as a victim. The victim's untruthful memory will be betraying his/her own past unless it was done on the base on "mature generosity aimed at forgiveness and reconciliation."[200] If the victim exaggerates what really happened by telling more than what he/she experienced, it would be accusing someone of doing something that he/she did not do.

For Volf, to remember truthfully is connected with justice and therefore is a precondition of reconciliation. Volf thinks that the truthfulness of one's memory does not eliminate other's truthfulness because it is dangerous to claim 'the truth' from one side of the story. This means that my truthful memory does not imply that it is the only truth. It is true for me because I experienced it, and that is what I can recall from the past. The other's memory can be true as well because they also experienced it that way. Different versions of memories can be dangerous if they are not truthful. Thus, the first rule has to be implemented, and that is to remember truthfully.

Remembering truthfully does not mean remembering fully what has happened in the past because this would be impossible, knowing the complex interaction between memory, perception, and truth. What Volf suggests is to remember truthfully to our best ability, even when it is not complete. It will be true in the sense that it is what we remember in the light of our honest feelings. In the end, Christ will "enable us truthfully and fully to remember our past as well as the past of those whose lives were intertwined with ours on account of wrongdoing."[201] Volf thinks that to remember the event on behalf of its victims is the moral responsibility of us as community. He argues that Christ will enable us to remember our past truthfully and fully. The truthful memory is "part of the larger obligation to speak well of our neighbors and thereby to sustain and heal relationships among people."[202]

Then Volf proposes the second rule, which is speaking the truth in love. Speaking the truth in love means not to mislead people by implying that the perpetrator is worse that he/she actually is. A loving act in remembering also demands remembrance of the good side of the perpetrator. By recalling the person's fullest self, one can balance the memory that he/she has about the perpetrator. This has to be done to reach the highest aim of lovingly truthful memory which "seeks to bring

---

[200] Volf, *The End of Memory*, 55.
[201] Volf, *The End of Memory*, 62.
[202] Volf, *The End of Memory*, 63.

about the repentance, forgiveness, and transformation of wrongdoers, and reconciliation between wrongdoers and their victims."[203]

Volf uses Paul Ricoeur's theory about two types of remembering: passive and active.[204] Passive remembering is when our memory comes back in our minds with no intentional effort. Active remembering is when we try to remember something intentionally. The two previous rules can only be applied when we are remembering in the active form. The passive form of memory could also trigger our actions, and Volf realizes this possibility by saying, "For not only do we act on memories of wrongs suffered: these memories act on us, too. They steal our attention, and they assault us with inner turmoil marked by shame, guilt, and maybe a mixture of self-recrimination and self-justification... such memories are not just clusters of information about the past—not even clusters of information stored for future use. They themselves are powerful agents."[205] We can see that Volf is insisting on truthfulness in the purpose of the use of memory. By choosing which memories are truthful we are separating the ones that are not; thus, truthfulness constitutes a just use of memory. When we remember truthfully, we also learn to remember therapeutically and by those memories, we can learn from the past. These are the basic rules that cover remembrance of the past wrongdoing.

3.4 A Community of Remembrance

Volf explains that it is difficult to remember truthfully when a person has been seriously wronged. That person needs outside help before he/she can achieve inner healing. This is when the exploration on memory takes its turn to outside of the self. Volf says, "Friends, family, or the public at large may need to acknowledge and condemn the wrongdoing; the offender may need to apologize and, if possible, offer restitution; the setting that made the injury possible may need to change so that the wronged person can feel safe."[206] People need help from outside when the hurtful past has become unbearable to remember.[207] Now we have

---

[203] Volf, *The End of Memory*, 65.
[204] See Paul Ricoeur, *Memory, History, Forgetting*.
[205] Volf, *The End of Memory*, 69.
[206] Volf, *The End of Memory*, 76. Volf also explains extensively how inner healings can happen within the person himself, which are done by integrating remembered wrongdoings into our life story (76); and the hope that some horrendous wrongs during our lives will be revealed at the end of history, and ascribe positive meanings to wrongs suffered (78).
[207] Volf also acknowledges the help of his community in keeping his traumatic memory

further questions: what is the role of community in remembering the hurtful past? What happens to the individual hurt when community acknowledges it? If the community acknowledges and accepts the story, can it become a part of the community's history? And later on, could this hurt be forgotten when they have become part of history?

Volf then advocates filtering memories of suffered wrongs through the lens of the sacred memories of the Exodus and Passion. The sacred memories of Exodus and Passion are connected to the identity of being Jew and Christian. They are communal memories, they shape the future of that community, and they are basically the memories of God. This lens can be used to reconcile the memories of today's traumatic past.

We will now briefly show how Volf connects the memory of the Exodus and Passion as a tool to help victims overcome their present suffering. This connection will be explored extensively in the following chapter in the light of the biblical theology analysis on what remembrance means in the Old Testament and New Testament, and how the meaning has progressed through time. Nevertheless his elaboration on the point should be mentioned here because Volf seems to make his analysis from an anthropological point of view.

Volf says that when Israel remembers the Exodus, they remember how God freed them from their suffering, and ordered them to be just and helpful towards the weakest and the needy. In this memory, God is being just and helpful to Israel in their time of need. However, this is not enough because Exodus has the tendency to remember the Egyptians and Amalekites acting at the expense of Israel's freedom. This means that the memory of the Exodus alone is not enough.

The memory of the Passion, which is historically and theologically connected with the memory of Exodus, is central in Christian theology. The memory of the Passion is the memory of God's saving action through a person towards the whole humanity, including the victims and perpetrators. Volf thinks that the Passion teaches to extend unconditional grace, affirm the claims of justice, and aim for communion. By learning from this memory, "We forgive out of God-like love for the wrongdoer; and by forgiving, we take one crucial step in a larger process whose final goal is the embrace of former enemies in a community of love."[208] The Lord's Supper is the ultimate remembrance that will change our attitude towards our negative remembrance. The Lord's Supper is a remembrance of the suffering Christ that can be

---

of interrogations from dominating his present and future, *The End of Memory*, 83.

[208] Volf, *The End of Memory*, 122.

used by the Church to foster reconciliation. Volf explains how this can happen by summing up his own thought,

> I will celebrate the Lord's Supper by remembering myself as a sinner and not as saint. I will celebrate the Lord's Supper by remembering my enemy not as this despicable person who has to be thrown into the pit of darkness, but as one for whom Christ has shed his blood. Therefore, I will be taken up into this action of Christ and hopefully emulate Christ in how I remember and treat the other person.[209]

Therefore, Volf continues, by remembering the wrongdoing through the memory of Passion, we will remember it as someone that has already been forgiven and with future hope that we will be reconciled with the perpetrators.

Because it is difficult to do such remembering especially when we are victims of a severe wrongdoing, it is very important to have a community that can support us to remember through the lens of the Exodus and the Passion. This is where Volf turns into how churches can offer to help remembering the memories of Exodus and Passion to get through the memories of present wrongdoing. He says, "Communities of sacred memory are, at their best, schools of right remembering—remembering that is truthful and just, that heals individuals without injuring others that allows the past to motivate a just struggle for justice and the grace-filled work of reconciliation."[210] By remembering within the community that has faith in the reconciling God through the memory of the Exodus and Passion, we can remember positively rather than negatively the wrongdoings that we suffered.

3.5 The End of Memory?

Volf's main focus of this book is the role of memory in the line of forgiveness and reconciliation. Volf explores how memory plays a crucial part in the conversation of forgiveness and reconciliation. Volf even continues further by saying that we could—even must—let go of the memories of a painful past when justice has been served.

Volf's thesis in his third part of the book is, "memories of suffered wrongs will not come to the minds of the citizens of the world to come, for in it they will perfectly enjoy God and one another in God."[211] In the end, we should let go of the memory of the wronged past. The "Final

---

[209] Hansen, "Redeeming Bitterness", 51.
[210] Volf, The End of Memory, 128.
[211] Volf, The End of Memory, 177.

Reconciliation" would be the goal of such remembering, and therefore would be the moment of the forgetting of hurtful past because justice has been done. He argues,

> What function would these memories serve in a secure world of perfect love? If those who wanted to keep such memories alive were the perpetrators, would we be wrong in suspecting that they could not forgive themselves for what they had done and therefore needed living memories to keep blaming themselves? If they were the victims, would it not be likely that they wanted to hold onto these memories because they cherished resentment against perpetrators or at least wanted to hold it in reserve? If we remembered wrongs suffered in a secure world of perfect love, might now our memory be doing the bidding of the desire for revenge—either on ourselves or on others?[212]

Volf's argument in letting go the memory of the hurtful past is because Christ has died for us. Christ shoulders the consequences of human sin; thus the sin has been detached from the sinner. When Christ died, sin died too. Forgiveness is an echo of God's grace. This is truly a scandal of non-remembrance of offences. Even so, Volf argues, "But if God's reconciling self-giving for the ungodly stands at the center of our faith, then nothing stands in the way of opting for grace, with its pain and delight, of forgiving and ultimately releasing the memory of suffered wrongs."[213] From his eschatological standpoint, Volf sees Christ as the final reconciler who will bring about the supreme memory—which will remember everything and eventually heal the past. Christ will not only heal your past but also remember and acknowledge your pain. The past identity which is full of pain can be changed into the identity of a person that has been redeemed by Christ.[214]

However, the real question is, can we really forget? Should we make

---

[212] Volf, *The End of Memory*, 207.
[213] Volf, *The End of Memory*, 209.
[214] Abraham van de Beek in "A Shared Story for Reconciliation—Which Story?" *Journal of Reformed Theology* Vol. 2 No. 1 (2008), 22, shares his doubt of forgetting the past by asking, "Can there be a sustainable story for the future if there is not a shared story of the past?" In his search for the sustainable story for the future that can be applied by both victims and perpetrators, and in line with what Volf suggested, van de Beek suggests to remembering the story of the cross. By placing his arguments on a biblical theological basis he argues that the only remembrance and thus a new identity for Christians is the death of Christ. The death of Christ brings a new story of life because it conquers death. He says, "We must give up our identity and share the story of God. We must share the cup He drank and be prepared to remember his death in the Lord's Supper we share his story, and we share it jointly. That is the only story that reconciles because it ends our identity (26)." This story of God is the whole story of the past, and it is the "remembrance of all human stories (26)."

it a goal in our journey of remembering in the light of forgiveness and reconciliation? Can we remember and forgive? Can we forgive and still remember the past wrongdoing? This is where our research questions Volf's idea of forgetting as the final act of reconciliation.

Volf is dealing with the problem of memory in relation with a forgiven past because he suggests that forgiveness is a gift by which the victims will treat the perpetrators as if the transgression never happened. The question raised and answered was on how we should remember. Now he tries to answer how to what length we should go to remember. Volf says that complete forgiveness will forget the past transgressions. This is the ultimate goal of forgiveness.

What about people who do forgive but not forget? Volf argues that there are two things happening when we forgive but not forget. First, the memory of the past will become stockpiled and could be used to wage battle. Second, the past will be forgiven, but the perpetrators will not be freed from his sin because the label "offender" is still attached to him in our memory.[215] But does it really work that way?

The fact is Volf still remembers exactly what had happened between him and Captain G. If he was to forgive the captain, based on his elaboration, he should be by now already have forgotten the traumatic event. Volf says,

> When I granted that I ought to love Captain G—love not in the sense of warm feeling but in the sense of benevolence, beneficence, and search for communion—much of what I wrote in the book followed, at least in rough outline if not in detail. But every time I wrote about loving Captain G. a small-scale rebellion erupted in my soul. "I love my parents and relatives; I love my wife and children; I love my friends; I love pets and wild geese. I might even love nosy neighbors and difficult colleagues, but I *don't love* abusers—I just don't and never will," screamed the leader of my internal insurrection. And at times it would not have taken much to make me switch sides—except that loving those who do me harm was precisely the hard path on which Jesus called me to follow him, a path that reflects more than any other the nature of his God and mine.[216]

The fact that he remembers it clearly, even when he was doing it as an example of his argument, leads to the question whether Volf can really achieve the ultimate goal in his reconciliation, which is the forgetting of the reconciled past. This shows that Volf has not really reconciled with his past with Captain G. He can still say that justice has not been

---

[215] Volf, *Free of Charge*, 176.
[216] Volf, "God Forgiveness and Ours", 225.

done because he never met the Captain anymore to have a full reconciliation act;[217] thus he cannot reach the ultimate act which is forgetting. Nevertheless, this gives us another question, does real forgiveness really demand forgetting and the letting go of memory? Is not what Volf does remembering and forgiving? Can we actually remember our traumatic past without any vengeance and still have forgiveness in place?

In his exploration on how God treats our past sins, he thinks that eventually God will forget our forgiven misdeeds. Volf says, "Scripture explicitly states that God doesn't even remember our sins. They don't come to God's mind (Jeremiah 31:34; Hebrews 8:12; 10:17)."[218] Later on Volf admits that he cannot fully grasp the nature of God's knowledge of forgiven sin. This is why he based his reasons on the history of Christianity where he suggests that spiritual writers and theologians have echoed that God doesn't remember our sin. This is why he says that in forgiving we will ultimately let it slip away; which initially generates the term "forgive and forget".

Repeatedly, Volf uses the idea of memory and remembrance of sin (and guilt) in the Old Testament in the anthropological meaning of the word, which is to recall an action or event back into one's mind. He says that eventually God will forget our sins based on Jeremiah 31:34 and Hebrews 8:12. He uses Psalm 25:7 to argue that to ask God not to remember our sin means we should treat the other the same too. We find that Volf's use of remembrance and memory in the Bible is not correct. We have seen in a previous chapter that the biblical idea of remembrance has a deeper meaning than just to recall something of the past into one's mind. In the Old Testament, remembrance means to remind humans of God's saving action towards them and to stay faithful to the covenant. In fact, the Old Testament is actually a book of remembrance of Israel's sins and God's grace, which keeps the record of Israel's sins, and how they remember their sins and ask for God's forgiveness. When God remembers Israel's sin, it is usually followed by punishment. After facing God's punishment, Israel will admit its iniquities and confess its sins. Their confessions will consist of a good remembrance of what they have actually done in the past, not merely their wrong actions in their own generation, but also in the generations

---

[217] In Volf, *The End of Memory*, 84, he argues that "Any healing of the wronged without involving the wrongdoer therefore, can only be partial. To complete the healing, the relationship between the two needs to be mended…Reconciliation with the wrongdoer completes the healing of the person who suffered the wrong."

[218] Volf, *Free of Charge*, 173.

before them. When God forgives them, God remembers their sins no more. Despite the repeated pattern, one thing is important to note: Israel *does* remember what they have done in the past. Thus, we can conclude that there is something lacking in Volf's idea of biblical use of memory and remembrance.

Therefore, we can now question Volf's conclusion that the past inequities should be forgotten when victims have been redeemed and the perpetrators transformed and their relationship has been defined through reconciliation. Noting that those steps Volf mentions are very difficult; is forgetting really possible? Can we really "no longer think of the injury?"[219] One can wonder if this should be the final goal of reconciliation, and think that if we can actually remember the past wrongdoing, and filter the negative feelings towards the memory that we have reached the goal.

4. *Metz, Schmemann, and Volf in Dialogue*

The three main theologians that we have analyzed represented three different Christian backgrounds: Catholic, Orthodox, and Protestant. The fact that all three come from different contexts provides a unique richness in theological understanding of remembrance. If we were to put them in a dialogue, what are the main theological arguments that we can bring from the three theologians to enrich our understanding of remembrance of the past conflict, and at the same time give a place for a redemptive memory both for victims and perpetrators? What do they have to say to the problem of remembrance of a past communal conflict?

We will start answering this question by pointing out their common ground; all three theologians agree that Christians should not forget their memory as God's people in the celebration of the Eucharist. This is the basis for the call to remember in the Christian tradition. The theologians agreed that the Eucharist is the source of our experience in the communion with God. This experience rooted in the memory of the cross is something that transforms the church as a community of believers.

Metz reminds us that the remembrance in the Eucharist is also to remember the suffering of Christ. The church as a community of believers cannot exclude the voices of the suffering from her context.

---

[219] Volf, *The End of Memory*, 209.

These voices resonate with the context in which we are living and remind us of the memory of the suffering on the cross. This memory of suffering brings an implication that the Church is expected to be inspired to act as a community that remembers the suffering. God's message in Christ speaks clearly to the communities who are insensitive to the situation of the world. And we have seen, what Metz did is giving a place to the voices of the voiceless to be heard. When we apply this to a context where communal conflict took place, then the remembrance of the suffering can be translated as remembrance of the past hurt. This means that the past hurts should be remembered, based on the theological foundation of the remembrance of the suffering. Thus, what Metz proposes is a theological basis of remembrance of the past hurt.

We can take this idea further by adding Keshkegian's point that the story of the cross should not only be about suffering, it is also about hope in the resurrection of Christ. There is hope in remembering the past suffering, which is the hope of healing. The remembrance of suffering is not a hopeless cause, it actually gives us hope in the thought that Christ has not only suffered but also has been resurrected. Although our suffering is not the same as the suffering of Jesus, his resurrection reminds us that the suffering is remembered in light of the resurrection. The important part is that the memory of the suffering should not be eliminated, rather it should be embraced with the hope brought by the memory of the resurrection.

What does it mean to a community in conflict, or in the HKBP case, to a community that was in conflict but decided not to talk about it? What would Metz say to the HKBP situation? Metz's theology gives suggestion that the memory of the past hurt should be brought to the presence of the memory of the cross. This means that the HKBP should start to remember what had happened in order to bring the memory of the suffering to the cross. The remembrance of the suffering, in this case the remembrance of the past conflict and the victims and perpetrators, is a transforming action by the Church as a community. The question is what we should do with the memory of the past hurt, and how we can prevent this memory to become a negative memory. How can we remember the past without falling into a perpetual remembrance, like what Metz seemed to suggest when he was talking about Germany's remembrance of the Holocaust? How long should we remember the painful past? Can the memory of past wrongs be transformed into a redemptive memory? More importantly, how can we find a place of doing this remembrance in our Christian tradition?

The place for remembrance in Christian tradition is in the liturgy. This is the contribution from Alexander Schmemann that we can incorporate. He brings the Eucharist to the fore as the most important sacrament because of its communal aspect. Schmemann also reminded us of the centrality of the Eucharist in worship and theology. Because of its central place, we should be aware of any hidden motives for using the Eucharist to anyone's own purpose.

The Eucharist gives us the place of communal remembrance. The church as a community celebrates the Eucharist together, with victims and perpetrators. What they remember is God's love in the life of Christ. This memory should be remembered in a joyous celebration, that God has given Christ for us. What Schmemann offers here is not necessarily in contrast with Metz's idea of the memory of the suffering. The memory of the suffering will be brought to God from the community, and then be transformed in a joyous celebration of God's saving action. This means that we can avoid a perpetual negative remembrance of the past hurt when it has been transformed in the joyous memory of the cross and resurrection.

One of the strong points, and at the same time his weakness, is Schmemann's understanding of the mystery of the Eucharist as one that can transform the church into becoming active in its context. However, he did not really explain how this mystery can lead the church into action except that we should be open to the Spirit. He warns us about the use of specific goals in celebrating the liturgy and rightly does so. The action of the church as a community of believers should come as the reflection of participating in the liturgy. For Schmemann, the action of the church as a community should be based on the encounter and experience of meeting God in liturgy.

What Schmemann would say to our specific case is that the remembrance of the cross is a joyous communal remembrance that transforms any painful memory, precisely because we know God remembers and meets us in liturgy of the Eucharist. We are invited to come to the Eucharist as a community of believers, both as victims and perpetrators. The Eucharist is the place where this encounter of memories and remembrance of victims and perpetrators can happen.

Nevertheless, there is still one problem, what happens with our own memory in the Eucharist? How can the Eucharist transform traumatic memory of the past to redemptive memory? This is where we can look at Volf's contribution on the role of memory in forgiveness and reconciliation.

What we can take from Volf is, for the sake of embracing and reconciliation and to bring it to the communal context, his plea to remember truthfully. This plea is not only addressed to the victims and perpetrators, but also for the sake of the entire community. There is a kind of handing over of personal memory to communal memory that is based on the theological ground that Christ will enable us to remember truthfully in love. Christ is the ultimate healer that remembers the pain. We can sense an eschatological hope in this idea. This hope of future in Christ does not turn us into a passive state of forgetting, rather it demands us to remember truthfully first as a condition to forgive and reconcile.

We appreciate Volf's insistence on forgiveness and reconciliation as the final goal of remembrance. In a way, Volf is saying that remembrance should not be the end goal of a past conflict. Remembrance in itself is not enough if we want to have healing of memory. His idea can also help us to give some presupposition in remembrance of communal conflict. We have to view our remembrance in the light of Christ as our Redeemer, the one who remembers. We can bring our pain and memory to Christ and know that in Christ, it is not forgotten, yet transformed as a healed memory.

What Volf and Schmemann relate is a plea to remember the past in the Eucharist. The Eucharist is exactly the place where we can remember the past truthfully and surrender the painful memories to Christ the redeemer. This remembrance will be done at a communal level, where it becomes communal memory. Communal remembrance means taking up the responsibility to remember as a community. The remembrance of past wrongs will be viewed from the Eucharist perspective that God remembers and ask us to remember the freedom from the pain. Here we can say that Volf would ask us to remember the past truthfully as a participant of the communal feast at the Eucharist.

The three theologians have supported and added depth to our plea for remembrance of the past conflict, especially in a communal context. It is important to note that their different theological backgrounds give us a rich ecumenical feeling in the development of our research. They all come from a different confessional context, yet they are speaking about the same idea of remembrance.

What we can conclude is that remembrance is a place where we can create a space for the victims to tell their story. It is also a place for communities to listen to stories of atrocities in the past. Personal stories can enter the public domain and stay there when they become part of one shared story for the community. It means that there is a possibility of having redemptive memory when the community gives a new meaning to it.

Our questions now are: how we can do this and bring the idea of communal remembrance in the life of the Church as community of believers. How can we actually remember 'truthfully' about the suffering in the mystery of the Eucharist? These are the points that we will discuss in our next chapter on remembrance in liturgy.

Chapter Five

Remembrance in the Liturgy of the Eucharist

We now have explored the notion of remembrance in various ways: as a new culture, in an actual communal conflict within the church, its varied presence in the Bible, and by ascertaining what several theologians have to say about remembrance. In this last major chapter, further questions now will be addressed, focusing on one overall major aspect. Since remembrance plays an important role in dealing with conflicts and trauma, how can we foster that process at a communal level? Can remembrance be practiced at a communal level in such a way that this remembrance will embrace everyone who is involved in the conflict?

Within the Christian tradition, liturgy is the place of communal remembrance; indeed, we can say that liturgy is an act of remembrance. It is the place of experiencing God's loving action through the life of Jesus Christ. After the Bible is considered as a place of the passing on of social memory, Christians are reminded of God's saving action through Jesus Christ, and how to be open to this experience in liturgy. The community remembers the experience in their liturgy and makes it as a social memory. Thus, liturgy is basically a communal remembrance of God's action, where God acts as the subject. In it we are being reconciled with God, and the reconciliation experience transformed us.

This chapter will explore the possibility of transformation of victims and perpetrators with their painful memories by way of the memory of the loving Christ in the liturgy of the Eucharist. We will explore what remembrance means in liturgy and how it can bring healing to past memories. We will explore ecumenical liturgical resources to find places in liturgy for communal remembrance and healing. Through liturgy, the transformation of the individual past hurt into communal memories of Christ can open a space of healing for both victims and perpetrators. Even so, this research will not go exhaustively into the history of liturgy in general, or even eucharistic liturgy, because it is a broad topic of its own. We will, however, look at some ecumenical resources of eucharistic theology and their significance in healing the memory of the past.

In the last parts of this chapter, we will return to the background and impetus of this research, which is the HKBP 1992–1998 conflict. We will look into the Church's liturgy of the Eucharist and its theological significance. What is the HKBP's theological understanding of remembrance in the Eucharist? What significance does it bring to our research with regard to remembrance of the past wounds? How do we optimize this theological understanding in the light of transforming and healing memory of the past wounds? How do we do all this and, at the same time, take into account Schmemann's warning about not using the Eucharist for our own willful ends, Metz's idea of memory of suffering, and Volf's theology of embrace? Such are the questions that we will address in this chapter.

1. *Liturgy and Remembrance*

Liturgy as an act of remembrance can be seen fully in the Eucharist. The Eucharist is a memorial of the life of Jesus Christ. It is not only a recalling of something that happened in the past, but it is the re-actualization of the event for the present. This is the mystery that exists and is made into effect in liturgy: a transformation of past events into our present. Paul says in Romans 16:25–27,

> Now to him who is able to establish you by my gospel and the proclamation of Jesus Christ, according to the revelation of the mystery hidden for long ages past, but now revealed and made known through the prophetic writings by the command of the eternal God, so that all nations might believe and obey him—to the only wise God be glory forever through Jesus Christ! Amen.

The phrase "revelation of the mystery" refers to the link between past and present. It also shows the revelation of God's plan in Christ. Geoffrey Wainwright, a Protestant theologian and liturgist says, "Mystery here denotes the divine purpose and plan to bring human beings to salvation, which has now been brought to light as never before through its embodiment in Jesus Christ, the incarnate Son."[1]

This mystery is also considered as a liturgical mystery. The mystery of the past has been revealed and made known so that everybody in the present will believe and obey God. Here, we see that the event in

---

[1] Geoffrey Wainwright, "Christian Worship: Scriptural Basis and Theological Frame" in *The Oxford History of Christian Worship*, eds. Geoffrey Wainwright and Karen B. Westerfield Tucker (New York, Oxford University Press, 2006), 8. See also *Eucharist and Eschatology* (New York: Oxford University Press, 1981).

the past is connected with the present, which later on will encourage action for the future. This liturgical memory is the actualizing of the past event. But what does it actually mean?

The remembrance in liturgy is mainly referring to the word *anamnesis* that Jesus instituted during the last supper with the disciples. As the words of institution that were instituted by Jesus himself, what do the words *eis tēn emēn anamnēsin* mean and what do they mean for the church? Max Thurian takes *eis tēn emēn anamnēsin* with the meaning "with a view to my memorial, in memorial of me, as the memorial of me."[2] Further he says that this memorial is not a simple subjective act of recollection; it is actually a liturgical action. Nevertheless, it is not just a mere liturgical action which makes the Lord present, it is a liturgical action which recalls the memorial before the Father concerning the unique sacrifice of the Son, and this makes Him present in His memorial, in his presentation of his sacrifice before the Father and in His intercession as heavenly High Priest. Thurian says, "The eucharistic memorial is a recalling to us, a recalling by us to the Father and a proclamation by the Church; it is a thanksgiving and intercession of Christ for the Church."[3] Thurian continues by concluding what the Bible means by memorial: "to recall before God what he has already done for his people so that he may grant us today all the benefits thereof. The memorial is the actualization of the work of God and at the same time it is the recalling in prayer to the Father of what he has done, in order that he may continue his work today."[4]

David Power says, "The sacramental action of Christian liturgy is the recovery, the creative perception of the human within the memory of Christ and of Christ within the human." He states that "such memorial

---

[2] Max Thurian, *The Eucharistic Memorial II: The New Testament* (London: Lutterworth Press, 1963), 35. This book is a continuation of the first book on the Old Testament; see *The Eucharistic Memorial I: The Old Testament* (London: Lutterworth Press, 1968).

[3] Thurian, *The Eucharistic Memorial II*, 35.

[4] Max Thurian, "The Eucharistic Memorial, Sacrifice of Praise and Supplication" in *Ecumenical Perspectives on Baptism, Eucharist and Ministry*, ed. Max Thurian (Geneva: World Council of Churches, 1983), 94. In connection with the remembrance in prayer, see Edward P. Blair, "An Appeal to Remembrance", 41–47. He says that praying in the name of Jesus, repeatedly mentioned in the New Testament, is a form of remembering Jesus. According to Hebrew thought, by making mention of the name, one keeps the soul of another alive and active in the present. The person ceases to exist when the name is forgotten. Thus to pray in the name of Jesus is to make him present in living power. And to remember him when one eats the bread and drinks the cup is to know him as living presence and to look forward to his coming triumph. To remember him is to surrender to him, to obey him, to live in harmony with his gracious redemptive purpose, and to share in his destiny.

needs to affirm, enlarge, and fill, what is lost. With the advent of a new millennium, a new evangelization, a new resurgence of hope, histories cannot be remembered, Christ is not embodied in a people, without remembrance of suffering, of time lost. Between time lost and time regained, there lies the art of sacramental remembrance."[5]

The Eucharist is the event where Christ's death is remembered, where in his self-emptying action, God takes form in a people who have suffered.[6] Jesus said, "Do this in remembrance of me!"[7] What is the meaning of remembering Christ's death? The Eucharist is an act of active remembrance in liturgy, for Jesus has given his very being for humanity. This act of remembrance is "guided by the power of the Spirit and focuses on the location of the memory of Christ within the memory of a people, and the memory of the people within the memory of Christ's *kenosis*."[8] The past has become the present for the future through the Eucharist. Therefore, the remembrance in the Eucharist does not mean a passive remembrance of the past, but it is also a recalling of the present for the future through the memorial of Christ.

There are different opinions on how remembrance is done in anamnesis. The question posed for the act of remembrance in anamnesis is, "what really happens in remembering?" Does it mean that we are going back in time and make present something that has happened before? Wainwright suggests that the anamnesis contains the polarity of the past and the future. He says,

> At the eucharist Christ is present to the eyes of faith: at His table in the final kingdom we shall see Him face to face (cf. 1 Cor. 13:12a). The eucharist is a periodic celebration: in the final kingdom the worship and rejoicing, as in the life of heaven, will be perpetual. In the eucharist, a part of mankind and a part of the world serve the glory of God. In the final kingdom God will be all in all. The people who celebrate the eucharist are imperfect in their obedience: in the final kingdom their submission to the rule of God will be total. Eucharistic joy is marred by our persistence in sin: the joy of the final kingdom will be full.[9]

---

[5] David N. Power, "Foundation for Pluralism in Sacramental Expression: Keeping Memory" in *Journal of Worship* 75 no. 3 May (2001), 198. David Power wrote his paper in connection with the church's actions in the past which have kept people away from their traditional roots. The Eucharist is the place of ritual and narrative of sacramental memorial and is faced with the memory of suffering and the call to confession and apology for past actions of the church.

[6] See Power, "Foundation", 199.

[7] Luke 22:19; 1 Cor. 11:26.

[8] Power, "Foundation", 199.

[9] Geoffrey Wainwright, *Eucharist and Eschatology*, 147.

Jesus is present through the eyes of faith and through it the community gains hope and joy for the future where the kingdom of God will reign after the return of Jesus. Again, here we see that the presence of Jesus is real for those who see it through faith. The Eucharist is a symbol of an event that happened in the past, yet actual for people of faith.

However, the remembrance of the past in the Eucharist has different meanings for different traditions. Lee Palmer Wandel, a historian of early modern Christianity, has done her research on the texts: "this is my body," "this do," and "remembrance of me" that divided Christendom in the sixteenth century. She focuses on the development of the interpretation of these words and what they meant to three main Christian traditions: the Catholic, Lutheran, and Reformed Church. Her research leads her to a conclusion that all three denominations have different interpretations of time in the eucharistic liturgy and this influences the way they remember the past and the present.

She found out that Lutheran and Catholic tradition have a more active concept of memory than Reformed tradition because for them Christ is really present in the Eucharist. For Lutherans, the remembrance in the Eucharist is an opportunity to reflect on Christ's salvific death. While remembering Christ's death in the past, Christ is corporeally present in the moment they celebrate the memory. In the Catholic Mass, Christ is present only after the consecration is being said by the priest. Memory of the past becomes an active presence after each consecration. The remembrance in the Eucharist in the Reformed tradition is more about a specific event that happened in the past that remains apart from the present. The congregation is being reminded of this specific event through the narrative action of the Eucharist so that people are reminded of that event.[10]

Based on her historical research, Wandel sees that the relation of the past memory of Jesus is related differently to the present sacrament of the Eucharist. This different interpretation of the past is connected with how churches perceive Jesus' presence in the Eucharist. It is not our intention to contribute to the confessional discussion on this issue. However, the HKBP is a church that belongs to the Lutheran tradition. Based on Wandel's conclusions, we see that Lutherans perceive in a more active way that Christ is corporeally present. This finding will be useful for our research when we come to the liturgy of the Eucharist in the HKBP.

---

[10] Lee Palmer Wandel, *The Eucharist in the Reformation: Incarnation and Liturgy* (Cambridge, New York: Cambridge University Press, 2006), 260–261.

How can we look beyond the different interpretations of the past and present in the eucharistic liturgy? One of the commonalities of the Christian tradition is precisely the hope of the *parousia*. While remembrance of the past might be different between active and passive memory, the expectation of the future is shaped by the same God of Christ Jesus.

Memorial celebration in the Eucharist is not only about the past, but also very much connects the community of believers to the future. The commemoration that Jesus instituted invites believers to think about the future and to learn about acting upon God's love in the world. The Eucharist cannot be separated from eschatology and ecclesiology. This is why the Eucharist is often intertwined with many of the struggles that the church has to deal with. Indeed, in our research it is the struggle of unity in the church in the Indonesian context. What we can learn from the liturgy of the Eucharist is a major point of a shared connection to the hope of the future without neglecting the concern about the past and present.

Wainwright noticed that the anticipation of the future in the Eucharist has been developed only thoroughly in the last century.[11] He says that the theological emphasis of the Eucharist as a mere remembrance of the cross has been broadened in three ways. Anamnesis is now used to mention "the birth, life, passion, resurrection, ascension, and heavenly intercession of Jesus Christ as well as his expected parousia."[12] A second change is the new emphasis on the church's calling in the midst of the world. A third change that he writes about is on the eschatological aspect of the Eucharist. This eschatological meaning in the Eucharist, as Morrill also wrote, had somehow been missing in the Catholic liturgy until its liturgical reform.[13]

---

[11] Wainwright wrote a part on "Recent Thinking on the Eucharist" in Max Thurian and Geoffrey Wainwright (editors), *Baptism and Eucharist: Ecumenical Convergence in Celebration*, (Geneva: World Council of Churches, 1983), 104–108. He wrote then that the new ideas are: The sacrament as sign, Transsignification, Memorial and Sacrifice, the eschatological dimension, the ecclesiological dimension, ecumenical agreement, the Eucharist and the world, and the Eucharist as blessings. He wrote another version in "Recent Eucharistic Revision," in *The Study of Liturgy*, eds. Cheslyn Jones et al. (New York: Oxford University Press, Revised Edition, 1992), 328–338.

[12] Wainwright, "Recent Eucharistic Revision", 335. See also Geoffrey Wainwright, "Sacramental Time" in *Liturgical Time*, Wiebe Vos and Geoffrey Wainwright (Rotterdam: Liturgical Ecumenical Center Trust, 1982), 135–146. Here Wainwright correctly suggests that this memorial of Christ has more ontological substance than a mere psychological event would be afforded.

[13] See Wainwright, *Eucharist and Eschatology*, 87. He says, "The first, and indisputable,

Wainwright firmly connects the Eucharist with this eschatological aspect. He shows from the early eucharistic prayers and liturgy that eschatology was never far from the mind of the first congregation when they celebrated the Eucharist. They believed and expected the return of Jesus Christ in the anamnesis of Jesus Christ in the celebration of the Eucharist.[14]

Wainwright notes that one of the evidences of the relation of the Eucharist and eschatology is found in the word *maranatha* (1 Cor. 11:26). The early churches were celebrating the Eucharist in two-fold expectations: the celebration of the memory of Jesus and the expectation of the *parousia*. The celebration of the meal would be repeated until the return of Christ. The remembrance of Jesus is kept with the expectation of hope in the Kingdom of God.

When it is connected with the expectation of the future, the Eucharist reminds us that Christ will come as both Savior and Judge.[15] Thus, even when we are remembering the future, we are also being reminded that "the Christian's baptismal incorporation into Christ breaks through: *present* judgment by the Lord (vv. 29–32a) is a gracious chastisement (v. 32a), whose purpose is to (bring us to repentance and so) save us from *final* condemnation (v.32b)."[16] This is why Wainwright mentions the early liturgies that "made this connection of parousia and the final judgment at the end of the institution narrative and the anamnesis."[17] Thus even when the eucharistic liturgy is celebrated to remember the whole story of Jesus in the past, it has a very strong expectation of the

---

difference (between the western and eastern early liturgy) is that there is practically never any reference in the Western texts of the Eucharist to the second coming of Christ."

[14] See Wainwright, *Eucharist and Eschatology*, especially chapter 3, "Maranatha".

[15] Here Wainwright, *Eucharist and Eschatology*, 82, quotes Ernst Käsemann, "Anliegen und Eigenart der paulinischen Abendmalslehre" in *Exegetische Versusche und Besinnungern Vol. I* (Göttingen: Vandenhoeck & Ruprecht, 1960), 25. Wainwright translates Käsemann saying, "When the Lord comes on the scene, it is also the universal Judge who appears…His presence never leaves us unaffected. We do not, by our own disrespect, render his gift ineffective or make the presence of Christ unhappen. We cannot paralyze God's eschatological action. Salvation scorned becomes judgment… Where the Saviour is despised, the universal Judge remains present and shows himself in that very place as the one from whose presence there is no escape…the sacramental coming of the Lord always sets men in the perspective of the Last Day and therefore itself bears the marks of what God will do at the Last Day. It is a kind of anticipation, within the church, of the Last Day."

[16] Wainwright, *Eucharist and Eschatology*, 83.

[17] Wainwright, *Eucharist and Eschatology*, 84. See the examples of the liturgies on 61–64.

future in the parousia, and the judgment that Christ then will bring.

It is worthy to note that the connection of the Eucharist with the future is always seen in the context of the community. We can see the resemblance of this communal factor with Schmemann's, although Wainwright also stresses the individual role in it. Wainwright sees that "At the eucharist, Christians "come together to eat" (1 Cor. 11:33), and the Lord confronts each individual (*antropos*, v.28) in judgment and salvation: so will every man be judged as part of the universal last assize."[18] When the time of judgment comes, Christians who are part of the community will still face the Lord as individuals.

Why is the expectation of the future that comes from the remembrance of the past so relevant? In the Eucharist, believers are given the promise of "righteousness, peace, and joy" and as consequence, "The eucharistic community will act in the world in such ways as to display the righteousness, peace and joy of the kingdom, and so it will bear witness to the giver of these gifts, cooperating in the establishment of the kingdom without ever thought of denying that the work is entirely God's and will be drastically completed by Him."[19] As a witness of God's work, the Eucharist asks the community to do the work of God in their lives, and —importantly— not only for the sake of the gathered community, but also for the sake of the whole world. Wainwright sees that the Eucharist demands the community to pay attention to their context and to act upon God's words to them. It shows that the eschatological character of the Eucharist points to the future, and that God wants the recipient of this celebration to be responsible for their historical context yet to come. The demand to remember the past and at the same time the future can transform our ways of dealing with the present.

Now the questions develop. What if the expectation of the future becomes a medium of keeping the *status quo*? How does the hope of the future judgment in Christ's return help not only victims but also perpetrators with their present and past pain? This is where the active memory of the Eucharist plays a part. Here a connection exists between the past, the present, and the hope of the future that transcends the present and past.

Again, memory in liturgical commemoration in the Eucharist is not only about the past; it transforms our present, and it also contains hope

---

[18] Wainwright, *Eucharist and Eschatology*, 148.
[19] Wainwright, *Eucharist and Eschatology*, 148. This supports the idea of witness that Keshkegian mentioned earlier.

for the future. When the memory of the past transforms our present it means that it influences the reaction of the church towards what is happening around it. This encourages action of churches who are dealing with past conflict, or members that have traumatic past. Liturgical commemorations will lead to transformation and hope for the future.

The transformation and hope are implemented in the spirit of unity, a very important element in the Eucharist. The Eucharist reflects a two-tiered communion: Christ and community and also between the community member themselves.[20] The unity with Christ means "to be a faithful covenant partner in the historical Jesus, i.e. to be a life-bearer in the remembrance of his death."[21] The relationship with Christ also demands us to be in unity with other members of the body of Christ. The Eucharist can be a source of transformation of memory of the past in the spirit of unity of the community of believers.

Transformation and hope are the result of faithful participation in liturgy. William R. Crockett's findings on the Eucharist as a symbol of transformation support our view. He said that the Eucharist not only has transcendent meaning, but also "serves as vehicles for social transformation."[22] It is a religious symbol that supports renewal in the community precisely because of its communal characteristic. He says, "Eucharistic participation must lead first of all to a new social vision, then to a critique of our existing society in the light of that vision, and finally to advocacy for the poor and disadvantaged members of society and to social change."[23] Such vision of the Eucharist gives us support in finding a place of communal remembrance in liturgy.

Naturally, Schmemann validly warned us of not using the liturgy as a means of our own. We shall take his warning into account. However, sharing in such liturgy and remembrance should be able to bring a change of heart. Transformation and hope are the result and not the purpose of the remembrance in liturgy. This change will not only will have effects in the church, but also will spread through the community of believers in the world.

---

[20] See Dong-sun Kim, *The Bread for Today and the Bread for Tomorrow: The Ethical Significance of the Lord's Supper in the Korean Context* (New York: Peter Lang Publishing Inc., 2001), 68–69. Kim writes about the tradition of the meal as a powerful language of unification.

[21] Kim, 68. This means that repentance and self-check is needed before coming to the table, See 1 Cor. 16:22.

[22] William R. Crockett, *Eucharist: Symbol of Transformation* (New York: Pueblo Publishing Company, 1989), 250.

[23] Crockett, *Eucharist*, 256.

1.1 The Contribution of the Three Theologians in the Liturgy of the Eucharist

We will now take note of how the three theologians contributed to the theological foundation of remembrance and see whether these ideas have a place in the liturgy.

Metz's main idea is to include the memory of the suffering in our remembrance in the church. The remembrance of the suffering means that the church should be sensitive to the things that are happening in her context. This also means that any conflict should be remembered for the sake of solidarity with the suffering. This is the idea that is comprised in the Eucharist's aspect of memorial of Christ, the communion of the faithful, and the meal of the kingdom in the BEM liturgy, that we will analyze later on. Concretely, Metz's idea fits in the liturgical elements of the sermon and of intercessory prayer. In both elements, combined with the element of anamnesis of Christ, we remember the people who are suffering in the world, especially those in our own community. This gives a theological foundation for remembering the suffering in prayer and sermon, thus bringing them in our memory of Christ.

Schmemann's contribution is to celebrate the joyous remembrance of the Eucharist in a communal context. He as well wanted to put liturgy as the central source for good theology, which based on the liturgy of the Eucharist. We will see that Schmemann's main idea is somehow integrated in the BEM document's understanding of the Eucharist. This is not a surprise since Schmemann was also involved in the post-conciliar Roman Catholic liturgical reform of 1969 which contributed to the BEM formulation of the understanding of the Eucharist. The idea of a joyous remembrance in the communal context is essential. Schmemann basically urges the church to give more emphasis on liturgy, especially the Eucharist, as the source of good theology and renewal energy. There is a transformation of the understanding of time in the mystery of the Eucharist. This transformation can happen when the Eucharist is truly experienced in the liturgy. We can translate Schmemann's idea in the importance of preparing a good eucharistic liturgy that makes the church actively experiences the memory of Christ. Liturgy is the place where we can surrender our memories in the knowledge that God remembers us. A good eucharistic liturgy will give place to the memories of the victims and the perpetrators. Thus, any church who wants to have a chance of memory transformation requires a good eucharistic liturgy.

We have also seen Volf's contribution in remembrance towards forgiveness and reconciliation. His idea also contains an eschatological hope for the coming of Christ as the one who remembers the pain. Coming to the table means to remember truthfully what has happened in the past, with the hope of God's embrace both towards victims and perpetrators. Individual memory of the past becomes communal memory in the liturgy of the Eucharist. We can connect this idea with the fourth and fifth aspect of the Eucharist which is communion of the faithful and the meal of the kingdom.

When remembrance of the past is linked to forgiveness and reconciliation as its main purpose, the memory of pain can be given a new meaning and place in the community. The memory of pain now belongs to the community, and the community gives it to Christ in the memory of the Eucharist. Concretely, we can implement this idea in the liturgical elements of the confession of sin by stating that asking for forgiveness of sins also means to remember truthfully what had happened in the past and bring the memory to God who remembers. This idea of forgiveness is also connected with the eschatological element of the Eucharist, namely that Christ will return as our redeemer. Thus, our remembrance in the Eucharist demands from us an acceptance of one another and become one in the communion of believers. We can find these elements in parts of the liturgy, especially in the sign of reconciliation and peace, and the eating and drinking of the bread. People who are not ready to be at the same table with their brothers and sisters in Christ should reconsider their participation. Even so, we should not reject people who want to come to be in communion with the Lord because it is a free invitation to a joyous and transformative memory of Christ.

After looking at the theological understanding of the Eucharist, the elements in it, and the possibility of doing it in the liturgy, we can say that it is absolutely necessary to carefully prepare the liturgy of the Eucharist since it can be a place where memories meet and are redeemed. Some liturgical elements are important for the transformation of past hurt memories. We will investigate these elements and look at how they can help us experience redemptive memory in the eucharistic liturgy.

1.2. Elements of the Eucharist

1.2.1 The Eucharist as an Act of Confession

One of the functions of the Eucharist is to be a foundation for pluralism in memory-keeping. This memorial for the people requires that they should discern, know, and re-examine themselves before coming to the table of the Lord. The act of confession comes to the fore at this moment. Gustaf Aulen, a Lutheran theologian, thinks that the Eucharist contains the idea of a confession of what has been happening to one's life. In the connection to the memorial in the sacrament and God's victorious love, he says, "The Lord's Supper as an *in memoriam* celebration brings the faithful back to "that night in which he was betrayed." Participation in this memorial feast has, therefore, a character of confession."[24]

Aulen explains further what he means by the character of confession. It is not only being recognized when it is being delivered orally; there are also confessional acts such as that of the Eucharist. He says, "This act is a confession which is concerned with the inner personal life and declares the confessor's desires to belong to the Lord's Supper…if in this connection we speak of being "worthy and well prepared," this "worthiness" and "preparation" consist only in this: that we are willing to have God judge our unworthiness."[25] This is to be connected with the self-examination process in the presence of God.

Mary Anne Coate seems to agree with the idea of confession within the celebration of the Eucharist. She says,

> The Eucharist or great thanksgiving stands as a remembrance and re-enactment of the redemptive work of Christ "through whom we are freed from the slavery of sin". As such it includes—as do all public services—prayers of penitence and confession and the proclamation of absolution… the service reiterates the truth of our human condition that we cannot live up to the ideal of living without sin. Confession and forgiveness are, as it were, routine parts of our relationship with God.[26]

---

[24] Gustaf Aulen, *The Faith of the Christian Church* (Philadelphia: Mulenberg Press, 1948), 385. This is Aulen's explanation on one of the characteristic and fundamental ideas of the Lord's Supper in Christian faith, which are remembrance, sacrifice, fellowship (communion), and Eucharist.

[25] Aulen, *The Faith*, 389.

[26] Mary Anne Coate, *Sin, Guilt, and Forgiveness: The Hidden Dimensions of a Pastoral Process*, (London: Society for Promoting Christian Knowledge, 1994), 152. She is connecting the Eucharist with the liturgy when the phrase "go in peace" is used. The phrase, "go in peace" at the end of rite of confession has a more personal approach to the hearer. Confession and forgiveness from a process that requires the taking of

Confession and forgiveness form a process that requires the worshipper to take personal responsibility in acquiring the knowledge—as far as possible—of what has gone wrong and what has caused the situation. The service of the Eucharist demands confession as part of our relationship with God.

What does the presence of Jesus mean for the memorial aspect of the Eucharist when it is connected with the aspect of confession? Wainwright suggests that the Eucharist should be approached with repentance. He says,

> The condemnation of sin which the divine justice demands have been carried out in the death of Jesus, in which Father and Son cooperated for the sake of man's salvation. It is therefore clearly the will of the Father, and of Jesus the savior that men should be acquitted. The only condition is (in Johannine terminology) to believe in the Son and in the One who sent Him (John 3:18; 5:24)—which includes recognition that the death of Jesus was the divine condemnation of all sin, a recognition manifested in repentance for one's own sin. The penitent believer is justified, acquitted; and at every eucharist the divine acquittal is pronounced that will be heard at the last assize.[27]

Remembering Christ and entering the table of the new covenant means a self-identification and a confession of sins. The call for confession is made clear when Paul warns the people who come to the table in an "unworthy" manner (1 Cor. 11:27 f). A person should check whether she or he is worthy to come to the table of the Lord. This means one must reconcile first with the self, one's neighbor, and with God before coming to the table. To be able to reconcile means to remember and to confess sins and guilt.

1.2.2 The Eucharist and Forgiveness of Sins

What is the connection between the Eucharist and the forgiveness of sins? Between the four stories available about the Eucharist (in the account of Matthew, Mark, Luke, and Paul), only Matthew puts in the phrase "the blood of the covenant, is poured out for many for the forgiveness of sins." This is a strong emphasis on sinfulness that is not explicitly available in the other accounts.

In Matthew 26:28, the blood of the covenant is said to be poured out for the forgiveness of sins. There seems to be a parallel between the

---

personal responsibility in the knowledge—as far as possible—of what has gone wrong.
  [27] Wainwright, *Eucharist and Eschatology*, 83. Note: "assize" is a British word for "inquest", "verdict".

memorial and forgiveness of sins in the Eucharist. This could mean that the Eucharist can be seen as a memorial of Christ who died and gave the atonement of sins. The atonement of sins in this context is the result of Jesus' unique act of sacrifice on the cross and thus the Eucharist has a memorial aspect of this sacrificial act on the cross.

M. Eugene Boring notes that the forgiveness of sins was one of the six main distinctive changes in the Markan meaning.[28] The whole action by Jesus was related to "the forgiveness of sins", the identical words dropped from Mark's description of John's baptism (Mark 1:4). Forgiveness is related to Jesus' covenant-renewing death. Boring says that Jesus' primary mission is the forgiveness of sins (Mark 1:21; 9:1-7). Forgiveness is accomplished by Jesus' death, in terms of the sacrifice that seals the bond between God and the covenant people (cf. Ex. 24:8; Isa. 53:12; but see Matt. 9:2). Matthew described Jesus' death as replacing the sacrificial blood of the old covenant law. The death of Jesus was linked with the suffering of the servant Isaiah (cf. Isa. 53:12) and with the new covenant prophecy of Jeremiah (31:34). That is why Jesus' words were connected with Isaiah 53, because without them, the eucharistic words of Jesus would remain incomprehensible.[29]

Jesus' words on the Eucharist can be interpreted to say that Jesus understood his position as the Passover lamb that has to be sacrificed. Jeremias argued that Jesus must have thought about the atoning effect of his death. He says that every death has an atoning power, even animals and criminals who repent at the end of their life. An innocent death has an atoning power for others. Jeremias says that this is what Jesus has in mind when he explains the meaning of his death, "His death is the vicarious death of the suffering servant, which atones for the sins of the many, the peoples of the world, which ushers in the beginning of the

---

[28] M. Eugene Boring, "The Gospel of Matthew", in *The New Interpreter's Bible Vol. 8*, in ed. Leander E. Keck (Nashville: Abingdon Press, 1995), 471-472. The other five are (1) The Markan narrator's word about the cup, "and they all drank of it", are made into a parallel command to the words over the bread, so that each action comprises a command of Jesus and the disciples' obedient response. (2) The command to "eat" is then added to the words over the bread, to enhance the parallelism to the newly formulated command to "drink". (3) In the phrase "for many," Matthew changes the Markan presupposition from *hyper* to *peri* which is more in line with the sacrificial context. (4) Matthew adds "with you" in v. 29 showing the emphasis on his connection with the disciples. (5) Mark's "Kingdom of God" becomes "my father's kingdom".

[29] See Donald A. Hagner, *World Biblical Commentary: Matthew 14-28* (Dallas: Word Books Publisher, 1995), 772-774. See also Joachim Jeremias, *The Eucharistic Words of Jesus* (New York: The Macmillan Company, 1955).

final salvation and which effects the new covenant with God."[30] Jesus' death has the atoning power for the sins of others.

The phrase that Matthew includes is not surprising since he has much stress on the fulfillment and new hope for present time and the future in the action and saying of Jesus (Matt. 1:23; 2:6, 15, 17, 23; 4:14, etc. Den Heyer suggests that Matthew must have really felt the action of Jesus by the adding of Jesus' words in the account of the Eucharist. This is probably because the writer has seen the connection between the suffering servant and Israel's sins which was already proclaimed by the prophet: "But he was pierced for our transgressions, he was crushed for our iniquities; the punishment that brought us peace was upon him, and by his wounds we are healed (Isaiah 53:5).... Therefore I will give him a portion among the great, and he will divide the spoils with the strong, because he poured out his life unto death, and was numbered with the transgressors. For he bore the sin of many, and made intercession for the transgressors (Isaiah 53:12)."[31]

Matthew was fully aware of what he wrote when he added the saying "for forgiveness of sins" in the proclamation of the Eucharist. He differs of opinion with the other Synoptic Gospel writers by not stating John the Baptist's baptism of repentance for the forgiveness of sins (see Mark 1:4; Luke 3:3). Matthew seems to think that the forgiveness of sins can only be connected with Jesus Christ. In the beginning of his gospel, he speaks about how the angel came to Joseph and spoke. "She (read: Mary) will give birth to a son and you are to give him the name Jesus, because he will save his people from their sins (Matt. 1:21)." Matthew has already stressed that Jesus came for the forgiveness of sins and thus it is not surprising when he stresses the same theme again in the institution of the Eucharist.

As noted in the BEM report, the Eucharist nourishes the hope of the forgiveness of sins for baptized member of the body of Christ. The Eucharist is a sacrament of hope, where the forgiveness of sins achieved through the sacrificial act of Christ that has happened once and for all, makes possible the reconciliation of people with their neighbor and God the Father. We are justified sinners who receive the gift of

---

[30] Joachim Jeremias, *The Eucharistic Words*, 152.
[31] Den Heyer, *De Maaltijd van de Heer*, 98–99. Compare to Léon-Dufour, *Sharing The Eucharistic Bread:*, 148, who says that Matthew reminds us of what is indeed an important aspect of the death of Christ, the forgiveness of sins, which is the very condition of an authentic covenant. Léon-Dufour thinks that forgiveness of sins is one of the dimensions of the mystery of Christ's death.

forgiveness in the memorial of Jesus. Therefore, it is essential for the people to be reconciled before coming to the table of remembrance. The account noted by Matthew is very important in the connection with the idea of forgiveness of sins in the Eucharist. The Eucharist is God's offer which comes as a memorial and is given in the power of the Spirit, which guarantees the hope for the forgiveness of sins.

1.2.3 *The Eucharist as Table of Reconciliation*

This idea can be connected with the fourth aspect in the Eucharist as communion of faithful, but it has a greater importance for our research. When brothers and sisters are in dispute, how can the Eucharist become the table of reconciliation? In the past, there were stories about disagreements in the church that made each group believe that only those in harmony with one another should celebrate the Eucharist, and therefore exclude those who are against them, or worse, both groups had a separate celebration of the Eucharist.[32] The argument used in such cases was that only they who are already at peace with their brothers and sisters may celebrate the Eucharist together before God, "Therefore, if you are offering your gift at the altar and there remember that your brother has something against you, leave your gift there before the altar and go; first be reconciled to your brother, then come and offer your gift (Matt. 5:23 f)."[33]

When brothers and sisters continued celebrating the communion separately, because of their dispute, they actually marked the disunity of God's people. This is because the Eucharist expresses among many other things also the unity of the people. Reconciliation must be made between the conflicting sides before they come before the Lord. Wainwright says,

> Common participation in the one eucharist must be allowed to promote reconciliation among the opposing groups. The eucharist's value as expression will not be entirely lost, for it will express both the measure of unity that still holds the two parties together and also the will to reconciliation that already exists in those who seek fellowship at the Lord's table even with their contemporary adversaries. But more important will be the fact that common participation in the one eucharist will allow the Lord creatively to bring us closer to the perfect peace and unity that will mark the final kingdom.[34]

---

[32] See Wainwright, *Eucharist and Eschatology*, 142.
[33] Compare to 1 John 4:20, "If any one says, I love God and hates his brother, he is a liar; for he who does not love his brother whom he has seen, how can he love God whom he has not seen?"
[34] Wainwright, *Eucharist and Eschatology*, 142–143.

In the light of the eschatological purpose, Wainwright understands that the Lord's invitation to all penitents among sinning people is to gather them up in the Eucharist and receive forgiveness for sins that have led to disunity, and be filled with a uniting love through the Lord's transforming presence. "Those who then refuse his invitation like the renegades in the parable of the Great Supper, are excluding themselves, and may be pre-enacting their own final judgment at the hands of a Lord whose offer of salvation they spurned."[35] Reconciliation must be made in order to celebrate the Eucharist.

However, how can victims and perpetrators come together at the table of the Lord? What if a perpetrator would not admit her/his guilt against the victim? What if the victim already reconciled with her/himself and is not able to reconcile with the perpetrator because he/she would not admit his/her guilt? What kind of forgiveness will be made if there is only one side that offers it? How much is the Eucharist of help to the victims?

2. The Elements of Eucharist in the BEM Document

The BEM document[36] describes the meaning of the Eucharist as follows:

> The eucharist is essentially the sacrament of the gift which God makes to us in Christ through the power of the Holy Spirit. Every Christian receives this gift of salvation through communion in the body and blood of Christ. In the eucharistic meal, in the eating and drinking of the bread and wine, Christ grants communion with himself. God himself acts, giving life to the body of Christ and renewing each member. In accordance with Christ's promise, each baptized member of the body of Christ receives in the eucharist the assurance of the forgiveness of sins (Matt. 26:28) and the pledge of eternal life (John 6:51–58). Although the eucharist is essentially one complete act, it will be considered here under the following aspects: thanksgiving to the Father, memorial of Christ, invocation of the Spirit, communion of the faithful, meal of the Kingdom (II, 2).

---

[35] Wainwright, *Eucharist and Eschatology*, 141.
[36] World Council of Churches, *Baptism, Eucharist and Ministry*, Faith and Order Paper 112 (Geneva: World Council of Churches, 1982). For a cross reference on the comments, see J. M. R. Tillard, "The Eucharist, Gift of God", in *Ecumenical Perspectives on Baptism, Eucharist and Ministry,* ed. Max Thurian (Geneva: World Council of Churches, 1993), 104–118. We recognizes the incompleteness of this interpretation on the rich text of the Lima Report, however it will be useful to suggest readers who are interested in this topic to go to Max Thurian (ed.), *Churches Respond to BEM: Official Responses to the "Baptism, Eucharist and Ministry" Text Vol. 1–6*, of Faith and Order Paper, Geneva: WCC, 1997). Baptism, Eucharist and Ministry is a document of the theological commission of the World Council of Churches. In it, among other things, theologians of various main Christian traditions, together explored the meaning of the Eucharist.

The Lima document understands the gift of Eucharist in a Trinitarian way; it is a gift of God, in Christ, and through the Holy Spirit. It is an event in which the Christian receives the gift of salvation through the communion in the body and blood of Jesus. The emphasis is on the understanding that Christ grants us the communion with himself. The Faith and Order document stated that through the Eucharist, each baptized member would receive the assurance of forgiveness and the pledge of eternal life. Because it is a gift of God through Christ, this celebration is the event where the assurance of forgiveness of sins is received. The forgiveness of sins is God's grace; the assurance is given through the eating and drinking the eucharistic meal, and the promise of Christ.

There are five aspects to any eucharistic celebration. We will discuss them briefly, with the exception of the element of the memorial of Christ.

1. Eucharist as thanksgiving to the Father. First, it is a thanksgiving to the Father; it is an expression of thankfulness to the Father of all that God has done for us. Through Christ, we thank God for God's saving action in the life of Christ. This first aspect brings meaning to our relation with God.

2. The second element in the Eucharist, which we will discuss rather extensively, is the Eucharist as anamnesis or memorial of Christ. The heart of the Eucharist is the anamnesis. It is the memorial of the "crucified and the risen Christ…accomplished once and for all on the cross and still operative on behalf all humankind" (II, 5). This memorial is not an "empty" memorial, a mere recalling of the past; in fact "Christ himself with all that he has accomplished for us and for all creation (in his incarnation, servant hood, ministry, teaching, suffering, sacrifice, resurrection, ascension, and sending of the Spirit) is present in this anamnesis, granting us communion with himself. The Eucharist is also the foretaste of his *parousia* and of the final kingdom" (II, 6). This means that the remembrance of Christ is done in the wholeness of the memorial of him, his life, works, death, and resurrection until his ascension, and the sending of the Spirit. This is the memorial which is "the Church's effective proclamation of God's mighty acts and promises" (II, 7).

Because the Eucharist is a unique gift and offers the entrance to the gift which also invokes a presence, the response of the church to this gift is expressed in thanksgiving and intercession through Christ the High Priest. "In thanksgiving, the Church is united with the Son, its great High Priest and Intercessor (Rom. 8:34; Heb 7:25)…It is the memorial of all that God has done for the salvation of the world…in the memorial of the Eucharist, however, the Church offers its intercession in communion with Christ, our great High Priest" (II, 8).[37]

The anamnesis is also believed to be the basis and source of all Christian prayer; it relies on the risen Lord, and "In the eucharist, Christ empowers us to live with him, to suffer with him and to pray trough him as justified sinners, joyfully and freely fulfilling his will" (II, 9). This shows that Christ empowers us to live and suffer with him even though we are still sinners, because we are now justified sinners. As justified sinners, we have to offer ourselves as a living sacrifice. "In Christ, we offer ourselves as a living and holy sacrifice in our daily lives (Rom. 12:1; 1 Pet. 2:5); this spiritual worship, acceptable to God, is nourished in the eucharist, in which we are sanctified and reconciled in love, in order to be the servants of reconciliation in the world" (II, 10). This is an important point in terms of forgiveness and reconciliation. We must offer ourselves, the justified sinners, in our daily love. This means we must not differentiate the day of the celebration of the Eucharist from any other days. We must keep ourselves as a living and holy sacrifice in our daily activities. By living our life as an offering, through the Eucharist, we are sanctified and reconciled in love, in order to be the agent of reconciliation of the world. In other words, without having offered ourselves in our daily activities, our remembrance will not be acceptable and we will not be sanctified through the Eucharist.

The communion is based on God's love and reconciliation. The offering of life will not become acceptable when there is no reconciliation among fellow humans. The Lima Report states, "The eucharistic celebration demands reconciliation and sharing among all those regarded as brothers and sisters in the one family of God and is a constant challenge in the search for appropriate relationships in social, economy, and political life" (II, 20). Further it says, "All kind of injustice, racism, separation, and lack of freedom are radically challenged when we share in the body and blood of Christ" (II, 20). In the Eucharist, there should be a commemoration of injustices, racism, separation, and lack of freedom, because leaving it out would be "inconsistent if we are not actively participating in this ongoing restoration of the world's

---

[37] This is where the document gives its commentary to the problem of intercession in reference to the Eucharist, the unique sacrifice of the cross, which is made actual in the Eucharist and presented before the Father in the intercession of Christ and of the church for all humanity.

situation and the human condition" (II, 20). This would also mean that the participants of the Eucharist should and must be against anything that challenges God's reconciliation and love to the whole world, and surely also among brothers and sisters. Reconciliation among brothers and sisters must be made as a part of the approach to the Lord's Table. Through the memorial in the Eucharist, the active communion senses the unique but real presence of Christ, "Jesus said over the bread and wine of the eucharist: "This is my body….this is my blood…" what Christ declares is true, and this truth is fulfilled every time the eucharist is celebrated. The Church confesses Christ's real, living, and active presence in the eucharist" (II, 13).

The document notes that in this memorial of the real presence of Christ in the Eucharist it is recognized that the liturgical rites embrace the "solidarity in the eucharistic communion of the body of Christ, and are responsible for one another and the world (in the mutual forgiveness of sins; the sign of peace; intercession for all; the eating and drinking together; the taking of the elements to the sick and those in prison or the celebration of the eucharist with them)" (II, 21). The celebration of the Eucharist is meant to transform the community into a servant community, just as Christ is the servant. There is a direct connection between the eucharistic communion of the body of Christ and being responsible for one another. One of the means of responsibility noted here is the mutual forgiveness of sins. The solidarity of the Eucharist demands a mutual forgiveness. A mutual forgiveness presupposes that there are people who are being forgiven and that there are those who are granting forgiveness. The document does not expound much on this; however, the restoration of the world does demand forgiveness. This can be experienced in the sharing of the Lord's Table, the remembrance of Christ, and through it, the forgiveness of sins for those who confess to be in the same body of Christ.

The Eucharist is also an offering of God's grace. It comes as a memorial of the ultimate sacrifice that is being offered once and for all for the salvation of the whole world. God's grace is being given in the power of the Spirit, inaugurated by the resurrection of Christ. Tillard says, "Implicit in this grace is care for the world, the commitment of the will to the transformation of this world into the world which God wills, and therefore the disappearance of injustice, war, hatred, exploitation and the sources of these evils."[38] In other words, through

---

[38] Tillard, "The Eucharist", 113.

the remembrance of Christ in the Eucharist, we should become a community of transformation of the world into God's will.

3. The third aspect is the Eucharist as invocation of the Spirit. This aspect means that through the Spirit we can actualize that the past event becomes present and alive to us now. In the Spirit, the church will be "sanctified and renewed, led into all justice, truth and unity, and empowered to fulfill her mission in the world (II, 17)." Thus, the Holy Spirit completes the presence of the Triune God in the Eucharist. It completes our relation with the Triune God by inviting the Holy Spirit.

4. The fourth element is the Eucharist as communion of the faithful. It means that "The sharing in one bread and the common cup in a given place demonstrates and affects the oneness of the sharers with Christ and with their fellow sharers in all times and places. It is in the eucharist that the community of God's people is fully manifested (II, 19)." It means that the Eucharist also make demands to people in conflict that are coming to the table. The Eucharist demands reconciliation and sharing among brothers and sisters in Christ (Matt. 5:23f; 1 Cor. 10:16f; 1 Cor. 11:20–22; Gal. 3:28).This point is also important in our reference to the Eucharist as a table of reconciliation among victims and perpetrators. Everyone who desires to receive the Eucharist is challenged to be in peace with one another. This can be seen in the liturgical elements such as forgiveness of sins, the sign of peace, intercession, eating and drinking together, celebrating the Eucharist with the imprisoned and the sick (II, 21). This fourth aspect is thus about our relation to fellow human beings.

5. The last aspect of the Eucharist is the kingdom meal. This is the aspect where the Eucharist is seen as a feast to give thanks to God and anticipates the coming of the Kingdom in Christ (1 Cor. 11:26; Matt. 26:29) (II, 22). This aspect calls "the members of the body of Christ to be servants of reconciliation among men and women and witnesses of the joy of resurrection (II, 24)." Thus, the participants of the Eucharist are asked to be in solidarity with the outcasts. This means that the participation in the meal of the kingdom, which means a communion of people that are forgiven and reconciled, gives us the strength to share this same message with the world. If this aspect is not accomplished, then the witnessing element of the church will be weakened. "Insofar as Christians cannot unite in full fellowship around the same table to eat the same loaf and drink from the same cup, their missionary witness is weakened at both the individual and the corporate levels (II, 26)." We are asked to be fully reconciled with our sisters and brothers

who shared the same feast to be able to show our witnessing task to the world. We can also say that reconciliation with one another is an important factor in doing our task as Christ's witness.

We can conclude that all aspects of the Eucharist in the Lima Document show a unity not only with the Triune God, but also with our fellow humans. It gives meaning to our vertical relation with God and our horizontal relation with fellow human beings. These five elements should be active and present in the liturgy of the Eucharist.

2.1 *The Elements of the BEM Eucharistic Liturgy*

What are the liturgical elements that give us the opportunity of retrieving and transforming the memory of the past? For this we have to go back to liturgies in the tradition. If we are to return to Protestant traditions, because it is the context of this research project, then we will face multiple challenges. While the Roman Catholic Church has its rites and Eucharistic Prayers,[39] and the Orthodox Churches have three liturgies for the Eucharist (the liturgy of St. James, the liturgy of St. Basil the Great, and the liturgy of St. John Chrysostom), there is no liturgy that can bridge the differences among Protestant denominations. If we were to choose a single tradition, we would immediately find ourselves in different streams of proceedings, liturgical differences, and even symbols.[40]

There are some common parts that can be seen in the ecumenical liturgies of the Eucharist celebrations of the major protestant traditions such as the Eucharistic Prayer and the service of the Word. These elements are common in Protestant liturgical celebrations of the Eucharist. We will now see how these two elements can contribute to how the joyous remembrance of the past can be implemented in liturgy.

With regard to finding elements in the Eucharist that are connected to remembrance, we will focus mainly on the elements of the Eucharist in the WCC Faith and Order Text concerning the Eucharist. The BEM Document, article 27, mentions the elements in the eucharistic liturgy as follows,[41]

---

[39] Resources for Eucharistic Prayer can be found online at http://catholic-resources.org/ChurchDocs/EP1-4.htm accessed January, 2010. We can also find eucharistic prayers for Masses of Reconciliation at http://catholic-resources.org/ChurchDocs/EPR1-2.htm, accessed January 2010.

[40] There is a concise and wonderful resource for these differences among different denominations. See Article "Liturgies" in *The New Westminster Dictionary of Liturgy and Worship*, ed. J.G. Davies (Pennsylvania: The Westminster Press, 1986), 314–338. See also Max Thurian and Geoffrey Wainwright (eds.), *Baptism and Eucharist*.

[41] WCC, *Baptism, Eucharist, and Ministry*, II. 27. For the purpose of this research,

Remembrance in the Liturgy of the Eucharist

27. The eucharistic liturgy is essentially a single whole, consisting historically of the following elements in varying sequence and of diverse importance:

1. hymns of praise;
2. act of repentance;
3. declaration of pardon;
4. proclamation of the Word of God, in various forms;
5. confession of faith (creed);
6. intercession for the whole Church and for the world;
7. preparation of the bread and wine;
8. thanksgiving to the Father for the marvels of creation, redemption and sanctification (deriving from the Jewish tradition of the *berakah*);
9. the words of Christ's institution of the sacrament according to the New Testament tradition;
10. the *anamnesis* or memorial of the great acts of redemption, passion, death, resurrection, ascension and Pentecost, which brought the Church into being;
11. the invocation of the Holy Spirit (*epiklesis*) on the community, and the elements of bread and wine (either before the words of institution or after the memorial, or both; or some other reference to the Holy Spirit which adequately expresses the "epikletic" character of the eucharist);
12. consecration of the faithful to God;
13. reference to the communion of saints;
14. prayer for the return of the Lord and the definitive manifestation of his Kingdom;
15. the Amen of the whole community;
16. the Lord's prayer;
17. sign of reconciliation and peace;
18. the breaking of the bread;
19. eating and drinking in communion with Christ and with each member of the Church;
20. final act of praise;
21. blessing and sending.

As mentioned, the diverse elements vary in the degree of importance and sequence for different churches. We can divide the elements into the following: opening (1), confession and absolution (2–3), service of the word (4–5), intercession prayer (6), the Eucharist service (7–19), blessing and sending (20–21).

We can also group the liturgical elements into the five aspects that we mentioned earlier. The first aspect of the Eucharist as thanksgiving to the Father can be seen in point 8 in the liturgy. The second aspect, Eucharist as anamnesis or memorial of Christ can be seen on liturgy

---

the original signs (-) on every element have been replaced by numbers.

element number 4, 10, 14. The Eucharist as invocation of the Spirit is at liturgical element number 11. Aspect of the Eucharist as communion of the faithful is in numbers 2, 4, 17, and 19. And the last aspect of the Eucharist as a meal of the kingdom can be found in liturgical elements 6 and 21. We will analyze these elements later in the proposed Lima eucharistic liturgy that was designed by Geoffrey Wainwright.

2.2.1 *Service of the Word*

The first part that can be used as a means of redemptive memory of the past conflict in the church lies in the strong Protestant tradition of the ministry of the Word. It can be used to remember Christ's life and at the same time to remember the life of the community and the message of Christ to that community.

Preaching is already rooted in the Jewish synagogue tradition of reading the scripture and giving an exposition. This tradition, which was continued as a normal part of liturgy after Nicaea, lost its connection with the liturgy in the Middle Ages. The reformation gave the sermon its place back in the liturgy; and the Liturgical Movement in the twentieth century brought the preaching back as an integral part in the Roman Catholic liturgy.[42]

---

[42] Despite the fact that liturgy and Christian worship have always considered the sermon as an important part of Christian life, it only received a central place as a result of the Liturgical Movement that started in the Catholic monastery Benedictine Abbey of Solesmes, France in the nineteenth century. The main purpose of this movement is to encourage active participation of the believers who celebrated the worship. This monastery started the study of the church's liturgical heritage and continued to reach the momentum needed for the actual start of the Liturgical movement in 1903 when Pope Pius X called for more active participation in the worship of the church. This movement enjoyed its apex in the liturgical renewal in the Conciliar Reform of the Vatican II and has "made an impact upon the worship of most of the Christian communions." Since this movement, Christian churches have encouraged more communal action in liturgy. The liturgical renewal and rediscovery also provide an ecumenical basis for different Christian denominations to celebrate and worship together. For concise information about the origin and spread of this movement, see H. Ellsworth Chandlee, "The Liturgical Movement, in *The New Westminster Dictionary of Liturgy and Worship*, ed. J.G. Davies (Pennsylvania: The Westminster Press, 1986), 307–314. See also André Haquin, "The Liturgical Movement and Catholic Ritual Revision, in *The Oxford History of Christian Worship*, eds. Geoffrey Wainwright and Karen B. Westerfield Tucker (New York: Oxford University Press, 2006), 696–720. Haquin explains that, "The Liturgical Movement refers essentially to the pastoral initiatives and efforts undertaken by groups and individuals to rediscover the meaning of the Church and the liturgy and the place of the liturgy in the Christian life, in order to encourage "the active participation" of all the baptized and improve the quality of the celebrations; for liturgy is neither the monopoly of the clergy nor a private matter but the celebration of the whole church."

We recall Keshkegian's idea in the previous chapter, that sermon can function as memory that can be redemptive and healing. The sermon can be a powerful tool of remembrance. It can function as part of the eucharistic celebration. Wainwright sees that different traditions have seen the importance of a sermon in the eucharistic memorial. "Catholic preachers have learned to expound the scriptures, while Protestant preachers have begun to relate their sermon more directly to the liturgical action."[43] Ministry of the word gives foundation to, and reminder of, what is going to happen at the table.

Wainwright explains that preaching as worship has four characteristics.[44] First, preaching is doxological because it encourages the hearers to a doxological life. Preaching "has its part to play in the renewing of minds to discern the will of God for the living of lives acceptable to God. The transformation of the believer means an end to conformity with this world."[45] Second, it is *anamnetic* because it is a constant reminder of the gospel that is embodied in the life of Jesus Christ. Third, preaching is *epikletic* because it needs to be connected with the current situation. Wainwright says, "Effective preaching to a concrete situation demands a "reading" of that situation. Since Pentecost, there is a sense in which all the Lord's people have indeed become prophets (cf. Num. 11:29). The faithful have the responsibility to read "the signs of the times" (Matt. 16:2f; cf. Luke 12:54–56)... The preacher then has the responsibility of bringing the word of God to bear on the great issues of the age, particularly as they affect the company of believers."[46] The last characteristic is eschatological. The preaching should be directed towards God's fulfillment in the return of Christ.

When connected to the liturgy of the Eucharist, the sermon plays an important role in delivering the gospel. The first and foremost place of the sermon in eucharistic liturgy is in the readings of the scripture. The sermon functions as "the vehicle of Christ's presence and address to the assembled congregation. Through the gospels the Lord once again proclaims his gospel."[47] The second place of the sermon is the creed. It is where "the faith confessed in baptism is now being professed again...

---

[43] Wainwright, *Baptism and Eucharist*, 109.

[44] See Geoffrey Wainwright, "Preaching as Worship," in *Greek Orthodox Theological Review* 28, no. 4: (1983), 325–336.

[45] Wainwright, "Preaching as Worship", 329. Wainwright uses a lot of examples from John Chrysostom in his paper.

[46] Wainwright, "Preaching as Worship", 334.

[47] Geoffrey Wainwright, "The Sermon and the Liturgy," *Greek Orthodox Theological Review* 28, no. 4: (1983), 340.

It expresses the faith which the Church proposes for the world's belief and salvation, and its acceptance signifies membership of the saved and saving community."[48]

Thus, the sermon holds a very important place as the center of God's words in the worship. It is also a remembrance of Christ in the church. Christ will lead worship and the Spirit will lead the preacher into delivering God's words. We must also remember that a human factor also plays a role. Preaching is about delivering God's promise of the future to God's people. Therefore, it is really important to be well prepared for the sermon. The preacher needs to learn about the current situation. The difficult part is how to balance and interpret what God is really saying to us in our own context.

The preaching of the Word and the Eucharist are two complementary elements in worship. Carol M. Norén, a homiletician, says that if the Roman Catholics are again finding the role of the sermon in Sunday worship, then Protestants are re-defining the meaning of the Eucharist more as "a personal encounter with Christ, a source of awakening a sense of Christian community and social responsibility, and a new awareness of the eschatological dimension of liturgy."[49] Norén then describes the relation between the sermon and the communion. She says, "The eucharistic theology attached the Church to salvation history, and the sermon reminds people of faith that the Church participates in that history in the midst of the world."[50] Thus preaching can function as a reminder how God has helped humanity to overcome sin through the work of Jesus, and at the same time it also reminds people about the stories of their present context in which God is at work.

Concretely, the sermon functions as a reminder of Christ's life and teaching and how we interpret that message into today's reality. The sermon is also a way of reminding people what the Eucharist actually means for individuals or communities in conflict. When the sermon is connected with the story of past hurts, it reminds the congregation of what has happened, and how we can prepare ourselves to enter the communion of the Lord. By giving this message and constantly reminding the congregation of the meaning of the Eucharist and its

---

[48] Wainwright, "The Sermon and the Liturgy", 341. See Acts 1:8; 2:1–11 as the statement of the necessity of the assistance of the Holy Spirit in the creed.

[49] Carol M. Norén, "The Word of God in Worship", in *The Study of Liturgy*, eds. Cheslyn Jones et al. (New York: Oxford University Press, (1978) Revised Edition: 1992), 39. One of Norén's most important publication on the issue is *The Woman in the Pulpit* (Nashville: Abingdon Press, 1991).

[50] Norén, "The Word of God", 41–42.

elements, the sermon will play an important role in the remembrance of the past hurt and how God remembers our pain.

We can conclude that the sermon is an element in liturgy that functions as a place of remembrance. The sermon should be connected with all aspects of the Eucharist, especially for a community in current conflict. The message should speak, to the victimized as well as to the instigators or perpetrators, that God is inviting everyone to be in the communion with God and fellow human. This will bring home a strong message when it is linked to the celebration of the Eucharist.

2.1.2 *Intercession Prayer*

Intercession prayer is praying on behalf of others. It follows the model in the Old Testament where the priest functions as the intercessor between Israel and God. In liturgy, intercession prayer is offered as a place of solidarity between the church and the world. In the liturgical form of Lima, we can find the prayer after the sermon and after the confession of faith.

This is also the part where the community will remember its context and ask for God's blessing through words of prayer. Here, Alexander Schmemann describes the meaning of intercession,

> To be in Christ means to be like Him, to make ours the very movement of His life. And as He "ever liveth to make intercession" for all "that come unto God by him" (Heb. 7:25), so we cannot help accepting His intercession as our own. The Church is not a society for escape-corporately or individually-from this world to taste the mystical bliss of eternity. Communion is not a "mystical experience": we drink of the chalice of Christ, and He gave Himself for the life of the world. The bread of the paten and the wine in the chalice are to remind us of the incarnation of the Son of God, of the cross and death. And thus it is the very joy of the Kingdom that makes us *remember* the world and pray for it is the very communion with the Holy Spirit that enables us to love the world with the love of Christ. The Eucharist is the sacrament of unity and the *moment of truth*: here we see the world in Christ, as it really is, and not from our particular and therefore limited and partial points of view. Intercession begins here, in the glory of the messianic banquet, and this is the only true beginning for the Church's mission. It is when, "having put aside all earthly care," we seem to have left *this world*, that we, in fact, recover it in all its reality. Intercession constitutes, thus, the only real preparation for communion.[51]

---

[51] Schmemann, *The World as Sacrament*, 44–45. Meanwhile, Wainwright mentions a small explanation about the intercessions as, "The fuller form will have occurred in the service of the word. The intercessions at this point are therefore resumptive. A commemoration of the saints is often woven here." See Wainwright, *Baptism and*

In other words, the intercession is a place where the church realizes the reality and its present context. It is the time of remembering the world and asking that God will help the church to love the world, where the church will see even its darkest situation, in the joy of God's Kingdom that was shown in the love of Christ. The prayer of intercession is the honest situational statement where the church will remember honestly and transform the memory into a joyous communal remembrance.

In the eucharistic liturgy of Lima, Wainwright states the function of this intercession prayer. He says, "The prayer of intercession unites the believing community, now nourished by the Word of God, in prayer for the needs of the Church and the world."[52] In short, intercessory prayer is a prayer for the church and the world. The attention towards others will come after hearing the service of the word.

Many Indonesian churches have given a different meaning to intercession prayer. Intercession prayer (Indonesian: *doa syafaat* or Dutch: *voorbede*) functions more as a prayer for the members and activities of the church.[53] It is also seen as a form of giving attention to the members of the church, especially the sick, those who mourn, or even birthday events. The prayer also contains petitions regarding current global situations. The pastor is seen as the intercessor who brings the situation of the community to God in prayer.

In this segment of the liturgy, we are able to see an opportunity to remember the current situation in the church and the world in the form of prayer. It is a place of remembering one's context and it is a sign of solidarity from the congregation to the people or circumstances that are mentioned in the prayer. In this part, we can see the aspect of the communion of believers and the table as the kingdom table. Connected with Metz's plea, we can also use this part to pray for those who suffer, not only in our immediate surroundings, but also the global context. Intercessory prayer is also a sign of unity of the church with the world as her context.

2.1.3 Eucharistic Prayer

The climax of remembrance in liturgy is the Eucharist proper, which puts the Eucharistic Prayer at the center. William R. Crockett, a Prot-

---

Eucharist, 103.

[52] Wainwright, *Baptism and Eucharist*, 244.

[53] It is worth mentioning here that *Syafaat* in Indonesian is coming from an Arabic word. It can be translated as prayer to Allah on behalf of others to receive good and reject bad things.

estant systematic theologian who also writes about the Eucharist and liturgy explains, "It was the Eucharistic Prayer that formed the heart of the liturgy, and the words of institution."[54] This tradition of a prayer over the bread and the cup can be traced back to the Jewish prayers of thanksgiving and blessing over the meal at the table. In other words, the Eucharistic Prayer is the heart of the liturgy of the Eucharist.

What does the Eucharistic Prayer consist of? David Power says that Eucharistic Prayer is "a memorial prayer of thanksgiving and intercession, proclaimed by the celebrant in the name of the congregation over the gifts of bread and wine. By this prayer those present approach the table of Christ's body and blood in the contemplation of the mystery of God's salvific work."[55]

The Eucharistic Prayer, also called *anaphora*, is not the same as prayer in general. It is indeed the heart of the eucharistic liturgy. The other parts of the liturgy are formed with the Eucharistic Prayer in mind.[56] There are several elements in the Eucharistic Prayer. The common elements that we can find are (1) The introductory dialogue; (2) The preface or (first part of the thanksgiving); (3) The Sanctus; (4) The Post Sanctus (thanksgiving); (5) preliminary epiclesis; (6) The narrative of the institution; (7) The anamnesis; (8) The epiclesis; (9) The eucharistic intercession; and (10) The doxology. We can find all these elements in a typical Eucharistic Prayer; however they may come in a different order and importance for different churches.[57]

According to Power, there are two places where we can deliver the prayer of recalling of the mystery. He says, "While the meaning of the prayer is expressed succinctly in the anamnetic acclamation, the basis to the more precise sense in which the mysteries are recalled in each prayer is its distinctive narrative foundation for thanksgiving and

---

[54] See Crockett, *Eucharist*, 39. Here Crockett gives a short historical development of the Eucharist, from Jewish tradition to contemporary ecumenism.

[55] David Noel Power, "A Prayer of Intersecting Parts: Elements of the Eucharistic Prayer," *Liturgical Ministry* 14 (2005), 131. See also David N. Power, *The Eucharistic Mystery: Revitalizing the Mystery* (New York: Crossroad Publishing Company, 1992).

[56] Eucharistic Prayer also known as Anaphora (ἀναφορά) which literally means "carrying back". See W. Jardine Grisbrooke, "Anaphora," in *The New Westminster Dictionary of Liturgy and Worship*, ed. J.G. Davies (Pennsylvania: The Westminster Press, 1986), 13–21.

[57] See also Max Thurian and Geoffrey Wainwright, eds., *Baptism and Eucharist*, 102–103, and Power, "A Prayer of Intersecting Parts", 120–131. Power divides the elements of Eucharistic Prayer into 7 parts: (1) Narrative foundation; (2) Epiclesis; (3) Anamnesis/offering; (4) Sanctus; (5) Supper narrative; (6) Intercessions; (7) Vocal Participation of the people.

intercession."[58] These two parts can be used as remembrance part of the present context of the congregation.

Because we have discussed the intercession part previously, we now will take a brief look at the thanksgiving portion. The thanksgiving is a part where the church gives thanks to God for the saving action in the past.[59] The Eucharistic Prayer, as derived from its original Jewish sense, is about giving thanks to God. Now that it becomes a remembrance of Jesus Christ in a Christian community, thanksgiving becomes a remembrance of what God has done in Jesus Christ.

The thanksgiving part enables the community to remember what happened in the past, not only the event of the cross, but also what has happened in their own past, as an individual and a community. The prayer of thanksgiving makes the church as a whole, and the individuals that are in the community personally, remember God's redeeming acts in their lives and give by their participation thanks for it.

Crockett, in his research on the historical development of the Eucharist, argues that thanksgiving can become specific for different communities for what God has done for them.[60] Just as the Jewish tradition also recounts God's mighty deeds to them specifically, so local communities can also recall what God has done for them. This remembrance of Gods saving act also reinforces the assurance that God has always been there for the congregation. Giving thanks means knowing and mentioning what God has done and at the same time realizing that God will stay with them. The thanksgiving part is universal, yet it is also personal and communal. It is a part where the congregation can recall something from the past and be thankful for it, and at the same time it also gives them courage to go on to the future remembering that God has always been there for them, and shall always be there for them.

2.2 *Lima Liturgy of the Eucharist*

In the development of liturgy, some differences arise concerning the eucharistic liturgy. As mentioned earlier, we will use the proposed eucharistic liturgy of Lima as an example of an ecumenical eucharistic

---

[58] Power, "A Prayer of Intersecting Parts", 131.

[59] Wainwright says that Thanksgiving is resumed with a sharp focus on God's gift of Jesus Christ to us. This culminates in the recollection of the institution of the sacrament at the Last Supper, unless the institution narrative is also preceded by a preliminary epiclesis. See Wainwright, *Baptism and Eucharist*, 103.

[60] See Crockett, *Eucharist*, 52–54.

liturgy. This liturgy aims to, in Wainwright words, "illustrate the solid theological achievements of the Faith and Order Document: Baptism, Eucharist and Ministry."[61] The liturgy models one example of the various developments of recent theological ideas of the Eucharist. One of the strong points of this eucharistic liturgy is that it accommodates several traditions. This eucharistic liturgy was composed with ecumenical diversity in mind.[62]

This liturgy is not intended as the only model for eucharistic celebration. Even so, we can consider it as a carefully developed example of a recent ecumenical theological eucharistic liturgy. It is part of a fully orbed Sunday service and is particularly suited to churches that are used to a certain solemnity in their worship services. However, here we will only look at the part of the liturgical order that is focused on the actual Eucharist that is specifically relevant to our research.[63] .

Liturgy of the Eucharist

17. Preparation
O (Another Celebrant): Blessed are you Lord God of the universe…
18. Dialogue
P (Presiding Minister): The Lord be with you!…
19. Preface
P: Truly it is right and good to glorify you, at all times and in all places, to offer you our thanksgiving O Lord, Holy Father, Almighty and Everlasting God. Through your loving Word you created all things, and pronounced them good. You made human beings in your own image, to share your life and reflect your glory. When the time had fully come, you gave Christ to us as the Way, the Truth and the Life. He accepted baptism and consecration as your Servant to announce the good news to the poor. At the last supper Christ bequeathed to us the Eucharist, that we should celebrate the memorial of the cross and resurrection, and receive his presence as food. To all the redeemed Christ gave the royal priesthood and, in loving his brothers and sisters, chooses those who share in the ministry, that they may feed the Church with your Word and enable it to love by your Sacraments. Wherefore, Lord, with the angels and all the saints, we proclaim and sing your glory:
20. Sanctus
21. Epiclesis I

---

[61] Wainwright, *Baptism and Eucharist*, 241.
[62] See the remark by Wainwright about the different traditions in *Baptism and Eucharist*, 242–248.
[63] Wainwright divides the full liturgy into three parts: Liturgy of Entrance (liturgical order 1–6), Liturgy of the Word (liturgical order 7–16), and liturgy of the Eucharist (liturgical order as mentioned above). See Wainwright, *Baptism and Eucharist*, 249–255. The final parts are final hymn (33), word of mission (34), and blessing (35).

P: O God, Lord of the universe, you are holy and your glory is beyond measure. Upon your Eucharist send the life-giving Spirit, who spoke by Moses and the Prophets, who overshadowed the Virgin Mary with grace, who descended upon Jesus in the river Jordan and upon the Apostles on the day of Pentecost. May the outpouring of this Spirit of Fire transfigure this thanksgiving meal that this bread and wine may become for us the body and blood of Christ.
C *(Congregation): Veni Creator Spiritus!*

22. Institution

P: May this Creator Spirit accomplish the words of your beloved Son, who, in the night in which he was betrayed, took the bread, and when he had given thanks to you, broke it and gave it to his disciples, saying: Take, eat: this is my body, which is given for you. Do this for the remembrance of me. After supper he took the cup and when he had given thanks, he gave it to them and said: Drink this, all of you: this is my blood of the new covenant, which is shed for you and for many for the forgiveness of sins. Do this for the remembrance of me. Great is the mystery of faith.
C: *Your death, Lord Jesus, we proclaim! Your resurrection we celebrate! Your coming in glory we await!*

23. Anamnesis

P: Wherefore, Lord, we celebrate today the memorial of our redemption: we recall the birth and life of your Son among us, his baptism by John, his last meal with the apostles, his death and descent to the abode of the dead; we proclaim Christ's resurrection and ascension in glory, where as our Great High Priest he ever intercedes for all people; and we look for his coming at the last. United in Christ's priesthood, we present to you this memorial: remember the sacrifice of your Son and grant to people everywhere the benefits of Christ's redemptive work.
C: *Maranatha, the Lord comes!*

24. Epiclesis II

P: Behold, Lord, this Eucharist which you yourself gave to the Church and graciously receive it, as you accept the offering of your Son whereby we are reinstated in your Covenant. As we partake of Christ's body and blood, fill us with the Holy Spirit that we may be one single body and one single spirit in Christ, a living sacrifice to the praise of your glory.
C: *Veni Creator Spiritus!*

25. Commemorations

O: Remember, Lord, your one, holy, catholic and apostolic Church, redeemed by the blood of Christ. Reveal its unity, guard its faith, and preserve it in peace. Remember, Lord, all the servants of your Church: bishops, presbyters, deacons, and all to whom you have given special gifts of ministry. (Remember especially …)
Remember also all our sisters and brothers who have died in the peace of Christ, and those whose faith is known to you alone: guide them to the joyful feast prepared for all peoples in your presence, with the blessed Virgin Mary, with the patriarchs and prophets, the apostles and martyrs

… and all the saints for whom your friendship was life. With all these we sing your praise and await the happiness of your Kingdom where with the whole creation finally delivered from sin and death, we shall be enabled to glorify you through Christ our Lord.
C: *Maranatha, the Lord comes!*

26. Conclusion
P: Through Christ, with Christ, in Christ, all honor and glory is yours, Almighty God and Father, in the unity of the Holy Spirit, now and forever.
C: Amen.

27. The Lord's Prayer

28. The Peace
O: O Lord Jesus Christ, you told your apostles: Peace I leave with you, my peace I give to you. Look not on our sins but on the faith of your Church. In order that your will be done, grant us always this peace and guide us towards the perfect unity of your Kingdom forever.
C: Amen.
P: The peace of the Lord be with you always.
C: And also with you.
O: Let us give one another a sign of reconciliation and peace.

29. The Breaking of the Bread
P: The bread which we break…

30. Lamb of God
C: Lamb of God, you take away the sins of the world, have mercy on us…

31. Communion

32. Thanksgiving Prayer
Presiding Minister: In peace let us pray to the Lord: O Lord our God, we give you thanks for uniting us by baptism in the Body of Christ and for filling us with joy in the Eucharist. Lead us towards the full visible unity of your Church and help us to treasure all the signs of reconciliation you have granted us. Now that we have tasted the banquet you have prepared for us in the world to come, may we all one day share together the inheritance of the saints in the life of your heavenly city, through Jesus Christ, your Son, our Lord, who lives and reigns with you in the unity of the Holy Spirit, ever one God, world without end.
C: **Amen**.

We see that the liturgy opens with the first aspect of the Eucharist which is the thanksgiving to the Father. It also shows the unity between Christ and the Spirit in the first Epiclesis and in the institution (liturgical element 21 and 22), which are the second and third aspect of the Eucharist. The whole life of Jesus is celebrated in the Anamnesis (element 23) as one of the new suggestions in the BEM document. Wainwright also tries to picture the relation of the Father, the Son, and the Spirit in the Anamnesis. "The eucharist, given in the Spirit to the church as a precious gift, is received by the Father as an intercession and a thanksgiving, one with the very offering of the Son which reestablishes us in the covenant with God."[64] The celebration of the Eucharist is not only to remember Christ's saving work, but also the relation of the Father, Son, and Spirit with the church (see element 24).

The commemoration (element 25) is the part where we remember those who we wish to pray about. Wainwright says that here we can "mention all those for whom we wish especially to pray, remember those who preceded us in the faith and all the cloud of witnesses by whom we are compassed about."[65] This is also the chance where we can pray about people who were hurt in past events of the church as a community. Metz's idea of remembering the suffering can also be incorporated here when the congregation remembers what has happened in the past to certain people or certain communities. In the prayer of thanksgiving (element 32) we ask for a visible unity in the church through the spirit of reconciliation. Remembrance of the past and the hope of the future are displayed in the liturgy.

The thanksgiving prayer indicates that the Eucharist gives joy to the congregants. Through this joy, the church will strive towards a visible unity and work on the reconciliation signs that have been granted by God. A request for the unity of the church is also shown in this thanksgiving prayer. This element fulfils the fourth and fifth aspect of the Eucharist. There are also some elements that are felt to be missing in this liturgy. This liturgy assumes that the part of confession and absolution are already included in the early section, thus it does not need to appear again in the eucharistic prayer. However, precisely because of that, we are lacking a sense of self-examination and self-preparation before the Eucharist takes place. The absence of a "self-check" can be expected, since Wainwright designed the liturgy based on the expectation that the Eucharist should be celebrated as often as possible. Thus, the confession and absolution in the beginning of the liturgy are enough without the part of self-check. By having confession and absolution at the very beginning, congregation members come to the table as forgiven sinners.

However, the personal—and at the same time communal—poignant awareness of confession and absolution are crucial aspects. We can imagine that Volf would have wanted to have this element in his liturgy of the Eucharist. He would say that it is important for the congregation to

---

[64] Wainwright, *Baptism and Eucharist*, 245.
[65] Wainwright, *Baptism and Eucharist*, 246.

come to the table as people who are forgiven, forgiving, and reconciled. We will keep this in mind while we explore the HKBP liturgy later on.

3. The Liturgy of HKBP

The initial question of this research project was to find out whether the HKBP took the right way of dealing with her 1992–1998 conflict. The church chose the path of reconciliation by having a 1998 Reconciliation General Synod. However, our investigation showed that the HKBP in fact actually chose for a way of forgetting.

We have investigated the importance of memory and remembrance in dealing with a past communal conflict. One of the opportunities of expressing a communal memory in the church is in liturgy. The place of remembrance in liturgy is central and also an active core, in the sense that it connects the past to the hope for the future in present reactions.

The three main elements in the liturgy—the sermon, intercession prayer, and the liturgy of the Eucharist—are the liturgical elements where the church remembers the past and give thanks for it. It is also a moment and a place where the church remembers the real context that it has to deal with and learns to love with a joyous remembrance of God's love.

These parts can be adjusted within the actual context where the church finds itself. In the context of conflict and past trauma, the church can offer written prayers that make a connection with the situation and recall the circumstances. The church will use this real event as part of the thanksgiving as well as the intercessory prayer. Thereby the memory of the past hurt belongs to the community. This memory will be remembered in the context of the joyous memory of God's saving act.

The celebration of the Eucharist gives us a place of communal remembrance. It is, as Schmemann puts it, a social sacrament, where all individual members of the church are brought together in the presence of the Lord's feast. This social sacrament offers a unique opportunity where victims and perpetrators all share the same bread and wine, the same memory of the life, death, and resurrection of Jesus Christ.

How can we apply this exploration on liturgy in the case of HKBP's conflict? How can liturgy, especially in the Eucharist celebration, help those in conflict to remember what has happened and come to terms with their past? How can the celebration of the Eucharist help the HKBP Church to remember her past and transform it into a healed memory? We shall look into the resources that the HKBP has in her liturgy of the Eucharist, and try to find out if it can help the Church in dealing with her past.

In this part we will do text analysis on the liturgy of the Eucharist in the HKBP based on several church documents such as the Confession, the Church Guide for Pastoral Care and Discipline, the Church Order, and the "Agenda" (The Liturgical Book of the Church). We will do a close reading, and look particular at finding out whether the Church has room for remembrance in her liturgy of the Eucharist. We will also compare our findings with what we have learned from Schmemann, Metz and Volf. In the end, we will point out the strong and weak elements of remembrance in the liturgy and propose some adjustments.

3.1 Order of the Sunday Service

Our opportunity of finding the place for a communal remembrance in the Eucharist is very relevant for the HKBP because the HKBP is a liturgical church. The HKBP uses a lectionary, daily bible text reading, and the right use of liturgical colors, Sundays, and Bible texts for each Sunday. This means that the HKBP's strong liturgical root will give us the opportunity to explore the possibility of transforming past conflict into redemptive memory in its eucharistic liturgy.

In order to look into the sources of the HKBP liturgy, we will look into the available resource, which is the HKBP so-called *Agenda*. It is an adoption of the German's *Agende* or *Kirchenagende* (German: *Agende* or *Kirchenagende* means "things to be done").[66] The HKBP Agenda is originally written in Batak and was later translated into Indonesian.

The agenda can be traced back to the Prussian Union of the Lutheran and Reformed churches. King Frederick William III (1770—1840) published the agenda in 1822 for various churches within the Prussian dominions. After going through debates and revisions, the agenda underwent a thorough revision in 1879. In 1895, the general Synod finally accepted a service book that was to be used in the Prussian churches.[67] The 1895 Service Book for the Protestant Church of Prussia (*Agende für die evangelische Landeskirche Preussens*) shows the following liturgy form for a normal Sunday.[68]

---

[66] The HKBP Agenda is a continued tradition that was handed over by the German missionaries. It is possible that it was an adaptation of the Agenda of the Prussian Union (Evangelical Christian Church).

[67] See also Paul F. Bradshaw, ed., "Lutheran" in *The New SCM Dictionary of Liturgy and Worship* (London: SCM Press, 2002), 79–80.

[68] As mentioned by Hans-Christoph Schmidt-Lauber, "The Lutheran Traditions

1895 Prussian Liturgy

   1. **Entrance Hymn**
"In the Name of the Father, and of the Son and of the Holy Ghost."
"Our help is in the name of the Lord … "
   2. **Opening sentence from Scripture.**
"Glory be to the Father…"
   3. **Confession of Sins, Kyrie, and word of grace**
"Glory be to God in the highest …"(on feastdays only)
"The Lord be with you …"
   4. **Collect**
   5. **Epistle**
   6. **Hallelujah**
   7. **Gospel** (with "Praise be to you, O Christ" and "Glory be to You, O Lord")
   8. **Apostles' creed** (or Luther's hymn "Wir glauben all an einen Gott")
   9. **Hymn before the sermon**
  10. **Greeting from the pulpit**
  11. **Sermon**
  12. **Verse of a hymn**
  13. **Requests for prayer and announcements**
  14. **Blessing from the pulpit**
  15. **Verse of a hymn**
[If there is to be no communion, the dialogue, preface, and Sanctus nevertheless may be said at this point]
  16. **Prayers of intercessions**
  17. **If there is to be no communion: conclusion with Lord's prayer, Aaronic blessing, Amen, and a closing hymn-verse**
The Prussian liturgy also notes the order of the communion as follows,

If communion:
Verse of a hymn for the Lord's Supper
"The Lord be with you…"
Communion exhortation (unless there has been preparatory confession and absolution directly before the main service)
Eucharistic Prayer: dialogue, preface, Sanctus, prayer for fruitful communion
Lord's Prayer (here or after the words of institution, where customary)
"Kneel and hear" **the words of institution**
Agnus Dei

---

in the German Lands" in *The Oxford History of Christian Worship*, eds. Geoffrey Wainwright and Karen B. Westerfield Tucker (New York: Oxford University Press, 2006), 411–412. Highlights are made and numbers are assigned to mark the parts of the liturgy. Compare the similarity to the 1888 Common Service in *The Book of Worship* that was published by the United Synod of the Evangelical Lutheran Church in the South (Charleston, SC: Committee of United Synod on Common Book Worship, 1907).

Peace
Prayer to Christ for forgiveness of sins and faithful obedience
Invitation (Matthew 11:28 or Psalm 34:8a)
Communion ("Take and eat/drink," based again on the words of institution)
Post communion prayer of thanks
Aaronic blessing, Amen, and a closing hymn verse

Liturgy is like a play which has an opening, climax, and closing. Our argument here is based on the elements that are put before and after the sermon in both liturgies. The BEM document proposes a few elements before the sermon which are the confession of sin and absolution in the liturgy. The Prussian liturgy, however, offers everything before the sermon in order to build up to the climax. The climax of the service is the sermon. Other liturgical elements, except the offering and intercessions are placed before the sermon, because they all lead to the full readiness of heart to hear God's word.

The Eucharist celebration brings another dimension to the regular service of the Word. It is the Eucharist that becomes the climax of the liturgy, instead of the sermon. It is celebrated immediately after the sermon, and there are no other liturgical elements afterwards. We will discuss this in more depth in the part of where we will look at the HKBP liturgy on this.

The Prussian liturgy also has a separate preparatory service before the main service. This has a connection with the command to examine oneself in 1 Corinthians 11:28. However, the preparatory service is an option, rather than a requirement for the actual communion. We will come back to this preparatory service later on when we focus on the HKBP service.

Because of limited time and resources, this research does not provide the exact history of HKBP's liturgical development, not even from the form of the Prussian liturgy until its present state. This is one of the challenges that can be explored further after this research. What we will do is to show the earliest order of service in the 1904 HKBP Agenda and compare it with the most recent one.

Below is the order of a regular Sunday Service based on the HKBP 1904 and the latest 1998 Agenda.[69]

---

[69] HKBP 1904 Agenda and HKBP 1998 Agenda.

HKBP 1904 Agenda	HKBP 1998 Agenda
1. **Opening Hymn**	1. **Opening Hymn**
2. **Votum** Liturgist: In the name of God the Father, The Son Jesus Christ, and the Holy Spirit. Amen.	2. **Votum** Liturgist: In the name of God the Father, the Son Jesus Christ, and the Holy Spirit, who created heaven and earth. Amen.
3. **Introit** (according to liturgical Sunday)	3. **Introit** (according to Liturgical Sunday) Congregational responses: Hallelujah! (3x) or Maranatha! (3x)
4. **Collect**	4. **Collect**
5. **Reading of God's Commandments** (as mirror of self to sin; taken from The Commandments, or Bible Text or Martin Luther's Catechism) Congregation responds: Lord God, please strengthen us to act according to your Commandment.	5. **Hymn based on the liturgical Sunday**
	6. **Reading of God's Commandments** (as mirror of self to sin; from The Commandments, or Bible Text or Martin Luther's Catechism) Congregation responds: Lord God, please strengthen us to act according to your Commandment.
6. **Hymn about Confession of Sin**	7. **Hymn about Confession of Sin**
7. **Confession of sin and Absolution**	8. **Confession of sin and Absolution**
8. **Response Hymn**	9. **Response Hymn**
9. **Epistle** (the bible text reading from the NT letters, the gospels and/or from the Old Testament). Liturgist: "Blessed rather are those who hear the word of God and obey it." (Luke 11:28)	10. **Epistle** (despite the name of the rubric, it is not limited to these; it refers to the entirety of bible text for Sunday). Liturgist: "Blessed rather are those who hear the word of God and obey it." (Luke 11:28). Congregational response: Amen!
10. **Hymn**: Your words, O Lord, are the most precious of all, Stay in my heart so I will never leave you. If we don't hold your holy word, what will be the foundation of believers? (HKBP Hymn Book no. 25)	11. **Hymn about the Epistle reading**
11. **Apostles' Creed**	12. **Apostles' Creed**
	13. **Reading of Congregation News** (followed by intercession prayer)
12. **Response Hymn**	14. **Hymn about the sermon** (while collecting first and second offering)
13. **Service of Word** Opens with "And the peace of God, which transcends all understanding, will guard your hearts and your minds in Christ Jesus." (Phil. 4:7) Closed with a prayer.	15. **Service of Word** Opens with "And the peace of God, which transcends all understanding, will guard your hearts and your minds in Christ Jesus." (Phil. 4:7) Closed with a prayer
14. **Reading of Congregation News**	16. **Offering** (third offering - while singing hymn)
15. **Offering** (while singing hymn)	17. **Offering Prayer**
16. **Offering Prayer**	18. **Offering Hymn**
17. **Lord's Prayer**	19. **Lord's Prayer**
18. **Aaronic blessing**	20. **Aaronic blessing**

As we can see, there is not much development between the 1904 normal Sunday liturgy and the one from 1998. The most notable difference is the reading of the congregation's news, which is after the sermon in 1904 Agenda; while in 1998 Agenda it is before the sermon. The other change is the place of the offering which is after the sermon and reading of congregation news in 1904 Agenda; while in 1998 Agenda it becomes two times: before and once after the sermon. It is important to note here that the liturgist and preacher are usually two different persons. The preacher will take over and lead the liturgy only after the sermon.

If we are to compare the 1998 HKBP liturgy to the 1895 Prussian liturgy, we will find more similarities than differences. All the elements are nearly the same, and the clear focus of the liturgy is the sermon. The elements that are now placed after the sermon are offerings, since the congregation news and the intercession were moved to a slot before the sermon.

We will now try to break down the HKBP liturgy into five clusters and explain the logic of the service. The first section is the opening. The service is opened in the name of the Father, Son and Holy Spirit as a seal and sign that God is present in the service. The next part is the reading of the bible text that is connected to the liturgical Sunday. It will be read as an opening text, followed by a prayer.

The following section is the confession of sins. This section is opened with the reading of God's commandments or a relevant bible text or a brief part of Martin Luther's catechism as a mirror to realize one's sin. After looking at ourselves in this mirror, we then know and confess our sins. The confession is followed by absolution.

The third section is the faith statement of the congregation that those who confessed indeed received the grace of forgiveness. The Epistle acts as a direction towards the new life in Christ. This is why a pastoral letter from the Apostles is often chosen for this part, but sometimes some other bible texts are also used. After receiving the direction, the congregation will then pledge the faith by reciting the Apostles' Creed. Next, there is a reading of congregational news, followed by intercessory prayer for the church and the world.[70]

---

[70] After intercession, the collection of offering while singing preparation hymns for the sermon seems out of place. Based on informal source, the change of place of offering from the 1904 liturgy to the 1998 (it was already changed in the earlier version of 1998 Agenda), from after the sermon to before and after the service, is basically a practical one. They wanted to have more offering baskets, thus putting them (three times) altogether after the sermon seemed too demanding, thus it was decided to separate the offering baskets into two parts: before and after the sermon.

The next cluster is the preparation hymn for the sermon followed by the sermon. This is the climax of the service. The sermon begins and closes with a prayer. Afterwards, the closing section is the offering, the Lord's Prayer and the blessing.

Such a Sunday service will be changed when there is a Communion. The Eucharist is celebrated after the sermon. There will be no confession and absolution before the sermon, because it is moved to be part of the eucharistic liturgy. We will analyze the eucharistic liturgy of HKBP in the following section.

3.2 *The Preparation Service for the Celebration of the Eucharist*

Before we analyze the liturgy, let us take a look at the theological understanding of the Eucharist within the HKBP. This body celebrates the Eucharist as part of the sacraments; that it is one of the signs of a true church.[71] The HKBP 1996 Confession Article 8 B believes and confesses that,

> The Eucharist is eating the bread as a passage of our Lord Jesus Christ's body and drinking the wine as a passage of our Lord Jesus Christ's blood, so we will receive forgiveness of sins, life and joy. The Eucharist is a joyous feast for everyone that participates, because it is the beginning of a true communion. It is also a sign of thanksgiving to remember Lord Jesus Christ's act of redemption, and the way to receive His grace (Matt. 26:20–30; Mark 14:17–26; Luke 22:14–20; 1 Cor. 11:17–34).
>
> With this we encourage people to participate more often in the Eucharist.
>
> We reject the manner that some churches only give bread without wine to the congregation.
>
> Also the idea that there are more than two sacraments."

The elements that are being stressed in the Eucharist are the passage of Christ's body and blood as source of forgiveness of sins, (new) life and joy. It looks like the HKBP considers the remembrance in the Eucharist as an active one. It does not only symbolize Christ's body and blood, it channels them. It is a way to be thankful and remember Christ's act of redemption and the way to receive Christ's grace. The means of remembering Christ is also the means to receive grace.

This understanding of the Eucharist in the Church Confession is more recent when compared to the understanding of the Eucharist in

---

[71] HKBP 1996 Confession, article 7E sub section b, based on the texts Matt. 28:19 and Mark 16:15–16.

the liturgy of the Agenda of the church. While a new Confession has already been accepted, the liturgy still bases the understanding of the Eucharist on the 1951 Confession. Thus, we can already see the new understanding of the Eucharist compared to the 1951 Confession.[72]

The new formula adds, "The Eucharist is a joyous feast for everyone that participates, because it is the beginning of a true communion." This part is an important statement that gives us the foundation of the communal event in the celebration of the Eucharist. The element of "feast" is also added, which means that the Church wants to set a different tone than the grim reality of sins. This is probably the reason why we see the sentence: "With this we encourage people to participate more often in the Eucharist." It is now considered a common celebration, a feast with other members of Christ's body, a beginning of the true community in Christ. The first sentence reminds us of Schmemann's idea of a joyous remembrance, and the fourth aspect of the Eucharist as the communion of believers.

The second sentence in the confession is also added recently: "It is also a sign of thanksgiving to remember the Lord Jesus Christ's act of redemption, and the way to receive His grace." This part shows the second aspect of the Eucharist as the memorial of Christ's life. The older Confession never mentioned the aspect of remembrance in the Eucharist. Thus, a more recent theological understanding of the Eucharist must have been added to the 1996 confession.

The HKBP Confession sees the Eucharist as both a personal and a communal event. It is meant for all members of the congregation (who already followed catechism class and made their confession of faith— as stated in the liturgy of the Eucharist for catechism). It is personal because of the forgiveness of sins which is promised to each individual believer, and it is communal because it is seen as the beginning of a true communion.

The HKBP encourages her members to participate more often in the celebration of the Eucharist, except for those who are under pastoral

---

[72] HKBP 1951 Confession, Article 10 B states, "The Holy Communion is eating the bread as the passage of our Lord Jesus Christ's body and drinking the wine as the passage of our Lord Jesus Christ's blood, so we will receive our forgiveness of sins, life and joy (1 Cor. 11:17–34; Matthew 26; Mark 14; Luke 22). With this teaching, we are against and reject the teaching that says that only bread shall be given to congregation and not the wine. This is what Jesus said when He instituted the Holy Communion: "You will all drink from the cup." It is what the early churches did (1 Cor. 11:24–25). There is no reason to conclude from God's Word that God is being sacrificed again in every Mass. Thus, we reject this teaching.

discipline of the Church.⁷³ It will be made public when people are placed under pastoral discipline so that the community will also help and be responsible for the teaching of the person.⁷⁴ Welcoming back the person is also announced in the community so that they may now participate again in the communion. This reflects that the Eucharist is an important sign of community. It is not only a place of forgiveness for individuals; it is also a sign of participation in communal celebration. Members who have admitted their sins and are willing to change their attitude are welcomed back in the celebration of the Eucharist. It signals the re-entry to the community.

Because of the aspects of community and remembrance, we will explore the liturgy of the Eucharist in the HKBP, as it is mentioned in the Agenda. There are two types of liturgies of the Eucharist in the HKBP Agenda. The first one is the service where the Eucharist service is held separately with a preparation service. This preparation service is also held as a separate service. In the second service the Eucharist is held together with the preparation. We will explore both services with more attention to the Eucharist liturgy with preparation. Even though the preparation service is rarely celebrated in the Church anymore—probably because of time constraints, it gives the opportunity to look at it as a service of reflection. The preparation service can also function as a self-check service so that people who enter the Eucharist will come prepared.

The preparation service can be held well before the actual Sunday service: commonly on the Friday or Saturday prior to the Communion Sunday, or even a week before the communion. The Preparation Service is an independent service apart from a Sunday service. It is important to note that the preparation service also acts as a kind of confession of sin service. The liturgical element of confession of sins is not included anymore in the eucharistic service when a Preparation Service has taken place. This, however, is different with the eucharistic liturgy that includes the preparation, where confession of sins is included in the formula.

---

⁷³ HKBP, *Ruhut Parmahanion dohot Paminsangion* (Eng: *Church Pastoral and Discipline*) (Tarutung: HKBP, 1987), 16. "The punishment to those who do not want to change his/her attitude or sins, will be the exclusion from the church for a period of time. It means, his/her heart cannot receive God's grace, and is not able to participate in the Communion."

⁷⁴ We can trace back the idea of communal exclusion to the idea of excommunication in the early church. HKBP based the guidelines of carrying out the discipline on Matt. 18:15–17.

The preparation service is held according the following order *(the parts in brackets are added to clarify the parts in the liturgy)*:[75]

1. **Hymn** (about confession of sins)
2. **Prayer**
3. **Sermon Connected with the Holy Communion**
4. **Preparation Formula**

(a. Invitation and Guidance)

God's beloved people! We intend to celebrate the Holy Communion. Accordingly, I invite you to reflect whether we are worthy to receive the Holy Communion. For the Word of God says, every person should examine him/herself before receiving the Holy Communion, whether he/she deserves it. If anyone receives the Holy Communion in an unworthy manner, he/she brings punishment upon him/herself (1 Corinthians 11:27–29), because he/she then had underestimated the body of Christ. Therefore check yourselves – each one of you, whether you have possessed what is expected of the Lord Jesus. Because those who are humble, who regret all the bad acts that he/she does, who confessed his/her sin, and those who believe in forgiveness of sins given by the Lord Jesus; they are the ones that are worthy to receive the Holy Communion. You shall meditate on the Word of God says Jesus: "'Love the Lord your God with all your heart and with all your soul and with all your mind.' This is the first and greatest commandment. And the second is like it: 'Love your neighbor as yourself.'" (Matthew 22:37–40).

(b. Counsel)

If you mirror your soul and action in the law above, then you will confess, that you are a sinner who violates the law of God through words and deeds. You should not come to the Holy Communion in such circumstances, because the Communion is Holy. Think of these words: God knows His own people; those who mention the name of God must abstain from all evil. Do not be misguided, because God does not want to be blasphemed. Whoever does not believe in the Lord Jesus, and who does not receive redemption because of sin, should not come to the Holy Communion, because it will bring punishment to him/her. However, those who repent of sin, and long for God's love in Jesus Christ, and ask for the power of the Holy Spirit so that he/she is cleansed of sin; he/she can be assured that his/her sins are forgiven because of the redemption in the Lord Jesus Christ. The Holy Communion stamps it into your heart.

The Communion is a reconciliation table where we come as sisters and

---

[75] This HKBP preparatory service has similar order as the Dutch Lutheran *Order for the Absolution* and the *Order for the Lord's Supper*, as found in the Dutch Lutheran *Formulierboek*. See Harry J. Kreider, *The Beginnings of Lutheranism in New York* (New York: *unpublished*, 1949), 53–60. This book was written for the United Lutheran Synod of New York in connection with its celebration of the three hundredth anniversary of the oldest Lutheran Church in America.

brothers, united in the same memory of God's love through Christ's life, death, resurrection, and ascension.

(c. Questions) **Let us examine ourselves and answer each question:**
1. Do you confess that you are a sinner since you were born and by the violations of The Law of God? If so, answer with "Yes!"
2. Do you confess that you should be punished by God because of your sins, either now or in the future? If so, answer with "Yes!"
3. Do you regret your sins and that you expect deliverance from him? If so, answer with "Yes!"
4. Do you confess that the Lord Jesus came into this world to save sinners? That He died for your sins and rose again from the dead? If so, answer with "Yes!"
5. Will you leave the malice and hatred, and do you want to make peace with those who sinned against you? Do you want to forgive him/her like you expect God will forgive your sins? If so, answer with "Yes!"
6. Are you going to try to fight against sin, and obey the Word of God with all your heart? If so, answer with "Yes!"

(d. Confession Prayer and Absolution) **Let us humble ourselves and confess our sins to each other. Follow this prayer in your hearts!**

O Lord God, Holy Father, who art in heaven, but also willing to be with humble people who regret their sins. You are the God, the Most Gracious! We are despicable and sinful, because we often violate your law. If you give back to us according to our sins, we will perish now and in the future. God have mercy on us. Forgive us our sins. Purify our hearts that have been blackened because of our sins and transgressions. Clean our hearts, and renew our mind with a strong spirit. Give us the Holy Spirit so that we can avoid sin and live our lives more holy. Let us even be more convinced of Your Son Jesus Christ, our Lord's act of salvation. Amen.

Listen to the consolation from the Word of God: For God so loved the world that He gave His only begotten Son, that whoever believes in Him should not perish but have everlasting life (John 3:16).

As servant of the Lord, I declare upon God's name, rest assured; you will receive what you believe. Rest assured, your sins are forgiven and you have become the heir of the love in the Lord Jesus Christ. Let everyone who long for their forgiveness of sins, respond with Amen.

5. **Hymn**
6. **Aaronic Blessings**

The preparation service starts with a sermon about preparation and the communion. The opening part of the preparation formula assumes that people already understand what the Communion is, based on the sermon that is being delivered beforehand. The formula asks for a self-reflection before receiving the Communion. There is a kind of process of how forgiveness is being offered. It asks humility, remorse, confession, honesty with oneself, and faith in the forgiveness of sins in Jesus Christ.

The formula also sounds more personal because it is for each person.[76] The attendees are asked to think about their relation to God and fellow human. Thus, even when it seems personally directed to personal forgiveness, it asks people to think about their relation with others. This incorporates the personal-communal aspect of the formula.

After a personal reflection, the attendees will realize that they are sinners, so they are asked to repent before coming to the table. This is the message of the second part. It also explains the consequence of not doing so.

The third part about the questions is an important factor in the formula because it helps and reminds people to realize and confess what they believe, their faith, and their past action. The questions are more on the personal level since it refers to "you" in second person singular form. We can put the logic of the questions as follow: 1. The participant is reminded of the original sin and his/her violation of the Law; 2. Admit the unworthiness because of sins; 3. After admitting, then we show remorse for sins; 4. Admit that Jesus is the redeemer; 5. The importance of forgiving others before asking for one's own forgiveness; and 6. They will not to commit sin in the future anymore (to fight sin).

After answering all questions, the congregation will hear the words of consolation from God and the minister will declare absolution. The absolution is again declared in the second person singular form. This means that forgiveness of sins is at a personal level. The service ends with blessings.

The preparation service focuses on self-preparation, especially on the forgiveness of sins and absolution. The formula stresses the holy and righteous aspects of the Eucharist a lot and does not mention the other aspects of the communion. There are a lot of such aspects that are involved in the Eucharist, such as the aspect of God's grace, an invitation to experience God's grace, the expectation of the *parousia*, or the fact that a communion should be celebrated together with the whole community. The formula seems to be a personal self-reflection, and lacking a communal feeling. However, since this is a part of the eucharistic liturgy, we have to look at the liturgy of the Eucharist as well so that we can get a sense of continuation of the whole process.

3.3 *The Eucharistic Liturgy after the Preparation Service*

This is the order of eucharistic liturgy if a preparation service exists *(the parts in brackets are added to clarify the parts in the liturgy)*:

---

[76] The Indonesian translation renders as: "to check each one of you."

1. **Opening Hymn** (about the Lord's Supper)
P: The grace of the Lord Jesus Christ, and the love of God, and the fellowship of the Holy Spirit, be with you all.
2. **Epiclesis Prayer**
3. **Sermon** (if a preparation service is held beforehand then a Sermon is not obligatory, but the decision lies in the hand of the minister if he/she wants to deliver a sermon),
4. **Formula**
(a. Invitation)
Beloved people of our Lord Jesus Christ! In accordance with the message of the Lord Jesus to His disciples, now we are going to receive the Holy Communion. Let us therefore examine ourselves, whether we are ready to accept it as desired by our Lord Jesus. Our Lord Jesus gave the Holy Communion as comfort to those who repented of their sins, to grow in their faith; moreover, our memory of Jesus Christ shall be refreshed through the Holy Communion.
(b. Anamnesis)
Let us remember our Lord, who came into this world to lift up our sins and pay our debts, so we will be spared from destruction. Our Lord Jesus has taken our place in undertaking the Law so that we might receive justification. Our sins are forgiven, we are reconciled to God. This is what our Lord Jesus has sealed into our hearts through the Holy Communion. Every time we celebrate Holy Communion, we receive the flesh and blood of Christ, we are in fellowship with Him, it means: He is in us, and we in Him. Therefore let us remember and proclaim His death, as a sign that we confess: Our Lord Jesus died for our sins and rose again from the dead, so we are justified. When we receive God's blessing and consolation, let us give our lives to Him, so that we become God's.
(c. Guidance)
Let us always follow our Lord Jesus and act on His Word to make our lives more holy, as the expression of our gratitude to Him. Other than that let us unite our hearts, love, and help one another as to what is appropriate in the Church of the Lord Jesus, because Jesus is the Head of the Church, and we are His members. The Lord Jesus gave us the Law of Love, when He said, "This is where you will be a real disciple, when you love one another." Therefore, let us humble ourselves before God.
(d. Epiclesis)
Let us pray!
O Lord and loving God, Our Father in heaven! Have mercy on us O God; come to us who have gathered here. While we receive Holy Communion, please give us the Holy Spirit, so that our faith in Lord Jesus Christ, Your Son, who died for our redemption, will be strengthened. You gave your Son Jesus for us. That is why we came to receive the flesh and blood of the Lord Jesus Christ through the Holy Communion. Set our heart to the Lord Jesus, so we surrender our lives to Him, because He is our life and protection. Renew our hearts in the world full of suf-

fering, that because of Your Name, we will persevere in the suffering that we endure. Strengthen us to deny ourselves, so we are able to follow the Lord Jesus Christ and proclaim His Holy name. Move our hearts to the longing for eternal life and waiting for His return to change our vile and mortal body to eternal future on the day of resurrection. Amen.
(e.) The Lord's Prayer
(f. Institution)
P: Now pray, as we listen to the proclamation of the Holy Communion! On the night in which Jesus was betrayed, he took the bread, and after giving thanks, he broke the bread, gave it to his disciples, and said, "Take and eat, this is my body, which is broken for you. Do this in remembrance of me!"
Likewise, after the supper he took the cup, and gave thanks and said to them, "Take and drink! This cup is the new covenant in my name, which is shed for the forgiveness of your sins. Do this in remembrance of me!" Now, let us come because everything is ready. See and taste the gift of God.
(g. Communion)
5. **Hymn** (congregation sings during the communion)

(Congregation comes to the altar in groups of people. The pastor reads out the following formula for each group until the last group is served.).

P: Lord Jesus Christ said, "Take and eat! This is My body which was given to redeem you. It is to maintain and strengthen your faith in Him so that you become the heir of eternal life." Amen.
The Lord Jesus Christ said, "Take and drink! This is my blood which is poured for the forgiveness of your sins. It is to maintain and strengthen your faith in Him so that you become the heir of eternal life." Amen.
Go in peace!
(After everybody receives the bread and wine, the pastor takes the bread and wine as the last person – when there are more than one pastors, they can serve each other. Only pastors are allowed to serve.)
6. **Hymn**
7. **Thanksgiving Prayer**
Praise the Lord my soul! Praise His holy name all my heart! Praise the Lord my soul, and forget not all His goodness; He who forgives all your iniquities, who heals all sickness; He who redeemed your life from the grave, who crowns you with loving kindness and grace. Praise the LORD, my soul; all my inmost being, praise his holy name. Praise the LORD, my soul, and forget not all his benefits— who forgives all your sins and heals all your diseases, who redeems your life from the pit and crowns you with love and compassion. The LORD is compassionate and gracious, slow to anger, abounding in love. He does not always demand, and not forever holds a grudge. He will not always accuse, nor will he harbor his anger forever; he does not treat us as our sins deserve or repay us ac-

cording to our iniquities. As a father has compassion on his children, so the LORD has compassion on those who fear him. God has expressed compassion for us while we were yet sinners, by the death of Christ on the cross, and now it is even more so, after we are justified through His blood. Therefore my mouth and my soul and my actions will praise the Lord my God forever and ever. Amen.
   8. **Aaronic Blessings.**

Because it is a service that is connected with the preparation service, the eucharistic liturgy has a very compact structure. It does not have the elements of confession and absolution. Here, we will try to see the structure and the content of the formula.

The invitation is a calling upon the congregation to have a self examination before coming to the table. The formula mentions three purposes of the Eucharist: to comfort, to grow faith, and to refresh our memory of Jesus Christ. One of the things that we notice is the use of "we" instead of you. This means that the purposes of the Eucharist applied to the minister as well as it is to the congregation. The use of "we" can also be understood as a sign that it is a communal happening that is being experienced as a communal event, instead of individuals.

The anamnesis part asks the congregation to remember the work of Christ to redeem the sins of man. This remembrance is an active one since the congregation receives the flesh and blood of Christ. Here, the HKBP seems to follow the Lutheran line of the Eucharist. Through this fellowship and active remembrance, Christ will come into the heart of the celebrant and *vice versa*.

The HKBP eucharistic formula seems to focus on the remembrance of Jesus' death for forgiveness of sins. Forgiveness of sins seems to be the main focus of the remembrance. The remembrance is to renew our memory of Christ—that is the memory that saves us from sins—to reconcile us with God. While this is true as one of the purposes for Christ's life, but it is not the only thing that needs to be remembered in the Eucharist. This memorial aspect focuses only on the second aspect of the Eucharist which is a memorial of the life of Christ.

Up to this point, we have seen that the focus of the Eucharist is to remember God's saving act through the life, death, redemption, passion, resurrection and ascension of Jesus Christ, and also the Pentecost. The anamnesis of Christ is not only to proclaim his death, but also his life and saving actions. Thus, the focus on Christ's death as forgiveness of sins alone seems to forget the other purposes of the anamnesis in the Eucharist.

The guidance part asks the congregation to act and live according to God's Word as an expression of gratitude of the forgiveness of sins.

The Eucharist asks the congregants to be united. This is a strong plea for unity in the community. Real disciples of Christ, who receive the Eucharist, will help and love one another.

The Epiclesis part shows the connection between God the Father, Jesus Christ and the Holy Spirit in the Communion. This is the third aspect of the Eucharist which is the invocation of the Holy Spirit. Through the Eucharist, the participants ask God for the Holy Spirit so that their faith in Jesus Christ will be strengthened. The congregation also asks for the power to endure the world of suffering.

We also find the part about the waiting for the parousia in this epiclesis. The hope for the parousia is connected with the perseverance in suffering in the world. The Spirit will enable and strengthen us to follow Christ and be faithful in the suffering in the world because of hope of eternal future in Christ. This point reminds us of Metz's idea of remembrance of the suffering. We can use this part for the remembrance of the suffering in liturgy.

The process of the communion in the HKBP is personal and at the same time communal. A group of participants will come to the table to be given the bread and wine by the minister. They will drink and eat together as a group, return to their seats, and another group will come in their place. The positive thing about this process is that everybody will come as a group, yet can still experience it as a personal event. However, the communal feeling does not really exist because the whole community cannot take the communion together at the same time.

We can see again the stress on forgiveness of sins in the HKBP eucharistic formula through the thanksgiving prayer that is taken from Psalm 103. This prayer tries to point out that the Lord is compassionate and does not hold grudge against humans; God has redeemed the lives of the congregants, and covered them in loving kindness and grace. At the end of the prayer, God's compassion is shown again towards us as sinners—through Christ's death on the cross. This shows the first element of the Eucharist: giving thanks to the Father.

Based on our findings on the meaning of the Eucharist, we find that the HKBP's eucharistic liturgy does not have the five aspects of the Eucharist. We found some aspect of thanksgiving of the father; an unbalanced focus of memorial aspect of Christ which mainly focuses on his death and forgiveness of sins; and the invocation of the spirit. The aspect of the communion of the faithful is not fully addressed in this formula. The last aspect about the meal of the kingdom can hardly be seen here.

In general, the HKBP eucharistic formula tends to stress too much the aspect of forgiveness of sins. The aspect of eschatological hope and the remembrance of suffering in the world is mentioned, but not significant enough compared to part of the remembrance of Christ's death. The anamnesis in the Eucharist is surprisingly lacking in highlighting the joyous remembrance of Christ's life and resurrection. Christ did not only die on the cross; the Son was also resurrected and returned to the Father.

In short, the HKBP liturgy of the Eucharist with a preparation service has describe neither the five aspects of the Eucharist, as BEM document has stated, nor the definition of the Eucharist in her own confession. It is indeed a pity that a liturgical church such as the HKBP, has not yet adapted the formula of the liturgy to more recent understanding of the Eucharist in its Confession.

The focus of self-awareness and forgiveness of sins makes the preparation service inseparable from the actual Eucharist. The preparation stressed the personal level, forgiveness of sins, and personal confessions the most. The preparation service is actually a confession of sin service. There is a shift from a personal level to a communal level in the communion itself. The second person singular form is then changed into a plural form.

Before we go any further in our analysis on this formula, let us also take a look at the HKBP eucharistic liturgy without preparation service, which means that the service of the Eucharist is included in the normal Sunday service.

3.4 The Eucharistic Liturgy without Preparation Service

Besides the eucharistic liturgy with the preparation service, the HKBP also has a eucharistic liturgy without the preparation. This means that both formulas will be put in the same liturgical order. In such event, the HKBP will use the same Sunday liturgical order (*see above*) without the confession of sins and absolution. The service will be held directly after the sermon. In a normal Sunday service, the Eucharist is celebrated in the following liturgical order *(the parts in brackets are added to clarify the parts in the liturgy)*.

1. **Hymn**
2. **Peace (blessings)**
"And the peace of God, which transcends all understanding, will guard your hearts and your minds in Christ Jesus." (Phil. 4:7)

(a. Epiclesis)
Let us pray,
O giving God, our Father in heaven. Be in our midst. In the time that we receive your Holy Communion, please send your Holy Spirit on each one of us, so we believe in your Son Jesus Christ our Redeemer. Help us to deny ourselves, so we can follow Lord Jesus Christ, and our faith is growing stronger. Please move our hearts that we are always longing for your second coming. Amen.

(b. Invitation and Guidance)
Beloved congregation of God, we are going to receive the Holy Communion. Let us therefore examine ourselves, whether we are proper to accept it so no one will receive God's punishment.

Because those who receive the Holy Communion are people who regret their evil actions, and who has confessed their sins, and who believe in forgiveness of sins that is given by the Lord Jesus Christ. And for those who have received the Holy Communion, do not serve the devil anymore, and stay away from sin. Keep yourself away from evil things, jealousy and hatred. But always remember the Lord Jesus Christ who died and is risen, so you deserve to receive the Holy Communion.

(c. Confession and questions) *(stand up)*
1. Do you confess that you are a sinner since you were born, and by your own violations of God's Law? If so, answer with "Yes!"
2. Do you regret your sins and that you expect deliverance from him? If so, answer with "Yes!"
3. Do you confess that the Lord Jesus has come into this world to save sinners? That He died for your sins and rose again from the dead? If so, answer with "Yes!"
4. Will you leave the malice and hatred, and do you want to make peace with those who sinned against you? Do you want to forgive him/her like you expect God will forgive your sins? If so, answer with "Yes!"

Now, let us humble ourselves and confess our sins. Follow this prayer in your heart!

O Lord God, our Father in the Lord Jesus Christ. We are sinners. We often violate your Law. If you are to reward our mistakes, then it is right that we receive your punishment. But it is because of your love and because of your Son Jesus Christ who was sacrificed for our sins that we are to ask you: have mercy on us, accept us, and forgive our sins. Please give us your Holy Spirit so we have the power to fight evil and act according to your will as long as we live. Amen.

(d. Absolution)
Sisters and brothers who have regretted your sins and who are longing for God's love, may you receive according to your faith, according to the saying of our Lord Jesus, I say to you: Be sure, your sins have been forgiven, in the name of God the Father, The Son, and The Holy Spirit. Amen.

***(e.)* The Lord's Prayer** *(Only presiding minister)*

3. **Hymn**
(f. Institution)
Now hear the institution of the Holy Communion,
On the night in which Jesus was betrayed, he took the bread, and after giving thanks, he broke the bread, gave it to his disciples, and said, "Take and eat, this is my body, which is broken for you. Do this in remembrance of me!"
Likewise, after the supper he took the cup, and gave thanks and said to them, "Take and drink! This cup is the new covenant in my name, which is shed for the forgiveness of your sins. Do this in remembrance of me!"
Now, let us come because everything is ready. See and taste the gift of God.
(g. Communion)
4. **Hymn** *(congregation sings during the communion)*
(Congregation comes to the altar in groups of people. The pastor read out the following formula for each group until the last group is served.).
The Lord Jesus Christ said, "Take and eat! This is My body which was given to redeem you." It is to maintain and strengthen your faith in Him so that you become the heir of eternal life. Amen.
The Lord Jesus Christ said, "Take and drink! This is my blood which is poured out for the forgiveness of your sins." It is to maintain and strengthen your faith in Him so that you become the heir of eternal life. Amen.
Go in peace!
(After everybody receives the bread and wine, the pastor takes the bread and wine as the last person – when there are more than one pastors, they can serve each other. Only pastors are allowed to serve.)
5. **Thanksgiving Prayer**
Praise the Lord my soul! Praise His holy name all my heart! Praise the Lord my soul, and forget not all His goodness; He who forgives all your iniquities, who heals all sickness, He who redeems your life from the grave, who crowns you with loving kindness and grace. Praise the LORD, my soul; all my inmost being, praise his holy name. Praise the LORD, my soul, and forget not all his benefits— who forgives all your sins and heals all your diseases, who redeems your life from the pit and crowns you with love and compassion. The Lord is compassionate and gracious, slow to anger, abounding in love. He does not always demand, and not forever He grudges. He will not always accuse, nor will he harbor his anger forever; he does not treat us as our sins deserve or repay us according to our iniquities. As a father has compassion on his children, so the Lord has compassion on those who fear him. God has expressed compassion for us while we were yet sinners, by the death of Christ on the cross, and now it is even more so, after we are justified through His blood. Therefore my mouth and my soul and my actions will praise the Lord my God forever and ever. Amen.
6. **Aaronic blessings**
7. **(Closing) Hymn**

The HKBP eucharistic liturgy includes the self-introspection formula from the preparation service. The liturgy started with peace-blessings, followed by the epiclesis prayer, asking for the guidance of the Holy Spirit.

The minister will then ask the congregation to self examine whether they are ready to receive the Communion. Just like the preparation service, the purpose of this self examination is to prevent God's punishment. Those who receive the Communion are people who have confessed their sins and believe in the forgiveness of sins by Christ. There is also an after-effect that is mentioned here, which is the command to stay away from sin.[77]

The questions that are being asked here are similar with to ones in the preparation service, except that here we do not find the questions, "Do you confess that you should be punished by God because of your sins, either now or in the future?" And, "Are you going to try to fight against sin, and obey the Word of God with all your heart?" By leaving out these two questions, this formula feels a bit lighter and less-threatening. These questions are later integrated in the prayer part of the confession. The prayer also asks God to send the Holy Spirit to give power so that people will be able to live according to God's will. This prayer is followed by absolution. The following parts, which are the communion process and the thanksgiving prayer, have the same form as the eucharistic formula after a preparation service.

What is surprising in this eucharistic liturgy is that the formula has no *anamnesis* part. After absolution, the liturgy goes directly to the institution, the communion, and the thanksgiving prayer. There is no part that mentions that the Eucharist is the remembrance of the whole story of Christ, except in a small part of the invitation and guidance that reminded the congregation about Christ who died and is risen. This is a serious lack of theological understanding in this eucharistic liturgical form.

---

[77] Based on personal observance, some members of the congregation choose to walk away from the Communion because of this request. They feel that they cannot keep away from evil things. They are afraid that their inability to keep themselves from sin will bring God's punishment on them. This is precisely a misunderstanding of the self-examination part because of the stress on the part of God's punishment. The HKBP eucharistic liturgy focuses so much on the aspect of forgiveness of sins, that it seems to have forgotten that the Eucharist is to be a joyous remembrance of Christ. The Eucharist is a communal celebration, rather than a depressive gathering, with self-examinations evoking punishing effects, only focusing on the element of the need for the forgiveness of sins.

In sum, we can point out that this eucharistic liturgy at most has only three aspects out of five regarding the Eucharist. The liturgy shows that it has the invocation of the spirit in its epiclesis part; the thanksgiving to the Father in the thanksgiving prayer, and a part about being in communion with believers, which is included in the confession of sins. We can see these three aspects in the liturgy, with the aspect of communion only vaguely displayed by the confession of sins which somehow more focused on individual guilt.

What we cannot find in the liturgy is the aspect on the memorial of Christ and the meal of the Kingdom where we are asked to be agents of reconciliation in the hope of Christ's return. These two aspects are missing from the entire liturgical formula.

What we can conclude now is that the HKBP's eucharistic liturgy is seriously lacking the theological understanding of what the Eucharist is. We do not see the confessional understanding of the Eucharist in the liturgy. The most worrying of all is that the liturgy does not have a part about the memorial of Christ and what it means for the congregation. We can probably trace this back to the HKBP 1951 Confession which did not mention the element of remembrance in the Eucharist. The more recent Confession mentions "joyous feast for everyone that participates, because it is the beginning of a true communion." Alas, this statement of faith cannot be found anywhere in the liturgy.

Based on our findings, we can only conclude that the HKBP eucharistic liturgy was based on the 1951 Confession—if not based on the 1904 liturgy (based on the Prussian liturgy brought by German missionaries)—and not on the 1996 Confession. The more recent theological basis for the Eucharist in the HKBP 1996 Confession was not followed with a renewal of the old eucharistic liturgy that focuses only on forgiveness and punishment of sins. It is a serious challenge and crucial task for this Church to translate her deeper theological understanding and her Confession in a new eucharistic liturgy.

Precisely because of this lack of development in the new eucharistic liturgy, we will now suggest a new formula for the HKBP while giving full attention to recent developments in the confession of faith, and the purpose of this research, which is to find a space for memory transformation of past communal conflict. This will be a good opportunity to translate our findings thus far on remembrance in the Eucharist, and empower it to functions as a place of, and for, redemptive memory in the context of a communal conflict. A good liturgy will provide the HKBP as a church that has strong roots in a full liturgy, a way of remembering the past and having a transformative experience in the mystery of the Eucharist.

4. *Eucharistic Liturgy: A Space for Healing Memories*

This part intends to find out whether the memorial practices in the liturgy, especially in the eucharistic celebration, can provide a space for redemptive memory for people who are in trauma from past hurt. Our exploration has shown that it is indeed possible.

The remembrance action in liturgy, especially in the Eucharist, is not only a celebration of God's saving action in the past, but it also connects the community of believers to the future. The emphasis in the Eucharist is on the whole life of Jesus Christ; how this remembrance of Christ calls the church into a hope of the parousia.

Our memory of Christ's saving action transforms how we view our present in light of the hope for the future. Because of its communal aspect, liturgy demands changes in our lives not only as individuals but especially also as a community. Celebrating Christ at the table leads to a change of hearts and to a new communal vision. Eucharistic liturgy also gives a new meaning to the past. Our past memories are now being remembered in the light of Christ saving action and the hope for the second coming.

What does all this mean in a case such as the HKBP 1992–1998 conflict? We can broaden the question to, "What does it mean for communities in conflict"? How does the remembrance in the Eucharist bring healing and change to the community? More important, how can we translate this in a redemptive eucharistic liturgy?

We have seen that there are some elements in the liturgy that function as a place of remembrance: the sermon, the intercession prayer, and elements in the Eucharistic Prayer which forms the liturgy of the Eucharist. The sermon speaks to the congregation about God's message and functions as a reminder of what has happened in the past and of the redemptive power of Christ's love. The intercession prayer can mention the situation of conflict in the congregation, and deliver it to the Lord as a communal prayer. The Eucharist as the memorial celebration of the life, death, and resurrection of Christ provides a communal celebration of the past, present, and future. Here, the memory of Christ is being actively remembered by the community of believers. First, when we are asked to remember Jesus, we are also remembering our identity and at the same time we are asked to live Christ like. Consequently, this memory will change the life of believers and demands that people will act accordingly in their lives. Coming together to the table as a community also shows the process of accepting each other in the same body of Christ. We will try to capture these processes in the liturgy that follows below.

The following eucharistic liturgy is designed with the HKBP Church and her tradition in mind. This liturgy is a proposal for a community in conflict, especially for those who are in deep trauma, so that the liturgy can help and function as a remembrance of the past hurt in a way that its memory is transformed in the memory of a loving God. By surrendering our memory to God, the community can be assured that the memory of the past hurt becomes a memory in God. Every time we celebrate the remembrance of Christ, we remember that God remembers.

We will mainly focus on the eucharistic liturgy with a preparation service because it seems to offer a chance for the community to reflect about what has happened in the past before coming to the Lord's table. The purpose of the preparatory service is to give space for people in conflict to prepare, especially when the community that celebrates the communion is in conflict. The tradition notes that a preparatory service is held on the preceding Friday, or Saturday. Alternately, the liturgy suggestion can also be adapted to a regular full service with the Eucharist service included.

4.1 *Proposed Preparation Service of the Eucharist*

There will be no new structure to the preparatory service. We will modify some of the formulas, adjusting them to the new understanding of the Eucharist in the HKBP 1996 Confession, and various theological understanding of the Eucharist that we have found in our research as presented in this study. We will especially take care that the five aspects of the Eucharist as enumerated earlier are integrated in this amended eucharistic liturgy, along with the foundational notions of Metz, Schmemann, and Volf on the theological basis of remembrance.

The invitation and guidance is taken from the meaning of the Eucharist in the HKBP 1996 Confession. This formula lays more stress on the elements of eating the bread and drinking the wine as a passage to Christ's body and blood, so that celebrants will be united in the body of Christ in a joyous feast, which is the beginning of a true communion, a thanksgiving filled memorial of Christ, and a way to receive Christ's grace. This invitation will give a clearer picture of what to expect from the celebration of the Eucharist.

The second part is the announcement about those who are worthy of the communion. This means that a self-check is required in coming to the table. This is necessary not only to examine whether we have sinned against God, but also sinned against our brothers and sisters in Christ. Afterwards, congregants are asked to remember what they have done and bring it to God as a sign or as repentance in the "counsel part" of the worship service.

The "questions part" is taken from the Dutch Lutheran preparatory service, with slight modifications. It starts with the acknowledgment of oneself as sinner; followed by the believer that God is full of mercy and love, and it closes with the promise to lead a better life in God's grace and leave the old life behind. The confession prayer is taken from the confession prayer of the service of preparation for Holy Communion by the Office of Theology and Worship, Presbyterian Church in United States. The absolution formula has not changed.

The proposed liturgy of the preparatory service for the eucharistic celebration is as follows:

> 1. **Hymn** *(about coming to God's presence, and preparing our hearts)*
> P: In the name of the Father, and of the Son, and of the Holy Ghost.
> 2. **Epiclese Prayer**
> 3. **Sermon** *(about the Eucharist and what it means to the believer's life)*
> 4. **Preparation Formula**
> *(a. Invitation and Guidance)*
> Sisters and brothers in Christ! We have heard God's Words in the sermon about coming to the table of the Lord. We intend to celebrate the Holy Communion. The Communion is eating the bread as a passage of our Lord Jesus Christ's body and drinking the wine as a passage of our Lord Jesus Christ's blood, so we will receive forgiveness of sins, life and joy, as a united body of Christ. The Eucharist is a joyous feast for everyone that participates, because it is the beginning of a true communion. It is also a sign of thanksgiving to remember the Lord Jesus Christ's act of redemption, and the way to receive His grace (Matt. 26:20–30; Mark 14:17–26; Luke 22:14–20; 1 Cor. 11:17–34).
> Accordingly, I invite you to reflect whether we are worthy to receive the Holy Communion. Therefore check yourselves – each one of you, whether you have possessed what is expected of the Lord Jesus. Because those who are humble, who regrets all the bad acts that he/she does, who confessed his/her sin, and those who believe in forgiveness of sins given by the Lord Jesus; and those who are ready to forgive others; they are the ones that are worthy to receive the Holy Communion. You shall meditate on the Word of God where Jesus says: "Love the Lord your God with all your heart and with all your soul and with all your mind. This is the first and greatest commandment. And the second is like it: Love your

neighbor as yourself" (Matthew 22:37–40).
(b. Counsel)
Preparing our hearts for the communion means to remember and bring our sins to God and ask for forgiveness. By acknowledging our actions, we truly regret our sins, long for God's love in Jesus Christ, and ask for the power of the Holy Spirit to guide our lives. Let us reflect and examine ourselves on these questions:
(c. Questions)
1) Do you acknowledge and confess with humble hearts that you are poor and lost sinners, who
have disobeyed the Lord your God, secretly and openly, knowingly and unknowingly, by thoughts, words, and deeds, and have also offended your neighbor in many ways. Are you heartily sorry for these your sins, and do you implore God to forgive you of the same?
2) Do you firmly believe that God, in his everlasting mercy and through the precious merits of Jesus Christ, His Son, not only forgives you all your sins, but also seals with His true Body and Blood those who shall, under the Bread and Wine, eat and drink in the holy, consecrated Communion?
3) Do you intend to better your sinful life by God's grace, to bring forth good fruit as evidence of your penitence and faith, to prove yourself a new creature in Christ, and to walk in the Spirit according to the new man; furthermore, will you from your hearts ask for forgiveness and also forgive your fellow neighbor their offenses against you, and make it manifest by showing them all your love; moreover, will you remain steadfast in the eternal Word of God and our true Christian faith until the second coming of our Lord?
(d. Confession Prayer) Let us humble ourselves, and follow this prayer in your hearts!
Holy and merciful God, we acknowledge and confess before you our sinful nature, prone to evil and slow to do good, and all our shortcomings and offenses. You alone know how often we have sinned— in wandering from your ways, in wasting your gifts, in forgetting your love. We confess our sins against our sisters and brothers - the hardness of our hearts towards those in suffering and need, our indifference toward justice and mercy, our arrogance and all the evil ways of our selfishness and pride.
Have mercy on us, O God, according to your loving kindness. In your tender mercy blot out our transgressions. Wash us thoroughly from our iniquity and cleanse us from our sin. Create in us clean hearts, O God, and renew a right spirit within us. Do not cast us away from your presence or take your Holy Spirit from us (Psalm 51:1–3, 10–12). Restore to us the joy of your salvation and uphold us with your Spirit; through Jesus Christ our Lord. Amen.
(e. Absolution) Listen to the consolation from the Word of God:
For God so loved the world that He gave His only begotten Son, that whoever believes in Him should not perish but have everlasting life

(John 3:16). As servant of the Lord, I declare upon God's name, rest assured: you will receive what you believe. Rest assured, your sins are forgiven and you have become the heir of the love in the Lord Jesus Christ. Let everyone who long for their forgiveness of sins, respond with Amen.

5. **Hymn** *(about God's grace and forgiveness of sins, or about unity in Christ)*

6. **Aaronic Blessings**

4.2 Proposed Eucharistic Liturgy after Preparation Service

The order of this service is significantly changed based on some of the factors that we have found so far. First of all, we are going to incorporate the service into a normal Sunday service, so a regular Sunday service will begin the celebration of the Eucharist. Next, we will apply some changes in the order of the formula and add some important elements that we can find in the Lima eucharistic liturgy.

The service will start with the usual HKBP order of service, without the reading of the Law, confession of sins, and absolution. We assume that people who are partaking in this eucharistic service already participated in the preparatory service. We have to note once again, that this liturgy is intended for a community that is in conflict with one another. The Sunday liturgy can be completed with elements that supports the liturgical Sunday and the theme of the service (for instance hymns, and reading of the bible texts).

An intercessory prayer will specifically mention the conflicts that are happening within the community and also pray for strength for the victims, and power of repentance for perpetrators, and unity for the congregation. The sermon will preach on the biblical reading of the Sunday, while mentioning the redemptive power of the Eucharist memorial and how God remembers God's people. This particular part is appropriate to the fourth and fifth element of the Eucharist, along with Metz's suggestion of remembering the suffering. We will ask God to remember those who suffer and thus offer our memories of the world to God the helper and redeemer.

The preface will declare what the Eucharist is and include the invitation to take part in it. This section also mentions the invitation to come as a band of sisters and brothers in faith. The fellowship in Christ that the congregants are about to receive demands of people to unite their hearts, to love and to help one another in the Church of Christ. This will be followed by a response through the Sanctus. The Sanctus will be a part of the first eucharistic aspect which is thanksgiving to the Father and to resonate with the knowledge that God is holy.

The anamnesis part is taken from the eucharistic liturgy of Lima because it resonates with the HKBP confessional statement about the memorial meaning of the Eucharist. This memorial also pictures new theological developments of the Eucharist. Next is the commemoration rubric. It is intended as a part where we can mention all of those whom we want to pray for, to remember the events that happened in the community, especially people who suffer for the Lord. This is the aspect of the memorial of Christ. It resonates with Schmemann's idea of a full mystery experience in the communal celebration of the Eucharist.

The next part is the aspect of invocation of the Spirit, where we ask God to send the Holy Spirit to strengthen the faith and memory of Christ. Here, we will also ask the Spirit to be with all suffering—as a sign of solidarity and a remembering of people who suffer in Christ's name. This part also resonates with Metz's notion of remembrance of the suffering. This part will be followed by the Lord's prayer.

The next rubric is the Peace, where everybody will give the sign of reconciliation and peace to one another. The greeting of peace is given by Christ and shared among sisters and brothers in Christ. This is a sign of unity before receiving Christ's body and blood. This peace sign is important, especially for a community that is or was in conflict, so that they know that they are sealed as one body that is forgiven in Christ. This very much resonates with the fourth aspect of the Eucharist, and with Volf's idea of embracing one another.

The communion and thanksgiving prayer still hold to the old text of HKBP formula. However, one of the suggestions that we can make is an alteration in how the bread and wine are distributed. In the HKBP's eucharistic celebration, congregations are called in groups to come to the table to receive bread and wine. As we have mentioned earlier, this has its own positive and negative sides. What we would like to do is to have a more communal celebration, where we can have as many congregants as possible – if not all – in the participation of the feast, eating and drinking at the same time. This, however, depends much on the flexibility of the worship space and the number of participants. Some Evangelical Lutheran Churches in Germany celebrate the Eucharist at the backside of the altar, where all congregants will stand in a circle, and the minister walks to everybody and offers bread and wine. This particular way of distribution gives a more communal feeling because everybody takes the bread and wine together while facing each other in a circle of the body of Christ. This might be difficult to implement in HKBP churches that have larger numbers of congregants per service with less space. However, this suggestion is worthy to be considered if and when we really want to get the sense of togetherness in the community.

The Great Thanksgiving prayer is the closing section of the liturgy where we give thanks to God for Baptism and Eucharist. Here, we ask God to remember our stories, which mean that we have given our stories of suffering, conflict, and sins, to God, and ask for God's blessings to lead us in living the signs of reconciliation in our lives. This will become an open ending to our celebration of the Eucharist.

The Sunday service begins as follow:

> **Opening Hymn**
> **Votum**
> P: In the name of God the Father, the Son Jesus Christ, and the Holy Spirit, who created heaven and earth. Amen.
> **Introit** (according to Liturgical Sunday)
> Congregation responded: Hallelujah! (3x) *or* Maranatha! (3x)
> **Collect**
> **Hymn based on the liturgical Sunday**
> **Epistle** (despite the name "Epistle", it is not limited to reading the NT letters alone, it is more the reading of bible text for the Sunday).
> P: "Blessed rather are those who hear the word of God and obey it." (Luke 11:28).
> C: Amen!
> **Hymn related to the Epistle reading**
> **Apostle Creed**
> **Reading of Congregation News** (followed by **intercession prayer**)
> **Hymn about the sermon**
> **Sermon**
> **Offering**
> And the eucharistic liturgy:
> **The Service of the Eucharist**
> *(a. Preface)*
> Beloved people of our Lord Jesus Christ! In accordance with the message of the Lord Jesus to His disciples, we now are going to receive Holy Communion. This is an invitation for everyone who has already examined themselves, who have confessed their sins, and are ready to come to the table together with sisters and brothers in faith.
> We give you glory Lord, almighty Father, eternal God, through Jesus Christ our Lord. Christ instituted the Eucharist at the last supper, as a memorial of the life, death, resurrection, and ascension of the Lord. We do this as a communal sacrament, as a continuation of baptism, as our entrance to God's kingdom. This is what our Lord Jesus has sealed into

our hearts through the Holy Communion we are about to receive. Every time we celebrate Holy Communion, we receive the flesh and blood of Christ, and we are in fellowship with Him, which means: He is in us, and we in Him. Thus, let us always follow our Lord Jesus and act on His Word, let us unite our hearts, let love flow, and help one another in all what is appropriate in the Church of Lord Jesus, for Jesus is the Head of the Church, and we are His members. O Lord, we unite our voices with the angels and all citizens of heaven, we proclaim and sing your glory:
(b. Sanctus)
C : "Holy, holy, holy is the LORD Almighty; the whole earth is full of his glory." (Isaiah 6:3)
(c. Anamnesis)
P: Wherefore, Lord, we celebrate today the memorial of our redemption: we recall the birth and life of your Son among us, his baptism by John, his healing ministry, his presence as Your Living Word, his last meal with the apostles, his death and descent to the abode of the dead; we proclaim Christ's resurrection and ascension in Your glory, where as our Great High Priest he ever intercedes for all people; and we look for his coming at the last. United in Christ's priesthood, we present to you this memorial: remember the sacrifice of your Son and grant to people everywhere the benefits of Christ's redemptive work.
C: *Maranatha, the Lord comes!*
(d. Commemoration)
P: Remember, Lord, your one, holy, catholic and apostolic Church, redeemed by the blood of Christ. Reveal its unity, guard its faith, and preserve your Church in peace. Remember, Lord, all the servants of your Church: ephorus, ministers, teacher preachers, bibelvrouw, diaconness, elders, and all to whom you have given special gifts of ministry.
Remember especially ... *(here we can mention names or event(s) that is/are in the mind of the congregation; and we can also mention the memory of the suffering for the name of the Lord)*
We give the memory of these people/event(s) to you O Lord. Guide them to the joyous feast prepared for all people in your presence. With all of them we sing your praise and await the blessedness of your Kingdom where with the whole creation finally delivered from sin and death, we shall be enabled to glorify you through Christ our Lord.
C: *Maranatha, the Lord comes!*
(e. Epiclesis)
Let us pray!
O Lord and loving God, Our Father in heaven! Have mercy on us O God; come to us who gather here. While we partake of Holy Communion, please grant us the Holy Spirit in the name of Your Son, so that our faith in our Lord Jesus Christ, who died for our redemption, will be strengthened. You gave your Son Jesus for us. Set our hearts with your Spirit as we partake in Christ's body and blood, so we too can surrender our lives to Christ. Renew our hearts in a world full of suffering,

especially for those who suffer in your name, so that we will be able to persevere. Strengthen us in denying ourselves for the sake of following the Lord Jesus Christ and proclaim His Holy name. Move our hearts to the longing for eternal life and to a hopeful waiting for His return on the day of resurrection. Amen.

(f. The Lord's Prayer)

(g. The Peace)

P: O Lord Jesus Christ, you told your apostles: Peace I leave with you, my peace I give to you.
Look not on our sins but on the faith of your Church. In order that your will be done, grant us always this peace and guide us towards the perfect unity of your Kingdom forever.
C: Amen.
P: The peace of the Lord be with you always.
C: And also with you.
P: Let us give one another a sign of reconciliation and peace.

(h. Institution & breaking of the bread)

P: Now pray, as we listened to the proclamation of the Holy Communion! On the night in which Jesus was betrayed, he took the bread, and after giving thanks, he broke the bread, gave it to his disciples, and said, "Take and eat, this is my body, which is broken for you. Do this in remembrance of me!" Likewise, after the supper he took the cup, and gave thanks and said to them, "Take and drink! This cup is the new covenant in my name, which is shed for the forgiveness of your sins. Do this in remembrance of me!"
Now, let us come because everything is ready. See and taste the gift of God.

(i. Communion)

(j. Hymn (*congregation sings during the communion*))

(*Where possible: all congregants form a circle in front of the altar. When not possible, congregants come to the altar in groups. The pastor reads out the following formula for each group until the last group is served.*)

 P: Our Lord Jesus Christ said, "Take and eat! This is My body which was given to redeem you." It is to maintain and strengthen your faith in Him so that you become the heir of eternal life. Amen.
Our Lord Jesus Christ said, "Take and drink! This is my blood which is poured for the forgiveness of your sins." It is to maintain and strengthen your faith in Him so that you become the heir of eternal life"
Amen.
Go in peace!
(*After everybody receives the bread and wine, the pastor takes the bread and wine as the last person – when there are more than one pastors, they can serve each other. Only pastors are allowed to serve.*)

(k. Thanksgiving Prayer)

Praise the Lord my soul! Praise His holy name, all my heart!
Praise the Lord my soul, and forget not all His goodness;

He who forgives all your iniquities, who heals all sickness,
He who redeemed your life from the grave, who crowns you with loving kindness and grace.
We give you thanks for uniting us by baptism in the Body of Christ and filling us with joy in the Eucharist.
Remember us, O Lord, remember our stories;
and help us to remember you in Christ through the guidance of the Spirit.
Lead us to show Your signs of reconciliation in our daily lives,
so that we become witnesses of your endless love. Amen.

13. Final Hymn

14. Sending and Aaronic blessing

When the Church wants to celebrate the communion without a preparatory service, then we can alternate the service by inserting some elements in it. The service without preparatory service beforehand will look like this:

15. The Service of Eucharist

(a. Preface)

Sisters and brothers in Christ! We have heard God's Words in the sermon about coming to the table of the Lord. We intend to celebrate the Holy Communion. The Communion is eating the bread as a passage of our Lord Jesus Christ's body and drinking the wine as a passage of our Lord Jesus Christ's blood, so we will receive forgiveness of sins, life and joy, as a united body of Christ. The Eucharist is a joyous feast for everyone that participates, because it is the beginning of a true communion. It is also a sign of thanksgiving to remember Lord Jesus Christ's act of redemption, and the way to receive His grace (Matt. 26:20–30; Mark 14:17–26; Luke 22:14–20; 1 Cor. 11:17–34).

(b. Counsel)

Preparing our hearts for the communion means to remember and bring our sins to God and ask for forgiveness. By acknowledging our actions, we truly regret our sins, long for God's love in Jesus Christ, and ask for the power of the Holy Spirit to guide our lives. Let us reflect and examine ourselves on these questions:

(c. Questions)

1) Do you acknowledge and confess with humble hearts that you are poor and lost sinners, who have disobeyed the Lord your God, secretly and openly, knowingly and unknowingly, by thoughts, words, and deeds, and have also offended your neighbor in many ways. Are you heartily sorry for these your sins, and do you implore God to forgive you of the same?

2) Do you firmly believe that God, in his everlasting mercy and through the precious merits of Jesus Christ, His Son, not only forgives you all your sins, but also seals with His true Body and Blood those who shall, under the Bread and Wine, eat and drink in the holy, consecrated Communion?

3) Do you intend to better your sinful life by God's grace, to bring forth

good fruit as evidence of your penitence and faith, to prove yourself a new creature in Christ, and to walk in the Spirit according to the new man; furthermore, will you from your hearts ask for forgiveness and also forgive your fellow neighbor their offenses against you, and make it manifest by showing them all your love; moreover, will you remain steadfast in the eternal Word of God and our true Christian faith until the second coming of our Lord?

(d. Confession Prayer) Let us humble ourselves and follow this prayer in your hearts!

Holy and merciful God, we confess our sins against our sisters and brothers - the hardness of our hearts towards those in suffering and need, our indifference toward justice and mercy, our arrogance and all the evil ways of our selfishness and pride. Have mercy on us, O God, according to your loving kindness. In your tender mercy, blot out our transgressions. Wash us thoroughly from our iniquity and cleanse us from our sin. Create in us clean hearts, O God, and renew a right spirit within us. Restore to us the joy of your salvation and uphold us with your Spirit; through Jesus Christ our Lord. Amen.

(e. Absolution) Listen to the consolation from the Word of God:

For God so loved the world that He gave His only begotten Son, that whoever believes in Him should not perish but have everlasting life (John 3:16). As a servant of the Lord, I declare upon God's name, rest assured: you will receive what you believe. Rest assured, your sins are forgiven and you have become the heir of the love in the Lord Jesus Christ.

***(f. Anamnesis) (g. Commemoration) (h. Epiclesis)**, followed by the next parts from the eucharistic liturgy.*

This eucharistic liturgy suggestion will provide a new experience of the Eucharist, not only for the HKBP, but also for churches who are interested in dealing with their past in the mystery of the Eucharist. This liturgy incorporates not only recent theological understandings of the Eucharist, but it also offers an ecumenical tone since it is a result of an ecumenical exploration of the theological understanding of the Eucharist. As a liturgical church, the HKBP can definitely use this suggestion in seeking to renew their liturgical formula of the Eucharist.

5. Conclusion

The remembrance in the Eucharist has provided a communal celebration of memory of the past. It functions as a place where everybody can share their stories of past hurt. Remembrance gives hope and a chance of healing to those who want their stories and identities to be acknowledged and heard. By remembering, we refuse to let the past stories of injustice and hurt to be passed by. The memory of the cross demands that we should remember all suffering. Therefore, this should come as a result of divine liturgy instead of being a goal of it.

Everyone needs to earnestly prepare themselves before coming to the table: those who see the need and are ready to be forgiven and reconciled; those who are willing by the grace of God to forgive and reconcile in communion with Christ; those who do not experience suffering much, in order to become more mindful of those who do. If there was conflict among the people, or a group of people, then this is the space and place for facing remembrance of what really happened, with the goal of reconciliation in mind.

The events that happened prior to coming to the table of reconciliation should be made clear and announced to everybody as a part of the story of the gathered community. This would help the individual victim to see and release the full pain by realizing that the community is acknowledging their pain. For the perpetrators, this is a very important step for them because it is the sign of the forgiveness of sins for them. This event can become, at the same time, a place of healing for both victims and perpetrators. It offers the opportunity for both sides to meet and hear each other's story told, with the purpose of reconciliation gathered at the Lord's Table.

When forgiveness happens around the table, then the memory of the event can be preserved with a different meaning. It is not a memory of pain alone, but more: it has become a memory and a life story, a life-lesson for the entire community. They will be enabled to give new meaning to what had happened in light of God's love and forgiveness upon all involved. The past is still there, the story is still there. Yet personal remembrance can diminish when the person realizes that the community has remembered their pain. Then the memory is not only a memory of pain, in fact it is on the way of being transformed into a memory of healing, for both victims and perpetrators.

The community of believers can, and should in fact, give a new meaning to pains of the past, traumatic events, and negative memories. The community of believers fully remembers what happened, brings it forth to the Lord's Table as a table of remembrance, and gives a new meaning to it. When the community remembers the past through the Eucharist, this memory of the painful past is transformed into a joyous feast of God's act of redemption in Jesus Christ. Stanley Hauerwas says, "Such remembering…saves us from being the eternal victim. For we know as Christians that we have been freed from being victimized because our savior has defeated death and death's lies."[78] In this remembrance the memory stays but it has been given a new meaning. The Eucharist is the place above all others of healing and redemptive memories through living the liturgy and the word preached and practiced.

This is what the attempt was in trying to achieve a deeper and broader understanding of communal reconciliation in a proposed eucharistic liturgy for the HKBP. The memory of the past should be remembered as a way of confessing our sinful actions to God in the hope of Christ's redemptive memory. The sermon, intercessory prayers, and Eucharistic Prayers give us exactly this opportunity to celebrate the memory of the past conflict and to come together as sisters and brothers in faith.

---

[78] Stanley Hauerwas, "Embodied Memory: Acts 5:27–32, Revelation 1:4–8, John 20:19–31," *Journal for Preachers* 19, no. 3: (1996), 23.

Chapter Six

God Remembers

1. The Importance of Remembrance

In this study we have researched many aspects of how the phenomena of remembrance and memory affect our personal and communal life. Philosophical and psychological definitions categorize remembrance as belonging to a declarative memory type. This is the kind of memory we explore in order to find the truth about events that we experienced and that drive us to find out what really happened. This declarative type of memory that we have explored proves to be very important for our self-understanding and our very being. For it not only enables us to shape a coherent narrative of ourselves, our lives, our experiences, and our past, it also tells us about who we now are and gives us an inkling of who we are going to be. Remembering does not merely mean to recall some past event or circumstance to one's mind, it actually gives us an anchored sense of our identity.

In our time, we have both the luxury and the curse of being able to preserve memories of the past by recording them in various ways. This may be wonderful in the case of happy events, but it can also assign us to become captives of Technicolor memories, visually documenting horrible experiences of injustice, losses and pain, that we are doomed to relive as though we are stuck in an everlasting pain of past hurts. In some respects it is a luxury and an advance, because the memory of the past is well preserved through the ways of modern technology. For instance we now have the opportunity to admit to, and process, our reflections as recorded versions of a story of the same occurrence other than our own version. We have easier access to accurate information from sources other than our own. On the whole, it is a good thing that perpetrators can be confronted with the voices, images and stories that were recorded through various means of those who were victimized. However, this advancement in technology can also become a curse because recorded memories will always be readily available. We do not have control over who is getting the information or the duration of the information in storage. Any story of pain can easily be exploited, and we do not have full control over our own information in a changing technological world.

The recent bankruptcy protection filed by Borders, the second largest book store chain in the United States of America, had for some time been expected as a result of readers' migration to digital formats.[1] This has marked a highly visible major consequence of the digital era with its ease of access to information, especially books. This new high tech medium is not only reducing our carbon footprint—which is a positive consequence—but also opening the possibility of ubiquitous access to information, including private or confidential documents, including history. Easier access also means a more open and varied source of information about an event. These memories of events are becoming available, and most of the time they remain accessible on the Internet. Technology has forced us to remember our past, whether we want it or not.

We have also seen that remembrances of past communal conflict can work in favor of victims. Twentieth century atrocities are now being remembered anew as an acknowledgement of the past. This can be a positive learning experience for the future, and be of help in moving forward as a nation, or even to restore broken relationships because of a more level playing field with regard to full disclosures. Recent establishment of the so-called truth commissions are examples of this tendency. More communities around the globe are choosing to preserve the memory of the victims to honor and respect the stories of the victims and to raise hopes that such things will not happen again in the future. To remember traumatic events, even to revisit them by means of video-recorded eyewitness accounts means to be able to grasp more fully about what happened in the past, and to be able to say 'never again' to such violence. Remembering is not always easy because memories are not like factual history, and our minds do not have the capacity to remember in all details what had happened. However, exchanging stories through storytelling is an important event in the process of remembrance in order to be able to hear other voices and share story of the painful past. Remembrance is an essential element for both the perpetrators and victims to acknowledge each other and find out what really happened in the past beyond one's own point of view.

---

[1] See News, "Borders Announces Liquidation, Closing 400 Stores," http://www.ktla.com/news/landing/ktla-borders-bankrupt,0,2928708.story, accessed on July 2011, and "Borders' Bankruptcy Shakes Industry" http://www.nytimes.com/2011/02/17/business/media/17borders.html?pagewanted=all, accessed on July 2011.

Instead of forgetting and suppressing past traumatic events, such communal remembrance is proven a much more adequate way of dealing with collective traumas and deep wounds. In order to address and possibly bring an old conflict to some sort of resolution, and to build a new future by going forward, a specific activity of remembrance might be needed rather than continued hushing or avoiding a problem, or suppressing evidence and truth. To remember in such a manner is to build the future. To reject the act of remembrance would cause trauma to persist and fester. Such trauma will perpetuate prejudices in the future, therefore no genuine forgiveness and reconciliation can be accomplished. When we do not remember the whole truth, trauma infects us inwardly and will influence every step that we take for the future. Therefore, a deliberate way of remembrance is better than forgetting.

The past that is being remembered in a community is formed as a collective memory. Collective memory helps the community to confirm and to form its identity. When the past is remembered as a painful memory only, it becomes a negative force for the present and the future. A negative remembrance is a memory of the painful past that is still being remembered as only pain and hurt. The identity as unacknowledged victim keeps making its mark even when those who inherit the memory are not the actual victims anymore. Such communities then still remember the past pain and injustice, and identify themselves as the victims. Negative remembrance can lead a group that considers itself as the victims to keep identifying the heirs of the offending group as being perpetrators themselves. The danger of negative remembrance is that it perpetuates open wounds without a hope for healing.

Memory of an event is open for a new meaning, based on how the groups involved perceive what is past. When a new meaning is attached to the same memories of the past events, it opens the possibility of a more redemptive memory, even if it is a resolution of 'never again!' Redemptive memory comes from a more positive framework for the remembrance of painful past where the pain—or shame, or injustice—is being remembered without inheriting the actual pain that was inflicted. Our research has shown that this is a possibility that is always needed to be further explored and pursued.

2. To Create a Redemptive Memory

The process of creating a redemptive memory is the field where our research can inform the current culture of remembrance by offering insights from the Christian core tradition of remembrance. We started this research with the question, "How can the current culture of remembrance be informed by a deeper understanding of remembrance in biblical, theological, and liturgical resources in Christian tradition in order to deepen reconciliation after the 1992–1998 conflict in the HKBP?" The research question was motivated by the conflicts during in the HKBP Church. It appears that the Church after 1998 refused to talk about her past for the sake of the future. The HKBP case is one of the examples of cases where the roles of victims and perpetrators are not clearly defined. It is also an example where the conflicting groups need to relate and acknowledge their differences to become truly one again in diversity, as also happened in the examples of South Africa and Australia. However, the HKBP took a different step by not addressing what actually happened in the past for the sake of a hopeful ongoing reconciliation.

The HKBP has good reasons for leaving the problem in the past. Batak culture has its positive and negative sides where dealing with conflict is concerned. The way of forgetting and moving on as in the traditional new year rite may have influenced the way in which the Church handled the matter by forgetting the past in order to move on to the future. However, Batak cultural history itself shows that it is not that easy to forget the past. The HKBP was fortunate that the conflicting sides decided to walk together again as one, instead of considering the other option of becoming two separate churches—which had happened in the stories of the past conflicts. This option to remain one church should now be followed with forging a way to deal with the memory because the specter of divisiveness will linger when it is not fully dealt with.

By simply trying to forget, the HKBP is risking losing a real and genuine reconciliation of the church. Leaving a problem behind does not mean that it is fully solved. We can see that the problem is still operative by looking at some congregations that refuse to re-unite, congregations that are still in conflict up to the day of writing this conclusion, the hesitance to even mention the past conflict, or—worse—even ignoring the tear that the deaconess shed in the bookshop in Pematangsiantar when asked about the documents of the past conflict. This is precisely an example of what we can call a negative remembrance in which the memory of the past lingers in the form of a painful memory. Such memory can come to the fore again and again in the future and threaten not only to compromise the genuine unity of the Church, but is dangerous fuel for possible future issues of disagreement. Given the research that has been gathered in this study, the Church's decision of leaving the case behind must be challenged with conviction.

Since remembering is a better way of dealing with the past hurt than forgetting, the HKBP could make a good beginning by truthfully remembering the past. A pressing reason for walking this path is not only that remembrance for Christians has a theological foundation, but that Batak culture has a strong appreciation for remembrance already, and is perfectly capable of incorporating later and further wisdom. We see that there is no germane reason for the Church not to talk about the past.

What we offer in this study is for the HKBP to significantly strengthen her basis for a kind of remembering that is based on the Scripture, theology, and liturgy. Our biblical exploration has shown that the command "remember" is the foundation of Israel in its identity as God's chosen people. To remember, in biblical terms of understanding and practice means much more than a psychological understanding of recalling something back into one's mind. When connected with God and God's covenant of grace, the command to remember projects an active sense of remembering, where the past is giving a contribution as to how the present will be understood and the future will be formed. The call to remember is connected with God's promises and to remember past mistakes and sins, and ask for forgiveness. A true reconciliation between God and God's people happened when Israel admitted its past sins and asked for God's forgiveness in the form of a sacrificial act. In addition, especially within the theme of remembrance and forgiveness, the Old Testament is very much a book of remembrance of both Israel's sins and God's grace, by keeping a record of Israel's sins, how they remember their sins, and how they ask for God's forgiveness that will not be withheld as with other capricious deities.

There is a repeated pattern of how remembrance is used in the relation of God and Israel. Israel's forgetfulness is connected with their disobedience towards the covenant. When God remembers Israel's sin, it is usually followed by punishment. After facing God's punishment, Israel will admit its iniquities and confess its sins. Israel's confessions consist of a comprehensive remembrance of what they have actually done in the past, not merely their wrong actions in their own generation, but also in the generations before them. When God forgives them, God remembers their sins no more. Despite the repeated pattern, one thing is important to note: Israel remembers what they have done in the past but also remembers God's compassion.

Remembrance has very strong biblical roots. It provides a practical way towards a real forgiveness and reconciliation, both with God or with fellow human beings. Biblical forgiveness demands a self-knowledge of one's own guilt, in which one must be able and willing to recall his/her past iniquities and show remorse for it. A suitable confession of sins has an important role in the remembrance of one's sin in order to be able to ask for real forgiveness.

A continuation of the same idea of remembrance that pervades the Old Testament is found in the New Testament, and especially in an actively remembered means of grace in the institution of the Eucharist. The Eucharist is a unique event, which was instituted by Jesus himself to remember him. Remembrance is the heart of the Eucharist, where Jesus is being present and remembered. Even so, the Eucharist is not a whole new tradition that Jesus creates. It is actually a continuation and a renewal of the remembrance done in the Passover meal. The past deliverance of Israel by God is brought forward to the present by the present redemptive act by God in Christ and they are both to be remembered for the sake of the future. Jesus is the paschal lamb that is to be sacrificed—sacrificed on the cross—and his sacrifice is a unique kairos-time event that embraces all chronological time.

The remembrance in the Eucharist is not a passive remembrance; it has the character of confession and reconciliation. Just as in the case of Israel's confessing of its sins, the Lord's Supper demands a confession as self-examination as to whether one is worthy to come to the table and be reconciled with God and his or her neighbor. Confession presupposes remembrance of one-self and a keeping in mind that it is only through reconciliation with the other that one can come to the table and share the communion with the Lord. Forgiveness will be achieved through the sacrificial act of Christ, which has happened once and for all, through the reconciliation of people with their neighbor and God the Father, and all this is infused and carried by the mighty breath of the Creator Spirit. All aspects of a full-fledged theology are operative in remembrance, and thus play an important role within the theological understanding of the Eucharist.

Three theologians, Johan Baptist Metz, Alexander Schmemann, and Miroslav Volf, helped us to see the theological underpinnings and implications of remembrance. Their different theological backgrounds have enriched our understanding of remembrance and offer a kind of ecumenical theological understanding of the Eucharist. Through anamnesis in the Eucharist, we remember the ministry of Jesus, but especially the suffering, and forgiveness of sins in the celebration of the liturgy of Eucharist. Based on our exploration, we can conclude that the purpose of remembering past hurts as well as other consequences of sin in the Eucharist is to give a place and create a space for the voice of victims and testimonies of healing. The remembrance of the past should be done with a longing for true forgiveness and reconciliation. It is only by such possibilities that we can avoid the danger of keeping hold of negative memory and can break open the vicious cycle of violence.

The Eucharist is the central sacrament where the whole community celebrates the event together as one body of Christ. It is the uniting sacrament for every individual. We therefore can also learn to see this as the place for victims and perpetrators to come and celebrate the table of the Lord together. This difficult yet possible action is the time and place where people will be brought together as one. A proper liturgy of the Eucharist should be able to offer redemptive memory for the liturgy of daily life of Christians in the world. In the liturgy of the Eucharist we remember the suffering. When we say suffering, it does not mean that we only remember the memory of the victims. In communal conflict, the pain of shame and regret for wrongdoing that cannot be undone, means that perpetrators recognize that they are in need of healing and a forgiveness for actions that can only come by unmerited grace. All who heed the invitation to come recognize themselves in the brokenness of Christ. The actuality of the Eucharist invites and embraces everybody to come together as one in a remembrance of Christ. It is His Peace we need and extend to one another. The Eucharist offers a safe place to let go of negative memory towards people who don't want to remember the past because it is too painful. At the same time, the Eucharist also offers a place of remembrance where memory of the past will not be lost. What is the meaning of such remembrance in the Eucharist?

In order to be able to remember the past, the Eucharist gives us the assurance that we don't have to have to hold on to the memories; nor do that such memories have a hold on us. It is the memory of God who remembers us in Christ that is the formative memory for our lives. The community of believers will remember and bring their lives to Christ in the Eucharist. Victims and perpetrators are invited to first remember and then bring their memory to God. When personal hurts are brought to the presence of God in the memory of the Eucharist, it becomes the memory of the community. Personal stories become the story of the community, thus giving the assurance that the personal memory of the past hurt becomes that of the community. To know that one does not have to take the burden of remembering the past alone is a liberating experience. The Eucharist is the place of daring to let the bad memory and the pain to be in God's presence with the hope of healing of memory.

The letting go of the pain does not mean that the memory will be gone. The Eucharist also acts as a place of communal remembrance, with the assurance that God remembers what has happened in our lives. When people bring their memory, they surrender it to the community, and the community brings it to God. The memory of the past becomes a communal story, and the story of God's saving action in the light of the Eucharist. The memory is still there, but is now given a new meaning. Thus, the person can let go of their personal hurt, knowing that the memory stays, and at the same time the pain is not in the memory anymore. It has become a redemptive memory of Christ's saving action and God's remembrance.

It is important to note that to forget should never become a goal in the letting-go process of the painful memory, rather, it should become a viable option. While appreciating Volf's experience and reflections, we reject Volf's ultimate argument that says forgetting is the ultimate goal. To forget is an option only after such redemptive memory takes place, nevertheless not a goal. Knowing that the memory is now being transformed and yet remembered, people can opt to forget, or to remember it with different meaning. Along these lines of thought, we have no need for the view that forgetting should be the final prize of eucharistic remembrance.

Even so, we still need to be aware that remembrance is not the final way of dealing with the past hurt. It opens up the way to true forgiveness and reconciliation. For remembrance is needed in order to forgive. Without the memory of the hurt you cannot forgive or even reconcile because you cannot forgive what you have forgotten. This is why remembrance is the way towards real reconciliation. The act of remembrance, especially in Christian theology, is often connected with forgiveness and reconciliation. Remembrance is a way towards real reconciliation. We suggest further research is needed on the ways of forgiveness after remembrance.

3. The Eucharist and Justice

In remembering, we are doing justice to the victims. Here justice does not mean retribution in a judicial system. The judicial system still needs to do its work in its own form. Remembrance helps victims because it is a chance that can be offered to victims and perpetrators—mostly victims—for their stories to be heard, to be acknowledged, and to get the opportunity to have a healing of memory. By listening to the voices of the voiceless and remembering them, we are bringing justice to the victims. The justice that we mean here is not a kind of restorative justice, but it is more of an act of giving the victims their voices back.

The place of transformative remembrance in the Christian tradition is in the liturgy of the Eucharist. The liturgy of the Eucharist, with all its elements, should help people, especially conflicting sides, to prepare themselves and discern, whether they are ready to be forgiven and reconciled, and also to forgive and reconcile. If there is, or was conflict among people, or groups of people, then—with the purpose of reconciliation in mind— this is the chance to share the remembrance of what really happened.

The HKBP can use this tool that is at her disposal all along, to deal with her past conflict. As a liturgical church, in terms of having strong liturgical elements in the life of the church, the HKBP should start first by deliberately improving her liturgy of the Eucharist with a purpose to allow reconciliation to happen between the conflicting sides. Thus, we very much reject the view that says that ritual elements of the church are not as strong as cultural elements. Bungaran Simanjuntak argues from an anthropological point of view that the liturgical rituals are not as strong as the cultural practices and other elements in terms of reconciling people. First, we can argue with his high regard for the reconciling potential and effect of the culture. The remembrance of the past conflict in Batak culture can just as well undergird negative remembrance when it is not given a new meaning. Indeed, conflicts often last precisely because of cultural elements. Secondly, we need to say that Christian theology and ritual indeed still offer a true reconciling effect. The liturgy of the Eucharist, the knowledge that God remembers, and the redemptive feeling of being liberated from the painful memory, can help the HKBP to have a true reconciliation, when it is truly and fully exercised. The Church is enabled to receive and practice reconciliation through the means of the Church's sacrament of the Eucharist.

We have also seen that remembrance in the Eucharist has an active meaning as does remembrance in Batak philosophy. Remembrance in both fields of understanding is done in an active way by getting a sense of identity and remembering the past in order to walk to the future. Because of this, we can propose that the remembrance in the Eucharist will be very much appreciated and accepted by the Batak culture that influences the Church. If it is done correctly, the liturgy of the Eucharist can speak to the HKBP both theologically and culturally.

However, this research was not intended to look for a contextual theology of remembrance. Our purpose is to find a theological foundation of remembrance and how it can inform and maybe offer something to the new culture of remembrance. This can also be seen as a recommendation for further research in how to find a way of doing a contextual theology of remembrance, and in our specific case, a contextual theology of remembrance in the HKBP which is more explicitly connected to Batak culture. Indeed, based on our findings, we can say that Batak culture indeed has some strong remembrance elements in its culture that can be related to our findings about the theological understanding of remembrance.

Churches can also use these elements of remembrance in the liturgy of the Eucharist as a new way of dealing with the past. Our proposal for a revised liturgy of the Eucharist was taken from the kind of ecumenical resources that will be insightful for churches that want to celebrate the Eucharist in the theological understanding of the BEM Document. We hope that the liturgy presented in this study will offer a new strong element of remembrance for true reconciliation in the case of communal conflict. This liturgy of the Eucharist could become a place of redemptive remembrance of past hurts.

The painful past can now be remembered with a new redemptive meaning, which still gives us the opportunity to learn from the past mistakes and yet at the same time freeing us from the burden of the pain. The experience of the redemptive memory of the Eucharist lies in the knowledge that God remembers. Our hope is that the Eucharist will get a more central place, along with the preaching of the word, as th place of healing and remembrance. They are the gathering places of remembering God's love and Jesus sacrificial act, and the fellowship of the Spirit in the life of the church.

Our research has shown such elements of redemptive memory in the liturgy of the Eucharist to help us reconcile with the painful past. In the new culture of remembrance, where—at least in the HKBP—memory will most likely stay entrapped. Eucharistic redemptive memory gives us fresh hope that our remembrance of the past will not be a negative one. It encourages us to remember and deal with our past. When past hurt is being remembered, it will be transformed into a redemptive memory of God's remembrance. We hope that our research can convince communities at conflict to deal with their past by remembering it with the purposes of acknowledging the victims and aim for a true reconciliation. The pain that the past brought can be transformed when it is fully dealt with.

The next step of this theology of remembrance is to invite communities in conflict to come together and share their stories in light of the possible transformation of their memory of past pain. In an ideal world, the following step thereafter would be to take the path of forgiveness and reconciliation not only in liturgy but also in daily life. However, we should not rush too hastily through the process of remembrance. Remembrance is not a flash of insight but a course of faith that opens vistas towards genuine reconciliation that takes time.

We have reached the point where we can responsibly conclude that the theology of remembrance can become the church's contribution to the memory of the suffering in the world. Like all liturgy, it is effective because its undergirding theology is sound and not because it is driven by a purposeful scheme of success. On the contrary, in a theology of remembrance the church is asked to act as an institution of remembrance of the suffering, and not the quick fix. Following this path, the church will be aware of the memoria passionis in its own context, and remembers it within the larger community of remembrance, thus giving birth to a new social memory that sees the hurt that was and still is in the light of hope of a memoria ressurectionis, that makes visible the contours of a healing reconciliation and the sure and certain knowledge that God remembers. The transformation of negative memory into positive memory can be experienced and thus celebrated in the liturgy of the Eucharist, where victims and perpetrators are invited to share their memories, together within the larger community of believers. It is to remember the fullness of Christ, and the God who remembers.

4. Epilogue

This research is both a scientific research and a personal journey into the importance of remembrance for the painful memory of the past communal conflict. As a person, the calling to remember and the temptation to forget the past are always in the air. We all have pain that we want to forget. The problem is that we cannot control our memory; sometimes we remember the things that we want to forget or vice versa. Since we cannot control our memory, what we can do as an alternative is to give another meaning to the memory, so that whenever it does come over us, we do not feel the hurt in the same way anymore.

It should be noted that painful memory does not necessarily make us re-experience the pain when we have changed our feelings toward the memory. Let me explain with my personal experience. It was New Year's evening, and according to the Batak's culture, we all should have gathered as a family to celebrate the coming New Year. We usually have several nuclear families come together. My father's brothers and mother's family stayed over for the night, praying at the start of the New Year and celebrating it together as family. But on this particular night at the end of 1996, only my mother, my brother, my sister and I had gathered. My dad was imprisoned because he had started a free trade union in Indonesia, and the Soeharto administration did not like him. He was accused of starting the July 27th 1996 riot in Jakarta, which was not true at all (he was released free of charges after Soeharto stepped down as President in 1998), and was being put in prison on accusation of overthrowing the government. I did not know back then why there were only four of us. My mother explained that other family members were afraid of the government and their relation with my father, so they had chosen not to come. It was the only New Year's evening when I felt really alone and responsible for my family. We cried during our New Year's prayer and sang hymns. My mother told us that we should stick together as family. I felt hurt, betrayed, and angry that evening. I was hurt by the absence of my dad, betrayed by the families who did not come in a time of trouble, and angry at the government for breaking my family apart. Since that evening, my understanding of family changed. For me, then, family was not decided by blood, but by their presence and help during times of trouble. This is not a normal Batak understanding of what family is all about. In Batak culture, there is a rule to take care of family, that blood is stronger than anything else. However, that evening was a turning point for me with regard to that view.

For two years, I did not really know that this event caused so much pain in me. My anger was directed towards my family members who did not show up because they were afraid of the government's pressure. I did not want to have anything to do with them, and my attitude changed. Strangely, I did not recall exactly why I felt that way towards them. Apparently I tried to forget the evening. I was able to forget the cause of my resentment, but I could not put the negative feelings aside. I remembered the pain but not the event.

A few years later, we had the same New Year's evening prayer. This time, my dad was out of prison, the family was back on track. We had more than 4 people in the gathering. However, I still felt the pain and resentment towards the other family members who were there. I didn't know why I felt such a feeling. After that evening, I traced back my memory and remembered the 1996 New Year's evening. I cried and prayed for the hold my resentment had on my feelings towards my extended family.

If I were to keep the pain, then I would still hate the family members who did not show up that evening, or I would hate Soeharto's government for breaking my family apart. However, after some years, I have come to the realization that my extended family did not have another option. Even my parents did not blame the relatives. They said that it was meant to happen that way, and that God would always be with the family. They said that no matter what, family is still family. I remembered praying hard one night and surrendering all to God.

The memory of that night is not causing the same pain that I felt when it happened anymore. When I tried to forget the event, the pain stayed. I can only begin the process of healing by remembering what truly happened and why I felt what I felt. When my memory was healed, it was made whole by my full remembrance, and only then I was able to remember the event without feeling the pain anymore. Now I can remember the evening without feeling the hurt, betrayal, or anger. My understanding of family is still changed. Now family is made up of those who help you when you need help the most. We have to help those in need, not because they are family, but because they need help. I had a change of feelings after my memory was healed. The healing comes from the realization that God knows how I feel and what I had experienced. Now, I still remember what happened that evening, but I have changed the meaning of that evening. It is not a painful evening anymore, it is now an evening where God has shown God's mercy on my family, and where I gained some of the wisdom of my mother.

I reflect on that event, and on my research. We are not asked to forget the past hurt in the sense of putting the memory out of our mind. We are asked to remember, to give all our pain to God when gathered in the community of believers, and be assured that God will remember. It is both comforting and challenging at the same time, to remember and to put trust in God. The element of communal togetherness in the liturgy of the Eucharist makes me remember and pass on that hurtful memory to God. When we truly know that God remembers, the memory takes on a different meaning. The memory becomes the memory of God who was there and remembers us and our situation. After this truth is realized, we can choose to let go of the painful memory or remember it in a new way. We should keep one thing in mind, while it is human to forget, God will not forget, God remembers.

Bibliography

1. Books

Arendt, Hannah. *The Human Condition: A Study of the Central Dilemmas Facing Modern Man.* Garden City: Doubleday, 1959.
Aritonang, J.S. *Sejarah Pendidikan Kristen di Tanah Batak.* Jakarta: BPK GM, 1988.
Ashley, James Matthew. *Interruptions: Mysticism, Politics, and Theology in the Work of Johann Baptist Metz.* Notre Dame, Indiana: University of Notre Dame Press, 1998.
Assman, Jan. *Religion and Cultural Memory: Ten Studies.* Translated by Rodney Livingstone. Stanford, California: Stanford University Press, 2006.
Augustine. *Confessions.* Harmondsworth: Penguin, 1961.
Aulen, Gustaf. *The Faith of the Christian Church.* Philadelphia: Mulenberg Press, 1948.
Baldwin, Joyce G. *Tyndale Old Testament Commentaries: Haggai, Zechariah, Malachi, an Introduction and Commentary.* Leicester: Inter-Varsity Press, 1973.
Barr, James. *The Semantics of Biblical Language.* London: SCM Press, 1991.
Baum, Gregory and Harold Wells (eds.). *The Reconciliation of Peoples: Challenge to the Churches.* Geneva & New York: WCC & Orbis Books, 1997.
Bauman, Zygmunt. *Modernity and the Holocaust.* New York: Cornell University Press, 2000.
Beeby, H. D. *International Theological Commentary: Hosea, Grace Abounding.* Grand Rapids: Wm. B. Eerdmans, 1987.
Blenkinsopp, Joseph. *Treasures Old and New: Essays in the Theology of the Pentateuch.* Grand Rapids, Michigan: Wm. B. Eerdmans Publishing Co., 2004.
Boangmanalu, Jusen. *Anamnesis: Study on the Anamnetic Meaning of the Communion Compared with The Ancestors Memorial Activities in the Batak Traditional Religion* Master Thesis: Faculty of the South East Asia Graduate School of Theology, 1992.
Brettler, M.Z. *The Creation of History in Ancient Israel.* London: Routledge, 1995.
Bridge, Donald. and David Phypers. *Communion: The Meal That Unites?* Illinois: Harold Shaw Publishers, 1981.
Bruce, F. F. *The Epistle to the Hebrews.* Grand Rapids: Wm. B. Eerdmans, 1964.
Bruce, F. F. *The New Century Bible Commentary: I & II Corinthians.* London: Marshall, Morgan & Scott, 1980.
Bultmann, Rudolf. *Jesus and the World.* New York: Charles Scribner's Sons, 1958.
Casey, Edward S. *Remembering: A Phenomenological Study.* Bloomington, Indiana: Indiana University Press, 2000.

Childs, Brevard S. *Memory and Tradition in Israel*. London: SCM Press, 1962.
Clements, R. E. *Interpretation: A Bible Commentary for Teaching and Preaching, Jeremiah*. Atlanta: John Knox Press, 1988.
Clines, D. J. *The New Century Bible Commentary: Ezra, Nehemiah, Esther*. Grand Rapids: Wm. B. Eerdmans, 1984.
Coate, Mary Anne. *Sin, Guilt, and Forgiveness: The Hidden Dimensions of a Pastoral Process*. London: Society for Promoting Christian Knowledge, 1994.
Colombo, J. A. *An Essay on Theology and History: Studies in Pannenberg, Metz, and the Frankfurt School*. Atlanta: Georgia: American Academy of Religion, 1990.
Coutsoumpos, Panayotis. *Paul and the Lord's Supper: A Socio-Historical Investigation*. New York: Peter Lang Publishing, 2005.
Crockett, William R. *Eucharist: Symbol of Transformation*. New York: Pueblo Publishing Company, 1989.
Crossan, John Dominic. *In Fragments: The Aphorisms of Jesus*. San Francisco: Harper and Row, 1983.
Dahl, Nils Alstrup. *Jesus in the Memory of the Early Church*. Minneapolis: Augsburg, 1976.
Dasuha, Juandaha Raya P. and Martin Lukito Sinaga (eds.). *Tole! Den Timorlanden Das Evangelium!" Sejarah Seratus Tahun Pekabaran Injil di Simalungun, 2 September 1903-2003*. Pematang Siantar: Kolportase GKPS dan Panitia Bolon 100 Tahun Injil di Simalungun, 2003.
Davies, Philip R. *In Search of 'Ancient Israel'*. Sheffield: Sheffield Academic Press, 1992.
Davies, Philip R. *The Origins of Biblical Israel*. New York: T & T Clark, 2007.
Dick, Johns Roger. *Man in the World: The Theology of Johannes Baptist Metz*. Missoula, Montana: American Academy of Religion, 1976.
van Dijk, Kees. *A Country in Despair: Indonesia between 1997 and 2000*. Leiden: KITLV Press, 2001.
Dunn, James D.G. *Jesus Remembered*. Grand Rapids: Wm. B. Eerdmans. 2003.
Esler, Philip Francis. *New Testament Theology: Communion and Community*. Minneapolis: Augsburg Fortress, 2005.
Fussell, Paul. *The Great War in Modern Memory*. New York: Oxford University Press, 2000.
Gerhardsson, Birger. *Memory and Manuscript: Oral Tradition and Written Transmission in Rabbinic Judaism and Early Christianity*. Copenhagen: Ejnar Munksgaard, 1961.
Gerhardsson, Birger. *Tradition and Transmission in Early Christianity*. Copenhagen: Ejnar Munksgaard, 1964.
Govier, Trudy. *Forgiveness and Revenge*. New York: Routledge, 2002.
Greenfeld, Howard. *Passover*. New York: Holt, Rinehart and Winston, 1978.
Gultom, Ibrahim. *Agama Malim di Tanah Batak*. Jakarta: Bumi Aksara, 2010.
Haaken, Janice. *Pillars of Salt: Gender, Memory, and the Perils of Looking Back*. New Brunswick, NJ and London: Rutgers University Press, 1998.
Hagner, Donald A. *World Biblical Commentary: Matthew 14-28*. Dallas: Word Books Publisher, 1995.

Halbwachs, Maurice. *On Collective Memory.* Edited and translated by Lewis A. Coser. Chicago: University of Chicago Press, 1992.
Harrison, R. K. *Tyndale Old Testament Commentaries: Jeremiah & Lamentations.* Leicester: Inter-Varsity Press, 1973.
Helmick, Raymond G. and Rodney L. Petersen (eds.). *Forgiveness and Reconciliation: Religion, Public Policy, and Conflict Transformation.* Pennsylvania: Templeton Foundation Press, 2001.
Hendel, Ronald. *Remembering Abraham: Culture, Memory, and History in the Hebrew Bible.* New York: Oxford University Press, 2005.
den Heyer, C. J. *De Maaltijd van de Heer: Exegetische en Bijbeltheologische Studie over Pascha en Avondmaal.* Kampen: J.H. Kok, 1990.
Heyward, Isabel Carter. *The Redemption God.* Lanham: University Press of America, 1982.
Higgins, A. J. B. *The Lord's Supper in the New Testament.* London: SCM Press, 1956.
HKBP Information Bureau. *Building The Truth: The Streamlining of the Information about the Batak Christian Protestant Christian Church (Huria Kristen Batak Protestan: HKBP).* Tarutung: HKBP, 1994.
HKBP. *Almanak HKBP 2010.* Tarutung: HKBP, 2010.
HKBP. *Almanak HKBP 2011.* Tarutung: HKBP, 2011.
HKBP. *Aturan dan Peraturan Huria Kristen Batak Protestan HKBP 1982-1992.* Tarutung: HKBP, 1982.
HKBP. *Minutes of HKBP Meeting of Ministers 20-24 August 2001.* Pematangsiantar: HKBP, 2001.
HKBP. *Minutes of HKBP Meeting of Ministers 26-28 September 1994.* Tarutung: HKBP, 1995.
HKBP. *Minutes of HKBP Meeting of Ministers 5-8 November 1991.* Tarutung: HKBP, 1994.
HKBP. *Minutes of Meeting of Ministers.* HKBP: not published, 1999.
HKBP. *Ruhut Parmahanion dohot Paminsangion (Church Pastoral and Discipline).* Tarutung: HKBP, 1987.
HKBP. *The Profile of HKBP Walking into the Third Millennium.* Tarutung: HKBP, 2002.
Hoffman, Lawrence A. and Paul F. Bradshaw (eds.). *Life Cycles in Jewish and Christian Worship, Vol. 4.* Notre Dame, Indiana: University of Notre Dame Press, 1998.
Holmgren, Fredrick Carlson. *International Theological Commentary: Ezra and Nehemiah, Israel Alive Again.* Grand Rapids: Wm. B. Eerdmans, 1987.
Hubbard, David Allan. *Tyndale Old Testament Commentaries: Hosea, an Introduction and Commentary.* Leicester: Inter-Varsity Press, 1973.
Hutagalung, W. M. *Pustaha Batak: Tarombo dohot Turiturian ni Bangso Batak.* Pematangsiantar: Tulus Jaya, 1991.
Hutauruk, J. R. *Kemandirian Gereja.* Jakarta: BPK GM, 1993.
Jacques, Geneviève. *Beyond Impunity: An Ecumenical Approach to Truth, Justice and Reconciliation.* Geneva: WCC Publications, 2000.
Jeremias, Joachim. *The Eucharistic Words of Jesus.* New York: The Macmillan Company, 1955.

Jones, L. Gregory. *Embodying Forgiveness: A Theological Analysis.* Grand Rapids: Wm. B. Eerdmans, 1995.
Käsemann, Ernst. *Exegetische Versuche und Besinnungen Vol. I.* Göttingen: Vandenhoeck & Ruprecht, 1960.
Keown, Gerald L, Pamela J. Scalise and Thomas G. Smothers. *World Biblical Commentary: Jeremiah 26-52.* Waco, Texas: World Books, 1984.
Keshkegian, Flora A. *Redeeming Memories: A Theology of Healing and Transformation.* Nashville: Abingdon Press, 2000.
Keshkegian, Flora A. *Time for Hope: Practices for Living in Today's World.* New York: Continuum, 2006.
Kidner, Derek. *Tyndale Old Testament Commentaries: Ezra & Nehemiah, an Introduction and Commentary.* Leicester: Inter-Varsity Press, 1973.
Kilpatrick, G. D. *The Eucharist in Bible and Liturgy.* Cambridge: Cambridge University Press, 1983.
Kim, Dong-sun. *The Bread for Today and the Bread for Tomorrow: The Ethical Significance of the Lord's Supper in the Korean Context.* New York: Peter Lang Publishing Inc., 2001.
Kim, Llyod. *Polemic in the Book of Hebrews: Anti-Judaism, Anti-Semitism, Supersessionism?* Orlando: Pickwick Publications, 2006.
King, Nicola. *Memory, Narrative, Identity: Remembering the Self.* Edinburgh: Edinburgh University Press, 2000.
Kirk, Alan and Tom Thatcher (eds.). *Memory, Tradition and Text, SEMEIA Studies 52.* Atlanta: Society of Biblical Literature, 2005.
Kreider, Harry J. *The Beginnings of Lutheranism in New York.* New York: *not published*, 1949.
Lane, William L. *Word Biblical Commentary Vol. 47: Hebrews 1-8.* Dallas, Texas: Word Books Publisher, 1991.
Lehman, Paul. *Ethics in a Christian Context.* New York: Harper and Bros., 1963.
Léon-Dufour, Xavier. *Sharing the Eucharistic Bread: The Witness of the New Testament.* New York: Paulist Press, 1986.
Limburg, James. *Interpretation: A Bible Commentary for Teaching and Preaching, Hosea-Micah.* Atlanta: John Knox Press, 1988.
Longenecker, Richard N. *Biblical Exegesis in the Apostolic Period.* Grand Rapids: Wm. B. Eerdmans, 1999.
Lumban Tobing, Philip Oder. *The Structure of the Toba-Batak Belief in the High God.* Amsterdam: Jacob van Campen, 1956.
Lumbantobing, Andar M. *Makna Wibawa Jabatan dalam Gereja Batak.* Jakarta: BPK GM, 1996.
Lyotard, Jean-François. *The Postmodern Condition: A Report on Knowledge.* Translated by Geoff Bennington and Brian Massumi. Minneapolis: University of Minnesota Press, 1984.
MacKeating, Henry. *The Cambridge Bible Commentary: The Books of Amos, Hosea and Micah.* London: Cambridge University Press, 1971.
Malpas, Simon. *Jean-François Lyotard.* London: Routledge, 2003.
Margalit, Avishai. *The Ethics of Memory.* Cambridge: Harvard University Press, 2003.

Martinez, Gaspar. *Confronting the Mystery of God: Political, Liberation, and Public Theologies*. New York: Continuum, 2001.
Metz, Johann Baptist and Jürgen Moltmann. *Faith and Future: Essays on Theology, Solidarity, and Modernity*. Maryknoll, New York: Orbis Books, 1995.
Metz, Johann Baptist Metz. *Love's Strategy: The Political Theology of Johann-Baptist Metz (Selection of Writings)*. Edited by John K. Downing. Harrisburg: Trinity Press, LTD., 1999.
Metz, Johann Baptist. *A Passion for God: The Mystical-Political Dimension of Christianity*. Translated by J. Matthew Ashley. New Jersey: Paulist Press, 1998.
Metz, Johann Baptist. *Faith in History and Society: Toward a Practical Fundamental Theology*. Translated by David Smith. New York: The Seabury Press, 1980.
Metz, Johann Baptist. *The Emergent Church*. New York: Crossroad, 1981.
Metz, Johann Baptist. *The End of Time: The Provocation Talking about God*. Edited by Tiemo Rainer Peters and Claus Urban, translated by J. Matthew Ashley. New Jersey: Paulist Press, 2004.
Metz, Johann Baptist. *Theology of the World*. Translated by William Glen-Doepel. New York: Seabury Press, 1969.
Minow, Martha. *Between Vengeance and Forgiveness*. Boston: Beacon Press, 1998.
Morrill, Bruce T. *Anamnesis as Dangerous Memory: Political and Liturgical Theology in Dialogue*. Collegeville, Minnesota: The Liturgical Press, 2000.
Mukesura, Celestine. *An Assessment of Contemporary Model of Forgiveness*. PhD dissertation: Dallas Theological Seminary, 2007.
Müller-Fahrenholz, Geiko. *The Art of Forgiveness: Theological Reflections on Healing and Reconciliation*. Geneva: WCC Publications, 1997.
Nadeak, Moksa et al. *Krisis HKBP: Ujian bagi Iman dan Pengamalan Pancasila*. Tarutung: Biro Informasi HKBP, 1995.
Niebuhr, H. Richard. *The Meaning of Revelation*. New York: Macmillan, 1967.
Norén, Carol M. *The Woman in the Pulpit*. Nashville: Abingdon Press, 1991.
North, C. R. *The Old Testament Interpretation of History*. London: Epworth Press, 1946.
Nyhus, Edward O.V. *An Indonesian Church in the Midst of Social Change: The Batak Protestant Christian Church 1942-1957*. PhD Dissertation: University of Wisconsin-Madison, 1987.
Ogden, Graham S. and Richard R. Deutsch. *International Theological Commentary: Joel & Malachi, a Promise of Hope – a Call to Obedience*. Grand Rapids: Wm. B. Eerdmans, 1987.
Parker, David C. *The Living Text of the Gospels*. Cambridge: Cambridge University Press, 1997.
Pedersen, Johs. *Israel: Its Life and Culture I-II*. London: Oxford University Press, 1946.
Pedersen, Paul B. *Batak Blood and Protestant Soul: The Development of National Batak Churches in North Sumatra*. Grand Rapids: William B. Eerdmans Publishing Company, 1970.

Pomazansky, Michael. *Selected Essays*. Jordanville, NY: Holy Trinity Monastery, 1996
Power, David Noel. *The Eucharistic Mystery: Revitalizing the Mystery*. New York: Crossroad Publishing Company, 1992.
Purwanto, L. H. *Indonesian Church Orders under Scrutiny: The Relation between the Church Members and the Church Office-Bearers: How It Is and How It Should Be*. Kampen: Theologische Universiteit van de Gereformeerde Kerken in Nederland te Kampen, 1997.
Puskas, Charles B. *The Letters of Paul: an Introduction*. Minnesota: The Liturgical Press, 1993.
von Rad, Gerhard. *God at Work in Israel*. Nashville: Abingdon, 1980.
von Rad, Gerhard. *Old Testament Theology Vol. II: The Theology of Israel's Prophetic Traditions*. Edinburgh: Oliver and Boyd, 1967.
von Rad, Gerhard. *The Message of the Prophet*. New York: Harper & Row Publishers, 1965.
Ricoeur, Paul. *Memory, History, Forgetting*. Translated by Kathleen Blamey and David Pellauer. Chicago: The Chicago University Press, 2006.
Sayadi (ed.), *Aceh Jakarta Papua: Akar Permasalahan dan Alternatif Proses Penyelesaian Konflik*. Jakarta: YAPPIKA, 2001.
Schimmel, Solomon. *Wounds Not Healed by Time: The Power of Repentance and Forgiveness*. New York: Oxford University Press, 2002.
Schmemann, Alexander. *Church, World, Mission*. New York: St Vladimir's Seminary Press, 1979.
Schmemann, Alexander. *For the Life of the World*. New York: St Vladimir's Seminary Press, 1973.
Schmemann, Alexander. *Introduction to Liturgical Theology*. Translated by Asheleigh E. Moorhouse. Portland, Maine: The Faith Press Ltd., 1966.
Schmemann, Alexander. *The Eucharist: Sacrament of the Kingdom*. Translated by Paul Kachur. New York: St Vladimir's Seminary Press, 1987.
Schmemann, Alexander. *The Journals of Father Alexander Schmemann 1973-1983*. Translated by Juliana Schmemann. New York: St Vladimir's Seminary Press, 2000.
Schottroff, W. "*Gedenken' im Alten Orient und im Alten Testament*." Neukirchener: Verl. Unbekannter Einband, 1967.
Schreiner, Lothar. *Adat dan Injil: Perjumpaan Adat dengan Iman Kristen di Tanah Batak* (Translated by . Jakarta: BPK GM, 2000.
Schwarz, Adam. *A Nation in Waiting*. Australia: Allen & Ulwin, 1999.
Shriver, Donald W. Jr. *An Ethic for Enemies: Forgiveness in Politics*. Oxford University Press, 1997.
Sihombing, Fridz Pardamean. *Versöhnung, Wahrheit und Gerechtigkeit: Die ökumenische Bedeutung der Barmer Theologischen Erklärung für den Weg der Kirchen in Indonesien*. Wuppertal: Neukirchener, 2007.
Simanjuntak, Bungaran Antonius. *Konflik Status dan Kekuasaan Orang Batak Toba*. Yogyakarta: Yayasan Obor, 2009.
Simanjuntak, Bungaran Antonius. *Melayu Pesisir dan Batak Pegunungan*. Jakarta: Yayasan Obor Indonesia, 2010.

Sirait, Saut. *Politik Kristen di Indonesia: Suatu Tinjauan Etis*. Jakarta: BPK-GM, 2001.
Smedes, Lewis B. *Forgive and Forget: Healing the Hurts We Don't Deserve*. New York: Harper & Row Publishers, 1984.
Smith, Ralph L. *World Biblical Commentary: Micah – Malachi*. Waco, Texas: World Books, 1984.
Smiths, Mark S. *The Memoirs of God: History, Memory, and the Experience of the Divine in Ancient Israel*. Minneapolis, Fortress Press, 2004
Sölle, Dorothee. *Political Theology*. Translated by John Shelley. Philadelphia: Fortress Press, 1974.
Stokhof, W.A.L. et al. (eds.), *Konflik Komunal di Indonesia Saat Ini*. Jakarta-Leiden: INIS & PBB, 2003.
Stuart, Douglas. *World Biblical Commentary: Hosea-Jonah*. Waco, Texas: World Books, 1984.
Thayer, J. H. *A Greek English Lexicon of The New Testament*. Edinburgh: T & T Clark, 1986.
Thompson, J. A. *The New International Commentary on the Old Testament: The Book Of Jeremiah*. Grand Rapids: Wm. B. Eerdmans, 1980.
Thurian, Max (ed.). *Churches Respond to BEM: Official Responses to the "Baptism, Eucharist and Ministry" Text Vol. 1-6*. Geneva: World Council of Churches, 1987.
Thurian, Max and Geoffrey Wainwright (eds.). *Baptism and Eucharist: Ecumenical Convergence in Celebration*. Geneva: World Council of Churches, 1983.
Thurian, Max. *Ecumenical Perspectives on Baptism, Eucharist and Ministry*. Geneva: World Council of Churches, 1983
Thurian, Max. *The Eucharistic Memorial I: The Old Testament*. London: Lutterworth Press, 1968.
Thurian, Max. *The Eucharistic Memorial II: The New Testament*. London: Lutterworth Press, 1963.
Tutu, Desmond. *No Future without Forgiveness*. New York: Doubleday, 1999.
Vanderkam, James C. *An Introduction to Early Judaism*. Grand Rapids: W. B. Eerdmans, 2001.
Volf, Miroslav. *After Our Likeness: The Church as the Image of the Trinity*. Grand Rapids: Williams B. Eerdmans, 1998.
Volf, Miroslav. *Exclusion and Embrace: A Theological Exploration of Identity, Otherness, and Reconciliation*. Nashville: Abingdon Press, 1996.
Volf, Miroslav. *Free of Charge: Giving and Forgiving in a Culture Stripped of Grace*. Grand Rapids: Zondervan: 2006.
Volf, Miroslav. *The End of Memory: Remembering Rightly in a Violent World*. Grand Rapids: William B. Eerdmans Publishing Co., 2006.
Wainwright, Geoffrey. *Eucharist and Eschatology*. New York: Oxford University Press, 1981.
Wandel, Lee Palmer. *The Eucharist in the Reformation: Incarnation and Liturgy*. Cambridge, New York: Cambridge University Press, 2006.
Wertsch, James V. *Voices of Collective Remembering*. Cambridge: Cambridge University Press, 2002.

Wiesel, Elie. *All Rivers Run to the Sea: Memoirs Volume 1, 1928-1969*. London: Harper Collins, 1996.
Wiesel, Elie. *From the Kingdom of Memory: Reminiscences*. New York: Schocken Books, 1995.
Wills, Garry. *St. Augustine's Memory [Introduction and Commentary]*. New York: Viking Penguin, 2002.
Wollaston, Isabel. *A War against Memory: The Future of Holocaust Remembrance*. London: SPCK, 1996.
World Council of Churches. *Baptism, Eucharist and Ministry*. Geneva: World Council of Churches, 1982.
Wyschogrod, Edith. *An Ethics of Remembering: History, Heterology, and the Nameless Others*. Chicago: The University of Chicago Press, 1998.
Yerushalmi, Yosef Hayim. *Zakhor: Jewish History and Jewish Memory*. Seattle and London: University of Washington Press, 1982.
Zerubabel, Yael. *Recovered Roots: Collective Memory and the Making of Israeli National Tradition*. Chicago: The University of Chicago Press, 1994.
Zurbuchen Mary S. (ed.). *Beginning to Remember: The Past in the Indonesian Present*. Singapore: Singapore University Press, 2005.

2. Articles in Books and Journals

Allen, Leslie C. "זכר", in *New International Dictionary of Old Testament Theology and Exegesis Vol. 1*, ed. Willem A. van Gemeren, 1100-1106. Grand Rapids: Zondervan Publishing House, 1996.
Anonymous. "Angka na Pinarungkilhon di na Mangula Raphon Ephorus Pdt. Dr. P.W.T. Simanjuntak," *not published*, June 1998.
Averbeck, Richard E. "Azkārāh," in *New International Dictionary of Old Testament Theology and Exegesis Vol. 1*, ed. Willem A. van Gemeren, 335-339. Grand Rapids: Zondervan Publishing House, 1996.
Bailey, Kenneth E. "Informal Controlled Oral Tradition and the Synoptic Gospels." *Asian Journal of Theology* 5 no. 1 (1991): 34-54
Bailey, Kenneth E. "Middle Eastern Oral Tradition and the Synoptic Gospels." *Expository Times* 106 no. 12 S (1995): 363-367.
Bartels, K. H. "Remember," in *The New International Dictionary of New Testament Theology*, ed. Colin Brown, 230-247. Grand Rapids, Zondervan Publishing House, 1981.
Beckwith, R.T. "The Jewish Background to Christian Worship," in *The Study of Liturgy*, ed. Cheslyn Jones et al., 68-80. New York: Oxford University Press, 1992.
Behm. "ἀνάμνησις" in *Theological Dictionary of The New Testament Volume I*, ed. Gerhard Kittel, 348-349. Grand Rapids: Wm. B. Eerdmans, 1972.
Blair, Edward P. "An Appeal to Remembrance: The Memory Motif in Deuteronomy." *Interpretation* Vol. XV (1961): 41-47.
Boring, M. Eugene. "The Gospel of Matthew," in *The New Interpreter's Bible Vol. 8*, ed. Leander E. Keck, 87-506. Nashville: Abingdon Press, 1995.
Brown, Colin. "Remember, Remembrance," in *The New International Diction-

ary of New Testament Theology, ed. Colin Brown, 234-240. Grand Rapids: Zondervan Publishing House, 1981.

Byrskog, Samuel. "A New Perspective on the Jesus Tradition Reflections on James D.G. Dunn's Jesus Remembered." *Journal for the Study of the New Testament* 26.4 (2004): 459-471.

Craddock, Fred B. "The Letter to the Hebrews," In *The New Interpreter's Bible Volume XII*, eds. Leander E. Keck et al. 1-174. Nashville: Abingdon Press, 1998.

Cribb, Robert. "Unresolved Problems in the Indonesian Killings of 1965-1966." *Asian Survey* 42 (2002): 550–563.

Del Colle, Ralph. "Communion and the Trinity: The Free Church Ecclesiology of Miroslav Volf – A Catholic Response." *Pneuma: The Journal of the Society for Pentecostal Studies*, Volume 22, No 2 (2000): 303-327.

de Vries, Simon J. "Remembrance In Ezekiel." *Interpretation* vol. XVI (1962): 58-64.

Dulling, Dennis C. "Social Memory and Biblical Studies: Theory, Method, and Application." *Biblical Theology Bulletin* 36 (2006): 2-4.

Dykstra, Craig R. "Memory and Truth." *Theology Today* 44, No.2 (1987): 159-163.

Eising. "Zākhar, Zēkher, Zikkārôn, 'Azkārāh," in *Theological Dictionary of the Old Testament Vol. IV*, eds. G. Johannes Botterweck and Helmer Ringgren, 64-82. Grand Rapids: Wm. B. Eerdmans, 1980.

Elson, R. E. "In Fear of the People: Suharto and the Justification of State-Sponsored Violence under the New Order," in *Roots Of Violence in Indonesia*, eds. Freek Colombijn and J. Thomas Lindblad, 173-195. Leiden: KITLV Press, 2002.

Grisbrooke, W. Jardine. "Anamnesis," in *The Westminster Dictionary of Worship*, ed. J. G. Davies, 10-19. Philadelphia: The Westminster Press, 1979.

Hansen, Collin. "Redeeming Bitterness: Miroslav Volf Tells How to Stop the 'Shield of Memory' from Turning into a Sword." *Christianity Today* 51 no 5 (2007): 50-51.

Haquin, André. "The Liturgical Movement and Catholic Ritual Revision," in *The Oxford History of Christian Worship*, eds. Geoffrey Wainwright and Karen B. Westerfield Tucker, 696-720. New York: Oxford University Press, 2006.

Hardiman, Fransisco Budi. "Melampaui Mengingat dan Melupakan." Paper presented at the 69th Dies Natalis of the Jakarta Theological Seminary, September 2003.

Hauerwas, Stanley. "Embodied Memory: Acts 5:27-32, Revelation 1:4-8, John 20:19-31." *Journal for Preachers* 19, no. 3 (1996): 20-24.

Hearon, Holly. "The Art of Biblical Reinterpretation: Re-Membering the Past into the Present." *Encounter* 66 no 3 (2005): 189-197.

Hearon, Holly. "The Construction of Social Memory in Biblical Interpretation." *Encounter* 67 no 4 (2006): 343-359.

Hutasoit, S.M.P. "Added Explanation on Statistical Recapitulation of HKBP that are Loyal to the Church Order until April 1997." Tarutung: *not published*, 1996.

Hutasoit, S.M.P. "Statistical Recapitulation of HKBP that are Loyal to the Church Order." Tarutung: *not published*, 1996.

Hyde, Clark. "The Remembrance of the Exodus in the Psalms." *Worship* vol. 62 (1988): 404-414.
Ingolfsland, Dennis. "Jesus Remembered: James Dunn and the Synoptic Problem." *Trinity Journal* 27 NS No. 2 (2006): 187-197.
Japhet, S. "Postexilic Historiography: How and Why?" in *Israel Constructs its History: Deuteronomistic Historiography in Recent Research*, eds. De Albert Pury et al., 155-166. Sheffield: Sheffield University Press, 2000.
Kelber, Werner H. "The Generative Force of Memory: Early Christian Traditions as Processes of Remembering." *Biblical Theology Bulletin* 36 (2006): 15-22.
Lorey, David E. and William H. Beezley. "Introduction," in *Genocide, Collective Violence, and Popular Memory*. Eds. David E Lorey and William H. Beezley, xi-xxxiii. Wilmington, Delaware: SR Books, 2002.
Martos, J. "Eucharistic Theology," in *A New Dictionary of Christian Theology*, eds. Alan Richardson and John Bowden. 187-190. London: SCM Press (1983), 2002.
Matthiesen, Michon Marie. "Narrative of Suffering: Complementary Reflections of Theological Anthropology in Johann Metz and Elie Wiesel." *Religion & Literature* Vol. 18, No. 2 (1986): 47-63.
Metz, Johann Baptist. "Toward the Second Reformation the Future of Christianity in a Postbourgeois World." *Cross Currents* (1981): 85-98.
Meyendorff, Paul. "Protopresbyter Alexander Schmemann: A Life Worth Living." *St Vladimir's Theological Quarterly* Vol. 28, No. 1 (1984): 3-10.
Michel, O. "μιμνήσκομαι, μνείαν, μνήμη, μνῆμα, μνημεῖον, μνημονεύω"" in *Theological Dictionary of the New Testament* Vol. 3, ed. Gerhard Kittel, 675-683. Grand Rapids: William B. Eerdmans, 1979.
Norén, Carol M. "The Word of God in Worship," in *The Study of Liturgy*, ed. Cheslyn Jones et al., 31-51. New York: Oxford University Press, 1992.
Oppenheimer, Mark. "Embracing Theology: Miroslav Volf Spans Conflicting Worlds." *Christian Century* 120 (2003): 18-23.
Pattiasina, J. M. "To Proceed with the Efforts of the Reconciliation of HKBP." Report presented in a meeting of representatives of the World Council of Churches (WCC), the United Evangelical Mission (UEM/VEM), the United Evangelical Lutheran Church of Germany (VELKD), the Christian Conference of Asia (CCA), and the Lutheran World Federation (LWF), Geneva, March 12, 1995.
PGI, "PGI Position Paper on the HKBP Problem." Paper presented during the PGI Annual Executive Committee Assembly, Kotamobagu, June 16, 1995.
Power, David N. "Foundation for Pluralism in Sacramental Expression: Keeping Memory." *Journal of Worship* 75 no 3 (2001): 194-209.
Power, David Noel. "A Prayer of Intersecting Parts: Elements of the Eucharistic Prayer." *Liturgical Ministry* 14 (2005): 120-131.
Rebecca, Lea Nicoll Kramer, and Susan A. Lukey. "Spirit Song: The Use of Christian Healing Rites in Trauma Recovery." *Treating Abuse Today* 5 and 6 (1995/1996): 39-47.
Ricoeur, Paul. Interview with Sorin Antohi, "Memory, History, Forgiveness: A Dialogue Between Paul Ricoeur and Sorin Antohi." Translated from French

and annotated by Gil Anidjar, http://www.janushead.org/8-1/Ricoeur.pdf, March 10, 2003.

Siahaan, S.M.. "Laporan dan Informasi Sinode Godang HKBP ke -51, Tanggal 23 s/d 28 Nopember 1992 yang Gagal & Notulen Pertemuan Fungsionaris HKBP Periode 1986-1992 dengan Ketua BAKORSTANASDA SUMBAGUT/Panglima KODAM I BB," *not published*.

Sirait, Saut and Gomar Gultom. "Kronologi Sinode Agung ke 51 HKBP," *not published*.

Schmemann, Alexander. "Confession and Communion", http://www.schmemann.org/byhim/ confessionandcommunion.html, accessed October, 2009.

Schmemann, Alexander. "Fast and Liturgy: Notes in Liturgical Theology." *St Vladimir's Seminary Quarterly* ns 3 no 1 (1959): 2-9.

Schmemann, Alexander. "Liturgical Theology, Theology of Liturgy, and Liturgical Reform." *St Vladimir's Theological Quarterly* 13 no 4 (1969): 217-224.

Schmemann, Alexander. "Liturgical Theology: Its Task and Methods." *St Vladimir's Seminary Quarterly* no. 1 no 40 (1957): 16-27.

Schmemann, Alexander. "Liturgy and Theology." *The Greek Orthodox Theological Review* No. 17 (1972): 86-100.

Schmemann, Alexander. "The Proclamation of Joy: An Orthodox View." *Living Pulpit* 5, no. 4 (1986): 8.

Schmemann, Alexander. "Theology and Eucharist." *St. Vladimir's Seminary Quarterly* no 5 (1961): 10-23.

Schuller, Eileen M. "The Book Of Malachi," in *The New Interpreter's Bible: A Commentary in Twelve Volumes: Volume VII, Introduction To Apocalyptic Literature, Daniel, The Twelve Prophets*, eds. Leander E. Keck, 843-877. Nashville: Abingdon Press, 1996

Siahaan, S.M. "Report on the 53rd General Synod of the HKBP." *not published*.

Siebert, Rudolf J. "Towards a Critical Catholicism: Küng and Metz part II." *Anglican Theological Review* (1983): 1-13.

Simanjuntak, P.W.T. "Barita Jujur Taon ni Ephorus HKBP 1994-1996," *not published*.

Simanjuntak, P.W.T. "Penjelasan dohot Pengarahan ni Ephorus ni HKBP Pdt. Dr. P.W.T. Simanjuntak tu Sinode Godang Istimewa, 09-12 Juli 1998," speech delivered during opening of Extraordinary General Synod July 9-12, 1998.

Simorangkir, O.P.T. "The Secretary General of HKBP Report to the 51st General Synod," *not published*.

Sitompul, Einar. "Kemandirian Gereja: Refleksi Singkat Krisis HKBP," in *Gereja di Pentas Politik: Belajar dari Kasus HKBP*, ed. Einar Sitompul. Jakarta: Yakoma-PGI, 1997.

Tihon, Paul. "The Theology of the Eucharistic Prayer," in *The New Liturgy*, ed. Lancelot Sheppard. 178-179. London: Darton, Longman & Todd, 1970.

Tillard, J. M. R. "The Eucharist, Gift of God," in *Ecumenical Perspectives on Baptism, Eucharist and Ministry*, ed. Max Thurian. Geneva: World Council of Churches, 1993.

Tim PGI Untuk Konflik HKBP. "Laporan Tim PGI Maret 1994." Jakarta: PGI – report document, *not published*.

van de Beek, Abraham. "A Shared Story for Reconciliation – Which Story?" *Journal of Reformed Theology* Vol. 2 No. 1 (2008): 17-27.
Verhey, Allen. "Remember, Remembrance," in *The Anchor Bible Dictionary Vol. 5*, ed. David Noel Freedman, 667-669. New York: Doubleday, 1992.
Villa-Vicencio, Charles. "Telling One Another Stories," in *The Reconciliation of Peoples: Challenge to the Churches*, ed. Gregory Baum and Harold Wells, 30-40. Geneva: WCC, 1997.
Volf, Miroslav. "Exclusion and Embrace: Theological Reflections in the Wake of 'Ethnic Cleansing.'" *Journal of Ecumenical Studies* vol. 29 (1992): 230-248.
Volf, Miroslav. "Fishing in the Neighbor's Pond: Mission and Proselytism in Eastern Europe" in *International Bulletin of Missionary Research* 20 No. 1 (1996): 25-31.
Volf, Miroslav. "Forgiveness, Reconciliation, and Justice: A Christian Contribution to a More Peaceful Social Environment," in *Forgiveness and Reconciliation: Religion, Publc Policy, and Conflict Transformation*, eds. Raymond G. Helmick and Rodney L. Petersen. Radnor: Templeton Foundation Press, 2001.
Volf, Miroslav. "God Forgiveness and Ours: Memory of Interrogations, Interrogations of Memory." *Anglican Theological Review* (2007): 218-219.
Volf, Miroslav. "Stob Lectures." Lectures that were presented fall 2002 at the campus of Calvin College or Calvin Theological Seminary in honour of Henry J. Stob's. http://www.calvinseminary.edu/continuingEd/stob/pastLectures.php, accessed August, 2008.
Volf, Miroslav. "The Social Meaning of Reconciliation." Paper presented at the Henry Martyn Lecture at the 1997 EMA annual conference. http://www.globalconnections.co.uk/ pdfs/reconciliation.pdf accessed September, 2008.
Vosloo, Robert. "Reconciliation as the Embodiment of Memory and Hope." *Journal of Theology for Southern Africa* 109 (2001): 25-40.
Wainwright, Geoffrey. "Christian Worship: Scriptural Basis and Theological Frame," in *The Oxford History of Christian Worship*, ed. Geoffrey Wainwright and Karen B. Westerfield Tucker, 1-31. New York: Oxford University Press, 2006.
Wainwright, Geoffrey. "Preaching as Worship." *Greek Orthodox Theological Review* 28, no. 4: (1983): 325-336.
Wainwright, Geoffrey. "Recent Eucharistic Revision," in *The Study of Liturgy*, eds. Cheslyn Jones et al. New York: Oxford University Press, 1992.
Wainwright, Geoffrey. "Sacramental Time." in *Liturgical Time*, eds. Wiebe Vos and Geoffrey Wainwright. Rotterdam: Liturgical Ecumenical Center Trust, 1982.
Wainwright, Geoffrey. "The Sermon and the Liturgy." *Greek Orthodox Theological Review* 28, no. 4: (1983): 337-349.
Yee, Gale A. "The Book of Hosea: Introduction, Commentary, Reflections," in *The New Interpreter's Bible: A Commentary in Twelve Volumes: Volume VII, Introduction to Apocalyptic Literature, Daniel, the Twelve Prophets*, ed. Leander E. Keck. Nashville: Abingdon Press, 1996.

Young, Pamela Dickey. "Beyond Moral Influence to an Atoning Life." *Theology Today* 52 (1995): 351-354.

3. Dictionaries and Encyclopedias

Baldwin, James Mark. et al. (eds.). *Dictionary of Philosophy and Psychology Vol. II*. 1901. Gloucester, Massachusetts: Peter Smith, 1960.
Borchert, Donald M. (editor in chief). *Encyclopedia of Philosophy* 2nd Edition Vol. 7. Michigan: Thomson Gale, 2006.
Bradshaw, Paul F. (ed.). *The New SCM Dictionary of Liturgy and Worship*. London: SCM Press, 2002.
Davies, J. G. (ed.). *The New Westminster Dictionary of Liturgy and Worship*. Pennsylvania: The Westminster Press, 1986.
Fohrer, Georg and Hans W. Hoffmann. *Hebrew and Aramaic Dictionary of the Old Testament*. New York: Walter de Gruyter, 1993.
Fowler, H. W. et al. (eds.). *The Concise Oxford Dictionary of Current English*. 9th edition. New York: Clarendon Press, 1995.
Rahner, Karl (ed.). *Encyclopedia of Theology*. London: Burns & Oates, 1981.
Richardson, Alan and John Bowden (eds.). *The New Dictionary of Christian Theology*. London : SCM Press Ltd. 1983.

4. Internet Resources

"Borders Announces Liquidation, Closing 400 Stores." http://www.ktla.com/news/landing/ktla-borders-bankrupt,0,2928708.story, accessed July 2011.
"Borders' Bankruptcy Shakes Industry." http://www.nytimes.com/2011/02/17/business/media/ 17borders.html?pagewanted=all, accessed July 2011.
"Insiden Warnai Malam Natal HKBP Bandung," http://www.detiknews.com/index.php/detik.read/tahun/2007/bulan/12/tgl/24/time/224146/idnews/870419/idkanal/10, accessed December 2007.
"Konflik HKBP Bandung Terus Berlanjut," http://www.suarakarya-online.com/news. html?id=184650, accessed December 2007.
Eucharistic Prayer resources. http://catholic-resources.org /ChurchDocs/EP1-4.htm, accessed January, 2010.
Eucharistic prayers for Masses of Reconciliation. http://catholic-resources.org/ChurchDocs/EPR1-2.htm, accessed January 2010.
Harahap Daniel T. *Blog*. "Gereja yang Luka dan Tak Menyerah (1): Sebuah Kesaksian Seorang Pendeta di Masa Konflik HKBP 1991-1998," http://rumametmet.com/2007/03/20/gereja-yang-luka-dan-tak-menyerah-1/, accessed January 2009.
Hull, Geoffrey. "The Proto-History of the Roman Liturgical Reform." http://pagesperso-orange.fr/civitas.dei/hull.htm, accessed January 2010.
http://pgi.or.id/home
http://www.gkpi.org
http://www.hkbp.or.id
http://www.lutheranworld.org/Directory/asi/Welcome-EN.html, accessed

May 17, 2010.
Sutton, John. "Memory" in *The Stanford Encyclopedia of Philosophy Summer 2010 Edition*. http://plato.stanford.edu/ archives/sum2010/entries/memory, accessed April 15, 2011.
van Klinken, Gerry. "Battle for the Pews." http://www.insideindonesia.org/edit49/hkbp.htm, accessed October 2007.

5. Newspaper Articles

"250 Preman Mengamuk di Binjai, 18 Terluka," *Mimbar Umum*, June 26, 1995.
"3 Sintua Penentang SAI Dikeluarkan dari HKBP Padangsidimpuan," *Sinar Indonesia Baru*, April 25, 1994.
"8 Tersangka Perusak Rumah dan Mobil Warga HKBP di Duri Ditahan Polisi," *Sinar Indonesia Baru*, April 25, 1994.
"Danrem 022/PT, Kolonel Inf. Sunarto: Korpri Unit Hankam Siantar-Simalungun Bersih dari SSA," *Sinar Indonesia Baru*, April 29, 1994.
"Dari Gereja ke Gereja," *Sentana*, Third Week December, 1993.
"Ephorus HKBP Pdt PWT Simanjuntak Mendukung Upaya Pemerintah Memberantas Premanisme," *Sinar Indonesia Baru*, March 28, 1995.
"Ephorus Pimpin Kebaktian di HKBP Tanjung Sari Dihadiri 3000 Orang," *Sinar Indonesia Baru*, April 25, 1994.
"GBKP Pinjamkan Gerejanya untuk anggota-anggota HKBP yang anti SAI," *Sinar Indonesia Baru*, March 22, 1994.
"Govt Has Confusing Stance on HKBP Rift," *Jakarta Post*, June 8, 1994.
"Hari Ini Rapat Pendeta HKBP Dimulai," *Sinar Indonesia Baru*, September 27, 1994.
"Herber Hutasoit dibunuh Sadis," *Sentana*, First Week of June, 1994.
"Jemaah HKBP Agar Hidup Dalam Kearifan Menghadapi Masalah yang Ada," *Sinar Indonesia Baru*, April 4, 1994.
"Kakansospol Taput Letkol N. Simanjuntak: Dr. SAE Nababan Sudah Dilarang Muspida Taput Berkotbah Tanpa Izin. Sekwilda: Pegawai Pemda Taput yang terlibat Kemelut HKBP akan Ditindak. Supir Mobil Pemda yang Mengangkut Massa SSA akan Dipecat," *Sinar Indonesia Baru*, March 18, 1994.
"Kapolres Taput: Tidak ada Larangan Laksanakan KKR," *Waspada*, October 13, 1998.
"Kebaktian Minggu Dua Kali di Gereja HKBP Resort Binjai/Langkat Ditiadakan," *Sinar Indonesia Baru*, April 25, 1994.
"Konflik di HKBP Kian Meruncing, Kerusuhan Massa Bisa Meletus," *Republika* October 13, 1998
"Mau Diusir Pendeta dari Gereja: Jemaat HKBP Pondok Bambu Mengadu ke Pimpinan HKBP," *Narwastu Pembaruan*, No. 20/2005, March 2005.
"Menggugat Bakorstanasda, Menangkap Pendeta," *Forum Keadilan*, No. 21, February 4, 1993.
"Pangdam III Siliwangi: Anggota ABRI yang Turut Perkeruh HKBP Akan Diceklek Batang Lehernya," *Sinar Indonesia Baru*, April 23, 1994.
"Pendeta Laurensius Maringan Napitu Dihukum Percobaan 1 Tahun Atas Ke-

matian St Drs Petrus Pakpahan di Helvetia Medan," *Sinar Indonesia Baru,* September 29, 1994.
"Penunjukan Pejabat Ephorus HKBP," *Suara Pembaruan*, December 28, 1992.
"Penunjukan Pj. Ephorus Undang Protes," *Sinar Pagi*, December 29, 1992.
"Rival Church Group Clash, 5 Injured," *Jakarta Post*, July 3, 1995.
"Rudini: Sejak Awal Saya menentang Campurtangan Pemerintah dalam Masalah HKBP", *Sentana,* 4th Week of February, 1994.
"Sengketa HKBP Hendaknya Diselesaikan Kekeluargaan," *Kompas,* June 8, 1994.
"State Should Stay Out of Church's Conflict: Rudini," *Jakarta Post*, January 2, 1993.
"Sudomo bans all comments on church conflict," *Jakarta Post*, January 11, 1993.
"Sudomo, Try to Seek Solution to Row over Bishop's Appointment," *Jakarta Post*, December 31, 1992.
"Tentang Kasus di HKBP Pondok Bambu: Pendeta Jangan Sok Berkuasa di Tengah Masyarakat," *Narwastu Pembaruan,* No. 20/2005, March 2005.
"The May Riots: Remembering the Terror," *Jakarta Post*, Monday May 16, 2005.
"Tidak Ada Lagi Kebaktian Bergilir di HKBP Tanjung Sari," *Sinar Indonesia Baru*, April 3, 1994.
"Ulah Oknum Camat dan Koramil: Bibelvrouw Manur Boru Panjaitan dan Hutapea Dipukuli," *Sentana,* Third Week of March, 1995.
"Wakil Ketua Tim Khusus HKBP Raja D.L. Sitorus: Mujizat, Jika Sisa Kemelut Tuntas dalam Waktu Singkat," *Suara Indonesia Baru*, March 15, 1995.
Sirait, Binsar T. H. "Jemaat Pagi HKBP Pondok Bambu Angkat Pendeta," *Reformata*, 25/Year III/April/2005.

Index of Names

Arendt, H.   6, 213
Ashley, J.M.   159, 160, 162, 169
Augustine   6, 15, 16

Bailey, K.E.   133–135
Barr, J.   101, 107
Beek, A. van de   223
Blenkinsopp, J.   96, 97, 99, 100
Bultmann, R.   133, 134

Childs, B.S.   99–103, 105–114, 116–120
Crockett, W.R.   239, 258–260
Crossan, J.D.   131

Dahl, N.A.   207
Davies, P.R.   93, 97–99
Dulling, D.C.   93
Dunn, J.D.G.   132, 133, 135, 136

Halbwachs, M.   93
Hardiman, F.B.   12
Hearon, H.   93, 94
Hendel, R.   99, 132
Hutauruk, J.R.   21, 22, 63, 73, 88

Jacques, G.   4
Jeremias, J.   145, 146, 148–150, 244, 245
Jones, L.G.   16

Keshkegian, F.A.   ix, 173, 177–185, 227, 238, 255
Kilpatrick, G.D.   149, 153, 154
King, N.   8, 9

Lyotard, J.F.   211
Margalit, A.   9–11
Metz, J.B.   ix, 18, 157–179, 184, 193, 202, 205–208, 226–228, 232, 240, 258, 264, 266, 280, 287, 290, 291, 304
Morrill, B.T.   163, 199, 202, 205–208, 236
Müller-Fahrenholz, G.   16

Nababan, S.A.E.   32–34, 36–63, 65–67, 69–73, 83–88
Nadeak, M.   13, 30, 32, 33, 37, 38, 40, 41, 45–47, 49, 53, 58, 66, 69, 70, 83
Norén, C.M.   256

Pedersen, J.   101, 105–107, 116
Pedersen, P.B.   23, 24
Power, David N.   234, 259, 260

Ricoeur, P.   5, 6, 93, 220

Schimmel, S.   5
Schmemann, A.   ix, 18, 157, 163, 177, 185–208, 226–229, 232, 238–240, 257, 265, 266, 272, 287, 291, 304
Shriver, D.W. Jr.   16
Siahaan, S.M.   vii, 38, 40, 42, 43–50, 52, 58, 59, 65–67, 70–72, 86–88
Sihombing, F.P.   27, 81, 83–86
Sihombing, P.M.   33
Simanjuntak, B.A.   24, 25, 77–81, 85, 307
Simanjuntak, P.W.T.   32, 34, 36, 38, 42, 47, 49–57, 59, 60, 62–65, 67–74, 86–88
Simarmata, W.T.P.   59, 73, 74
Simorangkir, O.P.T.   32, 35, 36, 38, 39-44, 52, 85, 86
Sitompul, A.A.   33, , 40, 42, 44, 62, 63
Sitompul, E.   30
Smedes, L.B.   4
Soeharto   44, 45, 54–56, 72, 81–84, 88, 310, 311

Thurian, M.   136, 140–142, 150, 151, 233, 236, 247, 252, 259
Tutu, D.   16

Villa-Vicencio, C.   11
Volf, M.   ix, 17, 18, 157, 158, 208–226, 228, 229, 232, 241, 264, 266, 287, 291, 306
von Rad, G.   114, 115, 118, 120, 121, 123, 124

Wainwright, G.   145, 232, 234, 236–238, 243, 246, 247, 252, 254–261, 263, 264, 267
Wertsch, J.V.   9
Wiesel, E.   1, 2, 169
Wollaston, I.   4
Wyschogrod, E.   9

Zerubabel, Y.   8
Zurbuchen, M.S.   82

Index of Biblical References

Genesis

9:15–16	108
30:22	109
40:14, 23	99
41:9	103

Exodus

3:15	103
12	104, 153
12:14	104, 118, 150
12:46	149
13:8	119
13:9	118
17:14	103, 104
20:16	217, 218
24:8	244
25:30	104
28:12	104
30:16	104
32:32–33	125
34:6	110
34:7	109
35:21	105

Leviticus

17:11	153
2:2, 9, 16	104
5:12	104
6:15	104
23:24	104
24:7	104

Numbers

5:15	140
5:26	104
10:8	119
11:29	255
15:39	102
22–24	153

Deuteronomy

7:18	115
8:11, 19	106
9:7	115
11:19	96
16:3	119
24:9	115
24:18, 22	119
25:17	115
25:19	103
32:26	103

Joshua

4:7	104

Judges

8:34	115
16:28	109
19–21	123

1 Samuel

1:11	109
1:19	108, 109
23:31	102

2 Samuel

19:19	102, 108

2 Kings

3	153
9:25	102
20:3	109

1 Chronicles

16:15	

Ezra

8:36	124
9	126

Index of Biblical References

Nehemiah

2:7	124
2:20	104
5:15	109
5:19	108
8:11c	64
9:1–37	viii, 114, 121, 126–128

Esther

2:1	102
6:1	104
3:12	124
8:9	124
6:1	125

Job

4:7	102
7:7	102
13:12	104
21:6	102

Psalms

6:5	103
9:6	103
9:12	109
20:3	109
22:28	102
25:6–7	111, 216, 225
30:5	103
34:8a	268
51:1–3, 10–12	289
63:7	106
69:28	125
78:12–16	114, 127
78:42	116
88:5	112
89:50	109
103	280
103:18	102
105:8	111, 112, 127
105:23–42	114
106:6–12	114, 127
106:45	112
111:4	103
111:5	111, 112
112:6	103
114	148
115	148
115:7, 12	106
118	148
132:	109
136:23	106, 109
137:7	109
139	125
145:7	103

Proverbs

10:7	103

Isaiah

4:3	125
6:3	293
23:16	103
38:3	109
43:18	110
43:25	110
47:7	102, 107
49:14	106, 108
53:5	245
53:12	244, 245
57:8	104
63:7	114
63:9	110
64:9	109
65:17	103, 110

Jeremiah

2:2	109
3:21	116
13:25	116
14	110
14:10	106, 109, 130
17:2	104
18:15	116
18:20	109
31:20	112
31:33	140
31:34	viii, 121, 129–130, 140, 225, 244
44:21	112

Index of Biblical References

Lamentations

1:7, 9	102
3:19	109
3:20	102

Ezekiel

22:12	116
23:35	116

Daniel

12:1	125

Hosea

2:13	116
4:6	108, 116
7:2	109, 111, 122
8:1–2	130
8:13	109, 111
9:9	109, 111, 123
11:1	114
12:6	74
14	123

Amos

9:7	114

Habakkuk

3:2	102

Haggai

1:1, 14	124

Zechariah

6:14	104

Malachi

2:17–3:5	124
3:13–4:3	124
3:16	viii, 121, 123–126

Matthew

1:21, 23	245
2:6, 15, 17, 23	245
4:14	245
5:23	137, 246, 251
9:2	244
11:28	268
16:2f	255
16:21	152
17:22–23	152
18:15	273
18:21–22	213
20:18–19	152
21:38–39	152
22:37–40	274, 289
26	272
26:13	145
26:20	148, 271, 288, 295
26:21	148
26:26–29	143, 251
26:28	243, 247
26:30	148
26:75	137
28:19	271

Mark

1:4	244, 245
1:21	244
8:31	152
9:1–7	244
9:30–32	152
10:33–34	152
12:7–8	152
14	272
14:7	148
14:9	145
14:17–26	271, 288, 295
14:18	148
14:22	143
14:22–25	143
14:26	148
14:30	148
14:72	137
16:15–16	271

Luke

1:54, 72	137, 140
3:3	245
7:36–50	144
9:22	152
9:43–45	152

10:38–42	144	3:16	26
11:28	269, 292	4:17	137
11:37–54	144	10:16	251
12:54–56	255	11:2	137
14:1–24	144	11:17–34	271, 272, 288, 295
17:32	137	11:20–22	251
18:31–33	152	11:22–23	147, 148
20:14–15	152	11:23–25	143, 272
22:14–20	144, 148, 271, 288, 295	11:24	138
		11:26	145, 146, 234, 251
22:19	234	11:27–29	268, 274, 153, 243
22:61	137	11:33	238
23:42	xiii	12:20	26
		12:1–11	32
		13:12a	234
		16:22	239

John

2:22	137		
3:16	275, 290, 296, 243	*2 Corinthians*	
3:18	243	5:18	73
5:24	243	7:15	137
6:51–58	247		
12:16	137	*Galatians*	
16:33	203	3:28	251
17:20–21	26		
17:21	73	*Ephesians*	
18:28	149	1:2, 22	25
19:14	149	2:14	62
19:31	149	2:22	26
19:36	149	4:4	26
20:19–31	298		

Acts

1:8	256	*Philippians*	
2:1–11	256	4:7	269, 281
5:27–32	298	*Colossians*	
10:4	138, 145	3:5	64
11:16	137		

Romans

		1 Thessalonians	
1:3f	138	1:2	138
8:34	249	*2 Timothy*	
12:1	249	2:8	138
16:25–27	232		
		Hebrews	

1 Corinthians

		1–8	142
1:2	25	2:5–8	137
3:11	25	7:25	257

Index of Biblical References

8:12	137, 140, 225	*2 Peter*	
9:14	140	2:7	137
10:3	139, 140, 146	3:2	137
10:8	142		
10:16–17	140	*1 John*	
10:17	225	4:20	246
10:31	137		
11:15	137	*Jude*	
13:8	198	5, 17	137
James		*Revelation*	
5:12	218	1:4–8	298
		1:6	26
1 Peter		3:5	125
1:12f	138	16:19	137
1:25	48	17:8	125
2:5	249	18:5	137, 140
2:9	25, 26	20:12	125
3:15	173		